American Red Cross

American Red Cross
Emergency Medical Response
Workbook

This *Emergency Medical Response Workbook* is part of the American Red Cross Emergency Medical Response program. By itself, it does not constitute complete and comprehensive training. Visit redcross.org to learn more about this program.

The emergency care procedures outlined in this book reflect the standard of knowledge and accepted emergency practices in the United States at the time this book was published. It is the reader's responsibility to stay informed of changes in emergency care procedures.

Published by StayWell Health & Safety Solutions

Printed in the United States of America

ISBN: 978-1-58480-328-7

Contents

Introduction

This workbook is designed to accompany the *Emergency Medical Response* textbook. Specific workbook activities were created to help you review the most important material in the textbook, to help you practice making appropriate decisions about emergency care and to help you prepare for the skills and written evaluations. The material in each unit of this workbook reinforces key concepts and skills taught in the textbook and the course. This affords you the opportunity to build on learned material and apply your knowledge to emergency situations. Most of the workbook activities allow you to work at your own pace and evaluate your progress at various stages.

To maximize the benefit of using the *Emergency Medical Response Workbook*, you are encouraged to first read the textbook, then answer the questions in the corresponding chapter of this workbook. You may need to refer to your textbook for questions you are unable to answer. After completing the activities in each workbook chapter, check your answers against those in the answer keys at the end of this workbook. For help with those questions that you answered incorrectly or with difficulty, return to the corresponding chapter in the textbook and review the relevant material. If you still do not understand why an answer is correct or have additional questions about the material you are studying, ask your instructor for help.

In each chapter of the workbook, you will find the following sections:

Learning Activities

This section is the heart of the workbook. It contains a variety of activities that test and reinforce your understanding and retention of the material in the textbook. The activities in this section consist of—

- Crossword puzzles.
- Matching exercises.
- Fill-in-the-blank questions.
- Short answer questions.
- Labeling exercises.

Case Studies

In the Case Studies, descriptions are given of specific emergency scenarios followed by questions that ask how you, as an *emergency medical responder* (EMR), would react to these situations and what care you would provide. These questions challenge you to apply the information you have learned to problems and situations you will likely encounter and help you to develop logical solutions.

Self-Assessment

Each workbook chapter contains questions on the material in the corresponding chapter of the textbook. These exercises give you practical experience in answering multiple-choice and ordering questions and help prepare you for the final written exams given at the end of this course.

Enrichment

Enrichment material is found at the end of certain chapters. The material in the enrichment has been included in the workbook for those needing or wanting additional information and skills.

Skill Sheets

Cross-references to skill sheets in the *Emergency Medical Response* textbook are included in some workbook chapters. The skill sheets contain photographs or illustrations and simple step-by-step directions on how to perform each skill.

End-of-Unit and Course Review Exams

Each workbook unit also includes End-of-Unit exams containing multiple-choice questions. This material revisits content in each chapter within a unit to allow you to test your knowledge of the material. In addition, the workbook includes a Course Review exam highlighting the most important content.

Completing these workbook exercises as you progress through the textbook will help to enhance your comprehension of the material in this course.

1 PREPARATORY

1 The Emergency Medical Responder

| REVIEW OF CONCEPTS AND TERMS |

Matching

Directions: *Write the letter of the description from Column 2 in the space next to the correct term in Column 1. Use each letter only once.*

Column 1

___ 1. Scope of practice

___ 2. Paramedic

___ 3. Protocols

___ 4. Standing orders

___ 5. Prehospital care

___ 6. Licensure

___ 7. Medical direction

___ 8. Certification

___ 9. Indirect medical control

___ 10. Emergency medical services

Column 2

A. The monitoring of care provided by out-of-hospital providers to injured or ill persons, usually by a medical director

B. Directions to provide certain care without talking to a physician

C. Care provided before a patient arrives at a medical facility

D. Credentialing at the local level

E. Off-line medical control

F. Range of duties and skills allowed and expected to be performed

G. Required acknowledgement of person with permission to practice in a specific state

H. Person with more in-depth training than an *advanced emergency medical technician* (AEMT)

I. Standardized procedures to be followed when providing care

J. Network of community resources and medical persons for the provision of emergency care

Short Answer

Directions: *Supply the information requested.*

1. List the five types of *emergency medical services* (EMS) in the United States.

_____

_____

_____

_____

_____

2. Describe the responsibilities of state EMS agencies.

_____

_____

_____

_____

_____

3. Explain the purpose of the *National Emergency Medical Services Education and Practice Blueprint.*

_____

_____

_____

_____

_____

4. Name four nationally recognized levels of training for pre-hospital care.

_____

_____

_____

_____

_____

5. State the level of credentialing that provides the highest level of public protection.

_____

_____

_____

_____

_____

| CASE STUDY |

Directions: *Read the case studies and answer the questions that follow.*

Scenario A

You are the first to arrive on the scene of a department store roof collapse. There are numerous people fleeing the building. Some are walking independently while some need assistance. Others are standing in the parking lot dazed and shocked.

1. What would be your primary responsibilities as an *emergency medical responder* (EMR)?

_____

_____

_____

_____

2. You provide care to patients based on standing orders. Which type of medical control would this be?

_____

_____

_____

_____

3. What secondary responsibilities would be appropriate?

_____

_____

_____

_____

Scenario B

You are among a group of professional EMS responders providing care to numerous patients at the scene of a building fire. Each of the responders has a different level of training and is providing the appropriate types of care.

1. Which of the following EMS personnel would be responsible for preparing the patient for transport?
   a. EMR
   b. *Emergency medical technician* (EMT)
   c. AEMT
   d. Paramedic

2. You are working alongside an AEMT. Which of the following would this person be allowed to do?
   a. Provide strictly basic emergency care
   b. Work to stabilize the patient
   c. Insert an *intravenous* (IV) line
   d. Perform an in-depth physical assessment

3. One group of responders is from a private company that has been hired to provide EMS services. This is an example of which type of EMS service?
   a. Fire-based services
   b. Hospital-based services
   c. Other services
   d. Third-party services

| SELF-ASSESSMENT |

Directions: *Answer the questions by selecting the correct letter(s) or by placing the answers in the proper order.*

1. Which of the following best describes the EMS system in the United States today?
   a. A group of varied, informal resources
   b. Multi-tiered, nationwide system
   c. Police and fire-based response systems
   d. Private organizations and companies providing care

2. Which of the following would be a primary responsibility for you in your role as an EMR?
   a. Ensuring the patient's safety
   b. Directing bystanders to help
   c. Recording what you did
   d. Reassuring the patient

3. An individual acting in which capacity would be least likely to act as an EMR?
   a. Lifeguard
   b. Athletic trainer
   c. Camp leader
   d. Paramedic

4. Scope of practice is best described as—
   a. Range of duties and skills an EMR is allowed and expected to perform.
   b. Credentialing that occurs at the local level.
   c. Protocols issued by the medical director.
   d. Permission to practice in a particular state.

5. An EMR who is required to be licensed will be licensed through the—
   a. National Highway Traffic Safety Administration.
   b. State EMS agency.
   c. Public safety department.
   d. Employing EMS agency.

6. Which of the following would be considered a component of an effective EMS system?
   a. Certification
   b. Scope of practice
   c. Medical oversight
   d. Core content

7. Which of the following would most likely have criminal implications for an EMR?
   a. Recording care that was provided
   b. Participating in continuing education classes
   c. Maintaining certification
   d. Performing a skill not trained to do

8. While at the scene of an accident, you speak to the physician via radio to obtain permission for a procedure not included in the standing orders. This is an example of which type of medical control?
   a. Off-line
   b. Indirect
   c. Direct
   d. Protocol

9. As part of a presentation for career day at a local high school, a participant asks you about the types of characteristics needed by an EMR. Which of the following would you be least likely to include in your response?
   a. Ability to remain inflexible
   b. Able to control personal fears
   c. Compassion
   d. Ability to stay current

10. An EMR is granted the right to practice via which mechanism?
   a. Certification
   b. Licensure
   c. Local credentialing
   d. Medical direction

11. Which of the following best emphasizes the importance of the role of an EMR?
   a. EMRs can provide care without input from a physician.
   b. EMRs have knowledge of advanced skills and techniques.
   c. EMRs function similarly in most areas across the country.
   d. EMR's actions may determine whether a seriously injured person survives.

12. The following are four nationally recognized levels of EMS training. Place them in the proper order from basic to most advanced.
   a. Paramedic
   b. EMR
   c. AEMT
   d. EMT

13. Which of the following would be addressed by the resource management component of the Technical Assistance Assessment Standard?
   a. Available supplies for care
   b. 9-1-1 communication system
   c. Specialty care centers
   d. Personnel training programs

14. You are the first to respond to the scene of a motor-vehicle crash involving a car that hit a utility pole head on. The car is overturned, and several wires are down on the ground. Which of the following would be the priority?
   a. Gaining access to the patient
   b. Ensuring the safety of the scene
   c. Providing care to the patient
   d. Recording your actions

2 The Well-Being of the Emergency Medical Responder

Crossword Puzzle

Directions: *Complete the crossword puzzle using the clues on the next page.*

ACROSS

5. Biological agent that can be harmful to those exposed
7. A disease-causing agent
9. Short, less formal method for discussing a traumatic event

DOWN

1. Type of infection that strikes a person with a weakened immune system
2. Group method of discussing the events of an incident
3. Type of immunity developed via exposure to disease or immunization
4. Rapid and severe onset that quickly subsides
6. Type of immunity with which we are born
8. Proteins in blood and body fluids used by immune system to neutralize pathogens

Matching

Directions: *Write the letter of the disease or condition from Column 2 in the space next to the correct pathogen in Column 1. Use each letter only once.*

Column 1	Column 2
___ 1. Viruses	A. Hepatitis
___ 2. Bacteria	B. Athlete's foot
___ 3. Fungi	C. Rocky Mountain
___ 4. Protozoa	Spotted Fever
___ 5. *Rickesttsia*	D. Thrush
___ 6. Prions	E. Meningitis
___ 7. Yeasts	F. Mad cow disease
	G. Malaria

Fill-in-the-Blank

Directions: *Write the correct word in the space provided.*

1. AIDS is caused by _____.

2. The flu virus can enter the body through _____ transmission when an infected person coughs from within a few feet.

3. Hepatitis causes inflammation and swelling of the _____.

4. _____ precautions combine *body substance isolation* (BSI) and universal precautions.

5. The most effective means to prevent the spread of infection is _____ _____.

6. The body's normal response to any situation that changes a person's existing mental, physical or emotional balance is called _____.

7. _____ _____ are highly stressful situations encountered by *emergency medical responders* (EMRs) that involve serious injury or death.

| CASE STUDY |

Scenario A

You arrive at an office building in response to a 9-1-1 call reporting that an individual has collapsed in the cafeteria. You observe the female patient lying face-down on the floor. There is blood oozing from a cut on her forehead and you notice what looks like urine on the floor. A bystander tells you that the patient hit her head on the table when she fell.

1. When providing care to this patient, which *personal protective equipment* (PPE) would be essential to use?
   a. Disposable gloves
   b. Safety glasses
   c. *High-efficiency particulate air* (HEPA) mask
   d. Disposable gown

2. As you provide care to the patient, some of the patient's blood gets on your forearm. Which of the following would you do next?
   a. Use alcohol to clean off the blood.
   b. Irrigate the area with sterile saline for 10 minutes.
   c. Clean the area thoroughly with soap and water.
   d. Wash the area with a diluted bleach solution.

3. Which of the following would be the most important for you to do to prevent disease transmission after you have completed caring for the patient?
   a. Report any potential exposures to blood and body fluids.
   b. Wash your hands thoroughly.
   c. Dispose of any biohazard materials.
   d. Disinfect the equipment and supplies.

Scenario B

You are called to the home of an elderly gentleman who has been diagnosed with terminal cancer. The family is at his bedside and tells you that he has an advance directive. You observe that the patient is not breathing.

1. Which of the following actions would be most appropriate?
   a. Ask the family if you can see the written directive.
   b. Begin to resuscitate the patient.
   c. Call the funeral director for the family.
   d. Tell the family that there is nothing that you can do.

2. One family member says that they were praying in the hopes that the patient "would hold on until his grandson graduated next month." This would suggest that the family member is in which stage of grieving?
   a. Denial
   b. Anger
   c. Bargaining
   d. Acceptance

3. Which of the following signs would be least likely to indicate obvious death in a patient?
   a. Dependent lividity
   b. Overly flexible joints
   c. Putrefaction
   d. Rigor mortis

| SELF-ASSESSMENT |

Directions: Answer the questions by selecting the correct letter(s).

1. Which of the following best reflects the stages of grief?
   a. Grief responses occur in a predictable pattern for everyone.
   b. Anger as a grief response usually is the first response to occur.
   c. Each person's reaction to death and dying is unique.
   d. Each person experiences every stage of grief.

2. Which of the following is the most effective natural defense against infection?
   a. Mucous membranes
   b. Intact skin
   c. Hand washing
   d. PPE

3. Which of the following is an example of disease transmission by indirect contact?
   a. Infected blood splashing into the eyes
   b. Touching an infected person's body fluids
   c. Touching a soiled dressing of an infected patient
   d. Inhaling particles from an infected person's sneeze

4. Which of the following diseases is most likely caused by bacteria?
   a. Hepatitis
   b. Measles
   c. Malaria
   d. Tuberculosis

5. You arrive at the home of a patient who has been ill for the past 3 weeks with what he thought was a respiratory infection. He also has had a bad cough throughout this time. You evaluate the patient and suspect that he may have tuberculosis. Which of the following symptoms might also be present?
   a. Yellowing of the skin
   b. Bloody sputum
   c. Abdominal pain
   d. Stiff neck

6. You are providing care to a patient who is thought to have rabies. You understand that this condition is transmitted by which method?
   a. Indirect contact
   b. Direct contact
   c. Respiratory droplet transmission
   d. Vector-borne transmission

7. When removing disposable gloves, which action would be most appropriate to do first?
   a. Pull the first glove off by pulling on the fingertips.
   b. Slide two gloved fingers under the first glove at the wrist.
   c. Pinch the outside of the second glove with bare fingers.
   d. Remove the second glove so that the first glove ends up inside of it.

8. Which of the following is considered to be a work practice control?
   a. Disinfecting work surfaces possibly soiled with blood or body fluids
   b. Ensuring that sharps disposal containers are available
   c. Providing biohazard containers
   d. Posting signs at entrances where infectious materials may be present

9. You are preparing to clean up a spill of blood that occurred while caring for a patient. Which solution would be most appropriate to use?
   a. Alcohol
   b. Chlorine bleach
   c. Hydrogen peroxide
   d. Liquid soap

10. You and a fellow EMR had responded to a *multiple-casualty incident* (MCI) several days ago. Which of the following would lead you to suspect that your colleague is experiencing critical incident stress?
    a. Increased attention span
    b. Enhanced concentration
    c. Unusually excessive silence
    d. Heightened job performance

11. You are with the family of a patient who has suddenly died as a result of a heart attack. You would do which of the following?
    a. Encourage the family to refrain from becoming angry
    b. Provide reassurance that may or may not be accurate
    c. Speak to them in a firm, authoritative voice
    d. Remain calm and nonjudgmental

12. After a critical incident, you are to participate in debriefing. Which of the following best describes this technique?
    a. Group discussion with a trained professional
    b. One-to-one interaction with a peer counselor
    c. Short informal discussion with others
    d. Brief interaction occurring immediately after the incident

13. You are providing care to a patient at the scene of a building explosion. The patient is lying on the ground and unconscious, but breathing. He has a large laceration on his upper leg, and blood can be seen spurting from the wound. Which PPE would you use? Select all that apply.
    a. Resuscitation mask
    b. HEPA mask
    c. Disposable gloves
    d. Gown
    e. Face shield

14. Which of the following diseases would you identify as being caused by a virus? Select all that apply.
    a. Mumps
    b. Chicken pox
    c. Avian flu
    d. Malaria
    e. Tetanus
    f. Anthrax

15. While caring for a patient, some blood splashes into your eyes. Which of the following would you do first?
    a. Wash your face with soap and water.
    b. Apply antiseptic eye drops.
    c. Flush the eyes with clean water for 20 minutes.
    d. Report the incident to the designated person in your agency.

16. Mucous membranes protect the body from infection by—
    a. Providing an intact barrier so pathogens cannot enter.
    b. Trapping pathogens to be forced out.
    c. Acting as part of the immune system.
    d. Destroying the pathogen before it can grow.

17. Which of the following would be a most likely route of transmission for hepatitis B?
    a. Drinking contaminated water
    b. Eating contaminated food
    c. Hugging an infected person
    d. Having sexual contact with an infected person

18. Which of the following would be an example of direct contact transmission?
    a. Patient's blood entering a cut on the responder's hand
    b. Touching a work surface soiled with a patient's body fluid
    c. Inhaling air and particles from a patient who sneezed nearby
    d. Getting bitten by an infected mosquito

19. When washing your hands, you should rub your wet hands vigorously with soap for at least—
    a. 5 seconds.
    b. 10 seconds.
    c. 15 seconds.
    d. 20 seconds.

20. You are providing care to a patient with hepatitis C. Which of the victim's body fluids can spread this infection? Select all that apply.
    a. Blood
    b. Semen
    c. Vaginal fluid
    d. Breast milk
    e. Saliva

| SELF-ASSESSMENT: ENRICHMENT |

Health of the Emergency Medical Responder

Directions: *Circle the letter that best answers the question.*

1. Which of the following would be most appropriate for you as an EMR to do to maintain physical fitness?
   a. Perform a limited amount of strength training.
   b. Engage in at least 30 minutes of physical exercise per day.
   c. Sporadically engage in stretching exercises.
   d. Workout once a week.

2. Which of the following would be least helpful in promoting your physical well-being?
   a. Limit your intake of foods high in sugar.
   b. Adhere to standard precautions.
   c. Use a sunscreen with a *sun protection factor* (SPF) of 10.
   d. Use proper lifting techniques.

3. A fellow EMR is exhibiting signs of stress. Which suggestion would be least appropriate as a means for managing stress?
   a. Reprioritizing work tasks
   b. Eating fast food meals to relax
   c. Practicing muscle relaxation
   d. Engaging in physical activity daily

| SKILL SHEET |

Refer to the *Emergency Medical Response* textbook for the following skill sheet for this chapter:

- Removing Disposable Gloves, page 37.

3 | Medical, Legal and Ethical Issues

| REVIEW OF CONCEPTS AND TERMS |

Matching

Directions: *Write the letter of the description from Column 2 in the space next to the correct term in Column 1.*

Column 1

___ 1.   Battery

___ 2.   Assault

___ 3.   Consent

___ 4.   Morals

___ 5. Abandonment

Column 2

A.   Principles related to issues of right and wrong

B.   Protection of a patient's privacy

C.   Ability to understand the questions of an *emergency medical responder* (EMR) and implications of decision making

D.   Written instructions documenting patient's wishes if the patient is unable to communicate

E.   Unlawful touching of a person without the person's consent

Column 1

___ 6. Confidentiality

___ 7. Advance directive

___ 8. Competence

Column 2

F.   Ending of care to an injured person without the patient's consent

G.   Attempt to physically harm another with the person feeling immediately threatened

H.   Permission to provide care

Short Answer

Directions: *Supply the information requested.*

1.   Define an EMR's scope of practice.

   _____

   _____

   _____

   _____

   _____

2. Explain the concept "duty to act."

_____

_____

_____

_____

3. List the three concepts associated with ethical responsibilities.

_____

_____

_____

_____

4. Name three principles that can be used with decision-making models.

_____

_____

_____

_____

_____

5. State the four components necessary to obtain consent.

_____

_____

_____

_____

_____

| CASE STUDY |

Directions: *Read the case studies and answer the questions that follow.*

Scenario A

You are the first to arrive at the home of a middle-aged couple in response to a 9-1-1 call made by the wife saying that her husband was having a heart attack. The patient is alert but complaining of severe chest pain and pressure. You summon more advanced medical personnel and you begin to provide care.

1. You obtain consent from the patient before touching him to prevent which of the following?
   a. Abandonment
   b. Battery
   c. Assault
   d. Negligence

2. You momentarily stop care before additional personnel arrive. You could be legally responsible for which of the following?
   a. Negligence
   b. Assault
   c. Abandonment
   d. Battery

3. More advanced medical personnel arrive and you inform them about the patient's condition and history. You understand that this action is appropriate because it does not violate the patient's—
   a. Consent.
   b. Advance directive.
   c. Competence.
   d. Confidentiality.

Scenario B

You are one of several EMRs called to the scene of an apartment fire. Your patient is a 16-year-old girl who has a 9-month-old infant. The 16 year old is breathing rapidly and the infant is crying. While talking with the 16 year old, she tells you that she is a legally emancipated minor.

1. You would obtain consent for treating the 16-year-old patient from—
   a. The patient.
   b. The patient's parents.
   c. The patient's guardian.
   d. The patient's next of kin.

2. The 16 year old nods her head in response to your request to care for her infant. This is an example of—
   a. Implied consent.
   b. Expressed consent.
   c. Informal consent.
   d. Parental consent.

3. Which of the following would be appropriate to do while caring for the 16-year-old patient if she tells you that she is fine and does not want any more care?
   a. Tell her you are legally required to continue to provide care.
   b. Honor her refusal, following local policies for such situations.
   c. Inform her that if you stop care, she cannot call the *emergency medical services* (EMS) system later.
   d. Notify more advanced medical personnel to obtain further assistance.

| SELF-ASSESSMENT |

Directions: *Answer the questions by selecting the correct letter(s) or by placing the answers in the proper order.*

1. Which patient would you expect to be competent?
   a. A patient with dementia who has wandered off
   b. A patient who appears to be intoxicated and has fallen on the sidewalk
   c. A patient who is alert and has an open fracture of his left leg
   d. A patient with a bleeding facial laceration who is not making any sense when conversing

2. Good Samaritan laws would most likely apply to individuals who—
   a. Provide advanced levels of care.
   b. Use a rash, hurried manner.
   c. Perform care above their skill level.
   d. Act in good faith.

3. When applying the principle of the patient's best interest, you would—
   a. Ensure that the patient remains free from harm.
   b. Help the patient regardless of what it involves.
   c. Show respect for the patient's human dignity.
   d. Provide care that focuses solely on helping the patient.

4. The following statements reflect the steps in obtaining consent from a patient. Place the statements in the proper sequence beginning with what you should do first.
   a. "I am going to loosen your sleeve to check your arm."
   b. "My name is Jane Smith."
   c. "I notice that you have a large cut on your arm. May I help you?"
   d. "I am an emergency medical responder."

5. You arrive at the home of a patient experiencing severe difficulty breathing. The patient's spouse tells you that the patient has terminal cancer and has a *Do Not Resuscitate* (DNR) order. However, the spouse is unable to find the written document. Which of the following would you do first?
   a. Notify medical direction about how to proceed.
   b. Prepare to perform the usual emergency care.
   c. Call the patient's physician for verification.
   d. Honor the spouse's statement and the patient's wishes.

6. Which of the following would identify a surrogate decision maker?
   a. Durable power of attorney for health care
   b. Living will
   c. DNR order
   d. Health care proxy

7. An EMR made an error when providing care to a patient that resulted in patient injury. Which aspect of negligence was involved?
   a. Duty to act
   b. Proximate cause
   c. Breech of duty
   d. Patient harm

8. Resuscitation efforts would most likely be necessary if you identified which of the following?
   a. Rigor mortis
   b. Absence of pulse
   c. Dependent lividity
   d. Body decomposition

9. Which of the following would require mandatory reporting? Select all that apply.
   a. Suspected child abuse
   b. Tuberculosis
   c. HIV infection
   d. Gunshot wound from a robbery
   e. Epilepsy
   f. Heart attack

10. The *Health Insurance Portability and Accountability Act* (HIPAA) Privacy Rule requires that identifying patient information cannot be shared with which of the following without the patient's specific consent? Select all that apply.
    a. Family members
    b. Media
    c. Employers
    d. Public health authorities
    e. Organ procurement agencies
    f. Colleagues

11. You arrive on the scene of a convenience store robbery in which the store clerk was stabbed. A knife is lying on the floor next to the patient. Law enforcement personnel have arrived and are searching for the robber who has already fled the scene. Which of the following must occur first?
    a. Moving the store clerk to a safer location
    b. Cutting away the clerk's clothing to check the wound more closely
    c. Picking up the knife to give to law enforcement
    d. Waiting to enter the scene until it is cleared by law enforcement.

12. A patient at the scene of a motor-vehicle crash refuses care. Which response would be most appropriate initially?
    a. Telling the patient that he or she needs to be checked out
    b. Respecting the patient's right to refuse care
    c. Contacting the local law enforcement agency for help
    d. Documenting the patient's refusal for care

13. Medical futility specifically is an exception to which of the following?
    a. Living wills
    b. Health care proxy
    c. DNR orders
    d. Durable power of attorney for health care

14. A patient who appears to be mentally incompetent is seriously injured and alone. You would—
    a. Begin to treat the patient based on implied consent.
    b. Attempt to contact the patient's guardian for consent.
    c. Summon law enforcement to control the patient.
    d. Try to talk the patient into giving consent.

15. After which age would you commonly ask for consent from the patient as opposed to the parent or guardian?
    a. 12 years
    b. 14 years
    c. 16 years
    d. 18 years

4 | The Human Body

∣ REVIEW OF CONCEPTS AND TERMS ∣

Matching

Directions: *Write the letter of the description from Column 2 in the space next to the correct term in Column 1.*

Column 1

_C_ 1. Inferior

_A_ 2. Proximal

_E_ 3. Prone

_B_ 4. Anterior

_D_ 5. Medial

Column 2

A. Description indicating any body part that is close to the trunk.

B. The term that refers to the patient's front.

C. Description of any body part toward the patient's feet.

D. Term that refers to any part toward the body's midline.

E. Position indicating that the patient is lying face-down.

Fill-in-the-Blank

Directions: *Write the correct term in the space provided.*

1. The brain, heart and lungs are examples of _____ organs whose functions are essential to life.

2. The ___circulatory___ system consists of the heart, blood and blood vessels.

3. The _____ or _____ plane divides the body vertically into the anterior and posterior planes.

4. A body part is described as _____ because it is located away from the midline.

5. The ___anatomical___ position is the position that serves as the basis for all medical terms that refer to the body.

6. ___Joints___ are the places where bones connect to each other.

7. External respiration or ___ventilation___ is the mechanical process of moving air in and out of the lungs to exchange oxygen and carbon dioxide between body tissues and the environment.

8. ___Arteries___ carry blood, mostly oxygenated blood, away from the heart.

9. The ___central___ nervous system is involuntary.

10. The body's largest organ is the ___skin___.

Short Answer

Directions: *Supply the information requested.*

1. List the five major body cavities.

    _____
    _____
    _____
    _____
    _____

2. Name the two main anatomical divisions of the nervous system.

    _____
    _____

3. Identify the six sections of the skeleton.

    _____
    _____
    _____
    _____
    _____
    _____

4. State the most common type of moveable joint located in the body.

    _____
    _____
    _____

5. List five functions of the skin.

    _____
    _____
    _____
    _____
    _____

Labeling

Directions: *Write the name of the appropriate anatomical structure in the space provided.*

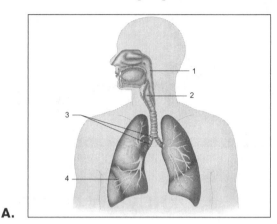

A.

1. _____

2. _____

3. _____

4. _____

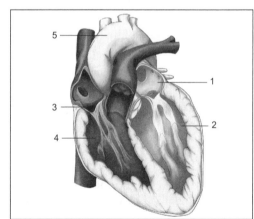

B.

1. _____

2. _____

3. _____

4. _____

5. _____

| CASE STUDY |

Directions: Read the case studies and answer the questions that follow.

Scenario A

You are called to the home of a patient who has fallen off of a ladder while painting the outside of his two-story house. The patient is lying on his back with his upper body elevated about 45 degrees. He is responsive but is moaning in pain and cannot move his left arm. He states, "When I fell, the ladder landed on my ribs but I pushed it off of me. But I think I broke my arm trying to break my fall." You observe what looks like a piece of bone protruding from his upper arm.

1. You would describe the patient's position as which of the following?
   a. Supine
   b. Prone
   c. Anatomical
   (d.) Fowler's

2. Which structure would you expect to be involved if his upper arm was broken?
   a. Radius
   b. Ulna
   (c.) Humerus
   d. Femur

3. Which body cavity would you suspect as being injured based on the patient's statement about the ladder hitting his ribs?
   a. Pelvic
   (b.) Thoracic
   c. Abdominal
   d. Cranial

4. What organs lie beneath the ribs that may be injured? Select all that apply.
   a. Stomach
   (b.) Lungs
   (c.) Heart
   d. Bladder
   e. Kidneys

5. When describing the patient's upper arm injury, you would identify it as which of the following?
   a. Lateral to the wrist
   b. Superior to the elbow
   c. Anterior to the ribs
   d. Medial to the sternum

Scenario B

You are called to a local office building where a woman has fainted. A co-worker tells you that the woman has problems involving blood glucose levels for which she uses insulin.

1. Based on the co-worker's information, you would suspect which body system as being involved?
   a. Circulatory
   b. Respiratory
   c. Endocrine
   d. Digestive

2. You recognize that insulin is an example of a—
   a. Hormone.
   b. Tendon.
   c. Ligament.
   d. Red blood cell.

3. What other structures would be involved with this system? Select all that apply.
   a. Liver
   b. Adrenal gland
   c. Ovaries
   d. Gall bladder
   e. Kidneys

| SELF-ASSESSMENT |

Directions: *Answer the questions by selecting the correct letter(s).*

1. You are checking the temperature of a patient and find it to be below normal. Which prefix would you use to describe this finding?
   a. Hyper-
   b. Hypo-
   c. Brady-
   d. Tachy-

2. You observe a patient straightening his leg. You identify this motion as which of the following?
   a. Extension
   b. Flexion
   c. Superior
   d. Proximal

3. A patient is placed in the Fowler's position. You would expect to find this patient—
   a. Face-down on his stomach.
   b. Sitting up slightly.
   c. Lying flat on his back.
   d. On his back with his legs elevated.

4. A patient was involved in a motor-vehicle crash and is experiencing problems breathing, suggesting an injury to his lungs. Which body cavity would you identify as being affected?
   a. Spinal
   b. Abdominal
   c. Cranial
   d. Thoracic

5. Which vertebrae would be involved if a patient experiences an injury to his neck?
   a. Thoracic
   b. Lumbar
   c. Cervical
   d. Sacral

6. You find that a patient is not breathing. The patient's brain cells will begin to die within which time frame if the oxygen supply is not re-established?
   a. 1 to 2 minutes
   b. 2 to 4 minutes
   c. 4 to 6 minutes
   d. 6 to 8 minutes

7. Which process does the body use to produce energy?
   a. External respiration
   b. Cellular respiration
   c. Ventilation
   d. Inspiration

8. Which of the following occurs during expiration?
   a. Relaxation of the diaphragm
   b. Contraction of the chest muscles
   c. Movement of ribs outward
   d. Expansion of the chest cavity

9. You are providing care to a patient who is bleeding from a puncture wound. Which blood component would be involved in helping to stop the bleeding?
   a. Red blood cells
   b. White blood cells
   c. Platelets
   d. Plasma

10. You obtain a patient's pulse based on the understanding that the pulse reflects which of the following?
    a. The amount of oxygen being delivered to the tissues
    b. The blood being pumped to the body from the left ventricle
    c. The force of blood flowing through the arteries
    d. The exchange of oxygen and carbon dioxide in the capillaries

11. You describe the elbow as being inferior to which of the following?
    a. Fingers
    b. Hand
    c. Wrist
    d. Shoulder

12. A patient is not breathing and does not have a pulse. You suspect that this may reflect a problem with which part of the nervous system?
    a. Brainstem
    b. Spinal cord
    c. Cerebellum
    d. Cerebrum

13. A patient has sustained a broken leg and is complaining of severe pain. Which nervous system is involved in a patient's response to pain?
    a. Autonomic
    b. Sympathetic
    c. Peripheral
    d. Parasympathetic

14. You are called to a scene involving an infant who is having difficulty breathing. Which of the following is most important for you to keep in mind about the infant's respiratory system in contrast to an adult's respiratory system?
    a. The trachea is wider but softer.
    b. The chest wall is more rigid.
    c. Infants are nose-breathers.
    d. The respiratory rate is slower.

15. Which of the following is the body's largest organ?
    a. Skin
    b. Brain
    c. Kidneys
    d. Heart

16. The stomach is located in which body cavity?
    a. Cranial
    b. Thoracic
    c. Abdominal
    d. Pelvic

17. When describing the location of the kidneys in relation to the lungs, you would identify them as—
    a. Superior.
    b. Inferior.
    c. Posterior.
    d. Anterior.

18. Which structure attaches bone-to-bone and is responsible for holding a joint together?
    a. Ligament
    b. Tendon
    c. Patella
    d. Coccyx

5 | Lifting and Moving Patients

| REVIEW OF CONCEPTS AND TERMS |

Matching

Directions: *Write the letter of the description from Column 2 in the space next to the correct term in Column 1.*

Column 1

___ 1. Log roll

___ 2. Position of comfort

___ 3. Restraint

___ 4. Backboard

Column 2

A. A posture used to help maintain a clear airway in an unresponsive, breathing patient.

B. Equipment used to immobilize a patient's head, neck and spine during transport

C. Method of moving a patient that keeps the body in alignment when a head, neck or spinal injury is suspected

D. Technique for moving a patient using a stretcher's bottom sheet

Column 1

___ 5. Body mechanics

___ 6. Draw sheet

___ 7. Recovery position

Column 2

E. Study of the action and function of muscles in maintaining posture

F. Physical means for limiting a patient's movement to prevent injury to him- or herself

G. Posture naturally assumed by a patient who is feeling ill or is in pain.

Labeling

Directions: *Write the name of the correct emergency move being depicted in the space provided.*

1. _____

_____

2. _____

_____

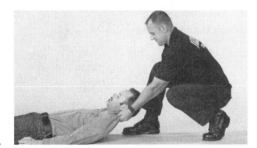

3. _____

_____

4. _____

_____

5. _____

_____

6. _____

_____

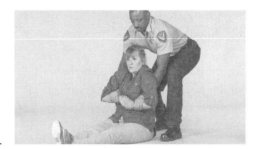

7. _____

_____

| CASE STUDY |

Directions: *Read the case studies and answer the questions that follow.*

Scenario A

You arrive at the scene of an apartment fire. A person has jumped from the balcony of a second-floor apartment and has landed face-up on the ground next to the building. The patient has a decreased level of consciousness (LOC) but is breathing. You determine that you need to move the patient, but you suspect that the patient has neck or spinal injuries.

1. Which emergency move would be appropriate to use for this patient?
    a. Clothes drag
    b. Firefighter's carry
    c. Ankle drag
    d. Shoulder drag

2. When preparing to move the patient, which of the following would be the most important for you to do?
    a. Make sure that a stretcher is readily available.
    b. Be aware of your own physical abilities.
    c. Keep your knees rigidly straight.
    d. Twist your back to reach the patient.

3. You know that your right leg is weaker than your left leg. Which technique would be most appropriate for you to use?
    a. Power grip
    b. Power lift
    c. Squat lift
    d. Log rolling

Scenario B

You and your partner arrive on the scene of a commuter train fire. The entire last car is engulfed in flames and smoke is billowing. The fire is beginning to spread to the adjacent car. People are running as they exit the train cars. One person has tripped and fallen down as she is crossing the train tracks, cutting her face and arm. She is sitting on the side of the train station walkway, coughing and breathing rapidly.

1. Based on the patient's status, which technique would be appropriate to use when moving this patient?
    a. Blanket drag
    b. Direct ground lift
    c. Extremity lift
    d. Walking assist

2. You and your partner are preparing the patient who is coughing and breathing rapidly for transport. You would expect to place the patient in which position?
    a. Supine
    b. Upright sitting
    c. Left lateral recumbent position
    d. Modified *High Arm In Endangered Spine* (H.A.IN.E.S) recovery position

3. When assisting patients at this scene, you demonstrate your understanding of body mechanics when you—
    a. Lift with your back, not with your legs.
    b. Keep the patient's weight away from, not close to, your body.
    c. Move backward rather than forward.
    d. Maintain a low center of gravity.

▮ SELF-ASSESSMENT ▮

Directions: Answer the questions by selecting the correct letter(s).

1. When placing a patient in a modified H.A.IN.E.S. recovery position, you would—
   a. Kneel at the patient's head.
   b. Place the farther arm over the patient's chest.
   c. Bend the leg up that is farthest from you.
   d. Turn the patient's head, then his or her back.

2. You and three other responders are preparing to log roll a patient. The person at which position would direct the move?
   a. Head
   b. Shoulders
   c. Hips
   d. Feet

3. Which patient would you identify as most likely in need of restraint?
   a. A patient who is lying face-down and unconscious
   b. A patient who is screaming loudly in pain
   c. A patient who is difficult to arouse
   d. A patient who is violently thrashing about

4. You never restrain a patient in the prone position because—
   a. This position will limit too much of his or her movement.
   b. You must have access to the patient's airway at all times.
   c. The patient can gain easy access to remove the restraints.
   d. You will have difficulty securing the restraints.

5. When preparing to restrain a patient, at least how many *emergency medical responders* (EMRs) should be available?
   a. 3
   b. 4
   c. 5
   d. 6

6. You are preparing to transport a patient who weighs 750 lb. Which type of stretcher would be most appropriate to use?
   a. Scoop stretcher
   b. Standard wheeled stretcher
   c. Orthopedic stretcher
   d. Bariatric stretcher

7. When using the clothes drag technique, you would be moving in which direction?
   a. Forward
   b. Backward
   c. To the right
   d. To the left

8. Which technique would require at least three responders to be present?
   a. Walking assist
   b. Pack-strap carry
   c. Direct ground lift
   d. Extremity lift

9. You and your partner arrive at the home of a patient who needs to be transported to the medical facility. You plan to move the patient from the bed to the stretcher using the direct carry technique. You position the stretcher—
   a. At a right angle to the patient's bed.
   b. With the stretcher's head parallel to the bed's head.
   c. Alongside the bed with the stretcher's head at the bed's foot.
   d. At the foot of the bed, parallel to the bottom of the bed.

10. You always begin lifting a patient with your—
    a. Head facing down.
    b. Feet close together.
    c. Flexed arms relaxed.
    d. Back in locked-in position.

11. Which of the following is appropriate to do when using the squat lift?
    a. Stand with your feet shoulder width apart
    b. Lift your upper body before your hips
    c. Place your right leg in front of the left leg
    d. Lead with your shoulders

12. You try to reposition a piece of equipment but find that this is not possible. You reach for the equipment with the understanding that you should reach no more than which distance in front of your body?
    a. 10 inches
    b. 15 inches
    c. 20 inches
    d. 25 inches

13. When preparing to move and lift a patient, you should—
    a. Estimate the weight of the patient and any equipment to be used.
    b. Refrain from talking with the patient who is being moved.
    c. Keep the weight of the patient as far away from your body as possible.
    d. Bend at the knees rather than at your hips and waist.

14. You reach under the patient's armpits from the back and grasp the patient's forearms to drag him. You are using which emergency move?
    a. Clothes drag
    b. Blanket drag
    c. Shoulder drag
    d. Ankle drag

15. You would place a patient in the supine position if the patient was experiencing which of the following? Select all that apply.
    a. Difficulty breathing
    b. No breathing or pulse
    c. Suspected head or neck injury
    d. Shock
    e. Abdominal pain
    f. Vomiting

| SKILL SHEETS |

Refer to the *Emergency Medical Response* textbook for the following skill sheets for this chapter:

- Clothes Drag, page 100
- Blanket Drag, page 101
- Shoulder Drag, page 102
- Ankle Drag, page 103
- Firefighter's Drag, page 104
- Firefighter's Carry, page 105
- Pack-Strap Carry, page 106
- Walking Assist, page 107
- Two-Person Seat Carry, page 108
- Direct Ground Lift, pages 109–110
- Extremity Lift, pages 111–112

2 | ASSESSMENT

6 | Scene Size-Up

| REVIEW OF CONCEPTS AND TERMS |

Fill-in-the-Blank

Directions: *Write the correct term in the space provided.*

1. A _____ injury due to an explosion may occur because of the energy released, debris or the impact of the person falling against an object or the ground.

2. Falls and motor-vehicle crashes are examples of a _____ of injury.

3. A person who falls against the steering wheel has experienced _____ trauma.

4. You identify a _____ as a large bluish lump formed by blood clotting under the skin.

5. The first priority when arriving at an emergency scene is _____.

6. The use of wooden blocks to help stabilize a vehicle is called _____.

Short Answer

Directions: *Supply the information requested.*

1. List six items or activities that could be used when implementing standard precautions.

    _____
    _____
    _____
    _____
    _____
    _____

2. Name four common *mechanisms of injury* (MOIs).

    _____
    _____
    _____
    _____

3. Define the term "kinematics of trauma."

    _____
    _____
    _____
    _____

4. State four indications that a vehicle is unstable.

_____

_____

_____

_____

5. List four factors that determine the severity of injuries caused by a fall.

_____

_____

_____

_____

6. Explain why a bullet from a handgun causes more bodily damage than a stabbing with a knife.

_____

_____

_____

_____

| CASE STUDY |

Directions: *Read the case studies and answer the questions that follow.*

Scenario A

You are called to the scene of a motor-vehicle crash on a dark, two-lane highway. The car crashed through the guardrail and landed on a slope of a small ravine. The driver, who said he "skid on a patch of ice and lost control of the car," is alert but complaining of pain in his chest and difficulty breathing. He was wearing a seat belt with a shoulder strap and the driver's front and side airbags were activated. You notice a strong smell of gasoline in the area.

1. Which of the following would be your priority when first arriving on the scene?
   a. Ensuring scene safety
   b. Providing patient care
   c. Determining the MOI
   d. Identifying the need for additional resources

2. Which of the following would be most important for you to do?
   a. Get the patient out of the car
   b. Stabilize the vehicle
   c. Put on *personal protective equipment* (PPE)
   d. Ask the patient if he can move his arms

3. Based on the patient's MOI, you might suspect injuries to which of the following? Select all that apply.
   a. Chest
   b. Face
   c. Abdomen
   d. Head
   e. Shoulders

Scenario B

You and your partner are called to a local tavern where a fight has broken out and has since progressed into the streets. When you arrive, you observe four to five individuals fighting on the sidewalk. Two individuals are lying on the ground and bleeding. Broken glass is all over the ground, and a crowd has gathered around the individuals, screaming and yelling at them.

1. Which of the following would be your initial action upon arriving at the scene?
   a. Walk quickly to the two injured individuals to provide care
   b. Wait for law enforcement personnel to arrive to secure the scene
   c. Set up barriers around the scene to keep bystanders back
   d. Notify personnel trained to deal with hazardous materials

2. You are providing care to one of the patients who is bleeding and find that he has sustained a stab wound. You would identify this as which of the following?
   a. Blunt trauma
   b. Contusion
   c. Penetrating injury
   d. Hematoma

3. When approaching this scene, whose safety would be of the highest priority?
   a. Yours
   b. The patients'
   c. The crowd's
   d. Law enforcement's

| SELF-ASSESSMENT |

Directions: *Answer the questions by selecting the correct letter(s) or by placing the answers in the proper order.*

1. Which of the following would be least likely to affect your decision about the number of additional resources needed at the scene?
   a. Nature of the illness
   b. Number of injured persons
   c. Evidence of any hazards
   d. Number of bystanders

2. When approaching an emergency scene, which of the following would lead you to suspect that hazardous materials are present? Select all that apply.
   a. Vapor cloud
   b. Broken glass
   c. Strange odor
   d. Spilled liquid
   e. Downed power lines

3. You determine that a patient requires assisted ventilations. Which of the following would you expect to use when adhering to standard precautions?
   a. Face mask
   b. Protective eyewear
   c. CPR breathing barrier
   d. Gown

4. When on scene, which individual is responsible for traffic control at an emergency scene?
   a. The *emergency medical responder* (EMR)
   b. A designated bystander
   c. Law enforcement personnel
   d. Driver of an emergency vehicle

5. You would suspect head, neck or spinal injuries if a patient who is 6 feet tall falls onto a hard surface from a height greater than—
   a. 2 feet.
   b. 4 feet.
   c. 5 feet.
   d. 7 feet.

6. Which vehicle is unstable?
   a. A vehicle that has been struck and has rolled over with its two side wheels over the guardrail
   b. A vehicle that has been struck from the rear and has ended up on the shoulder of the road
   c. A vehicle that has collided head-on with a telephone pole
   d. A vehicle that has been struck from the side and now is facing oncoming traffic

7. You are providing care to a patient involved in a motor-vehicle crash in which the patient was wearing a lap belt without a shoulder strap. The lap belt was fastened across the base of his pelvis. You would be alert for injury to which of the following?
   a. Chest
   b. Hip
   c. Abdomen
   d. Shoulder

8. A patient was hit in the leg with a baseball bat. You would identify this injury as which of the following?
   a. Blunt trauma
   b. Penetrating trauma
   b. Blast injury
   c. Chocking

9. During the primary phase of a blast injury, which body structures would most likely experience injury? Select all that apply.
   a. Stomach
   b. Muscles
   c. Lungs
   d. Bones
   e. Inner ear
   f. Skin
   g. Intestines

10. You arrive at the home of a patient in response to a 9-1-1 call made by his wife. On arrival you observe that the patient is in the tripod position. You would suspect which of the following?
   a. Abdominal pain
   b. Fracture
   c. Stroke
   d. Difficulty breathing

11. You suspect that *hazardous materials* (HAZMATs) may be present at an emergency scene, and you notify dispatch about the need for specialized personnel. While waiting for the specialized personnel to arrive, which of the following would you do?
   a. Attempt to approach the scene to identify the material.
   b. Put on a mask and gown so you can care for the patient.
   c. Stay uphill and upwind from the emergency scene.
   d. Await the arrival of law enforcement to clear the scene.

12. Which of the following is the highest priority when responding to a call involving domestic violence?
   a. Ensure that the suspected perpetrator is on the other side of the room when you are caring for the patient.
   b. Wait for law enforcement to secure the scene before attempting to enter.
   c. Use yes–no questions with the patient to prevent further escalation of violence.
   d. Ask questions, speaking directly to the patient and suspected perpetrator together.

13. A whiplash injury is associated with which type of motor-vehicle crash?
   a. Head-on
   b. Rear-end
   c. Side impact
   d. Rotational

14. When arriving on the scene of an emergency involving a person who has fallen from a ladder, you understand that the severity of the injury increases with the height of the fall because—
    a. The speed of the fall increases with greater heights.
    b. The landing is less likely to be soft and yielding.
    c. More objects are present to cause additional injuries.
    d. The patient is more likely to fall head first.

15. You are caring for a patient who has been involved in a chemical plant explosion and you notice effects from the secondary phase of the explosion. Which of the following would you identify?
    a. Difficulty breathing
    b. Hearing difficulties
    c. Head injuries
    d. Open wounds

16. You arrive at the scene of an emergency. Place the following steps in the proper sequence, starting with what you would do first.
    a. Ensure patient safety.
    b. Decide on necessary additional resources.
    c. Determine the MOI.
    d. Ensure personal safety.
    e. Call for additional support services.

17. When sizing up the scene of an emergency, which of the following would be most appropriate?
    a. Await the arrival of additional resource personnel.
    b. Ensure the safety of the patient above anything else.
    c. Use each of your senses to determine any hazards.
    d. Rely on the information provided to you by dispatch.

| SELF-ASSESSMENT: ENRICHMENT |

Dealing with Hazards at the Scene

Directions: *Answer the questions by selecting the correct letter(s).*

1. Which of the following is considered a primary cause of death among *emergency medical services* (EMS) workers?
    a. Fire
    b. Traffic on roadways
    c. Water
    d. Electricity

2. When responding to an emergency situation in which a conscious patient is in the water, which of the following would you do first?
    a. Throw the patient something that floats.
    b. Use a boat to get closer to the patient.
    c. Reach out to the patient with a pole.
    d. Go into the water to rescue the patient.

3. Which of the following would be considered a natural disaster? Select all that apply.
    a. Hurricane
    b. Refinery explosion
    c. Building collapse
    d. Earthquake
    e. Tornado

4. You are moving a crowd back from an area involving a downed electrical line. The length of the span of wire is 15 feet. You would establish a safe area at which distance?
   a. 15 feet
   b. 20 feet
   c. 25 feet
   d. 30 feet

5. Which of the following would be the priority when arriving at a hostage situation?
   a. Ensure that you do not become a hostage.
   b. Get information from the bystanders if possible.
   c. Attempt to calm the person who has taken the hostage.
   d. Try to restrain the hostage taker for law enforcement.

7 | Primary Assessment

| REVIEW OF CONCEPTS AND TERMS |

Crossword Puzzle

Directions: *Complete the crossword puzzle using the clues.*

DOWN

1 What the patient reports experiencing, such as pain
3 Major artery supplying blood to the brain
4 Isolated or infrequent gasping in the absence of other breathing in an unconscious person
7 Circulation of blood through the body or a body part
8 Main artery of the upper arm

ACROSS

2 Below-normal oxygen concentration in organs and tissues
5 Bluish discoloration of the skin
6 An observable evidence of injury or illness
9 A person's state of alertness; mental status

Fill-in-the-Blank

Directions: *Write the correct term in the space provided.*

1. The first step in the primary assessment is to determine what has occurred and what is happening with the patient. This is called a
_____
_____ , which will determine your immediate course of action.

2. Important information about the patient's condition obtained by checking responsiveness, breathing, pulse and circulation is called _____
_____.

3. A person's *level of consciousness* (LOC) can range from being fully _____ to being unconscious.

4. Try to approach a patient from the _____ so that the patient does not have to turn his or her head.

5. To open the airway of a patient with a suspected head, neck or spinal injury, use the _____ maneuver.

6. The normal breathing rate for an adult is between _____ and _____ breaths per minute.

7. The normal pulse rate for an infant ranges between _____ and _____ *beats per minute* (bpm).

Short Answer

Directions: *Supply the information requested.*

1. List five life-threatening conditions that you would assess for when performing a primary assessment.
_____
_____
_____
_____
_____

2. Name the three assessments that you would complete after assessing a patient's LOC.
_____
_____
_____

3. Explain how you assess a patient's breathing status.
_____
_____

4. Describe what capillary refill indicates.
_____
_____

5. Identify the two techniques that can be used to open a patient's airway.
_____
_____

| CASE STUDY |

Directions: *Read the case studies and answer the questions that follow.*

Scenario A

You are called to a home in response to a call that an adolescent who was swimming in the pool has been injured. Upon your arrival, you find a 17-year-old girl who is lying on her right side beside the pool and is not moving.

1. Which of the following would you do first?
   a. Open the patient's airway.
   b. Assess her LOC.
   c. Check her pulse.
   d. Begin to provide ventilations.

2. During your primary assessment, you assess that the patient can open her eyes when you ask her to do so. You would describe this as which of the following?
   a. The patient responds to verbal stimuli.
   b. The patient is alert and aware of surroundings.
   c. The patient responds to painful stimuli.
   d. The patient is unconscious.

3. The patient should be in which position when you assess her airway status?
   a. On her left side
   b. In the position that you found her
   c. Supine, face-up
   d. Prone, face turned to the side

4. Which of the following findings would you consider abnormal?
   a. Pulse of 70 bpm
   b. Capillary refill of 2 seconds
   c. Respiratory rate of 18 breaths per minute
   d. Bluish skin color

Scenario B

You arrive at the scene in which a 65-year-old man has fallen on an icy sidewalk and is unable to get up. His neighbor called 9-1-1. The man is talking and complaining of severe pain in his left upper leg. His left upper pant leg is torn, exposing a visible open wound that is oozing blood and with what appears to be a bone protruding from it.

1. When approaching this patient, you would proceed in a specific manner. Which of the following would be stated or asked first?
   a. "What is your name?"
   b. "I am an emergency medical responder here to help you."
   c. "Can you tell me what happened?"
   d. "Will you let me examine you?"

2. Based on the situation, you would expect to determine which of the following about the patient? Select all that apply.
   a. The patient has an open airway.
   b. The patient is unconscious.
   c. The patient lacks a pulse.
   d. The patient may be at risk for compromised airway.
   e. The patient is breathing adequately.

3. Your primary assessment reveals several signs and symptoms. Which of the following would be considered a symptom?
   a. Complaints of leg pain
   b. Open leg wound
   c. Respiratory rate of 22 breaths per minute
   d. Bleeding from the leg wound

| SELF-ASSESSMENT |

Directions: *Answer the questions by selecting the correct letter(s) or by placing the answers in the proper order.*

1. You perform a primary assessment for which reason?
   a. Ensure scene safety
   b. Identify possible immediate threats to life
   c. Help determine the *mechanism of injury* (MOI)
   d. Decide if you need additional resources

2. You would expect to summon more advanced personnel if you assess which of the following? Select all that apply.
   a. Prolonged chest pain
   b. Difficulty breathing
   c. Vomiting
   d. Intermittent abdominal pressure
   e. Seizure

3. Which of the following is considered a sign?
   a. Pain
   b. Nausea
   c. Bleeding
   d. Shortness of breath

4. The following stages indicate LOC. Place them in the order from highest to lowest level of awareness.
   a. Unconscious
   b. Verbal
   c. Alert
   d. Painful

5. You check a patient's pulse and count the number of beats occurring in 15 seconds and find it to be 20. What is the pulse rate in beats per minute?
   a. 240
   b. 120
   c. 80
   d. 40

6. A patient who is not breathing at all is said to be experiencing—
   a. Respiratory distress.
   b. Agonal gasping.
   c. Cyanosis.
   d. Respiratory arrest.

7. When assessing the pulse of an infant, you would place your fingers at which artery?
   a. Carotid
   b. Brachial
   c. Radial
   d. Femoral

8. You need to open an unresponsive patient's mouth to clear the airway of fluids. Which of the following would you use?
   a. Head-tilt/chin-lift method
   b. Jaw-thrust maneuver
   c. Cross-finger technique
   d. Neck hyperextension

9. When assessing a patient's breathing and pulse, look, listen and feel for no longer than—
   a. 5 seconds.
   b. 10 seconds.
   c. 15 seconds.
   d. 20 seconds.

10. While performing the head-tilt/chin-lift technique, tilt the patient's head just past neutral if the patient is a(n)—
    a. Adult.
    b. Adolescent.
    c. Child.
    d. Infant.

11. Which of the following would lead you to suspect that a conscious patient is experiencing a breathing problem? Select all that apply.
    a. Shrill whistling sounds with breaths
    b. Grunting with each breath
    c. Quiet, effortless breaths
    d. Gasping with breathing
    e. Deep, regular breathing

12. When evaluating perfusion, which of the following would you note about the skin? Select all that apply.
    a. Color
    b. Intactness
    c. Moisture
    d. Temperature
    e. Pulse
    f. Capillary refill

13. Which of the following would you expect to note first if a patient was developing shock?
    a. Weak pulse
    b. Irritability
    c. Pale skin
    d. Excessive thirst

14. Your assessment reveals that a drowning victim has a pulse but is not breathing. You prepare to use a resuscitation mask to give 2 initial ventilations. Which of the following would you do next?
    a. Apply even downward pressure on the mask
    b. Blow into the mask
    c. Attach a one-way valve to the mask
    d. Seal the mask

15. After you size-up the scene, the following are steps involved with performing a primary assessment for a child. Place them in the order in which they should occur.
    a. Summon more advanced medical personnel
    b. Check the patient for responsiveness
    c. Quickly scan for severe bleeding
    d. Check for breathing and a pulse

16. When checking a patient's pulse, you would use—
    a. Two fingers.
    b. The palm of the hand.
    c. The thumb.
    d. The back of the hand.

17. Your assessment reveals that a patient is stable. You would routinely reassess this patient every—
    a. 5 minutes.
    b. 10 minutes.
    c. 15 minutes.
    d. 20 minutes.

18. Which method is most appropriate to use when checking an infant for responsiveness?
    a. Asking the parent if the infant is okay
    b. Calling the infant by his or her name
    c. Flicking the underside of the foot
    d. Clapping your hands near the infant's ear

19. Your primary assessment reveals that the patient is moving air freely in and out of the chest and has pale, moist skin. Which action would be most appropriate?
    a. Providing 2 initial ventilations immediately
    b. Administering emergency oxygen to the patient if available
    c. Continuing to monitor for changes
    d. Clearing the airway of debris

20. When using a resuscitation mask, place the rim of the mask between—
    a. The lower lip and chin.
    b. The mouth and nose.
    c. The upper and lower lips.
    d. The bridge of the nose and lower jaw.

| SELF-ASSESSMENT: ENRICHMENT |

Glasgow Coma Scale

Directions: *Answer the questions by selecting the correct letter(s).*

1. Which parameters are evaluated when using the Glasgow Coma Scale? Select all that apply.
   a. Eye opening
   b. Painful stimuli
   c. Motor response
   d. Speech response
   e. Verbal response
   f. Posturing response

2. Which of the following patients would require the use of the Pediatric Glasgow Coma Scale?
   a. 12 year old
   b. 9 year old
   c. 6 year old
   d. 3 year old

| SKILL SHEETS |

Directions: Refer to the *Emergency Medical Response* textbook for the following skill sheets for this chapter:

- Jaw-Thrust (Without Head Extension) Maneuver, page 153
- Using a Resuscitation Mask—Adult, Child and Infant, pages 154–155
- Using a Resuscitation Mask—Head, Neck or Spinal Injury Suspected (Jaw-Thrust [Without Head Extension] Maneuver)—Adult or Child, pages 154–157
- Primary Assessment, pages 158–160

8 | History Taking and Secondary Assessment

| REVIEW OF CONCEPTS AND TERMS |

Short Answer

Directions: *Supply the information requested.*

1. Name the two pieces of equipment that are needed to measure blood pressure.

   _____

   _____

2. List the six areas of information that are collected with the SAMPLE history.

   _____

   _____

   _____

   _____

   _____

   _____

3. Explain the purpose of a secondary assessment.

   _____

   _____

   _____

   _____

   _____

   _____

   _____

   _____

4. Identify the six characteristics assessed when gathering information about a patient's complaint.

   _____

   _____

   _____

   _____

   _____

   _____

   _____

   _____

5. Explain the mnemonic, DOTS.

   _____

   _____

   _____

   _____

   _____

Fill-in-the-Blank

Directions: *Write the correct term in the space provided.*

1. _____ involves listening to the sounds within the body through a stethoscope.

2. The number of breaths per minute is referred to as the _____

   _____.

3. Abnormal lung sounds heard as small, popping, rattling or bubbly sounds are called _____.

4. Blood pressure measures the _____ of blood against the walls of the artery as it travels through the body.

5. _____ refers to the examination performed by feeling part of the body, such as feeling for a pulse.

Labeling

Performing a Physical Exam

Directions: *Review the photos and place the photos in their proper sequence. Write the number of the step in the box provided.*

A

B

C

D

E

F

G

H

Taking a Patient's Blood Pressure by Auscultation

Directions: *Review the photos and place them in their proper sequence. Write the number of the step in the box provided.*

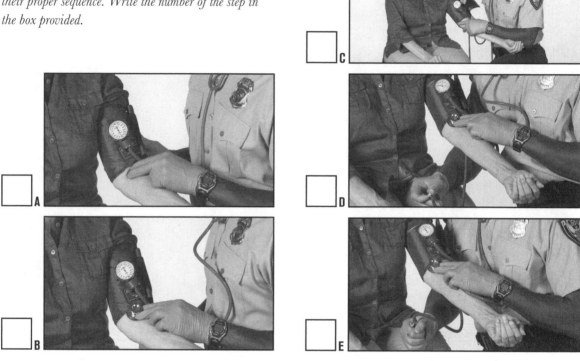

I CASE STUDY I

Directions: *Read the case studies and answer the questions that follow.*

Scenario A

You are called to the home of a couple in their 50s in response to a 9-1-1 call. Upon arrival, the wife states that her husband was mowing the lawn and "passed out." The patient is now alert and oriented, sitting on the porch step. He is pale and sweating profusely. The wife tells you that he has high blood pressure for which he takes medication. The patient denies any complaints of chest pain.

1. When obtaining the SAMPLE history, you would identify which of the following as the chief complaint?
   a. Pale skin
   b. Absence of chest pain
   c. High blood pressure
   d. Fainting

2. Which of the following would be most important for you to do before providing care to the patient?
   a. Obtain his vital signs.
   b. Determine the *mechanism of injury* (MOI).
   c. Obtain consent from the patient.
   d. Ask the patient what happened.

3. Which finding would correlate to the "E" in the SAMPLE history?
    a. The patient having high blood pressure.
    b. The patient mowing the lawn.
    c. The patient sweating profusely.
    d. The patient using medications for high blood pressure.

Scenario B

You arrive at the home of a young adult female whose roommate called 9-1-1 because the patient was having difficulty breathing. The patient has a history of asthma and allergies. She is responsive and alert.

1. Which of the following questions would you ask first?
    a. "When did this difficulty first start?"
    b. "Does anything make it better or worse?"
    c. "How would you rate your difficulty breathing?"
    d. "How long have you been experiencing this problem?"

2. You are assessing the patient's rate and quality of breathing. Which of the following is most appropriate for you to do?
    a. Tell the patient that you are going to count how fast she is breathing.
    b. Check her respiratory rate and quality without her knowing you are doing so.
    c. Count each inhalation and exhalation as two breaths.
    d. Know that noisy breathing is an expected normal finding with this patient.

3. You approximate this patient's systolic blood pressure to be 80 mmHg. When checking her blood pressure by auscultation, you would inflate the cuff to which reading?
    a. 80 mmHg
    b. 90 mmHg
    c. 100 mmHg
    d. 110 mmHg

| SELF-ASSESSMENT |

Directions: *Answer the questions by selecting the correct letter(s) or by placing the answers in the proper order.*

1. You would expect to obtain a trauma patient's history at which time?
    a. Before the physical exam
    b. During the physical exam
    c. After the physical exam
    d. Before transporting the patient

2. When obtaining a history from a child, which of the following is the most appropriate?
    a. Separating the child from the parent
    b. Positioning yourself at the child's eye level
    c. Asking the child the questions quickly
    d. Focusing the questions to the parent

3. When you obtain the SAMPLE history, the patient states that she drank a glass of water about 2 hours ago. You identify this as related to which of the following of the mnemonic?
    a. S
    b. M
    c. L
    d. E

4. You perform a secondary assessment on a responsive patient using the following steps. Place the steps in their proper sequence as you would perform them.
   a. Perform a focused medical assessment
   b. Assess baseline vital signs
   c. Obtain a SAMPLE history
   d. Perform components of a detailed physical exam
   e. Assess the patient's complaints
   f. Provide emergency care

5. When performing the physical exam, which of the following is most important for you to do?
   a. Manipulate the patient's clothing to access the area to be examined.
   b. Keep the area covered while you are examining it.
   c. Ask the patient questions about the area after examining it.
   d. Conduct the exam in a location that cannot be seen by bystanders.

6. You are assessing an injured patient using the mnemonic DOTS. The patient has a gunshot wound resulting in a fractured femur. You would consider the fractured femur as which component of the mnemonic?
   a. D
   b. O
   c. T
   d. S

7. You are examining the head of a patient. Which finding would you identify as normal?
   a. Both pupils are equal in size
   b. Clear fluid around the ears
   c. Pupil constriction on exposure to darkness
   d. Facial asymmetry

8. You are assessing an 8-month-old infant's respiratory rate. Which finding would you identify as normal?
   a. 18 breaths per minute
   b. 22 breaths per minute
   c. 34 breaths per minute
   d. 58 breaths per minute

9. When obtaining a patient's blood pressure, which of the following would be most appropriate?
   a. Apply the cuff over the patient's thickly clothed arm.
   b. Position the bladder of the cuff over the radial artery.
   c. Allow the patient's arm to hang down at his side.
   d. Ensure the cuff covers about two-thirds of his upper arm.

10. A patient's systolic blood pressure reflects—
    a. The force against arterial walls with heart contraction.
    b. The force against arterial walls between contractions.
    c. Occlusion of the pulse with compression of the brachial artery.
    d. The last sound heard with the release of air from the bulb.

11. You are caring for a child who is 5 years old. You would estimate the child's average blood pressure to be—
    a. 90 mmHg.
    b. 100 mmHg.
    c. 110 mmHg.
    d. 120 mmHg.

12. You provide an ongoing assessment for which reason?
    a. To identify life-threatening conditions
    b. To clarify the patient's history
    c. To further assess signs and symptoms
    d. To monitor changes in the patient's condition

13. When examining the abdomen during the physical exam, which of the following would you do? Select all that apply.
    a. Ask the patient about any pain.
    b. Observe for pulsations.
    c. Have the patient shrug his shoulders.
    d. Push in on the sides of the hips.
    e. Inspect for a protruding jugular vein.

14. Which of the following would you do first when performing a secondary assessment for a responsive medical patient?
    a. Obtain a SAMPLE history
    b. Perform a physical exam
    c. Assess the patient's complaints
    d. Assess baseline vital signs

15. You are assessing an 8 year old's vital signs. Which pulse rate would you identify as normal?
    a. 60 *beats per minute* (bpm)
    b. 75 bpm
    c. 90 bpm
    d. 140 bpm

| SELF-ASSESSMENT: ENRICHMENT |

Pulse Oximetry

Directions: *Answer the questions by selecting the correct letter(s).*

1. Which reading via pulse oximetry would indicate mild hypoxia?
   a. 98 percent
   b. 95 percent
   c. 92 percent
   d. 89 percent

2. At which frequency would you expect to record pulse oximetry for a stable patient?
   a. Every 5 minutes
   b. Every 10 minutes
   c. Every 15 minutes
   d. Every 20 minutes

3. Which factors may decrease the reliability of the pulse oximetry reading? Select all that apply.
   a. Shock
   b. Patient lying still
   c. Fingernail polish
   d. Carbon monoxide poisoning
   e Normothermia

4. You determine the need to use an alternate measuring site for obtaining a pulse oximetry reading. Which of the following would be appropriate?
   a. Finger
   b. Earlobe
   c. Elbow
   d. Lip

| SKILL SHEETS |

Refer to the *Emergency Medical Response* textbook for the following skill sheets for this chapter:

- How to Obtain a SAMPLE History, page 186
- How to Perform a Secondary Assessment for a Responsive Medical Patient, page 187
- How to Perform a Secondary Assessment for an Unresponsive Medical Patient, page 188
- Physical Exam and Patient History, pages 189–190
- How to Obtain Baseline Vital Signs, pages 191–192
- Taking and Recording a Patient's Blood Pressure (by Auscultation), pages 193–194
- Taking and Recording a Patient's Blood Pressure (by Palpation), pages 195–196

9 | Communication and Documentation

I REVIEW OF CONCEPTS AND TERMS I

Matching

Directions: *Write the letter of the description from Column 2 in the space next to the correct term in Column 1.*

Column 1

___ 1. Dispatch

___ 2. *Prehospital care report* (PCR)

___ 3. Minimum data set

___ 4. Medical control

___ 5. Echo method

Column 2

A. A standardized set of details about patients included in the PCR

B. Direction to *emergency medical responders* (EMRs) by physicians

C. Communication whereby listener repeats orders word for word

D. The point of contact between the public and responders

E. Document filled out for all emergency calls

Short Answer

Directions: *Supply the information requested.*

1. Identify the final element of emergency care.

   _____

   _____

   _____

   _____

   _____

2. List the four key components of radio communication for an *emergency medical services* (EMS) system.

   _____

   _____

   _____

   _____

3. Describe the important information that should be provided when communicating with medical control.

   _____

   _____

   _____

4. Identify the four sections of the PCR.

_____

_____

_____

_____

5. What is included in the run data section?

_____

_____

_____

_____

| CASE STUDY |

Directions: *Read the case studies and answer the questions that follow.*

Scenario A

You arrive at the scene of a motor-vehicle crash in response to a 9-1-1 call. A car has hit a guard rail head on, landing on an embankment. You are told that there are two passengers in the car.

1. The emergency call you received came from—
   a. Medical control.
   b. The receiving facility.
   c. The communications center.
   d. Other EMS personnel.

2. You are using radio communication. Which of the following is the most appropriate?
   a. Using any radio frequency available
   b. Speaking quickly with your mouth 10 inches away from the microphone
   c. Responding by saying "yes" or "no"
   d. Avoiding the use of "please" and "thank you"

3. You are preparing to transport one of the passengers to the hospital. Which information would you include in your communication with them? Select all that apply.
   a. The care provided to the patient and the patient's response
   b. The characteristics of the patient
   c. Questions about standing orders
   d. The patient's SAMPLE history
   e. The estimated time of arrival

Scenario B

You and your partner arrive at the scene of a fire in a senior citizen apartment complex. Fire personnel also are on the scene, having helped several of the tenants to safety across the street. You prepare to treat an older adult couple. The woman is sitting upright and coughing. She is holding her left arm and grimacing. The husband is standing next to her, visibly distraught about his wife.

1. When preparing to care for this couple, which of the following is the most important for you to do?
   a. Introduce yourself to the couple.
   b. Tell the woman that she fractured her arm.
   c. Address the couple by their first names.
   d. Have the husband describe the wife's problem.

2. You need to ask the wife a closed-ended question. Which of the following is an example?
   a. "Why did you call for emergency medical care?"
   b. "Are you having any pain in your arm?"
   c. "Can you tell me how you got out of the building?"
   d. "What can you tell me about yourself?"

3. You understand the need to be empathetic. Which of the following would you need to avoid?
   a. Awareness of cultural differences
   b. Sensitivity to the patient's situation
   c. Understanding of the patient's feelings
   d. Sporadic listening

| SELF-ASSESSMENT |

Directions: *Answer the questions by selecting the correct letter(s).*

1. When you are out of your vehicle, which component of radio communication would you expect to use?
   a. Base station
   b. Mobile radio
   c. Portable radio
   d. Mobile data terminal

2. *Emergency medical dispatchers* (EMDs) are responsible for which of the following? Select all that apply.
   a. Advising callers what to do until help arrives
   b. Contacting the appropriate emergency services
   c. Noting the time that the call was received
   d. Recording all conversations
   e. Providing an estimated time of arrival

3. When interviewing a patient, which of the following is most appropriate?
   a. Asking leading questions to get focused information
   b. Using why-type questions to gain insight
   c. Frequently interrupting the patient for clarification
   d. Allowing the patient to do most of the talking

4. The primary function of the run report is to—
   a. Serve as a legal document.
   b. Ensure high-quality care.
   c. Act as an educational tool.
   d. Allow for billing for services.

5. You would document the SAMPLE history in which section of the PCR?
   a. Run data
   b. Patient data
   c. Check boxes
   d. Patient narrative

6. When documenting patient information, which of the following is the most important?
   a. Not including care that you missed
   b. Being subjective
   c. Recording factual observations
   d. Making conclusions

7. You are reviewing a copy of a PCR. Where would you expect to find the patient's vital signs documented?
   a. Run data
   b. Patient data
   c. Check boxes
   d. Patient narrative

8. When providing care to a patient experiencing a medical emergency, which of the following would be the least effective in facilitating communication?
   a. Avoiding eye contact
   b. Minimizing distractions
   c. Ensuring adequate lighting
   d. Being on the same eye level with the patient

9. You are interviewing the daughter of an older adult patient who has fallen and hit his head. Which of the following is the most appropriate to say?
   a. "Can you tell me what happened?"
   b. "I'm sure your father will be fine."
   c. "Why was he walking without his cane?"
   d. "He really should be watched more carefully."

10. Which statement about documentation is most accurate?
    a. Documentation procedures are established by federal law.
    b. Procedures for documentation are fairly standardized.
    c. Documentation is as important as the care provided.
    d. Documentation provides minimal support if legal action occurs.

11. Control of the contents of a PCR falls within the—
    a. Responsibility of medical control.
    b. State in which the EMS system is located.
    c. *Health Insurance Portability and Accountability Act* (HIPAA).
    d. Facility to which the patient is transported.

12. Which aspect of the PCR is most frequently falsified?
    a. Chief complaint
    b. Vital signs
    c. Scene arrival time
    d. Time that the incident was reported

13. You are documenting information in the patient data section of the PCR. Which of the following would you include? Select all that apply.
    a. Level of alertness
    b. Respiratory rate
    c. Age
    d. Home address
    e. Time of arrival on the scene
    f. EMS unit number

14. You are communicating with medical control and receive an order for a specific treatment that you are qualified to perform. Which of the following is most appropriate when receiving the order?
    a. Repeat the order word for word.
    b. Tell medical control, "Affirmative."
    c. Have medical control repeat the order again.
    d. Tell medical control that you understand the order.

3 | AIRWAY

10 | Airway and Ventilation

| REVIEW OF CONCEPTS AND TERMS |

Matching

Directions: *Write the letter of the description from Column 2 in the space next to the correct term in Column 1.*

Column 1

___ 1. Wheezing

___ 2. Tidal volume

___ 3. Rhonchi

___ 4. Crackles

___ 5. Apnea

___ 6. Aspiration

Column 2

A. The act of taking in blood, vomit or saliva into the lungs

B. Air contained in the area between the pharynx and alveoli

C. Insufficient oxygen delivered to the body's cells

D. Normal amount of air breathed in at rest

E. Sudden blockage of an artery in the lung that is usually caused by blood clots that travel to the lungs from other parts of the body, for example, the legs

F. Rapid breathing often due to increased anxiety

Column 1

___ 7. Deadspace

___ 8. Hyperventilation

___ 9. Pulmonary embolism

___ 10. Hypoxia

Column 2

G. Popping or rattling sound also known as rales

H. High-pitched whistling sound on inhalation

I. Abnormal sound often heard without a stethoscope

J. Periodic cessation of breathing

Short Answer

Directions: *Supply the information requested.*

1. Explain the difference between respiratory distress and respiratory arrest.

   _____

   _____

   _____

   _____

   _____

2. List four underlying conditions that could lead to difficulty breathing.

_____

_____

_____

_____

3. Define the term "asthma trigger."

_____

_____

_____

4. Identify the two common methods used to open a patient's airway.

_____

_____

5. Name the two types of airway obstruction.

_____

_____

6. List two techniques used to remove visible foreign matter and fluid from the upper airway of an unconscious patient.

_____

_____

_____

_____

| CASE STUDY |

Directions: *Read the case studies and answer the questions that follow.*

Scenario A

You are summoned to a scene where you find a 25-year-old man unconscious on the floor with no suspected spinal injury. He vomited, and much of the vomit remains in his mouth. He does not appear to be breathing.

1. Which technique would you use to clear the mouth of the vomit?
   a. Abdominal thrusts
   b. Back blows
   c. Finger sweep
   d. Head-tilt/chin-lift

2. After clearing the mouth of vomit, you determine that the patient is not breathing but has a pulse. You prepare to give ventilations using a resuscitation mask, giving 1 ventilation about every—
   a. 1 second.
   b. 3 seconds.
   c. 5 seconds.
   d. 10 seconds.

3. As you are providing ventilations, the patient vomits. Which of the following would you do first?
   a. Turn the patient as a unit onto his side.
   b. Clear the airway of the vomit immediately.
   c. Reposition the patient's head to reopen the airway.
   d. Use greater force when ventilating to bypass the vomit.

Scenario B

You are called to the home of an 8-year-old child who is experiencing respiratory distress. On your arrival, the child's mother tells you that her son has a history of asthma.

1. When assessing this child, which of the following would you expect to find? Select all that apply.
   a. Wheezing noises
   b. Erect posture
   c. Slow, deep breathing
   d. Chest tightness
   e. Inability to talk and breathe at the same time
   f. Feelings of fear

2. You understand that the underlying problem associated with asthma is—
   a. Infection.
   b. Alveolar damage.
   c. Fluid build-up.
   d. Airway swelling.

3. The mother tells you that her son has certain asthma triggers. Which of the following might be included as triggers? Select all that apply.
   a. Dust
   b. Stable temperatures
   c. Upper respiratory infections
   d. Molds
   e. Animal dander

| SELF-ASSESSMENT |

Directions: *Answer the questions by selecting the correct letter(s) or by placing the answers in the proper order.*

1. When giving ventilations to an adult, you would recheck for breathing and a pulse after about—
   a. 1 minute.
   b. 2 minutes.
   c. 3 minutes.
   d. 4 minutes.

2. Which of the following indicates that you are giving effective ventilations?
   a. The chest clearly rises.
   b. The abdomen becomes distended.
   c. The mask is sealed tightly.
   d. Your breaths move easily into the mask.

3. Which structure is responsible for controlling the rate and depth of breathing based on oxygen and carbon dioxide levels in the body?
   a. Heart
   b. Lungs
   c. Brain
   d. Kidneys

4. Which of the following might occur if you provide ventilations with too much force?
   a. The patient will develop a blotchy skin discoloration.
   b. The stomach will become distended.
   c. The patient may experience a neck injury.
   d. The chest will fail to rise.

5. Which of the following is a likely cause of an anatomical airway obstruction?
   a. Food
   b. Swelling
   c. Blood
   d. Balloon

6. You determine that a child is breathing adequately based on which breathing rate?
   a. 12 breaths per minute
   b. 24 breaths per minute
   c. 36 breaths per minute
   d. 48 breaths per minute

7. Which of the following is least appropriate to use for a patient who is conscious and experiencing an obstructed airway?
   a. Back blows
   b. Chest thrusts
   c. Abdominal thrusts
   d. Finger sweep

8. You arrive on the scene of an emergency and find that a patient is hyperventilating. You determine that the patient is extremely anxious but is not experiencing any life-threatening symptoms. Which action is most appropriate?
   a. Encourage the patient to use pursed-lip breathing.
   b. Tell the patient to calm down since he is okay.
   c. Place the patient in a recovery position.
   d. Administer emergency oxygen as soon as possible.

9. When using a *bag-valve-mask resuscitator* (BVM), how many rescuers should be present to ensure effectiveness?
   a. 1
   b. 2
   c. 3
   d. 4

10. Which of the following would lead you to suspect that a patient's breathing is inadequate? Select all that apply.
   a. Lack of nasal flaring
   b. Midline trachea
   c. Rib muscles pulling in on inhalation
   d. Pursed-lip breathing
   e. Tripod positioning

11. You are caring for a patient who is not breathing and who has a significant injury to his mouth. Which method is most appropriate to use to give ventilations?
   a. Mouth-to-mouth
   b. Mouth-to-mask
   c. Mouth-to-nose
   d. Mouth-to-stoma

12. You are using a resuscitation mask to give ventilations to a child. Place the following steps in the order in which you would perform the skill.
   a. Open the airway.
   b. Position and seal the mask.
   c. Blow into the mask at a rate of 1 ventilation about every 3 seconds.
   d. Recheck for breathing and a pulse.
   e. Give ventilations for 2 minutes.

13. Which of the following is a limitation associated with using a BVM?
   a. It may interfere with the timing of chest compressions during CPR.
   b. It delivers only 16 percent oxygen.
   c. It cannot be connected to emergency oxygen.
   d. Three responders must be available.

14. You arrive on the scene of an emergency involving a 3-year-old child whose airway is obstructed. What is the most common cause of airway obstruction in this age group?
   a. Saliva
   b. Toy parts
   c. Tongue
   d. Airway swelling

15. Mouth-to-mask ventilations are advantageous over mouth-to-mouth ventilations because mouth-to-mask ventilations—
   a. Require less time to give.
   b. Deliver a higher percentage of oxygen.
   c. Require pinching the nose for a seal.
   d. Reduce the risk of disease transmission.

Assessing Breath Sounds

Directions: *Circle the letter that best answers the question.*

1. When listening to breath sounds from the front, you would place your stethoscope at which intercostal space?
   a. 2nd
   b. 3rd
   c. 4th
   d. 5th

2. When assessing a patient's breath sounds, you hear a snoring sound. You would identify this as—
   a. Wheezing.
   b. Rales.
   c. Rhonchi.
   d. Stridor.

Sellick's Maneuver (Cricoid Pressure)

Directions: *Circle the letter that best answers the question.*

1. Sellick's maneuver would most likely be used for a patient who—
   a. Is responsive.
   b. Is vomiting.
   c. Has no gag reflex.
   d. Will require a breathing tube.

2. You are asked to assist with the Sellick's maneuver. You would ensure that the patient is in which position?
   a. Supine
   b. Prone
   c. Semi-Fowler's
   d. Side-lying

Assisting the Patient with Asthma

Directions: *Circle the letter that best answers the question.*

1. While you are caring for a patient with asthma, the patient tells you that he uses a rescue inhaler. You understand that this medication provides which of the following?
   a. Long-term control
   b. Quick relief
   c. Allergy relief
   d. Infection control

2. A small-volume nebulizer delivers asthma medication in which form?
   a. Liquid
   b. Tablet
   c. Mist
   d. Dry powder

3. After the patient depresses the inhaler, the patient should hold his or her breath for a count of—
   a. 3.
   b. 5.
   c. 7.
   d. 10.

4. Which of the following is most important to do first when assisting a patient with an asthma inhaler for an acute attack?
   a. Obtain an order from medical direction.
   b. Help the patient to a comfortable position.
   c. Ensure that the prescription is for acute attacks.
   d. Shake the inhaler.

| SKILL SHEETS |

Refer to the *Emergency Medical Response* textbook for the following skill sheets for this chapter:

- Giving Ventilations—Adult and Child, pages 233–235
- Giving Ventilations—Infant, pages 236–237
- Giving Ventilations—Head, Neck or Spinal Injury Suspected—(Jaw-Thrust [Without Head Extension] Maneuver)—Adult and Child, pages 238–240
- Giving Ventilations Using a Bag-Valve-Mask Resuscitator—Two Rescuers, pages 241–243
- Performing the Sellick's Maneuver (Cricoid Pressure) *(Enrichment)*, page 246
- Assisting with an Asthma Inhaler *(Enrichment)*, pages 249–250

11 | Airway Management

| REVIEW OF CONCEPTS AND TERMS |

Fill-in-the-Blank

Directions: *Write the correct term in the space provided.*

1. Using a mechanical or manual device to remove foreign matter from the upper airway is called _____.

2. An oral or a nasal _____ _____ is a mechanical device used to keep the tongue from obstructing the airway.

3. A *bag-valve-mask resuscitator* (BVM) is an example of a _____ _____ _____.

4. The _____ is the most common cause of airway obstruction in an unconscious person.

5. A(n) _____ airway is inserted into the mouth.

Labeling

Inserting an Oral Airway

Directions: *Review the photos and place the photos in their proper sequence. Write the number of the step in the box provided.*

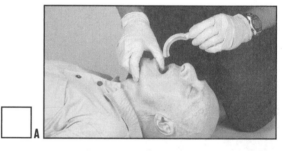
A

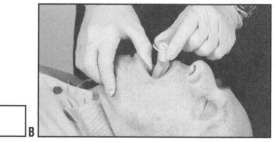
B

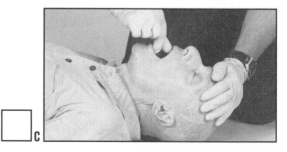
C

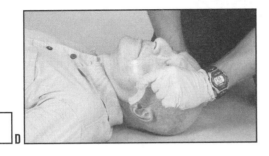
D

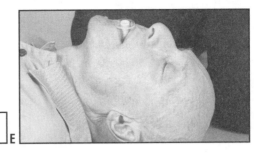
E

CASE STUDY

Directions: *Read the case studies and answer the questions that follow.*

Scenario A

You are called to a home where you find a 6-month-old girl in her crib who is struggling to breathe and is cyanotic. You do not see any rise and fall of the chest or hear or feel any air going in and out at the mouth and nose. She is conscious but not crying. You suspect an obstructed airway.

1. Which of the following would you do first?
   a. Give 2 slow ventilations.
   b. Tilt the head back.
   c. Perform 5 chest thrusts.
   d. Give 5 back blows.

2. During attempts to relieve the obstruction, position the infant's head—
   a. Lower than the chest.
   b. To the right or left side.
   c. Higher than the waist.
   d. At the same level as the rest of the body.

3. When performing chest thrusts, compress the chest to a depth of about—
   a. ¼ inch.
   b. ½ inch.
   c. 1½ inches.
   d. 2 inches.

Scenario B

You arrive at a restaurant in response to a call that a patron started choking on some food. The patient now is unconscious despite attempts by a bystander to help him.

1. Which of the following should you do first?
   a. Ensure that the patient is on a firm, flat surface.
   b. Attempt to ventilate the patient.
   c. Give 5 chest thrusts.
   d. Look inside the patient's mouth.

2. Which of the following is the most important for you to do when performing chest compressions on this patient?
   a. Compress the chest about 1 inch.
   b. Use your arms to compress the chest.
   c. Keep your fingers off of the chest.
   d. Place your fist in the center of the chest.

3. After 30 attempts, you check the patient's mouth and see the piece of food. You would remove the object with your—
   a. Thumb.
   b. Index finger.
   c. Little finger.
   d. Middle and ring finger.

Directions: *Answer the questions by selecting the correct letter(s).*

1. Which of the following best reflects manual suction devices?
   a. They are compact and lightweight.
   b. They require an energy source to function.
   c. They require sufficient suction for effective operation.
   d. They can provide positive pressure ventilations.

2. Which assessment is the highest priority when preparing to insert an *oropharyngeal airway* (OPA)?
   a. Evidence of airway obstruction
   b. Presence of a gag reflex
   c. Unresponsiveness
   d. Distance from the earlobe to the mouth

3. When preparing to suction a child using a mechanical suction device, you would limit each suction attempt to no more than—
   a. 5 seconds.
   b. 10 seconds.
   c. 15 seconds.
   d. 20 seconds.

4. You are inserting an OPA into an adult. As you reach the back of the patient's throat, he begins to gag. Which of the following would you do next?
   a. Rotate the airway 90 degrees.
   b. Continue to insert the airway.
   c. Give the patient a sip of water.
   d. Immediately remove the airway.

5. Which of the following would you identify as the universal sign that a conscious person is experiencing a foreign body airway obstruction?
   a. Coughing
   b. Clutching the throat
   c. Statement of "I'm choking."
   d. Inability to speak or cry

6. In which situation would it be appropriate for you to use back blows followed by chest thrusts for an adult?
   a. The patient is thin and frail.
   b. The patient is unconscious.
   c. The patient is pregnant.
   d. The patient is coughing.

7. Which of the following would indicate that an OPA is properly placed?
   a. The flange rests on the patient's lips.
   b. Resistance to the device is felt.
   c. No gagging occurs.
   d. The edge touches the patient's teeth.

8. You are using a mechanical suction device. You would apply the suction—
   a. As you insert the tip into the mouth.
   b. Upon reaching the back of the mouth.
   c. When touching the back of the tongue.
   d. As you withdraw the suction tip.

9. When giving abdominal thrusts to an adult, which of the following would be appropriate to do?
   a. Kneel behind the patient.
   b. Use the heel of your hand.
   c. Place a fist just above the navel.
   d. Use slow downward movements.

10. Which child would be at greatest risk for foreign body airway obstruction?
    a. 9-year-old girl
    b. 7-year-old boy
    c. 5-year-old girl
    d. 3-year-old boy

11. When giving chest compressions to an unconscious child with an airway obstruction, you would compress the chest at which rate?
    a. 80 compressions per minute
    b. 100 compressions per minute
    c. 120 compressions per minute
    d. 140 compressions per minute

12. You arrive at the local playground in response to a call that a child is choking. The 8-year-old child is responsive and coughing. His mother is standing next to him. Which of the following would you do first?
    a. Obtain consent from the mother to help the child.
    b. Encourage the child to continue coughing forcefully.
    c. Give 5 back blows followed by 5 abdominal thrusts.
    d. Lower the child to a flat, firm surface on the ground.

| SELF-ASSESSMENT: ENRICHMENT |

Nasopharyngeal Airway

Directions: *Answer the questions by selecting the correct letter(s).*

1. A *nasopharyngeal airway* (NPA) differs from an OPA in that an NPA—
   a. Cannot be used on an unconscious patient.
   b. Does not cause the patient to gag.
   c. Does not require measuring for size.
   d. Does not need to be lubricated for insertion.

2. When inserting the NPA, insert the airway with the bevel directed toward the—
   a. Nasal septum.
   b. Cheek.
   c. Roof of the mouth.
   d. Ear.

3. It would be inappropriate to use an NPA in which of the following conditions? Select all that apply.
   a. Heart attack
   b. Blunt chest trauma
   c. Suspected skull fracture
   d. Head trauma
   e. Penetrating abdominal injury

| SKILL SHEETS |

Refer to the *Emergency Medical Response* textbook for the following skill sheets for this chapter:

- Using a Mechanical Suctioning Device, pages 261–262
- Using a Manual Suctioning Device, pages 263–264
- Inserting an Oral Airway, pages 265–266
- Conscious Choking—Adult and Child, pages 267–268
- Conscious Choking—Infant, pages 269–270
- Unconscious Choking—Adult and Child, pages 271–272
- Unconscious Choking—Infant, pages 273–274
- Inserting a Nasal Airway (*Enrichment*), pages 275–276

12 | Emergency Oxygen

| REVIEW OF CONCEPTS AND TERMS |

Short Answer

Directions: *Supply the information requested.*

1. Describe how the oxygen content of air that is breathed in normally compares to that of the expired air in an exhaled breath.

   _____

   _____

   _____

2. List three essential pieces of equipment necessary to administer emergency oxygen.

   _____

   _____

   _____

3. Describe the typical oxygen cylinder found in the United States.

   _____

   _____

   _____

4. Explain the purpose of a pressure regulator attached to an oxygen cylinder.

   _____

   _____

   _____

   _____

   _____

5. Name the device that controls the amount of oxygen that is administered in *liters per minute* (LPM).

   _____

   _____

   _____

   _____

   _____

6. Identify the two major types of oxygen systems.

   _____

   _____

Labeling

Oxygen Delivery Devices

Directions: *Review the illustrations. Identify the type of oxygen delivery device being depicted in the space provided.*

1. _____

2. _____

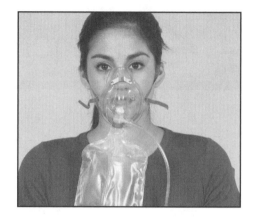

3. _____

4. _____

I CASE STUDY I

Directions: *Read the case studies and answer the questions that follow.*

Scenario A

You and your partner arrive at the scene of an emergency and find a woman lying on the floor, motionless. Your primary assessment reveals that the patient is unconscious and is not breathing, but she does have a pulse.

1. You are using a *bag-valve-mask resuscitator* (BVM) to ventilate the patient, and you attach emergency oxygen to it. You would expect to set the oxygen flowmeter to which setting?
   a. 5 LPM
   b. 10 LPM
   c. 15 LPM
   d. 13 LPM

2. You would expect that this patient is receiving which percentage of oxygen via the BVM that is attached to the oxygen delivery device?
   a. 24 percent
   b. 30 percent
   c. 55 percent
   d. 90 percent

3. Which of the following would you use to verify the oxygen flow?
   a. Movement of the flowmeter dial
   b. Audible hissing sound through the device
   c. Pressure gauge reading 190 *pounds per square inch* (psi)
   d. Absence of the O-ring gasket

Scenario B

You arrive at an office building in response to an emergency call about an employee who suddenly developed difficulty breathing. The patient, who is pale and anxious, has a respiratory rate of 26 breaths per minute. You notice that the patient is breathing through his mouth.

1. You decide to administer emergency oxygen to this patient. Which delivery device would be the least appropriate for this patient?
   a. Nasal cannula
   b. Resuscitation mask
   c. Non-rebreather mask
   d. BVM

2. A fixed-flow-rate oxygen system is available for use. Which statement best reflects this type of system?
   a. It is more practical than other types of systems.
   b. It requires minimal assembly for use.
   c. The flow rate can be adjusted as needed.
   d. The delivery device already is connected.

3. While administering emergency oxygen to this patient, you notice that the pressure gauge reads 1500 psi. Which action would be most appropriate?
   a. Increase the flow rate.
   b. Change the cylinder immediately.
   c. Continue administering emergency oxygen.
   d. Prepare to provide assisted ventilations.

| SELF-ASSESSMENT |

Directions: *Answer the questions by selecting the correct letter(s) or by placing the answers in the proper order.*

1. You determine that a child with which respiratory rate would benefit from emergency oxygen?
   a. 16 breaths per minute
   b. 22 breaths per minute
   c. 28 breaths per minute
   d. 36 breaths per minute

2. You determine that an oxygen cylinder needs to be changed when the pressure gauge reads—
   a. 2000 psi.
   b. 1000 psi.
   c. 500 psi.
   d. 200 psi.

3. When working with emergency oxygen systems, which of the following would be appropriate? Select all that apply.
   a. Checking the pressure regulator
   b. Handling the cylinder carefully
   c. Lubricating the connections
   d. Checking that the pin index is removed
   e. Hand-tightening the screw to ensure a snug regulator

4. You are preparing to use an emergency oxygen unit to provide first aid. Which of the following would be most important to keep in mind?
   a. A prescription must be obtained to use the unit.
   b. The flow rate can be adjusted to 10 to 15 LPM.
   c. The unit must contain at least a 15-minute oxygen supply.
   d. Federal regulations control how the unit is refilled.

5. When administering emergency oxygen by a fixed-flow-rate system, which of the following would be appropriate? Select all that apply.
   a. Turning on the system
   b. Opening the cylinder valve for 1 second
   c. Checking that the oxygen is flowing
   d. Placing the delivery device on the patient
   e. Attaching the regulator
   f. Opening the cylinder counterclockwise one full turn

6. Which oxygen delivery device provides the lowest concentration of oxygen?
   a. Nasal cannula
   b. Resuscitation mask
   c. Non-rebreather mask
   d. BVM

7. A nonbreathing patient is to receive emergency oxygen at 6 LPM. Which delivery device is most appropriate?
   a. BVM
   b. Resuscitation mask
   c. Nasal cannula
   d. Non-rebreather mask

8. An oxygen cylinder contains an oxygen concentration at what percentage?
   a. 25 percent
   b. 50 percent
   c. 75 percent
   d. 100 percent

9. You are using a non-rebreather mask to administer emergency oxygen. Which of the following is the most important to keep in mind?
   a. The patient exhales into the reservoir bag.
   b. The reservoir bag should be about two-thirds full.
   c. The device is inappropriate for a patient with a nasal injury.
   d. Several valves control the flow of oxygen in and out of the mask.

10. To prevent nosebleeds while administering emergency oxygen using a nasal cannula, avoid flow rates greater than—
    a. 2 LPM.
    b. 3 LPM.
    c. 4 LPM.
    d. 5 LPM.
    e. 6 LPM.

11. A patient is not breathing. Which emergency oxygen delivery device is appropriate to use? Select all that apply.
    a. Non-rebreather mask
    b. Resuscitation mask
    c. Nasal cannula
    d. BVM

12. When preparing to administer emergency oxygen using a variable-flow-rate system, which of the following would you do first?
    a. Open the cylinder valve after removing the O-ring gasket.
    b. Check the pressure regulator for the label "oxygen."
    c. Inspect the cylinder label for indication that it is oxygen.
    d. Open the cylinder counterclockwise for one full turn.

13. A patient has a respiratory rate of 36 breaths per minute. You are administering emergency oxygen using a BVM. Squeeze the bag—
    a. With each breath.
    b. Between each breath.
    c. On every second breath.
    d. With every fourth breath.

14. Which of the following would be appropriate when administering emergency oxygen? Select all that apply.
    a. Avoid using oxygen around sparks or flames.
    b. Use petroleum products to clean the regulator.
    c. Roll the cylinder when you need to move it.
    d. Check that oxygen is flowing before applying it to the patient.
    e. Use the valve or pressure regulator to carry the cylinder.

15. You are administering emergency oxygen to a child using the blow-by technique. Which action would you include?
    a. Holding the mask about 6 inches away from the child's face
    b. Waving the mask slowly from side-to-side like a game
    c. Placing the mask loosely on its side against the child's cheek
    d. Turning the flowmeter to the flow rate for 5 seconds then turning it off repeatedly

| SKILL SHEET |

Refer to the *Emergency Medical Response* textbook for the following skill sheet for this chapter:

- Oxygen Delivery, pages 286–287

4 CIRCULATION

13 | Circulation and Cardiac Emergencies

| REVIEW OF CONCEPTS AND TERMS |

Crossword Puzzle

Directions: *Complete the crossword puzzle using the clues.*

DOWN

1 A disturbance in the regular beating of the heart
2 High blood pressure
6 Fatty substance found in animal products
7 Conditions or behaviors that increase the chance that a person will develop a disease
8 Electrical shock to disrupt the heart's electrical activity

ACROSS

3 Device implanted under the skin to regulate the heartbeat
4 Condition in which the heart stops beating or beats too ineffectively to circulate blood
5 A test that measures and records the heart's electrical activity
9 Absence of electrical activity in the heart
10 Delivery of blood to body cells for gas, nutrient and waste exchange

Short Answer

Directions: *Supply the information requested.*

1. Explain *ventricular fibrillation* (V-fib).

   _____
   _____
   _____
   _____
   _____

2. Describe CPR.

   _____
   _____
   _____
   _____
   _____

3. List three situations in which you can stop CPR.

   _____
   _____
   _____
   _____
   _____

4. Name the two most common conditions caused by cardiovascular disease.

   _____
   _____
   _____
   _____
   _____

5. Trace the path of an electrical impulse in the heart.

   _____
   _____
   _____
   _____
   _____

6. Describe the major sign of a heart attack.

   _____
   _____
   _____
   _____
   _____

7. Identify the four links in the Cardiac Chain of Survival.

   _____
   _____
   _____
   _____
   _____

8. Explain how *automated external defibrillators* (AEDs) function.

   _____
   _____
   _____
   _____
   _____

| CASE STUDY |

Directions: *Read the case studies and answer the questions that follow.*

Scenario A

You are called to the scene of a drowning at a nearby lake. A 10-year-old child has just been removed from the water after being submerged for about 3 or 4 minutes. Your primary assessment reveals that the child is not breathing and has no pulse.

1. You are preparing to perform chest compressions. Where do you place your hands to be most effective?
   a. Uppermost portion of the sternum
   b. Atop the xiphoid process at the lower sternum
   c. In the middle of the chest
   d. Directly over the nipple area

2. You would compress the child's chest to which depth?
   a. About 1 inch
   b. About 1½ inches
   c. About 2 inches
   d. At least 2½ inches

3. Which of the following is most important for you to do when performing chest compressions on the child?
   a. Keeping the elbows flexed with each compression
   b. Pausing in between the up and down motion
   c. Rocking back and forth as you compress the chest
   d. Allowing the chest to recoil fully after each compression

4. An AED becomes available, and you prepare to use it. Which of the following is most important for you to do before using it with this child?
   a. Correctly placing the pads on the child's chest
   b. Ensuring that the child is not lying in a puddle of water
   c. Using pediatric defibrillation pads if available
   d. Checking to see if spare batteries are included

Scenario B

You arrive at an office building in response to a call about an employee who suddenly started complaining of chest pain. The patient also is complaining of shortness of breath and feeling sick to his stomach.

1. You obtain a SAMPLE history from the patient. Which of the following suggests that the patient is experiencing a heart attack? Select all that apply.
   a. The pain is described as squeezing and unrelieved by rest.
   b. The pain does not radiate.
   c. The patient has a history of hypertension.
   d. The patient is sitting up and leaning forward.
   e. The patient complains of feeling dizzy.
   f. The patient's face is flushed.

2. As the *emergency medical responder (*EMR) on the scene, which of the following would you do first if you suspect that the patient is having a heart attack?
   a. Get the patient to stop any activity and rest.
   b. Summon more advanced medical personnel.
   c. Closely monitor the patient's vital signs.
   d. Begin CPR.

3. Your local protocol allows you to administer medication to the patient. After asking the patient about the use of medications, you determine that it is safe to administer it. You would administer which of the following?
   a. 1 chewable baby aspirin
   b. A single dose of acetaminophen (Tylenol®)
   c. Two tablets of ibuprofen (Motrin®)
   d. One 5-grain adult aspirin tablet

Scenario C

You are on the scene of an apartment fire and are caring for a 6-month-old infant. After opening the infant's airway, you find that she is not breathing and does not have a pulse. You immediately give 2 ventilations, noting that the chest rises and falls, and you quickly scan for severe bleeding.

1. Which action would you do next?
   a. Begin chest compressions.
   b. Deliver 5 back blows.
   c. Give ventilations.
   d. Do a finger sweep.

2. You determine that the infant needs chest compressions. Which of the following would you use to perform chest compressions?
   a. The heel of your hand
   b. Two fingers of one hand
   c. Thumb side of your fist
   d. Both thumbs

3. Another EMR arrives on the scene to assist you with CPR. The cycle of compressions and ventilations that you would perform is—
   a. 30 compressions and 2 ventilations.
   b. 15 compressions and 1 ventilation.
   c. 15 compressions and 2 ventilations.
   d. 30 compressions and 1 ventilation.

| SELF-ASSESSMENT |

Directions: *Answer the questions by selecting the correct letter(s).*

1. Which of the following is the most common type of abnormal cardiac rhythm?
   a. Atrial fibrillation
   b. Sinus rhythm
   c. *Ventricular tachycardia* (V-tach)
   d. *Ventricular fibrillation* (V-fib)

2. You are assessing a child who has experienced a cardiac arrest. You understand that this is most likely the result of—
   a. Drowning.
   b. Breathing problems.
   c. Motor-vehicle injury.
   d. Poisoning.

3. You are the only EMR present and are performing CPR. Where would you position yourself to give chest compressions?
   a. At the patient's head
   b. Between the patient's legs
   c. Even with the patient's shoulders
   d. On the patient's side at the chest

4. You have been performing CPR on a patient and the patient begins to breathe. You also note a pulse. Which action is most appropriate?
   a. Cancel the call for more advanced medical personnel.
   b. Stop chest compressions but continue ventilations.
   c. Continue to monitor the patient while maintaining an open airway.
   d. Obtain an AED to check the heart rhythm.

5. To use an AED, which of the following must be present? Select all that apply.
   a. Absence of a pulse
   b. Obstructed airway
   c. No evidence of the chest rising and falling
   d. Pale or ashen skin
   e. Lack of responsiveness

6. You are applying AED pads to a child and notice that the pads may touch each other. Which action is most appropriate?
   a. Cut one of the pads in half, using a half instead of the whole.
   b. Use just one pad instead of both pads.
   c. Put one pad on the chest and the other pad on the back between the shoulder blades.
   d. Use both pads on the chest, overlapping the edges of the pads.

7. Which structure in the heart is responsible for initiating an electrical impulse?
   a. *Atrioventricular* (AV) node
   b. *Sinoatrial* (SA) node
   c. Right atrium
   d. Left ventricle

8. Which of the following would you least expect to find when assessing an older adult who may be having a heart attack?
   a. Shoulder aches
   b. Indigestion
   c. Fatigue
   d. Chest pain

9. You are called to a patient's home because the patient is complaining of chest pain. Which of the following would lead you to suspect that the patient is experiencing angina and not a heart attack?
   a. Pain spreading to the jaw and neck
   b. Pain that eases with resting
   c. Pain that is persistent
   d. Pain accompanied by difficulty breathing

10. You and another EMR are performing two-rescuer CPR. You would expect to switch positions approximately every—
    a. 2 minutes.
    b. 4 minutes.
    c. 6 minutes.
    d. 8 minutes.

11. You arrive on the scene where another EMR is performing CPR on a patient. Which of the following would you do first?
    a. Call for a position change at the end of the last compression cycle
    b. Immediately begin giving ventilations to the patient
    c. Confirm if more advanced medical personnel have been called
    d. Obtain an AED, if available

12. An AED has delivered a shock to the patient. Which of the following would you do next?
    a. Wait for the device to re-analyze the heart rhythm.
    b. Continue to monitor the patient's condition.
    c. Place the patient in a face-up position while maintaining an open airway.
    d. Begin performing CPR for about 2 minutes.

13. When interviewing a patient who is complaining of chest pain, which question is most appropriate to ask initially?
    a. "Have you ever had this type of pain before?"
    b. "Can you tell me how you feel right now?"
    c. "Does the pain move or spread anywhere?"
    d. "Is the pain crushing or squeezing?"

14. Which of the following statements best reflects the experience of a heart attack in a woman?
    a. Women often report their symptoms earlier than men.
    b. Women rarely experience shortness of breath.
    c. Chest pain in women typically is sudden and short-lived.
    d. Like men, women commonly experience chest pain as the main complaint.

15. You are preparing to apply AED pads to a patient's chest when you notice a transdermal medication patch. You should—
    a. Place the pads directly over the medication patch.
    b. Move the medication patch to another area on the chest.
    c. Remove the medication patch with a gloved hand.
    d. Apply the pads to a chest area away from the patch.

| SELF-ASSESSMENT: ENRICHMENT |

Preventing Coronary Heart Disease

Directions: *Answer the questions by selecting the correct letter(s).*

1. Which of the following statements about *coronary heart disease* (CHD) is the most accurate?
   a. CHD develops suddenly, leading to a decreased oxygen supply to the heart.
   b. CHD ranks second as the cause of death in adults in the United States.
   c. CHD involves arterial narrowing due to a buildup of fatty substances.
   d. CHD is primarily linked to genetics and family history.

2. Which of the following risk factors for CHD is a person unable to change?
   a. Diet
   b. Ethnicity
   c. Obesity
   d. Activity level

3. Which of the following is appropriate to do to control the risk factors for CHD? Select all that apply.
   a. Increase the intake of fast foods.
   b. Participate in a regular exercise program.
   c. Eat foods that are high in animal fats.
   d. Avoid cigarette smoking.
   e. Maintain blood pressure control.

| SKILL SHEETS |

Refer to the *Emergency Medical Response* textbook for the following skill sheets for this chapter:

- CPR—Adult and Child, pages 312–313
- CPR—Infant, page 314
- Two-Rescuer CPR—Adult and Child, pages 315–316
- Two-Rescuer CPR—Infant, pages 317–318
- AED—Adult, Child and Infant, pages 319–321

5 | MEDICAL EMERGENCIES

14 | Medical Emergencies

| REVIEW OF CONCEPTS AND TERMS |

Crossword Puzzle

Directions: *Complete the crossword puzzle using the clues.*

DOWN

1 Temporary loss of consciousness; syncope
2 Abnormal increase of fluid in the blood
3 Simple sugar used as the primary source of energy
5 Hormone produced by the pancreas
6 Brain disorder characterized by recurrent seizures

Matching

Directions: *Write the letter of the description from Column 2 in the space next to the correct term in Column 1.*

Column 1

___ 1. Aneurysm

___ 2. Aphasia

___ 3. Diabetes

___ 4. Embolism

___ 5. Seizure

___ 6. Sepsis

___ 7. Stroke

___ 8. Syncope

Column 2

A. Disruption of blood flow to a part of the brain
B. A disorder in the brain's electrical activity
C. A blockage in an artery or a vein caused by a blood clot that travels through the blood vessels until it gets stuck
D. Abnormal bulging of an artery due to weakness in the blood vessel
E. Condition in which the body is overwhelmed by its response to infection
F. Disorder involving the inability to produce or understand language
G. Loss of consciousness, commonly called fainting
H. Disease involving defects in insulin production and/or action

ACROSS

1 Acronym for remembering the signs of a stroke
4 Abnormally high levels of potassium in the blood
7 Decreased levels of oxygen in the blood
8 Generalized tonic-clonic seizure involving both hemispheres of the brain

Short Answer

Directions: *Supply the requested information.*

1. Identify five possible causes of altered mental status.

   _____

   _____

   _____

   _____

   _____

2. Explain what is meant by altered mental status.

   _____

   _____

   _____

   _____

3. Describe what occurs during generalized seizures.

   _____

   _____

   _____

4. List two causes of stroke.

   _____

   _____

5. Explain the two types of diabetes.

   _____

   _____

6. Describe the FAST mnemonic.

   _____

   _____

   _____

| CASE STUDY |

Directions: *Read the case studies and answer the questions that follow.*

Scenario A

You respond to an emergency call at a local fitness center. A woman who has been exercising is complaining of being light-headed and dizzy. She is breathing rapidly and her pulse is weak. Her skin is cool and clammy. You notice that she is wearing a medical ID bracelet. She tells you that she has diabetes and has not eaten since early this morning.

1. You understand that diabetes involves a problem with regulation of which of the following?
    a. Oxygen levels
    b. Brain electrical activity
    c. *Blood glucose levels* (BGLs)
    d. Fluid volume

2. You would most likely suspect which of the following?
    a. Seizure
    b. Hypoglycemia
    c. Hyperglycemia
    d. Transient ischemic attack

3. Which action is most appropriate?
    a. Have the patient give herself a dose of insulin.
    b. Offer the patient fruit juice or a non-diet soft drink.
    c. Place the patient in a supine (face-up) position.
    d. Use the head-tilt/chin-lift technique to open her airway.

Scenario B

You arrive at a shopping mall in response to an emergency call that a young man suddenly collapsed while trying on shoes in a shoe store. His friend who was with him reports that the patient mentioned hearing a strange sound before he collapsed. Additional bystanders report that the patient slumped to the floor and "then his whole body started shaking." His friend tells you that the patient has a history of seizures.

1. Which type of seizure is the patient experiencing?
    a. Simple partial seizure
    b. Complex partial seizure
    c. Generalized seizure
    d. Febrile seizure

2. You would interpret the patient's "hearing a strange sound" as indicating which of the following?
    a. Aura
    b. Tonic
    c. Clonic
    d. Post-ictal

3. The patient's seizure is ending. Which of the following is most appropriate?
    a. Positioning the patient on his side
    b. Inserting something into his mouth
    c. Restraining the patient's arms at his side
    d. Sitting the patient up in a chair

4. You would assess the patient as having status epilepticus if the seizure shows no signs of slowing down and lasts longer than—
    a. 2 minutes.
    b. 5 minutes.
    c. 8 minutes.
    d. 10 minutes.

| SELF-ASSESSMENT |

Directions: *Answer the questions by selecting the correct letter(s).*

1. Which of the following most accurately describes altered mental status?
   a. It occurs more commonly with a sudden rather than gradual change in *level of consciousness* (**LOC**).
   b. Altered mental status often can be attributed to a limited number of underlying causes.
   c. Fainting refers to an altered mental status occurring due to a sudden decrease in blood supply to the brain.
   d. Children experiencing altered mental status rarely show changes in behavior, personality or responsiveness beyond their age expectations.

2. Altered mental status due to which condition would require immediate action? Select all that apply.
   a. Sepsis
   b. Shock
   c. Hypoglycemia
   d. Poisoning

3. Seizures result from which of the following?
   a. Elevated BGLs
   b. Abnormal electrical brain activity
   c. Disrupted blood flow to the brain
   d. Abnormally low blood pressure

4. Which of the following would you expect to find in a patient experiencing an absence seizure?
   a. Rectal temperature above 102°F
   b. Jerking of one leg
   c. Blank staring
   d. Drooling

5. What is the priority when caring for a patient having a tonic-clonic seizure?
   a. Protecting the patient from injury
   b. Preventing tongue biting
   c. Clearing the airway
   d. Maintaining privacy

6. A patient has a history of seizures. Which of the following patients would least likely require summoning more advanced medical personnel?
   a. A patient who is currently pregnant
   b. A patient whose seizures are medically controlled
   c. A patient who has a seizure while in the water
   d. A patient who is known to have diabetes

7. Which of the following symptoms would you expect to assess when called to a scene in which the patient is experiencing a simple partial seizure?
   a. An extremely high body temperature
   b. Blank stare followed by random movements
   c. Unconsciousness followed by muscular rigidity
   d. Involuntary muscular contractions in one body area

8. A patient has hypoglycemia and is unconscious. Which of the following would you do?
   a. Give the patient 4 ounces of fruit juice through a straw.
   b. Crush 2 to 5 glucose tablets, placing them under his or her tongue.
   c. Summon more advanced medical personnel.
   d. Obtain another blood sample to recheck the glucose level.

9. Which of the following is the most common cause of stroke?
   a. Arterial rupture
   b. Embolism
   c. Tumor
   d. Swelling due to head injury

10. A *transient ischemic attack* (TIA) differs from a stroke in that a TIA—
    a. Has more symptoms.
    b. Has a different cause.
    c. Lasts for a shorter duration.
    d. Has a slower onset.

11. You arrive at the home of a 65-year-old man in response to a 9-1-1 call from his wife saying that he is having a stroke. The patient is conscious. Your SAMPLE history and physical exam might reveal which of the following? Select all that apply.
    a. Facial drooping
    b. Clear speech
    c. Mild headache
    d. Trouble walking
    e. Facial numbness

12. You are responding to an emergency call in which the patient is experiencing abdominal pain. Which of the following is the most important to note?
    a. The pain is serious enough to cause concern to the patient and/or others.
    b. The patient is most likely experiencing a problem in the digestive system.
    c. The pain is originating from the area involving the stomach.
    d. The intensity of the pain will indicate the severity of the situation.

13. You are called to the home of a patient with renal failure who is receiving dialysis at his home. When assessing this patient, you would be alert for which of the following as a possible complication? Select all that apply.
    a. Hypotension
    b. Air embolism
    c. Hypervolemia
    d. Bradycardia
    e. Hypokalemia

14. You arrive at the home of a patient whose spouse has called 9-1-1 because the patient is complaining of severe abdominal pain. When assessing the patient, which of the following would you do first?
    a. Check the patient's mental status and check for breathing and pulse.
    b. Obtain a general impression of the patient's appearance.
    c. Perform a physical exam using a hands-on approach.
    d. Gather a SAMPLE history from the patient and spouse.

15. When assessing a patient who you believe is having a stroke, which of the following would you assess first?
    a. Time of onset
    b. Speech
    c. Face
    d. Arm

| SELF-ASSESSMENT: ENRICHMENT |

Basic Pharmacology

Directions: *Answer the questions by selecting the correct letter(s).*

1. A drug profile typically describes which of the following about the drug? Select all that apply.
   a. Actions
   b. Serial number
   c. Side effects
   d. Route of administration
   e. Expiration date
   f. Manufacturer's name

2. Nitroglycerin is administered to—
   a. Relieve pain.
   b. Thin the blood.
   c. Dilate the blood vessels.
   d. Elevate BGLs.

3. When administering a drug authorized by medical direction, you would document which of the following? Select all that apply.
   a. Reason for and time of administration
   b. Drug name and dose
   c. Manufacturer's name and address
   d. Improvement and/or changes in the patient
   e. Route and time of administration

4. Aspirin acts by—
   a. Dilating blood vessels to enhance blood flow.
   b. Reducing platelets' ability to form clots.
   c. Increasing the amount of glucose in the blood.
   d. Increasing the amount of oxygen to the heart tissue.

5. Nitroglycerin is contraindicated in which of the following patients?
   a. A patient experiencing chest pain due to angina.
   b. A patient taking aspirin.
   c. A patient with early signs of a heart attack.
   d. A patient with a systolic blood pressure over 90 mmHg.

Blood Glucose Monitoring

Directions: *Circle the letter that best answers the question.*

1. Which value would you identify as an abnormal BGL before meals?
   a. 90 mg/dL
   b. 110 mg/dL
   c. 125 mg/dL
   d. 145 mg/dL

2. You suspect that a patient is experiencing hypoglycemia. You test the patient's BGL. Which result would confirm your suspicions?
   a. 62 mg/dL
   b. 76 mg/dL
   c. 88 mg/dL
   d. 100 mg/dL

15 | Poisoning

I REVIEW OF CONCEPTS AND TERMS I

Matching

Directions: *Write the letter of the description from Column 2 in the space next to the correct term in Column 1.*

Column 1

___ 1. Addiction

___ 2. Dependency

___ 3. Tolerance

___ 4. Withdrawal

___ 5. Overdose

Column 2

A. Effects of a substance on the body decrease due to continued use

B. The desire or need to continually use a substance

C. The compulsive need to use a substance

D. Mental and physical discomfort produced with the cessation of substance use or abuse

E. Use of an excessive amount of a substance leading to adverse, possibly life-threatening reactions

Chart Completion

Directions: *Complete the chart by writing the name of the drug from the list below in the correct column that identifies the category to which the drug belongs.*

Lysergic acid diethylamide (LSD)
Ecstasy
Ketamine
Morphine
Methamphetamine
Phencyclidine (PCP)
MDMA
Cocaine
Heroin
Diazepam (Valium®)

STIMULANTS	HALLUCINOGENS	DEPRESSANTS	NARCOTICS	DESIGNER DRUGS

| CASE STUDY |

Directions: *Read the case studies and answer the questions that follow.*

Scenario A

You respond to a call in which a passer-by noticed a middle-aged man lying on the sidewalk just in front of the doorway to a building. Upon arrival, you find that the patient is lying face-down and you notice vomit on the sidewalk and in his mouth. He is unresponsive. His chest is moving up and down in a shallow, slow fashion. You notice an empty bottle of liquor protruding out from under the patient's jacket.

1. You suspect alcohol poisoning. Alcohol is classified as which of the following?
   a. Stimulant
   b. Depressant
   c. Hallucinogen
   d. Narcotic

2. Which of the following would you do first?
   a. Call for more advanced medical personnel.
   b. Attempt to get the patient to sit up.
   c. Turn the patient onto his side.
   d. Assess his airway.

3. You would identify that the poison entered the body by which route?
   a. Inhalation
   b. Absorption
   c. Ingestion
   d. Injection

4. While caring for the patient, you also find a bottle of prescription medication next to him. The label reads codeine. You would identify this drug as which of the following?
   a. Depressant
   b. Hallucinogen
   c. Cannabis product
   d. Narcotic

5. You would suspect which effect if the patient has taken both drugs?
   a. Dependency
   b. Tolerance
   c. Synergistic
   d. Addiction

Scenario B

You arrive at the home of a young couple who called 9-1-1 because their 2 year old got into the cabinet under the sink and drank some liquid drain cleaner.

1. Upon arriving at the scene, which of the following is most appropriate to do first?
   a. Induce vomiting immediately.
   b. Call the national *Poison Control Center* (PCC) hotline.
   c. Have the child drink large amounts of water.
   d. Have the child eat a piece of bread.

2. Which of the following would least likely affect the severity of the poisoning in this child?
   a. Amount of substance ingested
   b. Child's weight
   c. Time elapsed since ingestion
   d. Child's gender

| SELF-ASSESSMENT |

Directions: *Answer the questions by selecting the correct letter(s).*

1. Which statement best reflects the most recent statistics about poisoning in the United States?
   a. The death rate is highest in the 6- to 10-year-old age group.
   b. Most poisonings occur in the home.
   c. A decrease in suicides has led to a decrease in adult poisoning deaths.
   d. The number of child poisonings has been gradually increasing.

2. Which of the following would be a source of chemical food poisoning?
   a. Lead
   b. Botulism
   c. *E. coli*
   d. *Salmonella*

3. You are called to the scene of an emergency involving several family members who may be experiencing food poisoning. Which signs and symptoms would you expect to find? Select all that apply.
   a. Vomiting
   b. Excessive eye burning
   c. Disorientation
   d. Fever
   e. Dehydration
   f. Seizures

4. A child is stung by a bee and experiences a reaction. This reaction is in response to a poison that has entered the body by which route?
   a. Absorption
   b. Injection
   c. Inhalation
   d. Ingestion

5. Which of the following would you identify as an inhaled poison?
   a. Poison ivy
   b. Contaminated water
   c. Snake bite
   d. Chloroform

6. You are called to a scene in which a patient was stung by a jellyfish. Which of the following would lead you to suspect that the patient is experiencing a severe allergic reaction?
   a. Itching
   b. Throat swelling
   c. Hives
   d. Rash

7. Which of the following terms related to use of a drug is used to characterize substance misuse?
   a. Improper
   b. Deliberate
   c. Persistent
   d. Excessive

8. Which substance category includes drugs that produce temporary feelings of alertness and bursts of energy?
   a. Hallucinogens
   b. Cannabis products
   c. Stimulants
   d. Inhalants

9. When providing care to a patient with suspected substance abuse, which of the following is most important?
   a. Determining which substance is involved
   b. Restraining the patient if he or she becomes aggressive
   c. Administering emergency oxygen if available
   d. Identifying potential life-threatening conditions

10. You suspect that a patient is experiencing cannabis intoxication. Which of the following would you most likely find?
    a. Drowsiness
    b. Bloodshot eyes
    c. Mood change
    d. Flushed face

11. Which of the following would you include when caring for a patient with substance misuse? Select all that apply.
    a. Apply several heavy blankets to prevent chilling
    b. Maintain an open airway
    c. Provide reassurance in a calm voice
    d. Avoid questions about what was used
    e. Summon more advanced medical personnel

12. You would suspect abuse of depressants in a patient exhibiting which of the following?
    a. Drowsiness, slurred speech and confusion
    b. Mood changes, flushing and hallucinations
    c. Tachycardia, hypertension and rapid breathing
    d. Excitement, restlessness and irritability

13. You are working with a group of other *emergency medical responders* (EMRs) on a program to prevent substance abuse in your community. Which of the following would the group need to address as possible contributing factors for substance abuse? Select all that apply.
    a. Traditional family structure
    b. Peer pressure
    c. Limited substance availability
    d. Media glamorization
    e. Low self-esteem

14. Which substance is considered the most commonly used stimulant?
    a. Ephedra
    b. Cocaine
    c. Nicotine
    d. Caffeine

15. When obtaining a SAMPLE history from a patient who is addicted to cocaine, he tells you that he has not used the drug in the last 12 hours. You would be alert for signs of—
    a. Dependency.
    b. Tolerance.
    c. Withdrawal.
    d. Overdose.

| SELF-ASSESSMENT: ENRICHMENT |

Administering Activated Charcoal

Directions: *Circle the letter that best answers the question.*

1. In which situations would the use of activated charcoal be indicated?
    a. The patient is unable to swallow.
    b. The patient is fully conscious and alert.
    c. The patient has overdosed on cyanide.
    d. The patient ingested bleach.

2. If a patient has ingested poison, activated charcoal may be recommended by the PCC or medical control. Activated charcoal ideally should be given within which time period of the patient swallowing a poison?
    a. 60 minutes
    b. 85 minutes
    c. 90 minutes
    d. 120 minutes

3. A patient weighs 75 kg. How much activated charcoal would you expect to be given?
    a. 7.5 g
    b. 15 g
    c. 75 g
    d. 150 g

Carbon Monoxide and Cyanide Poisoning

Directions: *Answer the questions by selecting the correct letter(s).*

1. You are called to the home of a family whose carbon monoxide monitor has gone off. The family is outside when you arrive. When interviewing them, which signs and symptoms would you expect them to report as initial complaints?
    a. Muscle weakness
    b. Shortness of breath
    c. Chest pain
    d. Dull headache

2. When providing care on the scene to a patient with carbon monoxide poisoning, which of the following is appropriate?
    a. Administering emergency oxygen
    b. Obtaining a blood sample for testing
    c. Giving an antidote
    d. Cleansing the skin thoroughly

3. Which of the following would increase a patient's risk for cyanide poisoning? Select all that apply.
    a. Smoking cigarettes
    b. Working in a plastics factory
    c. Cleaning metal equipment
    d. Farming
    e. Computer programming

4. Cyanide poisoning is least likely to occur by which route?
   a. Inhalation
   b. Injection
   c. Ingestion
   d. Absorption

5. You suspect cyanide toxicity in a patient with—
   a. Constricted pupils.
   b. Increased respiratory rate.
   c. Low systolic blood pressure.
   d. Decreased heart rate.

16 | Environmental Emergencies

| REVIEW OF CONCEPTS AND TERMS |

Crossword Puzzle

Directions: *Solve the crossword puzzle using the clues provided.*

DOWN

2 Control center of the body's temperature
3 Inadequate amount of fluids in the body's tissues
5 Freezing of body tissues
9 Acute infection that can occur with puncture wounds; also known as lockjaw

ACROSS

4 Body being colder than the usual core temperature
6 Injury due to pressure differences between body areas and the surrounding environment
7 Physical and chemical processes to convert oxygen and food to energy
8 Substance used to counteract the effects of venom
10 Electrically conductive substances, such as potassium and sodium

Short Answer

Directions: *Supply the information requested.*

1. List the five general ways that the body is cooled.

     _____
     _____
     _____
     _____
     _____

2. Name two factors than can increase the risk for heat-related illnesses.

     _____
     _____

3. Identify the two types of cold-related emergencies.

     _____
     _____

4. Explain how human bites differ from other bites.

     _____
     _____
     _____

5. Explain the cause of classic and exertional heat stroke.

     _____
     _____
     _____
     _____

6. Describe the four steps to follow for a water rescue.

     _____
     _____
     _____
     _____

| CASE STUDY |

Directions: *Read the case studies and answer the questions that follow.*

Scenario A

A 72-year-old woman goes out of her house in her bare feet, wearing only her pajamas and robe, to get the newspaper from the curb. There is snow on the ground, and the temperature is 20 degrees. When she tries to get back into the house, she finds the door is locked. She tries other entrances but they, too, are locked. Finally, a passerby sees her and calls 9-1-1. Upon arrival you find her sitting on the steps of her porch. The passerby is sitting with her and has his coat wrapped around her shoulders. She is conscious and alert but says that her feet are numb.

1. You would suspect which of the following as most likely?
   a. Hypothermia
   b. Stroke
   c. Frostbite
   d. Generalized seizure

2. Which of the following would provide further evidence to support your suspicion? Select all that apply.
   a. Waxy skin
   b. Skin cold to the touch
   c. Impaired judgment
   d. Glassy stare
   e. Decreased *level of consciousness* (LOC)

3. Which of the following is your priority?
   a. Ensuring scene safety
   b. Getting the patient out of the cold
   c. Reorienting the patient
   d. Rubbing the patient's feet vigorously

4. Which action is most appropriate for you to do when providing care to this patient?
   a. Gently warm the affected area in hot water.
   b. Bandage the affected area tightly with a clean dressing.
   c. Keep the toes secured closely together.
   d. Avoid breaking any blisters that have formed.

Scenario B

You and your partner are called to a rural camping site in response to a call about a camper being bitten by a snake on his lower leg. The patient tells you that it was a coral snake.

1. You inspect the bite wound, which reveals—
   a. A rectangular pattern of marks.
   b. A distinct single puncture wound.
   c. A star-like distribution of marks at the opening.
   d. A semicircular mark.

2. Which of the following would you do first?
   a. Elevate the leg.
   b. Wash the wound.
   c. Check for infection.
   d. Apply ice to the area.

3. You apply an elastic roller bandage to the area for which reason?
   a. Reduce swelling
   b. Provide support
   c. Slow venom spread
   d. Control pain

4. You are preparing to transport the patient. Which of the following methods is the least appropriate to use?
   a. Walking assist
   b. Stretcher carry
   c. Two-person seat carry
   d. Pack strap carry

| SELF-ASSESSMENT |

Directions: *Answer the questions by selecting the correct letter(s) or by placing the answers in the proper order.*

1. Which of the following is categorized as the most severe heat-related illness?
   a. Hyperthermia
   b. Heat cramps
   c. Heat exhaustion
   d. Heat stroke

2. To prevent heat-related illnesses, which of the following is appropriate? Select all that apply.
   a. Wearing dark colored clothing when outdoors
   b. Exercising for brief periods with frequent rests
   c. Avoiding activities during the late morning to afternoon
   d. Limiting intake of fluids to 3 to 4 glasses per day
   e. Increasing intake of caffeinated fluids

3. You suspect that a patient under your care is experiencing early signs of dehydration. Which of the following would you expect to find?
   a. Sunken eyes
   b. Rapid pulse
   c. Excessive thirst
   d. Decreased perspiration

4. The rationale for wearing a hat on the head during cold weather is based on the understanding that the body loses heat via which process?
   a. Radiation
   b. Convection
   c. Conduction
   d. Evaporation

5. Which mechanism for cooling the body is most affected by high humidity?
   a. Radiation
   b. Evaporation
   c. Conduction
   d. Convection

6. The body's core temperature is—
   a. 97.2° F.
   b. 98.2° F.
   c. 98.6° F.
   d. 99.0° C.

7. When the body becomes cooled, which of the following occurs as the first response?
   a. Superficial blood vessel constriction in the extremities
   b. Shivering
   c. Sweating
   d. Dilation of blood vessels

8. When exposed to the same conditions and based on your understanding of factors predisposing a person to heat-related illnesses, which individual would be at greatest risk for a heat-related illness?
   a. A 75-year-old diabetic with heart disease
   b. A 50 year old taking a diuretic agent
   c. A 30-year-old construction worker working outside
   d. A 25-year-old woman who drinks coffee throughout the day

9. You are providing care to a patient with a heat cramp. Which of the following would you do first?
   a. Massage the area gently.
   b. Have the patient rest.
   c. Stretch the area lightly.
   d. Give the patient water to drink.

10. You are called to the high school football practice facility where one of the athletes who has been practicing is complaining of dizziness and a throbbing headache. The weather is extremely hot and humid. You examine the athlete and suspect heat stroke based on which of the following? Select all that apply.
    a. Flushed, dry skin
    b. Rapid, bounding pulse
    c. Decreasing LOC
    d. Elevated blood pressure
    e. Body temperature of 102° F
    f. Heavy sweating

11. You are providing care for a patient with confirmed hypothermia. Place the following actions in the order in which you should perform them.
    a. Perform a primary assessment.
    b. Move the patient to a warmer environment.
    c. Call for more advanced medical personnel.
    d. Remove any wet clothing.
    e. Begin to rewarm the patient slowly.

12. An adolescent who has been stung by a wasp begins to exhibit signs and symptoms of anaphylaxis. Which of the following would least likely be found during the assessment?
    a. Localized skin rash
    b. Wheezing
    c. Chest tightness
    d. Facial swelling

13. You would treat all scorpion stings as medical emergencies based on the understanding that—
    a. Many species have a potentially fatal sting.
    b. Tissue destruction from the sting is highly likely.
    c. It is difficult to tell which scorpions are poisonous.
    d. Most people are allergic to scorpion venom.

14. Which of the following is the most important to consider before entering the water for a water rescue?
    a. Condition of the water
    b. Patient's condition
    c. Resources available
    d. Personal safety

15. A patient requires a water rescue. Which of the following are appropriate indications for removing the patient from the water to provide care? Select all that apply.
    a. The patient is conscious.
    b. The patient is face-down in the water.
    c. The patient has no spinal injury.
    d. The patient is unresponsive.
    e. The patient has a neck injury.

| SELF-ASSESSMENT: ENRICHMENT |

Assisting with an Epinephrine Auto-Injector

Directions: *Circle the letter that best answers the question.*

1. When assisting with an epinephrine auto-injector, which of the following is appropriate?
    a. Checking the expiration date on the device
    b. Ensuring that the liquid in the injector is cloudy
    c. Confirming that the patient has taken an antihistamine
    d. Removing the safety cap to read the device label

2. A patient is conscious but unable to self-administer the auto-injector. At which location would you administer the auto-injector?
    a. Lateral (outer) lower arm
    b. Lateral (outer) mid-thigh
    c. Either side of the abdomen
    d. Right side of the buttocks

Lightning

Directions: *Circle the letter that best answers the question.*

1. You are part of an emergency response team working an outdoor gathering and you notice that a thunderstorm is approaching. You see a flash of lightning and then approximately 20 seconds later, you hear thunder. Approximately how far away is the storm?
    a. 2 miles
    b. 4 miles
    c. 6 miles
    d   8 miles

2. You evacuate the crowd to a safe location until the storm clears. You would determine it is safe to leave the shelter when the last clap of thunder occurred—
    a. 15 minutes ago.
    b. 30 minutes ago.
    c. 45 minutes ago.
    d. 60 minutes ago.

SCUBA and Free-Diving Emergencies

Directions: *Circle the letter that best answers the question.*

1. Which of the following would occur if a *self-contained underwater breathing apparatus* (SCUBA) diver ascends too quickly?
    a. Pulmonary overinflation syndrome
    b. Pulmonary overpressure syndrome
    c. Decompression sickness
    d. Nitrogen narcosis

2. A patient experiences a diving emergency. The diver is alert. In which position would you place the diver?
    a. Supine
    b. Recovery
    c. Prone
    d. Fowler's

| SKILL SHEET |

Refer to the *Emergency Medical Response* textbook for the following skill sheet for this chapter:

■ Assisting with an Epinephrine Auto-Injector (*Enrichment*), pages 398–399

17 | Behavioral Emergencies

| REVIEW OF CONCEPTS AND TERMS |

Fill-in-the-Blank

Directions: *Write the correct term in the space provided.*

1. A _____ emergency is a situation in which a person behaves or responds to his or her environment in a manner that is unacceptable or intolerable.

2. A phobia is a type of _____ disorder.

3. Patients with clinical depression may have an emergency that may trigger thoughts of _____.

4. A person with _____ experiences feelings of persecution and exaggerated notions of perceived threat.

5. Hallucinations and delusions are characteristic of _____.

6. _____ are more likely to attempt suicide but less likely to die as a result of a suicide attempt.

Short Answer

Directions: *Supply the information requested.*

1. Identify the age group that has the highest risk of dying by suicide.

   _____

   _____

   _____

   _____

2. Describe how self-mutilation is an unhealthy coping mechanism.

   _____

   _____

   _____

3. Define sexual assault.

   _____

   _____

   _____

4. Define child abuse and child neglect.

   _____

   _____

   _____

   _____

   _____

5. Describe what can happen if you restrain a person without justification.

_____
_____
_____
_____
_____

6. Identify the assumption that must be made for any patient with a behavioral emergency.

_____
_____
_____
_____
_____

| CASE STUDY |

Directions: *Read the case studies and answer the questions that follow.*

Scenario A

You are called to the scene of a rape involving a 27-year-old woman. Upon arrival, you observe that she is distraught but quiet and controlled compared with her husband, who is nearby.

1. Which of the following is essential?
   a. Obtaining as much information from the patient as possible
   b. Removing the patient's clothing to inspect for injuries
   c. Offering the patient something to clean herself up
   d. Demonstrating sensitivity when interacting with the patient

2. When assessing a victim of rape, you would expect to assess which of the following?
   a. Psychological but not physical shock
   b. Lack of pain due to numbing
   c. A dazed, almost emotionally paralyzed state
   d. Intact clothing

3. When providing care, which of the following would you do with any evidence collected?
   a. Place wet clothing in a plastic bag.
   b. Bag each piece of evidence individually.
   c. Allow any wet clothing to dry first.
   d. Give any evidence to law enforcement personnel after the patient is transported.

Scenario B

You are called to a restaurant where a woman is disrupting the patrons. The woman is provocatively dressed. She is moving quickly from table to table and talking loudly, occasionally bursting into song. You notice that her thought patterns quickly change. You suspect that she is experiencing mania.

1. Which of the following would further confirm your suspicions of mania?
   a. Aggressiveness
   b. Feelings of hopelessness
   c. Inability to work
   d. Ability to complete a task

2. You understand that the patient's mania is a characteristic of which disorder?
   a. Schizophrenia
   b. Bipolar disorder
   c. Clinical depression
   d. Panic attack

3. When approaching the patient, which of the following is most appropriate to establish rapport? Select all that apply.
   a. Telling the patient to calm down
   b. Touching the patient on the shoulder
   c. Speaking directly to the patient
   d. Telling the patient who you are
   e. Avoiding eye contact as much as possible

| SELF-ASSESSMENT |

Directions: *Answer the questions by selecting the correct letter(s).*

1. A phobia is manifested by—
   a. An intense feeling of sadness.
   b. An exaggerated fear response.
   c. Bizarre behavior.
   d. Extreme body temperature increase.

2. Which statement best describes behavioral emergencies?
   a. Individuals are more likely to harm themselves than others.
   b. Signs and symptoms can range from agitation to withdrawal.
   c. Altered mental status often is not a finding.
   d. Manifestations usually develop slowly over a period of time.

3. Which of the following is considered a cause of behavioral emergencies? Select all that apply.
   a. Abdominal injuries
   b. Physical illness
   c. Adverse effects of prescribed medications
   d. Mental illness
   e. Extreme emotional distress

4. A patient is experiencing excited delirium syndrome. What would you expect to find?
   a. High body temperature
   b. Decreased body strength
   c. Increased pain sensitivity
   d. Relaxed demeanor

5. You would expect a patient's panic attack to last no longer than—
   a. 10 minutes.
   b. 20 minutes.
   c. 30 minutes.
   d. 40 minutes.

6. You are attempting to provide care to a patient experiencing paranoia when a friend mentions that the patient uses recreational drugs. You would suspect which drug group as being most likely involved?
   a. Narcotics
   b. Depressants
   c. Inhalants
   d. Stimulants

7. A patient in your care states, "The voices told me to do it." Which of the following would you suspect?
   a. Phobia
   b. Schizophrenia
   c. Self-mutilation
   d. Clinical depression

8. A patient has attempted suicide. Which of the following is your priority as an *emergency medical responder* (EMR)?
   a. Getting the patient to the medical facility
   b. Obtaining immediate on-site psychiatric care
   c. Treating any injuries related to the attempt
   d. Using medical restraints for transporting

9. Which statement best reflects the reason that older people are at a higher risk for suicide than the general population?
   a. Depression, common in this age group, often is misdiagnosed.
   b. Older adults have an increased tendency for impulsive actions.
   c. Older adults commonly experience more problems with alcohol abuse.
   d. This age group is more reluctant to seek help for mental health problems.

10. Which question is the least appropriate to ask a patient who is at risk for suicide?
    a. "How are you feeling?"
    b. "Are you thinking of hurting yourself?"
    c. "Have you suffered any trauma recently?"
    d. "You're not a threat to yourself, are you?"

11. Which of the following is appropriate when sizing up the scene for safety? Select all that apply.
    a. Identify the patient before entering the scene.
    b. Identify possible escape routes as necessary.
    c. Leave any objects as they are on the scene.
    d. Look for signs of more than one patient.
    e. Approach the scene even if you do not see a patient.

12. Which of the following is the least appropriate when involved with restraining a patient?
    a. Obtaining law enforcement authorization if required
    b. Seeking medical direction and approval before application
    c. Following local protocols related to the use of restraints
    d. Placing the patient in the prone position to ensure limited motion

6 | TRAUMA EMERGENCIES

18 Shock

| REVIEW OF CONCEPTS AND TERMS |

Fill-in-the-Blank

Directions: *Write the correct term in the space provided.*

1. Another term that is used to refer to shock is _____.

2. Reduced blood flow to the skin leads to a pale or _____ skin color.

3. The most common type of hypovolemic shock is _____ shock.

4. _____ shock may result from a pulmonary embolism or tension pneumothorax.

5. Bacteria releasing toxins into the bloodstream can lead to _____ shock.

Short Answer

Directions: *Supply the information requested.*

1. List three types of distributive shock.
   _____
   _____
   _____

2. Identify the three conditions necessary to maintain adequate blood flow.
   _____
   _____
   _____

3. Name the type of shock that can result from emotional distress.
   _____
   _____

4. Explain the reason for not giving any food or drink to a patient in shock.
   _____
   _____
   _____

5. Describe what happens in the body when shock occurs and give four possible conditions that could result in shock.
   _____
   _____
   _____
   _____
   _____

| CASE STUDY |

Directions: *Read the case studies and answer the questions that follow.*

Scenario A

You arrive at a factory warehouse. A 40-year-old man has fallen about 8 feet from a ladder, landing on a cement floor. On his way down, the side of his abdomen hit a shelf protruding from the wall. He is complaining of pain in his abdomen and left hip.

1. You suspect that the patient may be in the early stages of shock when he exhibits which of the following? Select all that apply.
   a. Apprehension
   b. Elevated body temperature
   c. Pale skin
   d. Elevated blood pressure
   e. Elevated respiratory rate

2. Which type of shock would you most likely suspect?
   a. Cardiogenic
   b. Distributive
   c. Hypovolemic
   d. Obstructive

3. You check the patient's pulse and find it to be 120 *beats per minute* (bpm) and weak. You would interpret this to indicate which of the following?
   a. Internal blood loss
   b. Low blood glucose levels
   c. Early signs of sepsis
   d. Cardiac trauma

4. As you check the rest of the patient's vital signs, you notice that his skin is moist, cool and a little pale. He complains of feeling light-headed. Which of the following does this best reflect?
   a. A normal stress reaction to injury
   b. The body's attempt to compensate for the injury
   c. A routine fear reaction
   d. Recovery from the initial injury

5. You are uncertain as to the extent of the patient's condition; therefore, you would—
   a. Have the patient sit up.
   b. Keep the patient flat.
   c. Raise his legs slightly.
   d. Place him in a recovery position.

6. While waiting for more advanced medical personnel to arrive, the patient's condition continues to deteriorate. His breathing rate is fast, his pulse is fast and weak, and he is responsive only to painful stimuli. Which of the following would you do first?
   a. Maintain an open airway.
   b. Cover him to prevent chilling.
   c. Elevate his head and chest.
   d. Immobilize his body.

| SELF-ASSESSMENT |

Directions: *Answer the questions by selecting the correct letter(s).*

1. Which type of shock is associated with a loss of body fluid due to a heat-related illness?
   a. Cardiogenic
   b. Metabolic
   c. Anaphylactic
   d. Neurogenic

2. Which of the following occurs with hypoperfusion?
   a. Shunting of blood flow to vital organs
   b. Failure of the blood vessels to constrict
   c. Increased flow of oxygenated blood to the skin
   d. Airway obstruction leading to respiratory failure

3. In anaphylactic shock, which of the following occurs?
   a. Airways dilate
   b. Blood vessels constrict
   c. Blood pools
   d. Tissues are damaged

4. Which measure would help to minimize shock?
   a. Covering the patient with a blanket
   b. Removing any excess patient clothing
   c. Immersing the feet in warm water
   d. Applying cool compresses to the neck and groin

5. A patient in shock appears pale and feels cool because—
   a. Shock damages the temperature control centers in the brain.
   b. The body responds by constricting blood vesssels in the extremities.
   c. Shock causes the heart to beat slower, reducing heat production.
   d. The body responds by cooling itself to decrease energy demands.

6. Which of the following would you do to minimize shock?
   a. Estimate the amount of blood loss.
   b. Elevate the patient's head.
   c. Give the patient a drink.
   d. Administer emergency oxygen if available.

7. A patient experiences a spinal cord injury. You would be alert for which type of shock?
   a. Septic
   b. Cardiogenic
   c. Vasogenic
   d. Obstructive

8. You determine that a patient in shock is deteriorating. Which of the following would you expect to find? Select all that apply.
   a. Increased blood pressure
   b. Dilated pupils
   c. Listlessness
   d. Deep, slow respirations
   e. Irregular, rapid pulse

9. A patient received a stab wound. He is bleeding profusely and develops signs and symptoms of shock. You would identify this type of shock as—
   a. Obstructive.
   b. Hypovolemic.
   c. Distributive.
   d. Cardiogenic.

10. When caring for a patient in shock, which of the following would you do first?
    a. Ensure the patient's airway is open.
    b. Control any visible bleeding.
    c. Immobilize any fractures.
    d. Elevate the lower extremities.

19 | Bleeding and Trauma

| REVIEW OF CONCEPTS AND TERMS |

Matching

Directions: *Write the letter of the description from Column 2 in the space next to the correct term in Column 1.*

Column 1

___ 1. Dressing

___ 2. Hemorrhage

___ 3. Tourniquet

___ 4. Pressure point

___ 5. Contusion

___ 6. Hemostatic agent

Column 2

A. Soft tissue injury resulting in blood vessel damage

B. Substances that remove moisture from blood and speed up the process of clot formation

C. Pad applied directly over a wound

D. Delivery of oxygen and nutrients to cells and removal of carbon dioxide and other wastes

E. Thickening of blood at a wound site to seal a blood vessel opening

F. Loss of a large amount of blood in a short time

Column 1

___ 7. Perfusion

___ 8. Clotting

Column 2

G. A tight band placed around an arm or leg to constrict blood vessels to stop blood flow to a wound

H. Sites on the body used to slow blood flow to a body part

Short Answer

Directions: *Supply the information requested.*

1. Name the most common cause of arterial bleeding.

   _____
   _____
   _____
   _____

2. List three characteristics of capillary bleeding.

   _____
   _____
   _____

3. Define occlusive dressing.

_____
_____
_____
_____

4. Identify two purposes of a triangular bandage.

_____
_____
_____
_____
_____

5. List the two main pressure points for controlling external bleeding in the extremities.

_____
_____
_____

| CASE STUDY |

Directions: *Read the case studies and answer the questions that follow.*

Scenario A

You are called to an emergency involving a young man who was stabbed in the leg on his way home from work. A passerby found him sitting on the curb and called 9-1-1. Upon arrival, the patient is conscious but holding his left calf area. His hands are covered in blood.

1. You determine that the bleeding is venous because it—
   a. Is bright red.
   b. Spurts from the wound.
   c. Fails to clot easily.
   d. Flows steadily.

2. When preparing to provide care for the patient, which of the following is most important for you to do to protect *yourself*?
   a. Use disposable gloves.
   b. Use a clean dressing on the wound.
   c. Prevent signs and symptoms of shock.
   d. Elevate the extremity.

3. When implementing measures to control this patient's bleeding, which of the following is least appropriate?
   a. Applying direct pressure with your hand
   b. Elevating the patient's leg above heart level
   c. Placing a sterile gauze dressing over the wound
   d. Using a tourniquet to stop the bleeding

Scenario B

You arrive on the scene of a motor-vehicle collision in which the car skidded and hit a telephone pole. The driver is in the car, alert but somewhat disoriented and complaining of a headache. He tells you that he hit his chest on the steering wheel and his face on the dashboard. His nose is bleeding.

1. Which finding would lead you to suspect internal bleeding from his chest impacting the steering wheel? Select all that apply.
   a. Rapid breathing
   b. Bruising on the chest
   c. Bounding pulse
   d. Warm, pink skin
   e. Coughing up blood

2. You suspect that the patient may have a skull fracture because he hit his head on the dashboard and is complaining of a headache. When caring for the patient's nosebleed, you would—
   a. Tilt his head forward slightly.
   b. Pinch his nostrils firmly together.
   c. Have the patient blow his nose.
   d. Cover the nostrils loosely with sterile gauze.

3. Which of the following would you do first when caring for this patient?
   a. Keep the patient as still as possible.
   b. Call for more advanced medical personnel.
   c. Assess the patient for signs and symptoms of shock.
   d. Apply direct pressure to the patient's chest.

| SELF-ASSESSMENT |

Directions: *Answer the questions by selecting the correct letter(s).*

1. When applying a dressing to an open bleeding wound, you use a sterile dressing primarily for which reason?
   a. To control the bleeding faster
   b. To absorb a greater amount of blood
   c. To prevent air from entering the wound
   d. To minimize the risk of infection

2. Which statement best describes a trauma system?
   a. Different components providing a seamless transition for patients to move between various phases of care
   b. A set of services designed to provide pre-hospital and acute care for patients with trauma
   c. The physical injury, wound or shock caused by an agent, force or mechanism
   d. The time encompassing the period when a severely injured patient requires surgery offering him or her the best chance of survival

3. A rural clinic in a remote area offering patient care until transport can be arranged describes which trauma system level?
   a. I
   b. II
   c. III
   d. IV

4. Which of the following is least appropriate in preventing disease transmission when providing care to a patient who is bleeding?
   a. Wearing disposable gloves
   b. Touching your mouth or nose during care
   c. Washing your hands before and after care
   d. Using protective eyewear

5. Which type of bleeding is the most urgent?
   a. External
   b. Arterial
   c. Internal
   d. Venous

6. Which of the following characteristics of blood denote arterial bleeding?
   a. Bright red color
   b. Steady flow
   c. Spontaneous clotting
   d. An increase in pressure corresponding to a decrease in blood pressure

7. A patient has a sucking chest wound. Which type of dressing would you use?
   a. Universal dressing
   b. Occlusive dressing
   c. Roller bandage
   d. Elastic bandage

8. When using a roller bandage, which of the following is appropriate?
   a. Cover the fingers and toes completely
   b. Secure the end of the bandage first
   c. Have the end match the edge of the dressing
   d. Use circular turns repeatedly over each other

9. You notice that blood has soaked through a dressing and bandage. You would—
   a. Elevate the body part above heart level.
   b. Apply additional dressings and another bandage.
   c. Reapply a new bandage leaving the dressings in place.
   d. Reapply direct pressure to the site over the soiled dressings.

10. A patient experiences internal capillary bleeding on his lower leg. Which action is most appropriate?
    a. Apply ice to the area.
    b. Elevate the body part.
    c. Apply direct pressure to the site.
    d. Maintain pressure at a pressure point.

11. You immobilize a limb while maintaining direct pressure for bleeding based on the understanding that this action—
    a. Slows blood clotting.
    b. Compresses the artery.
    c. Restricts blood flow.
    d. Removes moisture from the blood.

12. When applying direct pressure for serious bleeding, you would first use—
    a. Your thumb.
    b. Your hand.
    c. A pressure point.
    d. Your fingertips.

13. Which organ system is most quickly affected by changes in perfusion that may occur from bleeding?
    a. Renal system
    b. Musculoskeletal system
    c. Nervous system
    d. Digestive system

14. A patient has sustained trauma with a large open wound that is bleeding severely. Which of the following would be used to control the bleeding as a last resort?
    a. Direct pressure
    b. Elevation
    c. Pressure point
    d. Tourniquet

| SELF-ASSESSMENT: ENRICHMENT |

Mechanisms of Injury—The Kinematics of Trauma

Directions: Answer the questions by selecting the correct letter(s).

1. When a person falls feet first, injury would be less severe if which of the following occurs on impact?
   a. Hands are outstretched.
   b. Knees are bent.
   c. Buttocks hit first.
   d. Feet are flexed with toes up.

2. A patient experiences burns related to an explosion. You would identify this as which type of blast injury?
   a. Primary
   b. Secondary
   c. Tertiary
   d. Quaternary

3. A patient was involved in a rear-impact motor-vehicle collision. The airbags in the car did not deploy. Which of the following injuries would you expect to be the most common? Select all that apply.
   a. Facial injuries
   b. Head injuries
   c. Burns
   d. Abdominal injuries
   e. Neck injuries

4. Motorcycle accidents would least likely involve which of the following?
   a. Head-on impact
   b. Angular impact
   c. Rotational impact
   d. Ejection

| SKILL SHEET |

Refer to the *Emergency Medical Response* textbook for the following skill sheets for this chapter:

- Controlling External Bleeding, page 438
- Using a Manufactured Tourniquet (*Enrichment*), pages 442–443

20 | Soft Tissue Injuries

I REVIEW OF CONCEPTS AND TERMS I

Matching

Directions: *Write the letter of the description from Column 2 in the space next to the correct term in Column 1.*

Column 1

___ 1. Puncture wound

___ 2. Laceration

___ 3. Avulsion

___ 4. Crush injury

___ 5. Abrasion

___ 6. Burn

Column 2

A. An injury in which a portion of the skin and sometimes soft tissue is partially or completely torn away

B. An injury to the skin from heat, chemicals, electricity or radiation

C. An injury resulting from skin being pierced by a pointed object

D. An injury resulting in skin being rubbed or scraped away

E. An injury with smooth or jagged edges usually due to a sharp object

F. An injury to a body part usually due to a high degree of pressure

Short Answer

Directions: *Supply the information requested.*

1. Describe three functions of the skin.

   _____

   _____

   _____

2. List the two major layers of the skin.

   _____

   _____

3. Differentiate between an open and a closed wound.

   _____

   _____

   _____

4. List the three classifications of burns.

   _____

   _____

   _____

5. Describe the common method used to determine the extent of a burn in an adult and in a child.

   _____

   _____

   _____

   _____

Labeling

Directions: *Write the name of the appropriate layer of skin in the space provided.*

Structure of the Skin

A. _____

B. _____

C. _____

D. _____

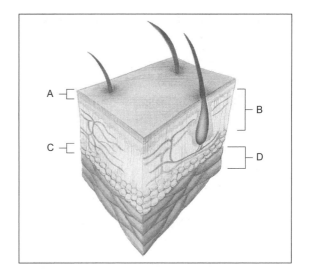

| CASE STUDY |

Directions: *Read the case studies and answer the questions that follow.*

Scenario A

You and your partner are called to a factory in which a worker's finger became caught in a cutting machine. The finger has been completely severed below the knuckle. The patient, who is conscious, is lying on the floor of the shop, crying in severe pain. The severed body part is on the floor about 10 feet away from the patient.

1. This situation involves which of the following?
   a. Avulsion
   b. Amputation
   c. Laceration
   d. Impalement

2. Which of the following is your priority?
   a. Controlling the bleeding
   b. Minimizing his pain
   c. Immobilizing the arm
   d. Recovering the body part

3. You would be alert for signs and symptoms of which of the following?
   a. Infection
   b. Cardiac arrest
   c. Shock
   d. Respiratory failure

4. Which of the following is appropriate to do when caring for the severed body part?
   a. Put the body part as is into a brown paper bag.
   b. Wrap the body part in sterile saline moistened gauze.
   c. Put the body part in a container of ice.
   d. Pour ice cold water onto the part continuously.

Scenario B

You are the first to arrive on the scene of a fire in a condominium complex. As you begin to approach the scene, a woman runs screaming from the building with her clothes on fire.

1. Which of the following would you do first?
   a. Perform a primary assessment.
   b. Cool the burn area.
   c. Extinguish the flames.
   d. Summon more advanced medical personnel.

2. You would identify this as which type of burn?
   a. Chemical
   b. Electrical
   c. Radiation
   d. Thermal

3. Which of the following would you use to cool the burn?
   a. Ice applied directly to the burned area
   b. Large amounts of cold running water
   c. Petroleum jelly liberally applied to the burned area
   d. Alternating warm and cool compresses on the burned area

4. The woman has partial-thickness burns covering her entire chest, abdomen and back. Inspection reveals no other burned areas. Approximately what percentage of her body is burned?
   a. 9 percent
   b. 18 percent
   c. 27 percent
   d. 36 percent

5. Which of the following is appropriate to use to cover the burned area?
   a. Dry, sterile dressing
   b. Pressure dressing
   c. Oil-based lubricant
   d. Antibiotic ointment

| SELF-ASSESSMENT |

Directions: Answer the questions by selecting the correct letter(s).

1. Which statement best describes a wound?
   a. Opening in the skin
   b. Destruction of the dermis
   c. Penetrating injury
   d. Soft tissue injury

2. When examining a patient you observe the simplest type of closed wound, identifying it as a—
   a. Contusion.
   b. Laceration.
   c. Burn.
   d. Puncture.

3. When providing care to a minor closed wound injury, you apply ice for which period of time and then remove it?
   a. 5 minutes
   b. 15 minutes
   c. 20 minutes
   d. 25 minutes

4. Which of the following would lead you to suspect that a closed wound involving an extremity requires more advanced medical care?
   a. The part is pink, warm and dry.
   b. The pain is out of proportion to the appearance.
   c. The patient can move it with little pain.
   d. There is some swelling of the area.

5. A patient receives a puncture wound. You would anticipate that this patient is at high risk for which of the following?
   a. Crush syndrome
   b. Shock
   c. Infection
   d. External hemorrhage

6. You are providing care for a minor superficial laceration on a patient's arm. Which of the following would you do first?
   a. Clean the wound with soap and water.
   b. Control the bleeding.
   c. Irrigate the wound with clear, warm running water.
   d. Apply antibiotic ointment.

7. You determine that a patient has a superficial burn based on which findings?
   a. Red and dry skin
   b. Blistering
   c. Mottling
   d. Blackened skin

8. You are estimating the amount of body area burned using the Rule of Nines. Burns to the genital area would account for which percentage of body area for an adult?
   a. 0 percent
   b. 1 percent
   c. 9 percent
   d. 18 percent

9. While assessing a burn patient, you notice soot around the mouth and nose. You would be alert for which of the following?
   a. Toxic inhalation
   b. Scarring
   c. Shock
   d. Airway closure

10. A patient experiencing which of the following types of burn would be referred to a burn unit? Select all that apply.
    a. Chemical burns
    b. Electrical burns
    c. Circumferential burns
    d. Superficial burns
    e. Full-thickness burn over 5 percent of the body surface

11. You are inspecting a patient's burn and determine it is a full-thickness burn based on which of the following? Select all that apply.
    a. Complaints of severe pain
    b. Reddened area that blanches (whitens) on touch
    c. Dry, leathery appearance
    d. Absence of hair
    e. Absence of sensation to touch

12. A patient has sustained a chemical burn to the eye. Which of the following is appropriate when flushing the eye?
    a. Use cold tap water.
    b. Position the head so water flows toward the nose.
    c. Continue to flush the eye for about 20 minutes.
    d. Use a brush to facilitate the chemical's removal.

13. Which of the following is a priority when providing care for a patient with an electrical burn?
    a. Performing a primary assessment for immediate life-threatening injuries
    b. Cooling the burn with large amounts of cold water
    c. Evaluating the entry and exit sites for the electrical burn
    d. Ensuring the source is de-energized with the patient free of the source

21 | Injuries to the Chest, Abdomen and Genitalia

I REVIEW OF CONCEPTS AND TERMS I

Matching

Directions: *Write the letter of the description from Column 2 in the space next to the correct term in Column 1.*

Column 1

___ 1. Pneumothorax

___ 2. Flail chest

___ 3. Subcutaneous emphysema

___ 4. Evisceration

___ 5. Hemothorax

___ 6. Percussion

Column 2

A. Accumulation of blood between the lungs and chest wall

B. Multiple rib fractures resulting in a loose section of ribs that does not move normally with the rest of the chest

C. Protrusion of abdominal organs through the wound

D. Collapse of a lung due to air in the chest cavity

E. Air entering the tissues under the skin covering the chest wall or neck

F. Complete lung collapse with air trapped in the pleural space

Column 1

___ 7. Tension pneumothorax

Column 2

G. Technique of tapping on the body surface and listening to sounds produced

Fill-in-the-Blank

Directions: *Write the correct word in the space provided.*

1. The abdominal cavity is lined with a thick membrane called the _____.

2. _____ injuries are the second-leading cause of trauma deaths each year in the United States.

3. Injury caused by the force of an object impacting with but not penetrating the body is called _____ trauma.

4. Chest injuries involving a strong crushing mechanism can lead to traumatic _____.

5. An embedded or _____ object is one that remains in an open wound.

6. A(n) _____ abdomen usually is a symptom of intra-abdominal disease, such as appendicitis or peritonitis.

| CASE STUDY |

Directions: *Read the case studies below and answer the questions that follow.*

Scenario A

You are called to the scene of an industrial accident. A worker was injured when a compressed gas cylinder being tested exploded, hitting her in the chest. She is lying on the floor, gasping. Her lips appear blue, and the front of her shirt on the left side is torn and soaked with blood. You notice a strange "whooshing" sound every time the patient takes a breath.

1. You would most likely suspect which of the following?
   a. Rib fracture
   b. Sucking chest wound
   c. Pneumothorax
   d. Flail chest

2. Which of the following would you need to do first?
   a. Apply an occlusive dressing.
   b. Control the bleeding.
   c. Assess for signs of shock.
   d. Begin ventilations.

3. As you complete your physical exam, you find a piece of the cylinder in another area of the left chest. Which of the following would you do?
   a. Immediately remove the protruding object.
   b. Press the surrounding clothing around the object.
   c. Stabilize the object with gauze at its current position.
   d. Wiggle the object to evaluate its depth of penetration.

Scenario B

You are called to a recreational center where a group of adults were playing baseball. One of the players was hit in the abdomen with a baseball bat. The player fell to the ground moaning in pain, grabbing his abdomen.

1. Based on the location of the injury, which organ is most susceptible to injury? Select all that apply.
   a. Liver
   b. Spleen
   c. Lungs
   d. Kidneys
   e. Stomach

2. Which of the following would you identify as least likely to indicate a serious abdominal injury?
   a. Complaints of vague pain
   b. Thirst
   c. Bruising
   d. Ashen skin

3. How would you position the patient?
   a. On his side with head elevated
   b. On his back with knees flexed
   c. Sitting up with his legs straight
   d. Prone with his legs elevated

4. When assessing this patient, you would begin to palpate the abdomen at which location?
   a. Directly at the point of impact of the bat
   b. Around the area of the navel (belly button)
   c. Starting from the furthest point away from the patient's pain
   d. Around the lower ribs on both sides

| SELF-ASSESSMENT |

Directions: *Answer the questions below by selecting the correct letter(s).*

1. Which of the following is most appropriate when caring for a male patient with a genital injury?
   a. Have a female *emergency medical responder* (EMR) provide the care.
   b. Ensure that bystanders are moved back slightly from the scene.
   c. Provide a drape to maintain the patient's privacy.
   d. Remove all of the patient's clothing to view the injury.

2. Which of the following typically characterizes a genital injury?
   a. Most often is an open wound.
   b. Extreme pain
   c. Profuse bleeding
   d. Result of sexual assault

3. Which structure separates the chest cavity from the abdominal cavity?
   a. Diaphragm
   b. Ribs
   c. Peritoneum
   d. Sternum

4. Which of the following is the most likely cause of a closed chest wound?
   a. Fractured rib breaking through the skin
   b. Knife wound
   c. Gunshot
   d. Blunt trauma

5. Which patient would be at greatest risk for traumatic asphyxia?
   a. A patient who was shot in the chest
   b. A patient who was pinned under a collapsed concrete wall
   c. A patient with broken ribs due to a fall
   d. A patient with a sucking chest wound

6. Which of the following would you expect to find in a patient with traumatic asphyxia? Select all that apply.
   a. Flattened neck veins
   b. Subconjunctival hemorrhage
   c. Pink neck and shoulders
   d. Black eyes
   e. Moon-like face

7. You suspect that a patient has fractured ribs when the patient attempts to ease the pain by leaning—
   a. Forward.
   b. Away from the side of the fracture.
   c. Toward the side of the fracture.
   d. Backward.

8. When providing care to a patient with broken ribs, which of the following is the priority?
   a. Ensuring adequate breathing
   b. Maintaining an open airway
   c. Controlling the bleeding
   d. Covering the wound

9. You suspect that a patient has a tension pneumothorax on the right based on which findings?
   a. Tracheal shifting to the left
   b. Increased breath sounds on the right
   c. Severe hypertension
   d. Abnormal percussion sounds on the left

10. When applying an occlusive dressing to a sucking chest wound, which of the following would you do?
    a. Use sterile gauze dressings and tape.
    b. Tape the dressing on three of the four sides.
    c. Cover the dressing with a disposable glove.
    d. Use a clean folded cloth for a dressing.

11. During your physical exam of a patient, you notice a portion of what looks like the patient's intestine protruding from the wound. You would identify this as which of the following?
   a. Flail chest
   b. Tension pneumothorax
   c. Evisceration
   d. Avulsion

12. A male patient experiences a blow to his scrotal area. Which of the following would you apply first?
   a. Sterile gauze dressing
   b. Ice pack to the area
   c. Saline-moistened dressing
   d. Warm compress

22 | Injuries to Muscles, Bones and Joints

| REVIEW OF CONCEPTS AND TERMS |

Crossword Puzzle

Directions: *Solve the crossword puzzle below using the clues provided.*

DOWN

1 Two or more bones together
3 A limb of the body
4 Type of muscle that attaches to bone
5 Partial or complete tearing or stretching of a ligament
7 Type of muscle found in the heart
10 Tissue that contracts and relaxes
11 Dense hard tissue that forms the skeleton

ACROSS

2 Type of muscle found in the hollow organs
6 Break in bone tissue
8 Excess stretching or tearing of a muscle or tendon
9 Band holding bones together at a joint
12 Band attaching muscle to bone
13 Use a splint to keep an injured body part from moving

Short Answer

Directions: *Supply the information requested.*

1. List the four basic types of injuries to muscles, bones and joints.

   _____

   _____

   _____

   _____

   _____

   _____

2. Describe the three basic *mechanisms of injury* (MOIs) for muscles, bones and joints.

   _____

   _____

   _____

   _____

   _____

3. Name five reasons for immobilizing an injury.

   _____

   _____

   _____

   _____

   _____

   _____

4. Explain the term "anatomical splint."

   _____

   _____

   _____

   _____

5. Identify the four general care measures for all musculoskeletal injuries.

   _____

   _____

   _____

   _____

| CASE STUDIES |

Directions: *Read the case studies and answer the questions that follow.*

Scenario A

You arrive on the scene of an emergency involving a pedestrian who has been struck by a car. The patient is lying on the ground nearby. The scene appears to be safe. On approaching the patient, you notice that the left forearm is visibly deformed with a bloody laceration near the deformity. The patient's left pant leg is torn, revealing that his left thigh also is bruised and deformed.

1. Which of the following would you do first?
   a. Perform a primary assessment.
   b. Immobilize the leg.
   c. Cover the laceration.
   d. Splint the forearm.

2. You prepare to care for the patient's forearm with the possible fracture. Which of the following would you do before applying the splint?
   a. Bandage the wound.
   b. Check for range of motion.
   c. Apply ice directly to the site.
   d. Straighten the arm.

3. Which bone would you suspect as being involved with this forearm fracture?
   a. Humerus
   b. Ulna
   c. Femur
   d. Tibia

4. Which type of splint is most appropriate to use?
   a. Vaccuum
   b. Traction
   c. Circumferential air
   d. Rigid

5. Which of the following would you expect if the patient's thigh injury is due to a femur fracture?
   a. Turning in of the leg
   b. Swelling
   c. Muscle relaxation
   d. Significant pain
   e. Unrestricted movement

6. After you apply the splint, which of the following is the least appropriate to assess?
   a. Proximal pulse
   b. Skin temperature
   c. Mobility
   d. Sensation

Scenario B

You arrive at a fitness center in response to a call that one of the patrons was working out and began to feel severe pain in his right ankle. You notice that the right ankle is visibly swollen compared with the left ankle. The patient states, "I sprained my ankle about 6 weeks ago."

1. The patient's statement is significant because—
   a. A previous sprain increases the risk for fracturing the same joint.
   b. The joint may be less stable, increasing the risk for re-spraining the joint.
   c. More force would be needed for the patient to reinjure the joint.
   d. A previous sprain increases the risk for bleeding with reinjury.

2. Which of the following is an appropriate action?
   a. Allow the patient to find a position of comfort.
   b. Apply ice directly to the skin of the ankle.
   c. Elevate the ankle about 6 inches.
   d. Apply a rigid splint for immobilization.

| SELF-ASSESSMENT |

Directions: *Answer the questions by selecting the correct letter(s).*

1. A fracture to which of the following places the patient at greatest risk for shock?
   a. Ulna
   b. Tibia
   c. Femur
   d. Collarbone (clavicle)

2. A patient who experiences an open fracture has the greatest risk for—
   a. Respiratory arrest.
   b. Dislocation.
   c. Sprain to a surrounding ligament.
   d. Infection.

3. Which body part is at highest risk for a dislocation?
   a. Elbow
   b. Knee
   c. Ankle
   d. Shoulder

4. Which of the following is appropriate to use as a soft splint?
   a. Cardboard box
   b. Pillow
   c. Rolled up magazine
   d. Shin guard

5. When applying a binder, which of the following would you do?
   a. Place a triangular bandage under the injury and over the uninjured part.
   b. Tie the ends at the side of the neck.
   c. Wrap a piece of cloth around the patient and the injured body part to hold it secure.
   d. Position the bandage around the injured area and fill with air.

6. Which statement would lead you to suspect that a patient has sustained a musculoskeletal injury?
   a. "I have no pain when I walk."
   b. "I have no feeling in my hand."
   c. "I didn't feel any popping sensation."
   d. "My wrist feels warm."

7. When providing care to a patient with a suspected elbow fracture, you should immobilize the arm—
   a. First and then correct any deformity.
   b. In the position in which you found it.
   c. After extending the arm.
   d. After correcting the deformity.

8. For which of the following would you summon more advanced medical personnel? Select all that apply.
   a. Suspected fracture of the toe
   b. Swelling of a joint
   c. Inability to walk
   d. Open femur fracture
   e. Suspicion of multiple traumatic injuries or medical conditions

9. When splinting the femur using rigid splints, you would extend the distal ends of the splint to which position?
   a. Just below the knee
   b. Just above the ankle
   c. Even with the bottom of the foot
   d. Past the bottom of the foot

10. A patient asks you why you are elevating his arm. Which response is most accurate?
    a. "It helps to reduce the swelling."
    b. "It helps to keep the bones aligned."
    c. "It makes the pain less noticeable."
    d. "It promotes healing."

11. You are assessing a patient's injury and you notice a grating sound when attempting to move the fractured part. You identify this as—
    a. Angulation.
    b. Crepitus.
    c. Deformity.
    d. Cravat.

12. You are preparing to apply a splint to a patient's forearm. Which of the following would you do first?
    a. Check for circulation and sensation beyond the injured area.
    b. Support the injured part above and below the injury.
    c. Obtain the patient's consent for treatment.
    d. Immobilize the wrist and elbow.

13. Which of the following is the final step when applying a sling and binder?
    a. Tying the ends of the sling at the side of the neck
    b. Rechecking for circulation and sensation
    c. Binding the injured body part to the chest
    d. Positioning the triangular bandage

14. When using a splint, which of the following is appropriate to do?
    a. Apply sterile pressure dressings over open wounds.
    b. Avoid padding splints to prevent further deformities.
    c. Remove any clothing around the injured site.
    d. Push any protruding bones back below the skin.

15. For which of the following would you expect to use a sling and binder to splint? Select all that apply.
    a. Collarbone
    b. Shoulder
    c. Elbow
    d. Forearm
    e. Pelvis

| SELF-ASSESSMENT: ENRICHMENT |

Agricultural and Industrial Emergencies

Directions: *Answer the questions by selecting the correct letter(s).*

1. When dealing with an emergency involving a confined space, which of the following is the most important to remember?
    a. The confined space is assumed to be hazardous.
    b. *Personal protective equipment* (PPE) is not required.
    c. Your sense of smell is adequate to determine air safety.
    d. An attendant must be present within 50 feet of the entrance.

2. Before trying to extricate a patient from agricultural equipment, which of the following is a priority?
    a. Digging a trench under the equipment
    b. Shutting down the equipment
    c. Ensuring ready access to a *self-contained breathing apparatus* (SCBA)
    d. Ensuring that the equipment is in reverse

3. Which of the following is required for Level B protection? Select all that apply.
    a. Hard hat
    b. SCBA
    c. Hooded chemical-resistant clothing
    d. Specialized gloves
    e. Face shields
    f. Boots

4. Which of the following is the most important when responding to an industrial emergency?
    a. Identifying the hazard
    b. Determining the number of victims
    c. Calling in specialized teams
    d. Sizing up the scene

| SKILL SHEETS |

Refer to the *Emergency Medical Response* textbook for the following skill sheets for this chapter:

- Applying a Rigid Splint, pages 492–493
- Applying a Sling and Binder, pages 494–495
- Applying an Anatomic Splint, pages 496–497
- Applying a Soft Splint, pages 498–499

23 | Injuries to the Head, Neck and Spine

| REVIEW OF CONCEPTS AND TERMS |

Fill-in-the-Blank

Directions: *Write the correct term in the space provided.*

1. The head is formed by the face and the
   _____.

2. A(n) _____ is a temporary loss of brain function caused by a blow to the head.

3. In-line stabilization is a technique to minimize _____ of the patient's head and _____ the patient's head and neck with the spine.

4. The _____ artery and jugular vein are located in the neck.

5. A(n) _____ _____ is a rigid device that is positioned around the neck of a patient to limit movement.

6. The _____ _____ is the series of vertebrae that extend from the base of the skull to the tip of the coccyx.

7. The cylindrical structure extending from the base of the skull to the lower back that consists primarily of nerve cells is known as _____ _____.

Short Answer

Directions: *Supply the information requested.*

1. Explain why the head is easily injured.
   _____
   _____
   _____
   _____

2. Differentiate a closed head injury from an open head injury.
   _____
   _____
   _____
   _____

3. Describe why a closed head injury is more challenging to detect.
   _____
   _____
   _____
   _____

4. Explain "raccoon eyes."

_____

_____

_____

_____

5. Define manual stabilization.

_____

_____

_____

_____

6. List four reasons for removing a helmet from an injured patient.

_____

_____

_____

_____

7. Identify the most common cause of death in patients with head injuries.

_____

_____

_____

| CASE STUDY |

Directions: *Read the case studies and answer the questions that follow.*

Scenario A

A member of a roofing crew has fallen from the roof of a two-story home, landing on his back. Upon arrival at the scene, you find the man unconscious but breathing. There is a small abrasion on his forehead, and blood is trickling from his mouth. One of his co-workers states, "I think he hit his head when he landed on his back." The patient's head is turned to the left.

1. Which of the following would you do first?
   a. Size-up the scene.
   b. Perform a primary assessment.
   c. Open his airway.
   d. Stabilize the head and neck.

2. You suspect a possible skull fracture is most likely based on which finding?
   a. Abrasion on the forehead
   b. Bleeding from the mouth
   c. Lack of responsiveness
   d. The bystander's statement

3. As you continue to assess the patient, which of the following would you interpret as indicative of a brain injury? Select all that apply.
   a. Hypotension
   b. Rapid pulse
   c. Clear fluid draining from the nose
   d. Bruising behind the ear
   e. Flaccid limbs

4. When stabilizing the head and neck, which of the following measures is the most appropriate?
   a. Maintain the head in the position found.
   b. Turn the head sharply to the front.
   c. Apply a *cervical collar* (C-collar).
   d. Secure the patient to a backboard.

5. As you are caring for the patient, you notice fluid draining from his ears. Which of the following would be appropriate?
   a. Apply gentle suction to the ears to remove the fluid.
   b. Cover the area loosely with a sterile gauze dressing.
   c. Elevate the patient's head approximately 30 degrees.
   d. Plug the ear canal with a small dressing.

Scenario B

You are called to a local athletic field where a youth football team has been playing a scrimmage game. One of the players, a 10-year-old boy, collided with another player, helmet to shoulder pads. The boy was knocked to the ground and lost consciousness for about 3 minutes. Upon your arrival, the boy is lying on the ground.

1. Which of the following is a priority in this situation?
   a. Performing a primary assessment
   b. Gathering information about what happened
   c. Obtaining the patient's vital signs
   d. Having the patient sit up

2. You suspect that the boy has a concussion. Which of the following would provide support for your suspicion? Select all that apply.
   a. Asymmetrical facial movements
   b. Inability to recall what happened
   c. Headache
   d. Confusion
   e. Pupils of unequal size

3. The boy is lethargic but responds to verbal stimuli. Which of the following is the most appropriate when providing care to the patient?
   a. Remove his helmet to assess his head more closely.
   b. Stabilize his head and neck with the helmet in place.
   c. Place the patient in a recovery position.
   d. Elevate the patient's legs about 12 inches.

| SELF-ASSESSMENT |

Directions: *Answer the questions by selecting the correct letter(s) or by placing the answers in the proper order.*

1. Which patient would you identify as having the lowest risk for sustaining a head, neck or spinal injury?
   a. A person who fell off of a 3-foot step stool
   b. A person who dove into 3 feet of water in a swimming pool
   c. A person who impacted the dashboard in a motor-vehicle collision
   d. A person who slipped off of a two-story platform

2. When controlling bleeding from an open head wound, which of the following is not appropriate?
   a. Elevating the head and shoulders if there is no spinal injury
   b. Pressing a sterile dressing gently over the wound
   c. Applying direct pressure to a spongy area
   d. Using a roller bandage to cover the dressing

3. A patient has a foreign body in the eye. Which of the following is appropriate?
   a. Tell the patient to rub his or her eye.
   b. Touch the eyeball directly with a gloved finger.
   c. Ensure that the patient refrains from blinking.
   d. Use the corner of a sterile gauze pad to remove the visible object.

4. You are providing care to a patient who splashed a cleaning solution into her eyes. You would irrigate both eyes for at least how long?
   a. 10 minutes
   b. 20 minutes
   c. 30 minutes
   d. 40 minutes

5. You feel resistance when attempting to align a patient's head and neck. Which of the following should you do next?
   a. Continue to move the head to align it with the neck.
   b. Apply a C-collar instead.
   c. Stabilize the patient's head and neck in the position found.
   d. Avoid any further attempts to stabilize the head and neck.

6. A patient has a piece of metal embedded in his eyeball from an industrial incident. Which of the following would you do?
   a. Remove the object immediately to prevent permanent damage.
   b. Secure a Styrofoam® cup over the embedded object.
   c. Apply a sterile dressing over top of the object.
   d. Encircle the eye with gauze dressing to stabilize the object.

7. When assessing a patient with a closed head injury, you notice fluid leaking from the patient's ear. Which of the following would you suspect?
   a. Skull fracture
   b. Scalp injury
   c. Concussion
   d. Penetrating skull injury

8. You are assessing a patient with a suspected head injury and observe bruising behind the ears. You would identify this as which of the following?
   a. Raccoon eyes
   b. Battle's sign
   c. Concussion
   d. Nosebleed

9. A patient incurred a facial injury in which a tooth was knocked out. Upon finding the tooth, which of the following is the most appropriate?
   a. Attempt to replace the tooth in the patient's mouth.
   b. Handle the tooth by its root.
   c. Rinse the tooth gently under running water.
   d. Place the tooth on ice for transport.

10. The guiding principle when dealing with any injury to the neck or spine is to—
    a. Treat the underlying cause.
    b. Establish the certainty of the injury.
    c. Rule out injury to the neck or spine if the patient can walk.
    d. Consider it to be a serious injury.

11. Which of the following would you do first when providing care to a patient with a head injury?
    a. Perform a primary assessment.
    b. Establish manual stabilization.
    c. Control any bleeding.
    d. Encourage the patient to talk to you.

12. You need to provide manual stabilization for a patient who is lying on his back. Place the following steps in the order in which you would complete them.
    a. Maintain an open airway.
    b. Control any external bleeding.
    c. Summon more advanced medical personnel.
    d. Position the head in line with the body.
    e. Place your hands on both sides of the patient's head.

| SELF-ASSESSMENT: ENRICHMENT |

Removing Helmets and Other Equipment

Directions: *Circle the letter that best answers the question.*

1. Removing a motorcycle helmet requires how many rescuers to be present?
   a. One
   b. Two
   c. Three
   d. Four

2. When removing a football helmet, you also remove the shoulder pads because—
   a. The patient also may have injuries to the chest.
   b. The shoulder pads interfere with completing a primary assessment.
   c. The patient could incur further spinal injury if they are not removed.
   d. Ventilations would be difficult to perform if needed.

3. When assisting with the removal of an athletic helmet, which of the following is accomplished first?
   a. Removal of the internal cheek pads
   b. Deflating the helmet's air bladder system
   c. Spreading the shoulder pads apart for removal
   d. Cutting away the chin strap

Cervical Collars and Backboarding

Directions: *Answer the questions by selecting the correct letter(s).*

1. To immobilize a patient's body, which equipment is appropriate to use? Select all that apply.
   a. Backboard
   b. C-collar
   c. Head immobilizer
   d. Straps
   e. Splints

2. When securing a patient to a backboard, you notice that the head is not resting in line with the rest of the body. Which of the following is appropriate?
   a. Elevate the head about 6 inches.
   b. Place a rolled blanket around the head.
   c. Put a folded towel underneath the patient's head.
   d. Crisscross straps across the forehead.

| SKILL SHEETS |

Refer to the *Emergency Medical Response* textbook for the following skill sheets for this chapter:

- Manual Stabilization, page 518
- Controlling Bleeding from an Open Head Wound, page 519
- Bandaging an Eye with an Injury from an Impaled Object, page 520
- Caring for Foreign Bodies in the Eye, page 521
- Immobilizing a Head, Neck or Spinal Injury (*Enrichment*), pages 526–527

7 | SPECIAL POPULATIONS

24 | Childbirth

| REVIEW OF CONCEPTS AND TERMS |

Matching

Directions: *Write the letter of the description from Column 2 in the space next to the correct term in Column 1.*

Column 1

___ 1. Crowning

___ 2. Bloody show

___ 3. Contraction

___ 4. Embyro

___ 5. Labor

___ 6. Implantation

___ 7. Dilation

___ 8. Dropping

Column 2

A. Engagement
B. Uterine rhythmic tightening and relaxation during labor
C. Baby's head visible at vaginal opening
D. Process of enlargement or stretching of the cervical opening
E. Discharge that often signifies the onset of labor
F. Birth process
G. Stage from fertilization to third month
H. Attachment of fertilized egg to uterine lining

Fill-in-the-Blank

Directions: *Write the correct term in the space provided.*

1. The _____ or the neck of the uterus is the lower, narrow portion that forms a canal that opens into the vagina.

2. The "organ of pregnancy" also is called the _____.

3. The developing fetus is contained in the uterus and surrounded by _____ _____.

4. A woman's due date usually is calculated as _____ weeks from the woman's last menstrual period.

5. During the _____ trimester, implantation and rapid development of the embryo occurs.

6. The fourth stage of labor, _____, occurs after childbirth and lasts approximately _____ hour(s).

7. False labor contractions also are called
   _____ _____ contractions.

8. The _____ scoring system is the universally accepted method of assessing a newborn at 1 minute and 5 minutes after birth.

| CASE STUDY |

Directions: *Read the case studies and answer the questions that follow.*

Scenario A

You arrive at a local department store in response to a call that a woman in the store is in labor. You find the woman lying on the floor in pain. She tells you that this is her first pregnancy and that her contractions started about an hour or so ago. "I just thought it was gas but then my water broke." The contractions, which are lasting about 30 seconds, are approximately 5 minutes apart. The baby's due date is 3 weeks away.

1. When assessing this patient, you determine that the patient is in labor when she reports that the contractions are—
   a. Occurring sporadically.
   b. Getting closer together.
   c. Lasting about the same length.
   d. Alternating between mild and strong.

2. Since this is the woman's first pregnancy, you would anticipate that labor would take between—
   a. 4 to 8 hours.
   b. 8 to 12 hours.
   c. 12 to 24 hours.
   d. 24 to 36 hours.

3. In which stage of labor is this woman?
   a. First stage
   b. Second stage
   c. Third stage
   d. Fourth stage

Scenario B

You arrive at a couple's home where the woman is pregnant and in labor. Your assessment reveals that the baby's head is crowning. You also observe a small loop of rope-like tissue protruding from the vaginal opening.

1. In which stage of labor is this woman?
   a. First stage
   b. Second stage
   c. Third stage
   d. Fourth stage

2. You interpret your findings to suggest which of the following?
   a. Breech birth
   b. Prolapsed umbilical cord
   c. Premature birth
   d. Meconium aspiration

3. You prepare to promptly intervene because you understand that—
   a. The blood flow to the baby can be cut off as the baby moves through the birth canal.
   b. The baby may aspirate amniotic fluid, which could lead to pneumonia.
   c. The mother is at high risk for hemorrhage and shock.
   d. The mother may experience a seizure because she has developed eclampsia.

4. Which action is most appropriate for this woman?
   a. Massaging her lower abdomen gently and frequently
   b. Having her assume a knee-chest position
   c. Avoiding any pulling on or touching of the baby
   d. Forming a "V" with your gloved index and middle fingers inserted into the vagina

| SELF-ASSESSMENT |

Directions: *Answer the questions by selecting the correct letter(s).*

1. Which of the following would you expect to see at the opening of the birth canal if the woman was experiencing a breech birth? Select all that apply.
   a. Head
   b. Buttocks
   c. Foot
   d. Shoulder
   e. Arm

2. Which of the following occurs first during pregnancy?
   a. Implantation
   b. Development of the embryo
   c. Development of the fetus
   d. Quickening

3. Which of the following occurs during the third trimester?
   a. Morning sickness
   b. Placental development
   c. Majority of weight gain
   d. Fetal movement

4. You have just assisted in the delivery of a newborn. You would expect the placenta to be delivered within which time frame?
   a. 15 minutes
   b. 30 minutes
   c. 45 minutes
   d. 60 minutes

5. You are assisting a pregnant woman who is in labor to cope with the discomfort and pain. Which of the following is the least effective?
   a. Encouraging her to breathe slowly and deeply
   b. Asking her to focus on an object to help her breathing
   c. Telling her that she has to learn to endure the discomfort
   d. Providing her with explanations about what is happening

6. You are assisting a woman with delivery and the baby is crowning. Which of the following would you do next?
   a. Place a hand on top of the baby's head and apply light pressure.
   b. Tell the mother to stop pushing and concentrate on her breathing.
   c. Check for looping of the umbilical cord around the baby's neck.
   d. Guide one shoulder out at a time without pulling on the baby.

7. You are assessing a newborn immediately after birth to determine the baby's APGAR score. The highest number score given to each area is—
   a. 1.
   b. 2.
   c. 3.
   d. 4.

8. A newborn has not yet made any sounds. Which method is the most appropriate to stimulate breathing and the cry reflex in a newborn?
   a. Gently slapping the newborn's back
   b. Placing the newborn with the head lower than his or her chest
   c. Mechanically suctioning the mouth and nose
   d. Flicking the soles of the feet with your fingers

9. Which of the following would indicate the need to begin resuscitation of the newborn?
   a. A respiratory rate greater than 30 respirations per minute
   b. A pulse less than 100 *beats per minute* (bpm)
   c. A pink body with bluish limbs
   d. No gasping movements

10. At which point in the pregnancy do most spontaneous abortions occur?
    a. During the first trimester
    b. Before 8 weeks
    c. Between 12 and 16 weeks
    d. After 20 weeks

11. An ectopic pregnancy mostly occurs in which location?
    a. Abdomen
    b. Ovary
    c. Cervix
    d. Fallopian tube

12. Which of the following would lead you to suspect that delivery is imminent?
    a. Strong contractions occurring every 3 to 4 minutes
    b. The woman's report of a strong urge to push
    c. The absence of crowning at the vaginal opening
    d. A sudden gush of fluid from the vagina

13. You would expect to begin resuscitation efforts for a newborn with which APGAR score?
    a. 2
    b. 4
    c. 6
    d. 8

14. When providing care to a newborn, which of the following is the least appropriate?
    a. Positioning him or her with the head slightly higher than the trunk
    b. Drying the newborn thoroughly
    c. Supporting the newborn's head whenever handling the newborn
    d. Clearing the mouth of secretions before the nose

15. Which of the following is considered to be the most common complication of childbirth?
    a. Breech birth
    b. Prolapsed umbilical cord
    c. Postpartum hemorrhage
    d. Premature birth

| SELF-ASSESSMENT: ENRICHMENT |

More Complications During Pregnancy and Delivery

Directions: *Circle the letter that best answers the question.*

1. Which of the following would you expect to find in a woman with placenta previa?
   a. Abdominal pain
   b. Abdominal rigidity
   c. Painless vaginal bleeding
   d. Uterine tenderness

2. While interviewing a pregnant woman, a history of which of the following would lead you to identify her as having an increased risk for uterine rupture?
   a. Prior cesarean section
   b. Young maternal age
   c. First pregnancy
   d. Previous vaginal deliveries

3. Which of the following would be noted with shoulder dystocia?
   a. Heavy vaginal bleeding
   b. Turtle sign
   c. Signs of shock
   d. Back pain

25 | Pediatrics

I REVIEW OF CONCEPTS AND TERMS I

Matching

Directions: *Write the letter of the description from Column 2 in the space next to the correct term in Column 1.*

Column 1

___ 1 Croup

___ 2. Epiglottitis

___ 3. Asthma

___ 4. Reye's syndrome

___ 5. Seizure

Column 2

A. Temporary abnormal electrical activity in the brain caused by injury, disease, fever, infection, metabolic disturbances or conditions that decrease oxygen levels

B. Illness brought on by the use of aspirin by a child or an infant to control a high fever

C. Illness often triggered by exposure to allergens

D. Bacterial infection associated with severe swelling that can lead to complete airway obstruction

E. Viral infection that is associated with a barking cough

Short Answer

Directions: *Supply the information requested.*

1. Describe the three general age groups developed for providing emergency care.

   _____
   _____
   _____

2. Identify the five child developmental groups and their corresponding ages.

   _____
   _____
   _____
   _____
   _____

3. Name the three components of the Pediatric Assessment Triangle.

   _____
   _____
   _____

4. Describe the process that occurs with respiratory emergencies in children.

   _____
   _____
   _____
   _____

5. List the most common causes of seizures in children.

_____

_____

6. Identify the most common type of child abuse reported.

_____

_____

| CASE STUDY |

Directions: *Read the case studies and answer the questions that follow.*

Scenario A

You are called to the scene of a motor-vehicle accident involving a car that has struck a utility pole head-on. Two adults and a 20-month-old child were in the car. The adults are being cared for by other emergency medical responders (EMRs). You are to provide care for the child who is in a safety seat in the backseat of the car.

1. You would identify this child as being at which developmental stage?
   a. Infant
   b. Toddler
   c. Preschooler
   d. School-age

2. Which of the following is of least importance when you are completing your primary assessment of the child?
   a. Appearance
   b. Breathing
   c. Skin
   d. Vital signs

3. The child is alert and crying. As you prepare to examine the child, he begins to scream and push you away. Which action is most appropriate?
   a. Ask another EMR to perform the exam
   b. Speak softly and calmly to the child, maintaining eye contact
   c. Delay the physical exam until more advanced medical personnel arrive
   d. Proceed with the exam in a head-to-toe manner

Scenario B

You arrive at the home of a family in response to a call that a 4-year-old child was climbing over a wooden fence in the backyard and fell. A piece of the fence has broken off and cut through the child's pant leg where you can see it protruding. There is blood on the pant leg and the ground. The child is crying and talking to his parents.

1. Which of the following is of greatest concern to you?
   a. Airway
   b. Breathing
   c. Skin
   d. *Level of consciousness* (LOC)

2. Which of the following conditions would you be most alert for at this time?
   a. Obstructed airway
   b. Shock
   c. Infection
   d. Seizure

3. While caring for the child, which of the following would lead you to suspect that immediate intervention is needed? Select all that apply.
   a. Strong, palpable pulse
   b. Increasing lethargy
   c. Cool, clammy skin
   d. Rapid breathing
   e. Increased crying

| SELF-ASSESSMENT |

Directions: *Answer the questions by selecting the correct letter(s).*

1. When providing care to an injured preschooler, which of the following is the most important to keep in mind?
   a. Preschoolers can understand complex sentences.
   b. Preschoolers' fears correspond to the severity of the injury.
   c. Preschoolers may feel that they caused the injury.
   d. Preschoolers readily cooperate with strangers.

2. When assessing an injured child, which of the following is the most appropriate?
   a. Use as much careful observation as possible to carry out the primary assessment.
   b. Use touch to convey a warm and caring attitude to the child.
   c. Refrain from interacting with the parents when gathering information.
   d. Perform a head-to-toe assessment for a child who is agitated.

3. You are using the Pediatric Assessment Triangle. At which time would you complete this assessment?
   a. After checking the patient's breathing and pulse
   b. During the scene size-up
   c. After obtaining the SAMPLE history
   d. Before beginning the physical exam

4. Which of the following is least appropriate to use to assess a child's LOC?
   a. AVPU scale
   b. Pupil assessment
   c. Evidence of spontaneous movement
   d. Vital signs

5. Which of the following patients would be considered a child when using an *automated external defibrillator* (AED) on a patient?
   a. 13-year-old boy
   b. 11-year-old girl
   c. 9-year-old boy
   d. 7 year-old girl

6. You are to provide care to a child who is having difficulty breathing. Which of the following would lead you to suspect that the child has a partial airway obstruction? Select all that apply.
   a. Drooling
   b. Frequent coughing
   c. Retractions
   d. Loss of consciousness
   e. Cyanosis

7. Which of the following is the most important to keep in mind when caring for a child compared with an adult?
   a. A child's tongue often is smaller than that of an adult.
   b. The epiglottitis is higher in children than in adults.
   c. Younger children breathe at a slower rate than adults.
   d. Children breathe more deeply than adults.

8. Which of the following is the most appropriate when caring for a child who is developing shock?
   a. Having the child assume a sitting-up position
   b. Covering the child with a light blanket
   c. Administering ventilations immediately
   d. Using back blows and chest thrusts

9. As you shine a pen light into a child's eye to assess the pupil response, which of the following would you expect to observe?
   a. Constriction before the light is applied
   b. Dilation when the light is applied
   c. Constriction when the light is applied
   d. No change when the light is applied

10. When attempting to open the airway of a child, you do not tilt the head as far back as that for an adult because—
   a. The smaller tongue will fall back more easily.
   b. The smaller airway will become obstructed more readily.
   c. The shorter trachea will become blocked due to the bending.
   d. Breathing through the nose will become the major way to inhale.

11. Which of the following should be avoided when providing care to a child with epiglottitis?
   a. Keeping the child calm
   b. Examining the throat
   c. Using the tripod position
   d. Monitoring for voice changes

12. You are called to the home where a child had a febrile seizure. Which temperature reading, as reported by the parents, would be an indicator of this condition?
   a. 100.6°F
   b. 101.4°F
   c. 102.2°F
   d. 103.8°F

13. Which of the following is a possible cause of seizures? Select all that apply.
   a. Head trauma
   b. Common cold
   c. Hypoxia
   d. Low blood glucose
   e. Respiratory distress

14. You arrive at a family's home to provide care for a child who has a fever. The child's temperature is 103.4°F. Which of the following would you do first?
   a. Call for assistance from more advanced medical personnel.
   b. Begin attempts to rapidly cool the child's body.
   c. Apply extra blankets and clothing to prevent chilling.
   d. Apply rubbing alcohol to the child's body to cool it.

15. You arrive on the scene and suspect that the patient, a child, is a victim of child abuse. Which of the following is a priority?
   a. Confronting the caregivers about the child's injuries
   b. Obtaining a thorough history of events from the child
   c. Providing care for the child's injuries
   d. Removing the child from the abusive situation

26 | Geriatrics and Special Needs Patients

I REVIEW OF CONCEPTS AND TERMS I

Matching

Directions: *Write the letter of the description from Column 2 in the space next to the correct term in Column 1.*

Column 1

___ 1. Alzheimer's disease

___ 2. Asperger syndrome

___ 3. Atherosclerosis

___ 4. Dementia

___ 5. Edema

___ 6. Mental illness

Column 2

A. Condition resulting from deposits of plaque

B. Condition involving significant impairment of intellectual functioning

C. Most common condition involving impaired thought, memory and language

D. Condition affecting a person's mood or ability to think, feel, relate to others and function in everyday activities

E. Condition on the autism spectrum

F. Swelling in body tissues due to fluid accumulation

Fill-in-the-Blank

Directions: *Supply the information requested.*

1. A guide dog, signal dog or other animal individually trained to provide assistance to an individual with a disability is called a(n) _____ animal.

2. The sensations of pain, taste and smell are _____ in an elderly person.

3. _____ impairment, exhibited by memory and other problems, is not a normal part of aging.

4. An extra copy of chromosome 21 results in the genetic condition known as _____ _____.

5. A problem with the outer or middle ear typically is associated with a _____ hearing loss.

6. A person becomes overwhelmed and starts throwing things and striking out. The person is exhibiting a(n) _____ _____.

| CASE STUDY |

Directions: Read the case studies and answer the questions that follow.

Scenario A

Early one evening, you are called to the home of an elderly couple. Upon arrival, the wife greets you at the door and tells you that her husband, who has Alzheimer's disease, suddenly went into the kitchen and then started screaming and shouting. "He even threw a dish at me, but luckily he missed," she explains.

1. Based on the patient's history, you would interpret this information as suggesting which of the following?
   a. Hallucinations
   b. Depression
   c. Catastrophic reaction
   d. Sundowning

2. Which statement or question is the most appropriate to use with this patient?
   a. "You have to stop screaming like this."
   b. "I'm not going to cause you any harm."
   c. "If you don't behave, I'll have to call the police."
   d. "Why are you acting this way?"

3. When assessing this patient, which of the following would you need to do?
   a. Deal solely with the wife because the patient is confused.
   b. Speak to the patient at eye level to show your interest.
   c. Turn off the lights in the room to prevent distractions.
   d. Avoid long explanations of what you are doing to prevent overstimulation.

4. In addition to the patient's current behavior, which of the following might his history also reveal? Select all that apply.
   a. Pacing
   b. Rummaging
   c. Abuse
   d. Nonsensical speaking
   e. Intellectual impairment

Scenario B

You are providing care to an elderly patient who has fallen in his home. When speaking to the patient, it seems like the patient does not hear. The patient is awake and alert, breathing and has a pulse. The patient's son is present and tells you that his father is hard of hearing.

1. When dealing with this patient, which of the following is the most important?
   a. Use a loud shouting voice when talking to the patient during the interview.
   b. Repeat the same question several times before allowing the patient to answer.
   c. Speak slowly and clearly to the patient when interacting with him.
   d. Approach the patient from behind rather than the front.

2. You understand that the patient's hearing problem differs from deafness in that—
   a. The patient has a problem in his middle ear.
   b. There is a problem with the nerve that transmits sound.
   c. The patient had difficulty hearing high-frequency sounds.
   d. The patient can rely on his hearing for communication.

| SELF-ASSESSMENT |

Directions: *Answer the questions by selecting the correct letter(s).*

1. Which of the following would you identify as a normal change related to aging?
   a. Thickening of the heart muscle
   b. Increased lung elasticity
   c. Increased movement through the digestive system
   d. Loss of the ability to learn

2. In older adult women, the risk of fractures is increased because their—
   a. Pain sensation is diminished.
   b. Tolerance to glare is reduced.
   c. Bones become less dense.
   d. Level of activity declines.

3. The *emergency medical services* (EMS) system for whom you work deals with a large elderly population. When talking with other *emergency medical responders* (EMRs) about this population, which statement indicates a lack of knowledge about this age group?
   a. "Older people might not really tell you how sick they feel."
   b. "You need to expect that they won't be able to remember things."
   c. "They are at greater risk for breathing problems."
   d. "Older adults experience sensory changes that put them at risk."

4. Which of the following might provide a clue to possible elder abuse?
   a. A patient who has someone providing care in the home 24 hours a day
   b. A patient who has been to the emergency room three times in 2 weeks
   c. A patient who has lost weight due to an underlying medical problem
   d. A patient who has experienced one fall in the last 12 months

5. You are caring for a patient with Down syndrome. Which of the following health problems might you find? Select all that apply.
   a. Heart disease
   b. Hearing loss
   c. Thyroid disorders
   d. Skeletal problems
   e. Vision difficulties

6. You are caring for an elderly patient who has a loss of visual field. Which of the following would you most likely observe?
   a. The need to wear glasses to see
   b. The use of a white cane
   c. The need to turn his or her head to see
   d. The use of other senses to compensate

7. You are called to the home of a patient who is receiving chemotherapy and radiation therapy as treatment for cancer. When providing care for this patient, which of the following is the most important?
   a. Inspecting the skin for rashes
   b. Noting the degree of hair loss
   c. Evaluating the severity of vomiting
   d. Observing standard precautions

8. Which of the following would you expect to find in a patient with cystic fibrosis?
   a. Fluid overload
   b. Constipation
   c. Frequent coughing
   d. Loss of appetite

9. You are providing care to a patient with multiple sclerosis. Which of the following would you need to keep in mind?
   a. This disorder is a progressive genetic disorder.
   b. Its symptoms appear and disappear over a period of years.
   c. The condition primarily affects skeletal muscles.
   d. Eventually, the patient will require assisted ventilation.

10. You are caring for a child with autism. Which of the following would you least expect to find?
    a. Consistent, direct staring at you
    b. Repetition of behaviors
    c. Intense focusing on one object
    d. Negative response to touch

11. Which of the following best reflects the focus of hospice care?
    a. The goal is to cure the patient using advanced medical technologies.
    b. The emphasis is on providing comfort, not cure, to the patient and family.
    c. Pain relief is provided through medication administered through needles.
    d. Care is provided to terminally ill patients in the final 12 months of life.

12. Which of the following is the most appropriate to keep in mind when caring for an elderly patient?
    a. Provide quick, short explanations about what you are doing.
    b. Handle the patient's skin gently to prevent tearing.
    c. Apply additional pressure when administering ventilations.
    d. Use an *oropharyngeal airway* (OPA) for the responsive patient.

13. Which of the following would you identify as a mental illness? Select all that apply.
    a. Depression
    b. Panic disorder
    c. Autism
    d. Down syndrome
    e. Cerebral palsy

14. Which of the following is considered a type of elder abuse?
    a. Family member uses the patient's money to purchase the patient's medications.
    b. Patient has numerous old and new bruises on his inner arms.
    c. Caregiver takes the patient to a senior center daily.
    d. Patient is clean and dressed appropriately for the weather.

15. Which condition is considered the least severe of the autism spectrum disorders?
    a. Asperger syndrome
    b. *Attention-deficit-hyperactivity disorder* (ADHD)
    c. Autism
    d. Alzheimer's disease

8 EMS OPERATIONS

27 | EMS Support and Operations

I REVIEW OF CONCEPTS AND TERMS I

Fill-in-the-Blank

Directions: *Write the correct term in the space provided.*

1. Athletic trainers and trip leaders are examples of _____ *emergency medical responders* (EMRs).

2. A typical *emergency medical services* (EMS) response has _____ phases.

3. Air medical transport via a(n) _____ can be the best transportation choice when dealing with severely injured or ill persons who need quick transport to specialty centers or large treatment facilities.

4. The siren and air horn are examples of _____ warning devices.

5. The bag or box that contains the equipment used by the EMR when responding to an emergency is called a(n) _____ _____.

6. You are _____ the patient when you get the patient ready for transport.

Short Answer

Directions: *Supply the information requested.*

1. Name the two types of roles that an EMR may assume.

   _____
   _____
   _____

2. Describe the first phase of a typical EMS response.

   _____
   _____
   _____

3. Explain the role of the communication center.

   _____
   _____
   _____

4. Identify the two main types of air medical transport.

   _____
   _____
   _____

5. Describe what is meant by a 360-degree assessment.

_____

_____

_____

6. Explain the reason for securing all moveable equipment in the vehicle during patient transport.

_____

_____

_____

7. List the four items that must be included in a jump kit.

_____

_____

_____

_____

_____

_____

_____

_____

_____

_____

_____

| CASE STUDY |

Directions: *Read the case studies and answer the questions that follow.*

Scenario A

You receive a call to go the scene of an emergency involving a multiple-vehicle collision on a rural highway. Snow has been falling throughout most of the day, and the roads are snow-covered and icy. A caller has reported that three cars and a pickup truck were involved. You observe that the truck is overturned on the side of the road and one of the cars has rolled over and landed in a shallow gulley. The driver and passenger of the car in the gulley are unresponsive with multiple injuries. Neither was wearing a shoulder restraint or seat belt. The pickup driver is responsive but unable to get out of the car. There is a strong odor of gasoline around the truck. The windshield of another car is shattered with pieces of glass covering the ground.

1. Which phase of the EMS response is occurring when the caller reports the accident?
   a. Preparation for the emergency call
   b. Dispatch
   c. En-route to the scene
   d. Patient contact

2. Which of the following is the most important when travelling to this scene?
   a. Getting as much information from the *emergency medical dispatcher* (EMD) as possible
   b. Ensuring that you have the appropriate equipment readily available
   c. Observing appropriate driving behavior for the weather conditions
   d. Notifying dispatch about the need for additional emergency services

3. You determine that the driver and the passenger of the car in the gulley need to be transported to a trauma facility. Which of the following is appropriate?
   a. Contacting dispatch to summon an additional emergency vehicle for transport
   b. Making a request for air medical transport to the trauma center
   c. Getting both patients ready for transport by ambulance
   d. Notifying law enforcement to clear the roadway for transport

Scenario B

You are assisting at the scene of an industrial chemical spill and are preparing a patient for transport to a nearby burn facility by helicopter.

1. Which of the following is the most important in preparation for the arrival of the helicopter?
   a. Ensuring a safe *landing zone* (LZ)
   b. Having the patient ready for transport
   c. Applying ear and eye protection to the patient
   d. Moving bystanders back at least 20 feet

2. You prepare to assist with patient transport to the helicopter. You determine that it is safe to approach the aircraft when—
   a. The pilot signals that it is safe.
   b. The tail rotors have stopped spinning.
   c. The medical crew begins exiting the craft.
   d. The helicopter comes to a stop.

| SELF-ASSESSMENT |

Directions: *Answer the questions by selecting the correct letter(s).*

1. During which phase of the EMS response would the crew members give information about the scene and the patient to the nurses and doctors?
   a. Phase 5
   b. Phase 6
   c. Phase 7
   d. Phase 8

2. Ideally, what is the minimum size of a safe LZ?
   a. 100 square feet
   b. 1000 square feet
   c. 10,000 square feet
   d. 100,000 square feet

3. Which of the following would be an appropriate reason for requesting air medical transport?
   a. Head-on motor-vehicle collision
   b. Pedestrian struck by a speeding car
   c. Patient who fell from a height of 5 feet
   d. Patient with a fracture of the leg

4. Which of the following best describes rotorcrafts?
   a. Rotorcrafts are difficult to maneuver into tight areas.
   b. Rotorcrafts are used for transporting patients over long distances.
   c. Rotorcrafts can be used with hoisting procedures.
   d. Rotorcrafts can move up and down but not side to side.

5. When calculating the amount of space available in a helicopter, which of the following is of least importance?
   a. Number of patients to be transported
   b. Number of rescuers accompanying the patient(s)
   c. Life-saving equipment needed
   d. Weight of the fuel load

6. Which of the following sites makes the most appropriate LZ?
   a. Open soccer field
   b. Frozen lake
   c. Dry, barren pasture
   d. Field with powdery snow

7. When approaching a helicopter for transporting a patient, which of the following is important to do?
   a. Approach the helicopter from the back.
   b. Maintain a somewhat crouched posture.
   c. Wear a hat on your head.
   d. Carry an *intravenous* (IV) pole at a 90-degree angle to the ground.

8. You are checking the jump kit for the necessary supplies. Which of the following must be included?
   a. Maps
   b. Protective eyewear
   c. Stethoscope
   d. Wound dressings

9. You would check the jump kit during which phase of the EMS response?
   a. Phase 1
   b. Phase 2
   c. Phase 3
   d. Phase 4

10. Which of the following is considered a high-risk situation impacting safety during an emergency response? Select all that apply.
    a. Going through an intersection
    b. Exiting from a highway
    c. Driving in inclement weather
    d. Turning off a vehicle's stereo
    e. Responding alone

11. While driving a vehicle on a long transport, you find yourself feeling sleepy. Which of the following is the most appropriate for you to do?
    a. Drink a large cup of coffee.
    b. Eat one or two chocolate candy bars.
    c. Open the window to breathe fresh air.
    d. Chew on some gum.

12. You arrive at the scene of a crash involving a car that has struck an electrical pole. An electrical wire has fallen across the car and onto the ground. The wire is 100 feet in length. Which of the following actions is appropriate? Select all that apply.
    a. Tell the occupants of the vehicle to get out of the car immediately.
    b. Move the wire off the car onto the ground.
    c. Set up a safety area at least 150 feet from the car.
    d. Notify the power company to cut off the power.

13. You are providing CPR to a patient while he is being transported. Which of the following is the least appropriate?
    a. Stand freely using the stretcher for balance.
    b. Spread your feet to shoulder width for stability.
    c. Bend your knees to lower your center of gravity.
    d. Ask the driver to warn you of any uneven road surfaces.

| SELF-ASSESSMENT: ENRICHMENT |

Operational Safety and Security Measures

Directions: *Circle the letter that best answers the question.*

1. Which of the following should occur at the beginning of each shift?
    a. Briefing about any crew safety issues
    b. Discussion of security measures
    c. Remedial training for protocols
    d. Discussion of vehicle monitoring

2. Which of the following is the most important to maintain vehicle safety?
    a. Leaving the vehicle running when at an emergency scene
    b. Removing the key from the ignition when the vehicle is unattended
    c. Maintaining the emergency markings on a vehicle if it is no longer in use
    d. Removal of tracking devices from ambulances and rescue vehicles

28 | Access and Extrication

| REVIEW OF CONCEPTS AND TERMS |

Crossword Puzzle

Directions: *Complete the crossword puzzle using the clues.*

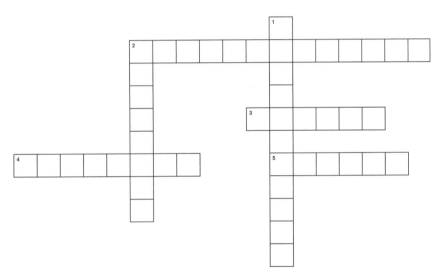

DOWN

1 Safe and appropriate removal of a patient trapped in a dangerous situation
2 Use of wood or supports, arranged diagonally to the vehicle's frame, which creates a stable environment for a motor vehicle by safely propping it up.

ACROSS

2 Type of extrication process that uses specialized tools to gain access to a patient
3 Type of extrication process that does not use equipment to gain access to a patient
4 Use of wooden blocks against the car's wheels to stabilize it
5 Attempt to reach a patient trapped in a motor vehicle, for the purpose of extrication and providing medical care.

Short Answer

Directions*: Supply the information requested.*

1. List five examples of basic extrication equipment.

   _____

   _____

   _____

   _____

   _____

2. Identify five pieces of equipment that an *emergency medical responder* (EMR) must have at a minimum when responding to a situation involving extrication.

   _____

   _____

   _____

   _____

   _____

3. Describe blocking.

   _____

   _____

   _____

4. Explain the meaning of the term "rule of thumb."

   _____

   _____

   _____

5. Name two indications that a vehicle is unstable.

   _____

   _____

| CASE STUDY |

Directions: *Read the case studies and answer the questions that follow.*

Scenario A

You are called to the scene of a construction site in which a worker has fallen from the first level of a scaffold to the ground. As he fell, several large pieces of plywood also fell, landing on top of him. The scaffold then fell, landing on top of the plywood. The patient is trapped from the waist down.

1. Which of the following is your primary role as an EMR?
   a. Providing care to the patient
   b. Extricating the patient
   c. Establishing a chain of command
   d. Ensuring crowd control

2. Your first priority is to—
   a. Control traffic at the scene.
   b. Ensure that the scene is safe.
   c. Complete a primary assessment.
   d. Request additional law enforcement.

3. Which type of equipment would you most likely expect to use during extrication?
   a. Ropes
   b. Pliers
   c. Shovel
   d. Pneumatic tool

Scenario B

You are called to the scene of a motor-vehicle collision involving two cars, one of which is a hybrid vehicle. You determine that both vehicles are unstable.

1. Which of the following suggests that a vehicle is unstable?
   a. It is positioned on a flat surface.
   b. It is on its side.
   c. It is on a dry surface.
   d. It is side by side with the other vehicle.

2. Which of the following would you do first to stabilize the vehicles?
   a. Put the car in "park."
   b. Set the parking brake.
   c. Turn off the ignition.
   d. Disconnect the battery source.

3. When working to stabilize a hybrid vehicle, which of the following would you need to keep in mind?
   a. Removing the ignition key is sufficient to stabilize the vehicle.
   b. The vehicle still can be operational even if silent.
   c. Cribbing should be placed under the high-voltage cables.
   d. Chocking the wheels should be avoided.

4. When using a simple access method, you would—
   a. Use a ratcheting cable.
   b. Try opening the door.
   c. Break the window glass.
   d. Remove the car roof with a tool cutter.

5. Emergency vehicles, including fire apparatus and ambulances, arrive on the scene. Which of the following is the most appropriate?
   a. Traffic cones placed at 25-foot intervals
   b. Ambulances parked on the outside of the fire engines
   c. Large fire apparatus positioned at an angle to the traffic lane
   d. A safety zone radius of at least 100 feet around the scene

| SELF-ASSESSMENT |

Directions: *Answer the questions by selecting the correct letter(s) or by placing the answers in the proper order.*

1. You are caring for a patient who is pinned inside of a vehicle directly behind the air bags, which have not deployed. Which of the following is the most appropriate?
   a. Mechanically cutting through the steering column
   b. Drilling into the air bag module
   c. Applying heat to the steering wheel hub
   d. Waiting for deactivation of the system

2. You put an unstable vehicle, which contains no passengers, in "park" and prepare to perform the following steps. Place the steps in the order in which you would perform them.
   a. Turn off the ignition.
   b. Set the parking brake.
   c. Move the seats back.
   d. Remove the key.
   e. Identify hazardous vehicle safety components.
   f. Disconnect the power source.

3. You use cribbing to provide further vehicle stabilization. You would make sure that there is no more than how much distance between the cribbing and the vehicle?
   a. 2 inches
   b. 4 inches
   c. 6 inches
   d. 8 inches

4. You arrive on the scene of an emergency involving *hazardous materials* (HAZMATs). Which of the following is the least appropriate?
   a. Avoiding low-lying areas
   b. Approaching the area quickly
   c. Staying upwind of the scene
   d. Going to the designated cold zone

5. Which of the following would lead you to suspect that a HAZMAT is involved? Select all that apply.
   a. Fire
   b. Vapor cloud
   c. Leaking container
   d. Spilled liquid
   e. Smoke
   f. Unusual odors

6. Throughout the extrication process, which principle is the most important?
   a. Moving the patient, not the device
   b. Using the path of greatest resistance
   c. Maintaining cervical spinal stabilization
   d. Using the least number of personnel possible

7. You place blocks against the wheels of a vehicle to prevent it from moving. This is called—
   a. Blocking.
   b. Cribbing.
   c. Extricating.
   d. Chocking.

8. Which of the following is the most commonly used extrication tool?
   a. Power hydraulic tool
   b. Pneumatic tool
   c. Manual hydraulic tool
   d. Tool cutter

9. To ensure that an upright vehicle does not roll, which of the following could be done?
   a. Turn the wheels away from the curb.
   b. Cut the tires' valve stems.
   c. Overinflate the tires.
   d. Tie the car frame to a tree branch.

10. You gained access to a patient who is to be extricated and begin to provide care. Which of the following is the most important for you to do first?
    a. Assess the patient's breathing and pulse.
    b. Administer emergency oxygen.
    c. Ensure that the neck and spine are stabilized.
    d. Obtain a SAMPLE history.

11. Undeployed air bags can become a hazard during extrication because if they suddenly deploy—
    a. Hazardous materials can be released.
    b. Extrication tools can become projectiles.
    c. The patient's spine will be crushed.
    d. Extrication will fail.

29 | Hazardous Materials Emergencies

| REVIEW OF CONCEPTS AND TERMS |

Fill-in-the-Blank

Directions: *Write the correct term in the space provided.*

1. Federal law requires that _____ or signs be placed on any vehicle that contains specific quantities of *hazardous materials* (HAZMATs).

2. Drivers transporting hazardous materials are required to carry _____ _____, documents that list the names, associated dangers and four-digit identification numbers of the substances.

3. The hot zone or _____ zone is the area in which the greatest danger exists.

4. _____ decontamination occurs as the person enters the warm zone.

5. The _____ _____ _____ _____ is a document provided by the manufacturer and identifies the substance, physical properties and any associated hazards for a given material.

6. The degree to which a substance is poisonous refers to its _____.

7. _____ refers to the degree to which a substance may ignite.

8. When assuming command at a HAZMAT incident, an *emergency medical responder* (EMR) remains in command until relieved by someone _____ in the chain of command.

9. Life-saving emergency care occurs in the _____ zone or contamination reduction zone.

10. The first step to follow when first arriving on the scene of a possible HAZMAT spill is _____.

Labeling

Safety Zones

Directions: *Write the name of the correct safety zone in the appropriate area on the illustration.*

A. _____

B. _____

C. _____

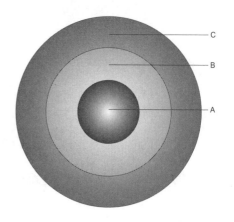

| CASE STUDY |

Directions: *Read the case studies and answer the questions that follow.*

Scenario A

You are the first to arrive at the scene of a tanker truck crash. As you near the scene, you notice a sign on the rear door of the truck indicating the presence of HAZMATs. You also see a small trickle of fluid oozing out of the rear door of the tanker. The driver is in the cab of the tanker and is not moving.

1. Which of the following would you do first?
   a. Contact dispatch to inform them of your findings.
   b. Establish a clear chain of command.
   c. Create safety zones.
   d. Access the patient.

2. Which of the following would be important when on the scene of a HAZMAT incident?
   a. Staying out of higher areas of elevation
   b. Remaining downwind of the scene
   c. Keeping yourself uphill and upwind of the scene
   d. Moving closer to the scene as time goes on

3. In addition to the placard on the tanker, you could gain additional information about the substance in the tanker at the scene from which of the following? Select all that apply.
   a. Warning signs
   b. *National Fire Protection Association* (NFPA) numbers
   c. Shipping papers
   d. *Emergency Response Guidebook*
   e. CAMEO®

4. To be able to enter the hot zone established by the HAZMAT team, which of the following would be the least appropriate?
   a. *Occupational Safety and Health Administration* (OSHA) training at the first responder awareness level
   b. Double gloves applied over work gloves
   c. *Personal protective equipment* (PPE)
   d. Positive-pressure *self-contained breathing apparatus* (SCBA)

| SELF-ASSESSMENT |

Directions: *Answer the questions by selecting the correct letter(s) or by placing the answers in the proper order.*

1. Which statement best describes a hazardous material?
   a. A substance that is primarily radioactive
   b. Any chemical posing a threat to an individual
   c. Toxic waste products from manufacturers
   d. Gases supplied in any form

2. You are reading about a hazardous substance that is considered highly poisonous. You would identify this as referring to the substance's—
   a. Flammability.
   b. Toxicity.
   c. Reactivity.
   d. Radioactivity.

3. Which of the following would be the first step in preparing for the worst-case scenario that may develop at a HAZMAT incident?
   a. Establishing a receiving facility close to the scene
   b. Assigning a single command officer for decision making
   c. Establishing a clear chain of command
   d. Establishing an accessible system of communication

4. Which information would you likely find on the shipping papers for a hazardous material?
   a. Physical properties of the substance
   b. Specific hazards of the substance
   c. Emergency first aid information
   d. Four-digit identification number

5. When establishing a clear chain of command, which of the following is the most accurate?
   a. There is one command officer responsible for decision making throughout the rescue.
   b. The communication system is based on each rescue team's preference.
   c. Each rescue team has a command officer that communicates with other team commanders.
   d. Individual rescue team members are able to choose to work with certain other members.

6. When dealing with a HAZMAT incident, which of the following would least likely suggest that the incident involves a possible terrorist attack?
   a. Numerous patients are exhibiting signs and symptoms of an unidentifiable illness.
   b. Strange odors, such as bitter almonds or garlic, are absent.
   c. The incident has occurred in a highly populated area.
   d. The animals in the area appear incapacitated.

7. Which of the following activities occur in the warm zone?
   a. Rescue
   b. Treatment of life-threatening conditions
   c. Initial decontamination
   d. Airway management

8. You suspect possible radiation exposure. Which of the following would be appropriate? Select all that apply.
   a. Put on PPE.
   b. Don a positive-pressure SCBA.
   c. Seal off all openings in protective clothing with duct tape.
   d. Apply triple gloves to your hands.
   e. Wear two pairs of paper shoe covers under heavy rubber boots.

9. Which of the following would increase your risk of radiation exposure?
   a. Short exposure time
   b. Close proximity to the source
   c. Minimal amount of materials
   d. Increased protective equipment

10. The support zone also is called which zone?
    a. Hot
    b. Exclusion
    c. Contamination reduction
    d. Cold

11. In your role as an EMR who is first on the scene of a possible HAZMAT incident, your last step would be to—
    a. Recognize the presence of a HAZMAT.
    b. Show awareness of the impact of the material to safety.
    c. Identify the specific material and its characteristics.
    d. Determine if the material is responsible for injuries at the scene.

12. A patient may become contaminated by which route? Select all that apply.
    a. Respiratory
    b. Gastrointestinal
    c. Topical
    d. Neurological
    e. Parenteral

13. You are assisting with decontamination efforts in which the patient is being cleaned with large amounts of soap and water after his clothing was removed and left in the hot zone. Which type of decontamination is being done?
    a. Dilution
    b. Gross
    c. Absorption
    d. Neutralization

30 | Incident Command and Multiple-Casualty Incidents

| REVIEW OF CONCEPTS AND TERMS |

Fill-in-the-Blank

Directions: *Write the correct term in the space provided.*

1. In an emergency, the first responder on the scene becomes the _____ _____, responsible until a more senior or experienced person arrives.

2. The _____ officer arranges for ambulances and other vehicles while tracking priorities, identities and destinations of all injured or ill people leaving the scene.

3. _____ is a vital link in the smooth running of a *multiple-casualty incident* (MCI); however, it may not always be as smooth and effective as desired.

4. The START triage system classifies injured or ill people into one of _____ levels.

5. The _____ _____ _____ is a guide to how the nation conducts all-hazards response.

6. You would use _____ to identify which patients need urgent care in an MCI.

7. A person who is decapitated would receive a triage tag that is _____ in color.

Short Answer

Directions: *Supply the information requested.*

1. Describe the *National Incident Management System* (NIMS).

   _____
   _____
   _____
   _____
   _____

2. Explain the function of the *incident command system* (ICS).

   _____
   _____
   _____
   _____
   _____

3. List three functional positions that may be required for a large incident.

   _____
   _____
   _____
   _____

4. Identify four examples that may be considered MCIs.

_____

_____

_____

_____

5. Describe the METTAG™ triage system.

_____

_____

_____

6. Name the four colors commonly used for triage.

_____

_____

_____

_____

7. List the three areas assessed using the START system.

_____

_____

_____

| CASE STUDY |

Directions: *Read the case studies and answer the questions that follow.*

Scenario A

You arrive on the scene of an apartment complex fire involving over 15 apartments. Numerous people have exited or have been pulled out of the building. Several people are burned severely, with varying levels of consciousness. Others are coughing and having difficulty breathing. Still others are sitting on the ground, stunned and sobbing. Fire personnel arrived just minutes before your arrival.

1. Which of the following would you do first?
   a. Assume the role of the *incident commander* (IC).
   b. Identify yourself to the IC.
   c. Begin assisting the patients.
   d. Determine the number of ambulances needed.

2. You are assisting with triage and identify patients who are able to walk with which colored tag?
   a. Red
   b. Yellow
   c. Green
   d. Black

3. One of the patients is a child. Which triage system would be the most appropriate to use?
   a. JumpSTART
   b. Smart Tag™
   c. METTAG™
   d. START

4. While triaging, you tag a person red based on which findings? Select all that apply.
   a. Unconsciousness
   b. Unable to ambulate
   c. Evidence of a spinal injury
   d. Capillary refill greater than 2 seconds
   e. Pulselessness

5. An individual alerts you and other responders to potential dangers that might cause injury. This person is functioning in which role?
   a. Treatment officer
   b. Triage officer
   c. Staging officer
   d. Safety officer

6. You notice that one of the patients is tagged white. You interpret this as an indication that the patient has—
   a. Life-threatening injuries needing attention.
   b. Some injuries but is ambulatory.
   c. Severe injuries that could wait for treatment.
   d. Minor injuries not needing a doctor's care.

Scenario B

You are the first to arrive at the scene of a commuter plane that crashed into a farm house. The plane was carrying 10 passengers and three crew members. No one was in the farm house when the plane hit. Other units of emergency responders and several fire departments are en-route with an estimated time of arrival of 10 minutes.

1. Which action would you perform first?
   a. Assess the safety of the scene.
   b. Identify calls that need to be made.
   c. Decide tasks that need to be done.
   d. Assign tasks to the arriving rescuers.

2. The other emergency personnel arrive on the scene. Which role would you need to assign first?
   a. Transportation officer
   b. Safety officer
   c. Triage officer
   d. Staging officer

3. A more experienced *emergency medical responder* (EMR) arrives on the scene. Which of the following would be the most appropriate?
   a. Assign the EMR specific patient care tasks to be completed.
   b. Transfer command to the EMR after giving a verbal report.
   c. Have the EMR assume responsibility for traffic control.
   d. Tell the EMR to set up a staging area for patient treatment.

4. Several of the patients have burns involving several body parts. You would expect these patients be triaged as which level?
   a. Minor
   b. Delayed
   c. Immediate
   d. Deceased/non-salvageable

| SELF-ASSESSMENT |

Directions: *Answer the questions by selecting the correct letter(s).*

1. You are working with the triage officer and identifying patients' status using symbols. Which triage system are you using?
   a. START system
   b. METTAG™
   c. Smart Tag™
   d. JumpSTART

2. Which color for triage would indicate that the patient requires urgent care?
   a. Red
   b. Yellow
   c. Green
   d. Black

3. Which of the following patients would you least expect to be at increased risk for severe stress reactions?
   a. A 10-year-old child involved in a bus accident
   b. An 82-year-old woman involved in a house fire
   c. A 55-year-old man involved in a factory explosion
   d. An ill 40-year-old woman involved in a train derailment

4. Which of the following is the most important for reducing responder stress after an MCI?
   a. Allowing for down time
   b. Encouraging the EMRs to talk among themselves
   c. Having a debriefing
   d. Ensuring clear expectations

5. Which of the following is the most appropriate in helping to manage and reduce stress of the patient and those around them? Select all that apply.
   a. Reuniting family members
   b. Providing information to the media
   c. Explaining events simply and honestly
   d. Limiting questions and discussions
   e. Having others available who are able to assist with tasks

6. The establishment of which of the following is essential to manage the emergency situation and provide care in an MCI?
   a. Triage
   b. *National Response Framework* (NRF)
   c. START system
   d. ICS

7. Which of the following positions would most commonly be required when dealing with an MCI? Select all that apply.
   a. Supply
   b. Extrication
   c. Treatment
   d. Safety
   e. Staging
   f. Logistics

8. Which of the following would be considered a large-scale MCI?
   a. Motor-vehicle crash involving a driver and passenger
   b. A fire involving a family of four
   c. A flood affecting a metropolitan area
   d. A building collapse affecting 10 workers

9. Secondary triage is performed at which time?
   a. Immediately after primary triage
   b. After patients are moved to the treatment area
   c. Before transporting patients to a receiving facility
   d. Upon arrival at the receiving facility

10. You are using the START system to assess an adult patient. You find that the patient is breathing at a rate of 42 breaths per minute. You would tag this person with which color?
    a. Yellow
    b. Red
    c. Green
    d. Black

11. When performing triage for each patient, assessment and tagging should take no longer than—
    a. 10 seconds.
    b. 20 seconds.
    c. 30 seconds.
    d. 40 seconds.

12. The staging officer is responsible for which of the following?
    a. Designating an organized parking area for multiple rescue units
    b. Communicating with the receiving hospitals about incoming patients
    c. Assigning patients to the proper transport mechanism
    d. Creating an area where ambulances can enter and leave adequately

13. You are using a triage system that uses symbols. You tag a patient as a rabbit to indicate that this patient needs which of the following?
    a. No care
    b. No urgent transportation
    c. Delayed care
    d. Urgent care

14. When using the JumpSTART triage system, which parameter would you assess first?
    a. Ambulatory status
    b. Respiratory status
    c. Perfusion status
    d. Mental status

15. The *Sort-Assess-Lifesaving Interventions-Treatment and/or Transport* (SALT) Mass Casualty Triage prioritizes patients for treatment using which of the following categories? Select all that apply.
    a. Immediate
    b. Expectant
    c. Ambulatory
    d. Delayed
    e. Minimal
    f. Dead
    g. Non-salvageable

31 | Response to Disasters and Terrorism

I REVIEW OF CONCEPTS AND TERMS I

Matching

Directions: *Write the letter of the description from Column 2 in the space next to the correct term in Column 1.*

Column 1

___ 1. Bioterrorism

___ 2. Atropine

___ 3. Mortality

___ 4. Incendiary weapon

___ 5. Organophosphate

___ 6. Morbidity

Column 2

A. Used in antidotes to counteract nerve agent effects

B. Effects of a condition or illness

C. Chemical compounds found in many common insecticides and used to produce toxic nerve agents, such as sarin

D. Death caused by a certain condition or disease

E. Deliberate release of an agent found in nature to cause illness or death

F. Device designed to burn at extremely high temperatures

Fill-in-the-Blank

Directions: *Write the correct term in the space provided.*

1. *Low-order explosives* (LEs) create a(n) _____ explosion.

2. Incident command is structured in _____ main functional areas.

3. The three main categories of disasters are _____, _____ and _____.

4. A(n) _____ approach is the type of approach that is used when responding to any kind of large-scale disaster.

5. Weapons of mass destruction are classified by the acronym _____.

6. Blister agents, also called _____, cause the skin and mucous membranes to form blisters on contact.

7. A class _____ biological agent poses the greatest threat to public health and national security.

8. _____ _____ is the most common fatal primary blast injury. It is caused by the over-pressurization wave from *high-order explosives* (HEs).

9. _____ _____ are the results of individuals being thrown by the blast wind caused by explosive and incendiary devices; they can involve any body part.

10. A(n) _____ _____ is a type of kit with premeasured doses of antidote to counteract the effects of nerve agents.

| CASE STUDY |

Directions: *Read the case studies and answer the questions that follow.*

Scenario A

You are called to the scene of an emergency at a government office building following a small explosion. Several of the workers are in extreme respiratory distress. Two workers have collapsed and are not breathing. A worker from a nearby building reports that there was a strange smell immediately after the explosion, stating that it smelled like "freshly cut hay."

1. Based on the worker's description, which of the following would you suspect?
   a. Sulfur mustard
   b. Cyanide
   c. Phosgene
   d. Tabun

2. Which of the following is the most appropriate for you to do?
   a. Administer an antidote such as sodium thiosulfate
   b. Begin resuscitative measures
   c. Initiate decontamination procedures to remove the agent
   d. Use bleach to clean the exposed area

3. Which of the following is the most important for you to use to protect yourself?
   a. *Hazardous materials* (HAZMAT) suit
   b. Chemical protective mask with charcoal canister
   c. Disposable gown, gloves and mask
   d. *High-efficiency particulate air* (HEPA) filter mask

Scenario B

You and your partner are called to the scene of an emergency involving an explosion at a shopping mall. An HE is suspected. You are among several emergency medical services (EMS) units that have arrived on the scene.

1. Which of the following would you identify as a possible example of an HE? Select all that apply.
   a. Nitroglycerin
   b. Pipe bomb
   c. Gunpowder
   d. Dynamite
   e. C-4

2. When triaging patients, which of the following would you identify as a primary effect of the explosion?
   a. Tympanic membrane perforation
   b. Lacerations due to flying debris
   c. Penetrating wound from a bomb fragment
   d. Fracture of the arm from hitting the wall

3. When providing care to the patients, which of the following is the most important for you to remember?
   a. Any fatalities need to be removed from the area.
   b. The primary responsibility is to evacuate ambulatory patients.
   c. The site of a bomb blast is considered a crime scene.
   d. Evidence of the blast is collected simultaneously as you provide care.

| SELF-ASSESSMENT |

Directions: *Answer the questions by selecting the correct letter(s).*

1. Which of the following is considered a biological disaster?
   a. Flu pandemic
   b. Nuclear explosion
   c. Chemical exposure
   d. Tornado

2. Which of the following would you identify as a Class B biological agent/disease?
   a. Hantavirus
   b. *Salmonella*
   c. Yellow fever
   d. Tick-borne virus

3. Which of the following is ultimately responsible for coordinating the response to and recovery from large-scale disasters in the United States?
   a. *National Response Framework* (NRF)
   b. *National Incident Management System* (NIMS)
   c. *Federal Emergency Management Agency* (FEMA)
   d. *Incident command system* (ICS)

4. Which *emergency support function* (ESF) would address damage and impact assessment?
   a. Communications
   b. Emergency management
   c. Public health and medical services
   d. Transportation

5. *Weapons of mass destruction* (WMDs) typically include which of the following? Select all that apply.
   a. Chemicals
   b. Guns
   c. Explosive agents
   d. Biologicals
   e. Radioactive material

6. Which type of agent attacks the body's cellular metabolism?
   a. Blister agent
   b. Nerve agent
   c. Blood agent
   d. Incapacitating agent

7. A patient has been exposed to cyanide. Which of the following would you least likely expect to administer as an antidote?
   a. Hydroxocobalamin
   b. Sodium nitrite
   c. Sodium thiosulfate
   d. Atropine

8. You would anticipate a high mortality rate if patients were exposed to which of the following biological agents?
   a. Q fever
   b. Ricin toxin
   c. Anthrax
   d. Brucellosis

9. Which of the following is the most important when providing care to patients exposed to biological agents?
   a. Using infection control procedures
   b. Providing required antibiotics
   c. Administering an antidote
   d. Decontaminating the patient

10. A group of patients was exposed to radiation. You first suspect that a patient is developing acute radiation syndrome when he exhibits which of the following?
    a. Nausea and vomiting
    b. Gingival bleeding and bruising
    c. Headache and hair loss
    d. Anorexia and partial thickness skin damage

11. When arriving on the scene of an incident potentially involving WMDs, which of the following is your top priority?
    a. Identifying the weapon
    b. Ensuring personal safety
    c. Assessing the patients
    d. Following appropriate protocols

12. You are assessing a patient who was exposed to a small droplet of nerve agent. The agent was in liquid form. Which of the following would you expect to find? Select all that apply.
    a. Sweating
    b. Blanching
    c. Loss of consciousness
    d. Seizures
    e. Apnea

13. You are working with the triage officer to classify patients who have been exposed to a nerve agent in vapor form. The patient you are assessing is unconscious and convulsing. You would classify this patient as—
    a. Delayed.
    b. Expectant.
    c. Immediate.
    d. Minimal.

14. You and a partner are working with patients exposed to a nerve agent. Your partner begins to show signs of exposure. You report this to medical direction and receive authorization to administer a nerve agent auto-injector kit. You would administer the auto-injector into which site?
    a. Upper arm
    b. Buttocks
    c. Abdomen
    d. Mid-outer thigh

15. Which medications would you expect to find in the DuoDote™ auto-injector kit? Select all that apply.
    a. Sodium thiosulfate
    b. Atropine
    c. Pralidoxime chloride
    d. Hydroxocobalamin

| SELF-ASSESSMENT: ENRICHMENT |

Preparing for a Public Health Disaster—Pandemic Flu

Directions: *Answer the questions by selecting the correct letter(s).*

1. Which statement best describes pandemic influenza?
   a. The cause is a virulent form of human influenza A virus.
   b. Outbreaks typically are limited to small regions in the United States.
   c. Responsibilities for controlling the flu are built on five pillars.
   d. Vaccination is of little benefit in preventing the flu.

2. Which of the following is the most helpful when planning for pandemic influenza? Select all that apply.
   a. Ensuring early detection
   b. Treating with antibiotic medications
   c. Isolating individuals with probable infection
   d. Increasing social interaction among children and adolescents
   e. Quarantining infected individuals in specialized flu centers

Personal Preparedness

Directions: *Answer the questions by selecting the correct letter(s).*

1. Which of the following is the most appropriate when assembling your personal emergency kit?
   a. Storing at least a week's supply of food and water
   b. Keeping the kit in an easily accessible location
   c. Checking your kit every month for outdated items
   d. Using a bag that is large enough to fit all of the supplies

2. When making a plan, you should include which of the following? Select all that apply.
   a. Learn how to turn off the utilities.
   b. Put a note about where to find emergency supplies.
   c. Perform practice evacuations.
   d. Predetermine at least three meeting places.
   e. Identify a person out of the area to contact.

32 Special Operations

| REVIEW OF CONCEPTS AND TERMS |

Fill-in-the-Blank

Directions: *Write the correct term in the space provided.*

1. Drowning is the _____ most common cause of death from unintentional injury in the United States.

2. The age group with the highest rate of drowning is children younger than _____ years.

3. A(n) _____ swimmer is able to stay afloat and breathe and possibly call for help.

4. The most common equipment used for evacuating a person from hazardous terrain is the _____.

5. A high-angle rescue may involve a slope greater than _____ degrees.

6. Any space with limited access that is not intended for continuous human occupancy is considered a(n) _____ space.

Short Answer

Directions: *Supply the information requested.*

1. Compare and contrast a drowning victim who is active with a drowning victim who is passive.

   _____
   _____
   _____
   _____
   _____

2. Name the three types of non-swimming rescue assists.

   _____
   _____
   _____
   _____
   _____

3. Explain the effects of icy water on body temperature.

   _____
   _____
   _____
   _____
   _____

4. Describe the reason for needing 18 to 20 people to carry a patient over rough terrain.

_____

_____

_____

_____

5. List five guidelines to follow when faced with a fire and you do not have the necessary training or equipment.

_____

_____

_____

_____

_____

| CASE STUDY |

Directions: *Read the case studies and answer the questions that follow.*

Scenario A

You are called to the scene of an emergency in which an 8-year-old boy has fallen through the ice while he and his brother were skating on a pond. The older brother and parents are at the scene. You identify the patient as a distressed swimmer.

1. Which finding would support your assessment?
    a. The patient is floating face-down.
    b. The patient is able to stay afloat.
    c. The patient is struggling to keep his mouth and nose above water.
    d. The patient is motionless.

2. Which events are occurring in the boy's body as a result of being in icy water?
    a. Cellular activity is increasing.
    b. The metabolic rate has increased.
    c. Oxygen is being diverted to the brain and heart.
    d. The patient requires increased amounts of oxygen.

3. Upon arrival, which of the following should you do first?
    a. Call dispatch to summon an ice rescue team.
    b. Go onto the ice to rescue the child.
    c. Attempt to calm the parents and brother.
    d. Use the wading assist to reach the child.

4. The child is removed from the water. You would provide care for—
    a. Seizures.
    b. Fever.
    c. Hemorrhage.
    d. Hypothermia.

Scenario B

You arrive on the scene where a farm worker has fallen into a tall, cylindrical silo that is filled with grain. The worker is alert and responsive, stating that he is trapped up to his chest.

1. Which of the following is the least likely hazard for this patient?
    a. Engulfment by the grain in the silo
    b. Lowered oxygen levels within the silo
    c. Possible exposure to poisonous gases
    d. Potential for drowning

2. You would identify this situation as one involving a(n)—
    a. Cave-in.
    b. Confined space.
    c. Hazardous terrain.
    d. Special event.

SELF-ASSESSMENT

Directions: *Answer the questions by selecting the correct letter(s).*

1. During a high-angle rescue, the team uses a secured rope to approach a patient. This is called—
   a. Reaching.
   b. Rappelling.
   c. Shoring.
   d. Throwing.

2. You are part of a team that is evacuating a patient over hazardous terrain. Which of the following would you expect to do after traveling a short distance?
   a. Rotate positions.
   b. Stop to rest.
   c. Switch hands.
   d. Get a replacement.

3. You are working at a major league baseball game with an expected attendance of approximately 37,000 people. You would expect to have how many ambulances readily available?
   a. 1
   b. 2
   c. 3
   d. 4

4. You would use the wading assist to reach a swimmer as long as the water is safe and no higher than your—
   a. Ankles.
   b. Knees.
   c. Waist.
   d. Chest.

5. A woman is struggling in the water at the deep end of a swimming pool. Which method would be the most appropriate to use to rescue her and pull her to the side of the pool?
   a. Lie down at the side of the pool and reach her with your arm.
   b. Enter the water and extend your hand or foot to her.
   c. Remove your shoes and jump into the pool to pull her to safety.
   d. Call for help and wade toward the deep end to grab her.

6. Which of the following most accurately describes drowning?
   a. Females are much more likely to drown than males.
   b. Most people who drown call for help.
   c. Young children can drown in as little as an inch of water.
   d. People who are drowning spend their energy making swimming motions.

7. Which of the following would be noted in a drowning victim who is passive?
   a. The arms are at the person's side.
   b. The person is floating face-up or face-down.
   c. The person is treading water.
   d. The person has a vertical body position.

8. Which of the following would be appropriate to use for a throwing assist?
   a. Paddle
   b. Tree branch
   c. Towel
   d. Ring buoy

9. Which of the following special operations units would be involved in an emergency involving *weapons of mass destruction* (WMDs)?
   a. Tactical *Emergency Medical Services* (EMS) Unit
   b. *Hazardous Materials* (HAZMAT) EMS Response Unit
   c. Fire Rehabilitation Unit
   d. Specialized Vehicle Response Unit

10. You are responding to the scene of a shooting involving a convenience store robbery. The clerk has been shot in the abdomen and the suspect has been apprehended. You are preparing to provide care to the clerk. Which of the following would you do first?
    a. Check with law enforcement for permission to enter the scene.
    b. Call for additional advanced medical personnel.
    c. Move the patient to another area to provide care.
    d. Remove any obstacles that are blocking access to the patient.

11. You arrive on the scene of an office building fire where local firefighters are present. Which of the following would you expect to do? Select all that apply.
    a. Assume the role of the *incident commander* (IC).
    b. Gather information to help the fire units.
    c. Prevent others from approaching the fire.
    d. Obtain information about the number of possible victims.
    e. Ask about the possible cause of the fire.

12. You are providing care to a patient at a crime scene. The patient has been stabbed and is bleeding. Which of the following would be an appropriate way to handle the patient's clothing?
    a. Roll the patient's clothes up into a ball.
    b. Put the patient's wet clothes in a plastic bag.
    c. Cut through the patient's clothes near the stab wound.
    d. Allow the bloody clothing to dry.

13. You are working as part of a team at a special event that is expected to draw about 30,000 people. Which of the following would be required? Select all that apply.
    a. An on-site treatment facility
    b. Beds for at least eight simultaneous patients
    c. Communication capabilities at the site
    d. On-site coordination of EMS activities
    e. Equipment for at least six simultaneous patients

CHAPTER ANSWER KEYS

Chapter 1: The Emergency Medical Responder

REVIEW OF CONCEPTS AND TERMS

Matching

1. F; 2. H; 3. I; 4. B; 5. C; 6. G; 7. A; 8. D; 9. E; 10. J

Short Answer

1. The five types are fire-based, third-party services, hospital-based, police system and private systems.
2. State *emergency medical services* (EMS) agencies are responsible for the overall planning, coordination and regulation of the EMS system within the state as well as licensing or certifying EMS providers. Their responsibilities may include leading statewide trauma systems, developing and enforcing statewide protocols for EMS personnel in addition to the national requirements, administering or coordinating regional EMS programs, operating or coordinating statewide communications systems, coordinating and distributing federal and state grants and planning and coordinating disaster and mass casualty responses, as well as homeland security medical initiatives.
3. The purpose of the *National EMS Education and Practice Blueprint* is to establish nationally recognized levels of EMS providers and scopes of practice. It provides a framework for future curriculum development projects and a standardized way for states to handle legal recognition and reciprocity.
4. The four nationally recognized levels of training are *emergency medical responder* (EMR), *emergency*

medical technician (EMT), *advanced emergency medical technician* (AEMT) and paramedic.
5. Licensure is an acknowledgement that the bearer has permission to practice in the state granting the licensure, has the highest level of public protection granted by the state and is the final authority for public protection.

CASE STUDY

Scenario A

1. Primary responsibilities include ensuring the safety of yourself and the bystanders, gaining access to the patient, determining any threats to the patient's life, summoning more advanced medical personnel as needed, providing medical care for patients and assisting more advanced medical personnel.
2. Indirect medical control involves the use of standing orders, which allows EMS personnel to provide certain types of care or treatment without speaking to the physician.
3. Secondary responsibilities would include summoning additional help and directing bystanders or asking them for help; taking additional steps if necessary to protect bystanders from danger; recording what you saw, heard or did at the scene; and reassuring the patient's family and friends.

Scenario B

1. **b.** The EMT takes over the care from EMRs and works on stabilizing and preparing the patient for

transport. The EMR has the basic knowledge and skills needed to provide emergency care to people who are injured or who have become ill. EMRs are certified to provide care until a more highly trained professional—such as an EMT—arrives. AEMTs receive more training than EMTs, which allows them to insert IVs, administer medications, perform advanced airway procedures and set up and assess *electrocardiograms* (ECGs or EKGs). Paramedics have more in-depth training than AEMTs, including more knowledge about performing physical exams. They also may perform more invasive procedures than any other prehospital care provider.

2. **c.** An AEMT is allowed to insert IVs, administer medications, perform advanced airway procedures and set up and assess EKGs. EMRs are allowed to provide basic emergency care. An EMT takes over the care from EMRs and works on stabilizing and preparing the patient for transport. Paramedics have more in-depth training and would be capable of performing more in-depth physical exams.

3. **d.** Third-party services are private companies that have been hired to perform EMS services. Fire-based services depend on fire departments to provide emergency services. Hospital-based services are those that are backed up, monitored and run by a local hospital. Other service systems include police and private systems.

SELF-ASSESSMENT

1. **b.** In 1973, the Emergency Medical Services Act created a multi-tiered, nationwide system of emergency care with standardized training within the system. Firefighters were the first group to be trained in CPR and basic first aid. Police, fire and private systems are the different types of EMS services available in this multi-tiered formal, nationwide system.

2. **a.** A primary responsibility is to ensure the safety of yourself and that of the patient. Directing bystanders to help, recording what you did and reassuring the patient are secondary responsibilities.

3. **d.** A paramedic, the highest level of training for an EMS responder, has more in-depth training than an AEMT, EMT or EMR. Lifeguards, athletic trainers and camp leaders may be EMRs.

4. **a.** Scope of practice refers to the range of duties and skills that an EMR is allowed and expected to perform. Certification refers to the credentialing

that occurs at the local level. Standing orders are protocols issued by the medical director. Licensure is the permission to practice in a particular state.

5. **b.** EMRs must be licensed through the state EMS office. The National Highway Traffic Safety Administration is responsible for overseeing the National EMS system. Each state has a lead EMS agency that can fall under the individual state health or public safety department. The employing EMS agency is not involved with licensure.

6. **c.** Medical oversight or medical direction, in which a physician acts as the medical director, is one of the 10 components of an effective EMS system. Certification, scope of practice and core content are components of the Education Agenda.

7. **d.** Legal implications may arise if you perform procedures or skills outside what you are trained to do. Proper recording of care, participating in continuing education classes and maintaining certification allow you to fulfill your role competently and effectively.

8. **c.** Other procedures that are not covered by standing order require EMRs to speak directly with the physician via mobile phone, radio or telephone. This kind of medical direction is called direct medical control or online medical direction. The use of standing orders is called indirect medical control or offline medical direction. Protocols are standardized procedures to be followed when providing care and are not a type of medical control.

9. **a.** An EMR needs to be flexible, maintain a caring and professional attitude by showing compassion and providing reassurance. An EMR also needs to be able to control his or her fears and keep his or her knowledge and skills up to date.

10. **b.** Licensure is the acknowledgement that the bearer has the permission to practice in the licensing state. Certification ensures that the EMR maintains a high degree of proficiency by upgrading knowledge, skills and ability, but it does not grant the EMR the right to practice. Local credentialing involves meeting specific local requirements to maintain employment or obtain certain protocols so that he or she may practice, but it does not grant the right to practice. Medical direction is the process by which a physician directs the care provided by out-of-hospital providers.

11. **d.** As the first trained professional on the scene, your actions as an EMR often are critical, determining whether a seriously injured or ill person survives. EMRs require medical direction for providing care. EMRs have the basic knowledge and skills needed to provide emergency care to people who are injured or who have become ill. The role of the EMR can vary depending on the state and location of practice.

12. **b, d, c, a.** The four levels of EMS training from basic to most advanced are: EMR, EMT, AEMT and paramedic.

13. **a.** Resource management includes planning for adequate numbers of trained personnel along with the equipment necessary to provide emergency care, including vehicles for transportation and the tools and supplies necessary to provide care. A 9-1-1 communication system would be addressed under the communications component. Specialty care centers would be addressed under the facilities component. Personnel training programs are an aspect of the human resources and training component.

14. **b.** The first priority would be to ensure the safety of the scene, which might entail summoning additional medical personnel to assist with the scene. Once the scene is safe, then gaining access to the patient and providing care would be important. Recording your actions is important but not the priority at this time.

Chapter 2: The Well-Being of the Emergency Medical Responder

REVIEW OF CONCEPTS AND TERMS

Crossword Puzzle

Matching

1. A; 2. E; 3. B; 4. G; 5. C; 6. F; 7. D

Fill-in-the-Blank

1. HIV
2. droplet
3. liver
4. Standard
5. hand washing
6. stress
7. Critical incidents

CASE STUDY

Scenario A

1. **a.** Although safety glasses, masks and disposable gowns may be appropriate in certain situations, disposable gloves would be the most important to use in this situation to prevent infection transmission that may occur with exposure to the patient's blood and urine. Safety glasses would be appropriate if there was a potential for splashing; a *high-efficiency particulate air* (HEPA) mask would be appropriate if there was a risk of inhaling potential infectious particles. A CPR breathing barrier, such as a resuscitation mask, might be appropriate if the patient required CPR or ventilations. A gown would be appropriate if there was a large amount of blood or body fluids present.

2. **c.** You should wash the contaminated area thoroughly with soap and water. Alcohol is not used. Irrigating the area with sterile saline for 20 minutes would be appropriate if the blood had splashed into the eyes. A diluted bleach solution is used to clean up spills such as on surfaces or in vehicles.

3. **b.** Although reporting potential exposures, disposing of biohazard materials, and disinfecting equipment and supplies are important, a major aspect of preventing infection transmission is to always wash your hands thoroughly after providing care.

Scenario B

1. **a.** In situations involving advance directives, you should honor the wishes of the patient if they are expressed in writing. Therefore, asking to see the written directive would be appropriate. In addition, since state and local laws vary, you should summon more advanced medical personnel immediately to provide care. If there is doubt about the validity of the directive, then you should attempt to resuscitate the patient. Telling the family that there is nothing that you can do is uncaring. Rather, you should provide support and remain calm and nonjudgmental.

2. **c.** The family member's statement reflects an attempt to negotiate with a spiritual higher being in an effort to extend life, a characteristic of the bargaining stage of grief. In the denial stage, the patient or family discounts or ignores the seriousness of the situation to buffer the pain. In the anger stage, the patient or family member projects feelings of anger toward others. In the acceptance stage, the patient and family accept the situation and incorporate the experience into the activities of daily living.

3. **b.** Obvious signs of death include dependent lividity, rigor mortis (joint stiffening), putrefaction or tissue decay and obvious mortal wounds. Joints become stiff (rigor mortis) with death; they do not become overly flexible.

SELF-ASSESSMENT

1. **c.** Although there are some predictable responses to grief, everyone's reactions to death and dying is unique. People do not always experience responses to grief in any particular order. Not everyone will experience every stage of grief responses, nor will every person experience grief in the same order.

2. **b.** The body has a series of natural defenses that prevent germs from entering the body and causing infection. Intact skin is the body's most effective natural defense. Mucous membranes are another natural defense but they are less effective than intact skin at keeping pathogens out of the body. Hand washing and the use of *personal protective equipment* (PPE) are effective means for preventing disease transmission, but they are not natural defenses.

3. **c.** Indirect contact occurs when a person touches an object, such as soiled dressings or equipment and work surfaces that contain the blood or other body fluids of an infected person, and that infected blood or other body fluid enters the body through a correct entry site. Infected blood splashing into the eyes or touching an infected person's body fluid would be examples of direct contact transmission. Inhaling particles from an infected person's sneeze would be an example of droplet transmission.

4. **d.** Tuberculosis is a bacterial infection. Hepatitis and measles are viral infections. Malaria is caused by a protozoan.

5. **b.** Tuberculosis is manifested by a respiratory infection, bad cough lasting 3 weeks or more, pain in the chest, weight loss, loss of appetite, weakness or fatigue, fever and chills, night sweats and bloody sputum or coughing up blood. Yellowing of the skin and abdominal pain are more commonly associated with hepatitis. A stiff neck would be associated with meningitis.

6. **d.** Rabies is transmitted via the bite of an infected animal and is an example of vector-borne transmission. Indirect contact can occur when a person touches an object that contains the blood or other body fluid of an infected person and that infected blood or other body fluid enters the body through a correct entry site. Direct contact occurs when infected blood or body fluid from one person enters another person's body at a correct entry site. Respiratory droplet transmission occurs when a person inhales droplets propelled from an infected person's cough or sneeze from within a few feet.

7. **d.** When removing disposable gloves, the second glove is removed so that the first glove ends up inside of it. To accomplish this, you should pinch the palm side of the first glove near the wrist and carefully pull the glove so that it is inside out. While holding this glove in the palm of the gloved hand, you would slip two fingers under the glove at the wrist of the remaining gloved hand, pulling it off, inside out, so that the first glove ends up inside the glove just removed. At no time during the removal should bare skin come in contact with the outside of either glove.

8. **a.** Work practice controls reduce the likelihood of exposure by changing the way a task is carried out. Disinfecting work surfaces that are possibly soiled with blood or body fluids would be an example. Ensuring that sharps disposal containers and biohazard containers are readily available and posting signs at entrances where there may be infectious materials are examples of engineering controls, measures that isolate or remove a hazard from the workplace.

9. **b.** When a spill occurs, the area should be flooded with a fresh disinfectant solution, most commonly

1½ cups of liquid chlorine bleach to 1 gallon of water (one part bleach per 9 parts water, or a 10 percent solution). Other commercial disinfectant/antimicrobial solutions are available and may be used. However, alcohol, hydrogen peroxide and soap would not be appropriate.

10. **c.** Signs and symptoms of critical incident stress include uncharacteristic, excessive humor or silence, confusion, guilt, poor concentration, decreased attention span, inability to do a job well, denial, depression, anger, a change in interactions with others, increased or decreased eating and any other unusual behavior.

11. **d.** When dealing with the family of a patient who has died suddenly, you should listen empathetically and remain calm and nonjudgmental; allow them to express their rage, anger and despair; speak in a gentle tone of voice; and not give false reassurance.

12. **a.** Debriefing usually takes place in a group setting within a controlled environment with a trained professional. Defusing is a less formal, less structured interaction that usually occurs within the first few hours after an event and lasts 30 to 45 minutes. It is done on a one-to-one basis between the responder and a peer counselor.

13. **c, d, e.** In addition to disposable gloves, you should wear a gown to protect your clothing and a face shield to protect yourself from splashing. A resuscitation mask would be appropriate if you were performing CPR or giving ventilations to a patient.

14. **a, b, c.** Viruses are responsible for causing mumps, chicken pox and avian flu. Malaria is caused by a Protozoan. Tetanus and anthrax are bacterial infections.

15. **c.** If the eyes are involved in an exposure, you should irrigate the eyes with clean water, saline or a sterile irrigant for 20 minutes. Other areas that are exposed, such as the skin, should be washed with soap and water. Antiseptic eye drops would not be appropriate. Reporting the incident to the appropriate person is important, but the eyes need to be flushed first.

16. **b.** The mucous membranes work to protect the body from intruding germs, often by trapping them and forcing them out through a cough or sneeze. The skin provides an intact barrier that prevents the pathogens from entering. Antibodies and white blood cells are part of the immune system and prevent and fight infection. Antibodies attack the pathogens and weaken or destroy them.

17. **d.** Hepatitis B, a bloodborne pathogen, is spread by sexual contact through infected body fluids. It is not spread by contaminated food or water or by casual contact, such as hugging an infected person.

18. **a.** Direct contact transmission occurs when infected blood or body fluid from one person enters another person's body, such as infected blood or body fluid entering the other person's body through a cut in the skin. Touching a soiled work surface would be an example of indirect contact transmission. Inhalation of air and particles from a person's sneeze is an example of droplet transmission. Being bitten by an infected mosquito is an example of vector-borne transmission.

19. **c.** When performing hand washing, you should rub your hands vigorously with soap for at least 15 seconds, making sure to cover all surfaces of the hands and fingers to ensure proper cleansing.

20. **a, b.** The infective body fluids of a patient with hepatitis C would include blood and semen. Vaginal fluid and breast milk would be considered infective body fluids for a patient with HIV. Saliva is not considered to be infective for a patient with hepatitis C in the absence of visible blood.

SELF-ASSESSMENT: ENRICHMENT

1. **b.** To maintain physical fitness, you need regular cardiovascular training. The American College of Sports Medicine recommends at least 30 minutes of physical activity per day. Strength training and stretching also need to be done on a regular basis.

2. **c.** To promote physical health, you should use a sunscreen with a *sun protection factor* (SPF) of at least 15, try to cut down on foods that are high in sugar and caffeine, adhere to standard precautions and use proper lifting techniques.

3. **b.** Stress management techniques include making sure that you eat regular meals and avoid fast food, reprioritizing work tasks, performing physical activity every day and practicing muscle relaxation.

REVIEW OF CONCEPTS AND TERMS

Matching

1. E; 2. G; 3. H; 4. A; 5. F; 6. B; 7. D; 8. C

Short Answer

1. An EMR's scope of practice refers to the range of duties and skills that an EMR is allowed and expected to perform.
2. Duty to act refers to an EMR's obligation to respond to an emergency and provide care at the scene.
3. The three concepts associated with ethical responsibilities are morals, ethics and applied ethics.
4. The three principles that can be used for decision making include do no harm, act in good faith and act in the patient's best interest.
5. To obtain consent, you must identify yourself to the patient, give your level of training, explain what you observe, ask if you may help and explain what you plan to do.

CASE STUDY

Scenario A

1. **b.** Touching a patient without first obtaining that patient's consent could be considered battery. Abandonment refers to the stoppage or cessation of care once is it started. Your obligation for care ends when more advanced medical personnel take over. However, if you stop your care before that point without a valid reason, you could be legally responsible for abandonment. Assault is a threat or an attempt to inflict harm on someone with the patient feeling threatened with bodily harm. Negligence refers to a failure to follow a reasonable standard of care thereby causing or contributing to injury or damage to another. It can involve acting wrongly or failing to act at all.
2. **c.** Abandonment refers to the stoppage or cessation of care once it is started. Your obligation for care ends when more advanced medical personnel take over. However, if you stop your care before that point without a valid reason, you could be legally responsible for abandonment. Negligence refers to a failure to follow a reasonable standard of care, thereby causing or contributing to injury or damage to another. It

can involve acting wrongly or failing to act at all. Assault is a threat or an attempt to inflict harm on someone with the patient feeling threatened with bodily harm. Touching a patient without first obtaining that patient's consent could be considered battery.

3. **d.** Information about a patient is considered private and confidential and is not shared with others except in certain cases, such as providing information to medical personnel who will take over care, for mandatory reporting or in certain legal circumstances.

Scenario B

1. **a.** The patient states that she is an emancipated minor and as such has been granted the legal right to make her own decisions. If the patient was not an emancipated minor, then consent would need to be obtained from her parents or guardian.
2. **b.** Expressed consent is given verbally or through a gesture. Implied consent is consent that is obtained from patients who are unable to give expressed consent, recognizing that the patient would give informed consent for care if he or she was able to do so. Informal consent is not a type of consent. Parental consent, which would most likely be expressed consent, would be obtained if the patient was considered a minor.
3. **b.** Although you are legally responsible for continuing to provide care once initiated, emancipated minors have the legal right to make their own decisions and therefore have a right to refuse care at any time during this period. You should honor her refusal and follow local policies for refusal of care. You also should remind the patient that she can call EMS personnel again if the situation changes or if she changes her mind. In addition, you should try to convince the patient that care is needed and notify medical direction and local EMS personnel.

SELF-ASSESSMENT

1. **c.** Competence refers to the patient's ability to understand an EMR's questions and the implications of decisions made. Therefore, the patient who is alert with a fractured leg would be considered competent. Patients with drug or alcohol intoxication or abuse and cognitive impairment, such as dementia, would not be considered competent.

2. **d.** If a responder acts in a reasonable and prudent way while providing care, he or she usually will be protected from lawsuits under most states' Good Samaritan laws. These laws require that the responder use common sense and a reasonable level of skill and provide only the type of emergency care for which he or she is trained.

3. **c.** To act in the patient's best interest refers to providing competent care with compassion and respect for human dignity, implying that the care provided serves the integrity of the patient's physical well-being while at the same time respecting the patient's choices and self-determination. The principle of do no harm means that people who intervene to help others must do their best to ensure that their actions will not harm the patient or patients. The principle of acting in good faith means to act in such a way that the goal is only to help the patient and that all actions serve that purpose.

4. **b, d, c, a.** When obtaining consent, you should first identify yourself to the patient ("My name is Jane Smith.") and then give your level of training ("I am an emergency medical responder."). Next you should explain what you observe, ask if you can assist the victim ("I notice that you have a large cut on your arm. May I help you?") and then explain what you plan to do ("I'm going to loosen your sleeve to check your arm.").

5. **b.** In the out-of-hospital setting, unless you are provided with written documentation (or unless your state laws and regulations allow acceptance of oral verification [which most states' laws do not]) or if there is any doubt as to whether a *Do Not Resuscitate* (DNR) order is valid or in effect, care should proceed as it would in the absence of a DNR order. You need to be aware of the DNR laws in your state. Notifying medical direction is important in order to inform them of the situation but not for direction about how to proceed. Calling the physician for verification would not be appropriate at this time. Although you would want to honor the spouse's statement and patient's wishes, you need to be presented with a valid written DNR order.

6. **a.** A surrogate decision maker is a third party who has been given the legal right to make decisions regarding medical and health issues on another person's behalf through a durable power of attorney for health care. A living will is a legal document that outlines the patient's wishes about certain kinds of medical treatments and procedures that prolong life in the event that the patient cannot communicate health care decisions. A DNR order protects a patient's right to refuse efforts for resuscitation. A health care proxy is a person named in the durable power of attorney for health care to make medical decisions on the patient's behalf.

7. **c.** Breach of duty occurred with the error in providing care. The duty to act is the obligation to respond to emergency calls and provide emergency care. Proximate cause refers to the injury that resulted from the breach of duty. Patient harm is the end result of the EMR's actions.

8. **b.** Rigor mortis, dependent lividity and body decomposition are signs of obvious death, indicating that resuscitative efforts may not be required. Absence of a pulse indicates the need for resuscitation.

9. **a, b, c, d.** Mandatory reporting must be done in cases of abuse and violence, such as child abuse and a gunshot wound from a crime, as well as certain infectious diseases, such as tuberculosis, HIV infections, AIDS and hepatitis B. Epilepsy and heart attack are not conditions that require mandatory reporting.

10. **a, b, c, f.** According to the *Health Insurance Portability and Accountability Act* (HIPAA) rule, you cannot relay any identifying information about a patient to anyone without the patient's specific consent. This includes the media, employers, colleagues, other family members or co-workers. Health information may be disclosed to public health authorities in cases of mandatory reporting, such as for abuse, neglect or domestic violence, and organ procurement agencies for the purposes of facilitating a transplant.

11. **d.** A crime scene should be entered only after law enforcement has cleared the area when someone is in need of your help. You should obtain permission to do anything that may interfere with the investigation, taking care not to disturb any item at the scene unless emergency medical care requires it. You should not cut through holes in clothing because they are part of the evidence collected during the investigation.

12. **b.** All patients have the right to refuse care and as an EMR you must honor the patient's refusal. In addition, you should follow local policies for refusal of care and tell the patient what treatment is needed and why, trying to convince them but not arguing with them. You also should remind the person that they can call EMS personnel if the situation changes or if they change their minds. Finally, you should notify local EMS personnel and medical direction according to local protocols and document the patient's refusal according to local policy.

13. **c.** Medical futility is an exception to the need for written proof of a DNR order and providing care. It is not involved with living wills or durable power of attorney for health care documents. It is unrelated to a health care proxy, which is the person named in a durable power of attorney for health care to make medical decisions.

14. **a.** A mentally incompetent person who is seriously injured falls under implied consent when a parent or guardian is not present. You should attempt to verify if there is a guardian present with the legal right to consent to treatment, but the priority here is to provide care to the patient. Enlisting law enforcement may be necessary to help notify or contact the guardian while you provide care. Trying to talk the patient into giving consent is inappropriate because his or her consent would be invalid.

15. **d.** Although it may vary by state, a minor usually is considered anyone younger than 18 years. In such cases, permission to give care must be obtained from a parent or guardian.

Chapter 4: The Human Body

REVIEW OF CONCEPTS AND TERMS

Matching

1. C; 2. A; 3. E; 4. B; 5. D

Fill-in-the-Blank

1. vital
2. circulatory
3. frontal, coronal
4. lateral
5. anatomical
6. Joints
7. ventilation
8. Arteries
9. autonomic
10. skin

Short Answer

1. The five major body cavities are the cranial, spinal, thoracic, abdominal and pelvic cavities.
2. The two main anatomical divisions of the nervous system are the central nervous system and the peripheral nervous system.
3. The skeleton is made up of six sections, including the skull, spinal column, thorax, pelvis, and upper and lower extremities.
4. The most common type of moveable joint in the body is the ball-and-socket joint.
5. The skin protects the body from injury and pathogens, regulates fluid balance, regulates body temperature, produces vitamin D and stores minerals.

Labeling

A

1. Larynx
2. Trachea
3. Bronchi
4. Alveoli

B

1. Right atrium
2. Right ventricle
3. Left atrium
4. Left ventricle
5. Aorta

CASE STUDY

Scenario A

1. **d.** The patient is in the Fowler's position because he is lying on his back with his upper body elevated 45 to 60 degrees. In the supine position, the patient is lying face-up on his or her back. The prone position would indicate that the patient is lying face-down on his stomach. The anatomical position is the position used as the basis for all medical terms that refer to the body; it is used to describe the position when the patient stands with the body erect and arms down at the sides, palms facing forward.

2. **c.** The humerus is the bone in the upper arm. The radius and ulna are bones in the forearm. The femur is the bone in the upper lower extremity.

3. **b.** The ribs are part of the chest cavity, which is located in the trunk between the diaphragm and the neck, and contains the lungs and heart. The pelvic cavity is located in the pelvis and is the

lowest part of the trunk, containing the bladder, rectum and internal female reproductive organs. The abdominal cavity is located in the trunk below the ribs, between the diaphragm and the pelvis. It contains the organs of digestion and excretion, including the liver, gallbladder, spleen, pancreas, kidneys, stomach and intestines. The cranial cavity is located in the head and contains the brain.

4. **b, c.** The ribs are part of the chest cavity and act to protect the heart and lungs. The stomach and kidneys would be located lower than the ribs, specifically, in the abdominal cavity. The bladder would be located in the pelvic cavity, the lowest part of the trunk.

5. **b.** The injured part is the patient's upper arm, which would be toward the patient's head, which is above, or superior to, the elbow. Lateral to the wrist would indicate an injury away from the midline of the body or in this situation away from the wrist. Anterior to the ribs would indicate that the injury is toward the front of the body or in front of the chest. Medial to the sternum would indicate that the injury was closer to the midline of the body.

Scenario B

1. **c.** The endocrine system is one of the body's regulatory systems. One of its critical functions is the control of blood glucose levels via production and secretion of insulin. The circulatory system is responsible for delivering oxygen, nutrients and other essential chemical elements to the body's tissue cells and removing carbon dioxide and other waste products via the bloodstream. The respiratory system delivers oxygen to the body, and removes carbon dioxide from it, in a process called respiration. The digestive system consists of organs that work together to break down food, absorb nutrients and eliminate waste.

2. **a.** Insulin is a hormone secreted by the cells of the pancreas to regulate blood glucose levels. A tendon is part of the musculoskeletal system that connects muscle to bone. A ligament is part of the musculoskeletal system that holds bones at a joint together. Red blood cells are a type of cell that makes up the blood, responsible for carrying oxygen to the cells of the body and taking carbon dioxide away.

3. **b, c.** The system involved is the endocrine system and includes glands, such as the adrenal glands and the gonads (ovaries and testes), as well as the hypothalamus and pituitary glands, thyroid gland, pineal gland and the islets of Langerhans

in the pancreas. The liver and gall bladder are part of the digestive system. The kidneys are a part of the urinary system.

SELF-ASSESSMENT

1. **b.** Hypo- is the prefix used to describe a less than normal finding, such as temperature. Hyper-indicates something that is excessive, above, over or beyond. Brady- means slow or dull. Tachy-indicates fast, swift, rapid or accelerated.

2. **a.** Extension refers to a straightening movement. Flexion describes a bending movement. Superior does not describe a movement but rather describes any part toward the patient's head. Proximal does not describe movement; it refers to any part close to the trunk.

3. **b.** The Fowler's position is one in which the patient is lying on his or her back with the upper body elevated at a 45- to 60-degree angle. In the prone position, the patient is lying face-down on his or her stomach. In the supine position, the patient is lying face-up on his or her back.

4. **d.** The thoracic cavity or chest cavity is located in the trunk between the diaphragm and the neck and contains the heart and lungs. The spinal cavity extends from the bottom of the skull to the lower back and contains the spinal cord. The abdominal cavity is located in the trunk below the ribs and contains the organs of digestion and excretion. The cranial cavity is located in the head and contains the brain.

5. **c.** The cervical vertebrae are located in the neck. The thoracic vertebrae are in the upper back, the lumbar vertebrae are in the lower back and the sacral vertebrae are in the lower spine.

6. **c.** Brain cells will begin to die in about 4 to 6 minutes unless the patient's oxygen supply is re-established.

7. **b.** Cellular respiration or internal respiration refers to respiration at the cellular level and involves metabolic processes which are carried out to obtain energy. External respiration or ventilation is the mechanical process of moving air in and out of the lungs. Inspiration is the process of breathing in air.

8. **a.** During expiration, the diaphragm relaxes and moves up. During inspiration, the chest muscles contract moving the ribs outward and upward allowing the chest cavity to expand.

9. **c.** Platelets are a solid component of blood used by the body to form blood clots when there is bleeding. Red blood cells carry oxygen to the cells of the body and take carbon dioxide away. White

blood cells are part of the body's immune system and help to defend the body against infection. Plasma is the straw-colored or clear liquid component of the blood that carries the blood cells and nutrients to the tissues, as well as waste products away from the tissues to the organs involved in excretion.

10. **b.** As the heart pumps blood from the left ventricle, it causes a wave of pressure referred to as the pulse. The wave of pressure carries blood which contains oxygen and nutrients to the tissues. This is called perfusion and occurs at the cellular level where oxygen and nutrients are delivered to the cells and carbon dioxide and other wastes are taken away. Blood pressure refers to the force of blood flowing through the arteries. Capillary exchange of oxygen and carbon dioxide occurs at the cellular level and reflects perfusion.

11. **d.** The elbow would be inferior (toward the patient's feet) to the shoulder but superior (toward the patient's head) to the fingers, hand and wrist.

12. **a.** The brainstem is the control center for several vital functions, including respiration, cardiac function and vasomotor control. The spinal cord consists mainly of nerve cells and carries information from the body to the brain. The cerebellum is responsible for coordinating movement and balance. The cerebrum is the largest and outermost structure.

13. **b.** The sympathetic nervous system controls the body's response to stressors such as pain, fear or a sudden loss of blood. The sympathetic nervous system along with the parasympathetic nervous system, which works to balance the sympathetic nervous system, are the two divisions of the autonomic nervous system. The autonomic nervous system is involuntary and controls the involuntary muscles of the organs and glands. The peripheral nervous system is located outside the brain and spinal cord.

14. **c.** Children, especially infants, are nose breathers, increasing the ease at which the airway can become blocked. The trachea is narrower and softer than an adult's trachea. The chest wall is softer and infants breathe faster.

15. **a.** The skin is the body's largest organ. Neither the brain, kidney nor heart is considered the body's largest organ.

16. **c.** The stomach is contained in the abdominal cavity. The cranial cavity contains the brain. The thoracic cavity contains the lungs and the heart. The pelvic cavity contains the bladder, rectum and internal female reproductive organs.

17. **b.** The kidneys are located in the lumbar region behind the abdominal cavity just beneath the chest; therefore they would be inferior to the lungs (beneath or toward the feet). The lungs would be superior to the kidneys. They would be posterior to the abdominal cavity and anterior to the spine.

18. **a.** Strong tough bands called ligaments hold the bones of a joint together. Tendons attach muscle to bone. The patella is the knee cap. The coccyx is the tailbone.

Chapter 5: Lifting and Moving Patients

REVIEW OF CONCEPTS AND TERMS

Matching

1. C; 2. G; 3. F; 4. B; 5. E; 6. D; 7. A

Labeling

1. Blanket drag
2. Ankle drag
3. Clothes drag
4. Firefighter's drag
5. Pack-strap carry
6. Shoulder drag
7. Firefighter's carry

CASE STUDY

Scenario A

1. **a.** For a patient with a suspected head, neck or spinal injury, only the clothes drag move would be appropriate to use. The firefighter's carry, ankle drag and shoulder drag can be used if there is no suspected head, neck or spinal injury.

2. **b.** When preparing to lift any patient, you need to be aware of your own physical abilities to prevent injury to yourself. Although having a stretcher is helpful, it is not most important. Your knees should be bent, and your back should be in the locked-in position.

3. **c.** The squat lift is an alternative to the power lift and is especially useful if one of your legs or arms is weaker than the other. The power grip always is

recommended for use because it allows for maximum stability and strength from your hands. The power lift would be appropriate to use when both legs or arms are of equal strength. Log rolling usually is used for patients with suspected spinal injury and ideally requires four people working in tandem.

Scenario B

1. **d.** The patient is alert and able to walk. Therefore, the walking assist would be the most appropriate. This technique frequently is used to help patients who simply need assistance to walk to safety. It can be done with one or two responders. The blanket drag is a good way to move a patient with a suspected head, neck or spinal injury in an emergency situation when stabilization equipment is unavailable or the situation dictates that there is not enough time or space to use the equipment. This patient has been walking and as such, a head, neck or spinal injury would not be suspected. The direct ground lift requires at least three responders. Although two responders are available for the extremity lift, the patient is able to walk with assistance. So this lift would be less appropriate to use.

2. **b.** The patient should be allowed to assume a position of comfort, which in this case would most likely be an upright sitting position due to her breathing difficulties. The supine position would be appropriate if the patient was not breathing rapidly or coughing. The left lateral recumbent position would be used if the patient were pregnant or had abdominal pain. The modified *high arm in endangered spine* (H.A.IN.E.S.) recovery position is used if you are alone and have to leave the person (e.g., to call for help), or you cannot maintain an open and clear airway because of fluids or vomit.

3. **d.** Applying the principles of body mechanics includes maintaining a low center of gravity, lifting with the legs not the back, keeping the patient's weight as close to your body as possible and moving forward rather than backward.

SELF-ASSESSMENT

1. **c.** When placing a patient in the modified H.A.IN.E.S. recovery position, you would kneel at the patient's side; reach across the body and lift the arm farthest from you up next to the head with the person's palm facing up; take the person's

arm closest to you and place it next to his or her side; grasp the leg farthest from you and bend it up; using your hand that is closest to the person's head, cup the base of the skull in the palm of your hand and carefully slide your forearm under the person's shoulder closest to you; place your other hand under the arm and hip closest to you; using a smooth motion, roll the person away from you by lifting with your hand and forearm, making sure the person's head remains in contact with the extended arm and be sure to support the head and neck with your hand; stop all movement when the person is on his or her side; bend the knee closest to you and place it on top of the other knee so that both knees are in a bent position; and make sure the arm on top is in line with the upper body.

2. **a.** The responder positioned at the head will be the lead for the move and will stabilize the head and neck during the move. The second responder stands at the patient's shoulders and upper back area. The third responder stands at the patient's hips. The fourth responder stands on the opposite side to position the backboard.

3. **d.** If a patient is aggressive or violent and in need of emergency care, he or she may need to be restrained. However, restraints are used only when the patient presents a danger to him- or herself or to others. A patient who is violently thrashing about poses a threat to the EMR and to him- or herself. A patient who is unconscious, screaming loudly in pain or difficult to arouse is not violent or aggressive and does not pose a danger to him- or herself or to others.

4. **b.** You should never restrain a patient in the prone position because you must have access to the patient's airway at all times. A patient in the prone position will not be able to adequately breathe because the weight of the body will force the organs toward the diaphragm, which could lead to hypoxia and other conditions. This lack of oxygen could cause the patient to become more aggressive. Limitation of movement is desired with the use of reasonable force and restraints. Easy access is not promoted by the prone position. Difficulty securing the restraints is not the reason for never using the prone position.

5. **c.** When preparing to restrain a patient, you will need at least four responders trained in the use of restraints plus an additional EMR who can advise the patient about what is taking place.

6. **d.** A bariatric stretcher is designed to accommodate a weight of up to 1600 lbs and

would be appropriate for this patient. A scoop or orthopedic stretcher is designed for patients who weigh up to 300 lbs and are made to be assembled and disassembled around the patient. A standard wheeled stretcher is most commonly used when moving patients from a situation in which transport by ambulance for more advanced medical care is required.

7. **b.** The clothes drag is done with the EMR moving backward. The firefighter's drag, firefighter's carry and pack-strap carry are done moving forward. None of the moving techniques involve the EMR moving to the right or left.

8. **c.** The direct ground lift would require at least three responders lining up on one side of the patient. The walking assist can be done with one or two responders. The pack-strap carry can be done with one responder. However, if the patient is unconscious, then a second responder is necessary to help position the patient on the other responder's back. The extremity lift requires two responders.

9. **a.** When performing the direct carry, you would position the stretcher at a right angle to the bed with the head of the stretcher at the foot of the bed and two responders placed beside the bed on the same side as the stretcher. The stretcher is not positioned with the stretcher's head parallel to the head of the bed, alongside the bed with the stretcher's head at the bed's foot or at the foot of the bed, parallel to the bottom of the bed.

10. **d.** When beginning to lift a patient, you should always begin your lift facing the patient and with your back in a locked-in position. Your legs should be shoulder-width apart, head up, back straight and shoulders square. Your arms should be locked.

11. **b.** To perform the squat lift, you should stand with your weaker leg slightly forward, keeping the foot on the weaker side flat on the ground throughout the lift sequence. You should lead with your head, lifting your upper body before your hips.

12. **c.** If you cannot reposition an object or patient to reduce the risk of injury, you should reach no more than 20 inches in front of your body.

13. **a.** To minimize injury, you should estimate the total weight to be lifted or carried, including the weight of any equipment to be used in addition to the patient. You should communicate clearly and frequently with your partner, patient and other responders. When carrying the patient, you should keep the weight as close to your body as possible and bend and flex at the hips and knees rather than at your waist.

14. **c.** With the shoulder drag, reach under the patient's armpits from the back, grasp the patient's forearms and drag the patient. With the clothes drag, gather the patient's clothing behind the neck and using the clothes, pull the patient to safety. With the blanket drag, position a blanket or tarp, drape or sheet next to the patient and then gather half of the blanket and place it against the patient's side. Then roll the patient toward your knees, reach across and position the blanket directly next to the patient. Finally, roll the patient as a unit onto the blanket, wrap it around the patient, gather up the excess at the head and drag the patient slowly. With the ankle drag, firmly grasp the patient's ankles and move backward, pulling along the long axis of the body.

15. **b, c, d.** The supine position is used when assessing an unconscious patient, when a patient needs CPR or assisted ventilation or when a patient has a suspected head, neck or spinal injury. A patient with difficulty breathing may be more comfortable sitting up and is normally transported in a sitting up position of comfort. A patient with abdominal pain will be more comfortable lying on the side with the knees drawn up. A patient who is vomiting should be allowed to remain in whatever position is most comfortable for that patient.

Chapter 6: Scene Size-Up

REVIEW OF CONCEPTS AND TERMS

Fill-in-the-Blank

1. blast
2. mechanism
3. blunt
4. hematoma
5. safety
6. chocking

Short Answer

1. Six items or activities that could be used when implementing standard precautions include hand washing, gloves, gowns, masks, protective eyewear and CPR breathing barriers.

2. Four common *mechanisms of injury* (MOIs) include motor-vehicle crashes, blunt trauma, penetrating trauma and falls.

3. Kinematics of trauma refers to the science of energy of motion (kinetics) and the resulting damage to the human body (trauma).

4. A vehicle is considered unstable if it is positioned on a tilted surface, stacked on top of another vehicle, positioned on a slippery surface, overturned or on its side.

5. Four factors that determine the severity of injuries from a fall include the distance fallen by the patient, the surface on which the patient landed, any objects in the way that may have slowed the fall or injured the patient and the position of the patient's body on landing.

6. A bullet enters the body at a greater speed than a knife, causing damage well beyond its actual pathway. It carries with it a wave of pressure that compresses surrounding tissues as it speeds through the body. Stabbing with a knife harms only the tissue that it actually contacts. The length of the knife indicates the depth of the injury.

CASE STUDY

Scenario A

1. **a.** The priority on arrival at any emergency scene is safety, both personal safety and the safety of others. Once you have sized-up the scene, you then would determine the MOI or nature of the illness. You then can decide what additional resources are needed to keep you and the patient safe and to provide care.

2. **b.** In this situation, the vehicle is tilted and considered unstable; therefore, it would be most important to stabilize the vehicle because any movement of the vehicle during patient care or extrication can prove dangerous or even fatal to the patient and rescue personnel. Once the vehicle is stabilized and the scene is safe, other measures may be taken, including putting on PPE, gathering information about the patient's injuries and attempting to remove the patient from the vehicle.

3. **a, c, e.** The patient was involved in a head-on crash while wearing his seatbelt with a shoulder strap. Although the seatbelt prevents head and facial injuries, it can cause injuries to the shoulder, chest and abdomen. The patient's complaints of pain in the chest and difficulty breathing support the suspicion that these areas may be injured.

Scenario B

1. **b.** If you arrive at the scene of violence or a crime, you should not try to reach a patient until you are sure that the scene is safe. Law enforcement personnel must make it secure. Once the scene is secured, you then can walk quickly to the patient while demonstrating calmness. It may be necessary to set up a barrier around the scene but only after law enforcement personnel have made the scene secure. There is no evidence of *hazardous materials* (HAZMATs), so notifying HAZMAT personnel is unnecessary.

2. **c.** Penetrating injury occurs when the patient is hit by or falls onto something that can penetrate or cut through the skin, causing an open wound and bleeding. Blunt trauma occurs when someone falls against or is struck by an object with no sharp edges or points, often resulting in closed wounds, such as a contusion or a hematoma.

3. **a.** Your first priority is your safety. Your next priority is the safety of the patients and bystanders. Law enforcement personnel would ensure their own safety and that of the scene.

SELF-ASSESSMENT

1. **d.** The number of resources needed depends on whether there are any hazards at the scene, the number of injured or ill persons, and the MOI or nature of the illness. The number of bystanders would not impact your decision about the need for additional resources.

2. **a, c, d.** HAZMATs are any chemical substances or materials that can pose a threat to the health, safety and property of an individual. Clues suggesting the presence of hazardous materials include clouds of vapor, spilled liquids or solids, unusual odors, leaking containers, bottles or glass cylinders and signs (placards) on vehicles, storage facilities or railroad cars. Broken glass or downed power lines would not indicate hazardous materials.

3. **c.** As part of standard precautions, CPR breathing barriers, such resuscitation masks and *bag-valve-mask resuscitators* (BVMs), would be used when providing ventilations to a patient. Masks block potentially infectious body fluids from reaching your face; however, they would interfere with your ability to provide ventilations. Protective eyewear is used to protect the eyes from debris, heat and body fluids. They would not protect you from the exposure to blood and body fluids that may occur with ventilations. Gowns provide protection from fluids that may be splashed onto the clothing or skin.

4. **c.** When on scene, the responsibility for directing traffic at an emergency scene lies with law enforcement.

5. **d.** A fall from a height greater than the height of the victim can result in head, neck or spinal injuries. For a patient who is 6 feet tall, a fall from a height of 7 feet could result in severe injuries.

6. **a.** A vehicle is unstable if it is positioned on a tilted surface or on its side. The vehicle that has rolled over with its two side wheels over the guardrail is unstable because it is on its side and tilted. The vehicle that has landed on the shoulder of the road, the one that has collided with a telephone pole and the one that is facing oncoming traffic all are on flat surfaces. Subsequently, the risk of these vehicles moving is minimal.

7. **b.** If a lap belt is fastened too low on a person's body, across the base of the pelvis, it can dislocate the hips. If worn without a shoulder strap, head injury from striking the dashboard may occur. If a lap belt is fastened too high, it can cause injury to the abdomen. A shoulder strap can cause injuries to the shoulder, chest or abdomen.

8. **a.** A blunt injury occurs when someone is struck by or falls against a blunt object—one with no sharp edges or points, such as a baseball bat. Typically, a closed wound results. Penetrating trauma occurs when a patient is hit by or falls onto something that can penetrate or cut through the skin, causing an open wound. A blast injury occurs with an explosion. Chocking is not an injury but a method for stabilizing an unstable vehicle.

9. **a, c, e, g.** In the primary phase of a blast injury, energy is released during the explosion, sending a wave of pressure expanding outward from the center of the blast. Individuals hit by this pressure can experience injury to any body part that is air filled, especially the lungs, stomach, intestines and inner ears. Blunt or penetrating injuries are common during the secondary phase of a blast injury, causing injury to the skin. Bones and muscles may be injured during the secondary phase as debris is blown outward and strikes the person and also during the tertiary phase, as the person is knocked to the ground or hit by another object by the force of the explosion.

10. **d.** Patients with chest pain or difficulty breathing often lean forward while sitting in what is called a tripod position. A patient with abdominal pain often pulls his or her knees up toward the chest while lying down or sitting with his or her back against a hard surface. Inability to move a body part, such as an arm or a leg, pain with movement or a visible deformity all suggest a fracture. Loss

of bladder or bowel control can indicate that the patient has had a stroke.

11. **c.** While awaiting the arrival of specialized personnel to deal with the HAZMATs, you should remain uphill and upwind at a safe distance from the scene and not approach the scene unless you are trained to do so and have appropriate PPE, such as a *self-contained breathing apparatus* (SCBA) and a chemical protective suit. A mask and gloves would not be appropriate PPE to use in a HAZMAT situation.

12. **b.** In a domestic disturbance, you should not approach until law enforcement has arrived and secured the scene. Once inside, you must be continually aware of your surroundings and take nothing for granted. Speak directly to the patient and ask open-ended questions that allow the patient to talk. If possible, separate yourself and the patient from the suspected perpetrator.

13. **b.** In a rear-end collision, the rear vehicle pushes the vehicle in the front forward and the driver, and any passengers will feel their heads and necks whipped back at first, then they will be jolted forward when the car stops. This backward motion often leads to a strained neck or what is called a whiplash injury. A head-on collision often is associated with head, face and chest injuries. A side-impact collision can cause injuries to any part of the person's body, including both sides of the body if the person was not wearing a seat belt. A rotational impact can cause a variety of injuries, usually from the person being struck by stationary objects inside the vehicle.

14. **a.** The severity of injuries caused by falls is determined by the distance fallen by the patient because the speed of the fall increases when the person falls from a greater height. The height has no effect on landing or vice versa. Objects may or may not be present to slow the fall or cause additional injury. Height and the direction of the fall, such as head first, are unrelated.

15. **d.** In the secondary phase, debris around the center of the blast is blown outward and can cause injury when it strikes the person, leading to blunt and penetrating injuries that are generally visible. Difficulty breathing suggests injury to the lungs, and hearing difficulties suggest injury to the ears, which typically are affected during the primary phase of the explosion. Head injuries are commonly associated with the tertiary phase as the person is knocked to the ground or against a wall by the force of the explosion or when other objects propelled by the force of the explosion strike the head. Often these injuries are similar

to those sustained by someone ejected from the vehicle during a car crash.

16. **d, a, c, b e.** Once you have ensured your personal safety, then you need to ensure the patient's safety. Once you have sized-up the scene and determined the MOI, you need to decide what additional resources are needed to keep you and the patient safe or to provide care. Finally, call for the needed assistance.

17. **c.** In an emergency, use each of your senses to size-up the scene. The priority is safety, but personal safety comes before patient safety. If you determine that the scene is safe, you do not need to wait for additional personnel to arrive. Information provided by dispatch, although helpful, is likely to be incomplete and may not be entirely accurate.

SELF-ASSESSMENT: ENRICHMENT

Dealing with Hazards at the Scene

1. **b.** The roadway is the number-one cause of death among EMS workers because traffic is often the most common danger encountered by EMRs and other emergency personnel. Major hazards, such as fires, water, electricity and downed power lines, are less likely to be associated with EMS fatalities.

2. **c.** To help a conscious patient in the water, always follow the basic rule of "reach, throw, row and then go." First, attempt to reach out to the person with a branch, pole or even your hand being careful not to be pulled into the water. If you cannot reach the person, try to throw the person something nearby that floats. If possible, use a boat to get closer (row) and then enter the body of water (go) only if you have been trained in water rescue and only as a last resort.

3. **a, d, e.** Natural disasters include tornadoes, hurricanes, earthquakes, forest fires and floods.

4. **d.** The safe area should be established at a point twice the length of the span of the wire. In this situation, the span of the wire is 15 feet; therefore, the safe area would be established at 30 feet.

5. **a.** If you encounter a hostage situation, your first priority is to not become a hostage yourself. You should not approach the scene unless you are specially trained to handle these situations. Assess the scene from a safe distance and call for law enforcement personnel. You can try to get information from the bystanders that may help law enforcement; however, you must remain at a safe distance until law enforcement personnel summon you.

Chapter 7: Primary Assessment

REVIEW OF CONCEPTS AND TERMS

Crossword Puzzle

Fill-in-the-Blank

1. general impression
2. vital signs
3. alert
4. front
5. jaw-thrust
6. 12, 20
7. 80, 140

Short Answer

1. Five life-threatening conditions include lack of consciousness, abnormal breathing, blocked airway, no pulse or severe bleeding.

2. After assessing the patient's *level of consciousness* (LOC), the next thing to do is to check for breathing, a pulse and severe bleeding.

3. To assess a patient's breathing status, look for the rise and fall of the patient's chest and listen and feel for signs of breathing.

4. Capillary refill is an estimate of the amount of blood flowing through the capillary beds. With a serious injury or illness, the body attempts to conserve blood in the vital organs. The capillaries in the fingertips are among the first blood vessels to constrict, thereby limiting their blood supply. If

the area does not return to pink within 2 seconds after squeezing and then releasing the tip, circulation is insufficient.

5. The two techniques that can be used to open a patient's airway are the head-tilt/chin-lift technique and the jaw-thrust (without head extension) maneuver.

CASE STUDY

Scenario A

1. **b.** The first step is to determine the patient's LOC. Then summon more advanced medical personnel, if necessary, and open the patient's airway if the patient has no response. Next, assess the patient's breathing and pulse.

2. **a.** Using the mnemonic AVPU (alert, verbal, painful, unresponsive), you would describe this patient as responding to verbal stimuli, that is, the patient reacts to sounds, such as your voice. A patient who is alert and aware of his or her surroundings is able to acknowledge your presence and respond to your questions. A patient who does not respond to verbal stimuli or commands but does respond when someone inflicts pain, such as pinching the skin between the patient's thumb and forefinger, is described as responding to painful stimuli. A patient who does not respond to any stimuli is described as being unconscious or unresponsive to stimuli.

3. **c.** A patient who is not moving may be unconscious; therefore, you would assess the patient in the supine (face-up) position, so that you can see the chest rising and falling. This observation would be difficult in the side-lying position and impossible if the patient was lying prone. Turning the patient's head to the side when prone could lead to further injury, especially if the patient has a head, neck or spinal injury.

4. **d.** Bluish skin color is not a normal finding and typically indicates inadequate blood flow and insufficient levels of oxygen in the blood. A pulse rate of 70 *beats per minute* (bpm), capillary refill of 2 seconds and a respiratory rate of 18 breaths per minute are normal findings.

Scenario B

1. **b.** When approaching a patient, speak to the patient, first identifying yourself as a rescuer and that you are there to help the patient. Then obtain consent from the patient before beginning the

primary assessment and providing care. Next, ask the patient about what happened and additional questions, such as, "What is your name?" and, "Where are you?" to form an idea about the patient's LOC.

2. **a, d, e.** A patient who can speak or cry is conscious, has an open airway, is breathing and has a pulse. However, the patient may still be at risk for a compromised airway.

3. **a.** Symptoms are what the patient reports experiencing, such as pain in the left leg. Signs are evidence of injury or illness that you can observe, such as the open leg wound, respiratory rate and bleeding from the wound.

SELF-ASSESSMENT

1. **b.** The primary assessment is used to quickly identify those conditions that represent an immediate threat to a patient's life. Ensuring scene safety, determining the MOI and deciding which additional resources are needed all are components of sizing up the scene.

2. **a, b, e.** As a general rule, you should summon more advanced medical personnel for prolonged chest pain, difficulty breathing and seizures, as well as for vomiting of blood and persistent abdominal pain or pressure.

3. **c.** A sign is evidence of an injury that you can observe, such as bleeding. A symptom is what the patient reports, such as pain, nausea or shortness of breath.

4. **c, b, d, a.** Using the mnemonic AVPU, the highest stage of awareness is alert followed by verbal, painful and finally unresponsive.

5. **c.** When counting the pulse over 15 seconds, take the number of beats obtained (in this case, 20) and multiply it by 4 to arrive at a pulse rate of 80 bpm.

6. **d.** A person who is not breathing at all is said to be in respiratory arrest. Respiratory distress refers to a condition in which the patient is having difficulty breathing or requires extra effort to breathe. Isolated or infrequent gasping in the absence of other breathing in an unconscious person may be agonal gasps, which can occur after the heart has stopped beating. Cyanosis is a bluish discoloration of the skin and mucous membranes due to insufficient levels of oxygen in the blood.

7. **b.** For an infant who is conscious or unconscious, check the brachial artery located in the inside of the upper arm, midway between the shoulder and elbow for a pulse. For adults and children, check the radial pulse on the thumb side of the patient's

wrist. If the adult or child is unconscious, check the carotid pulse located in the neck. The femoral pulse is located in the groin area and is not typically used to assess pulse.

8. **c.** If you need to open the mouth to clear the airway of fluids, use the cross-finger technique. The head-tilt/chin-lift technique and jaw-thrust (without head extension) maneuver are techniques for opening the airway. Neck hyperextension is not used to open the mouth or airway.

9. **b.** Look, listen and feel for breathing and a pulse for no longer than 10 seconds.

10. **c.** When performing the head-tilt/chin-lift technique, tilt the head slightly past neutral if the patient is a child. Tilt the head further back for an adult or adolescent. Tilt the head to the neutral position for an infant.

11. **a, b, d.** Indicators that a patient is having difficulty breathing include shrill whistling sounds, grunting and gasping with breaths. Normal (effective) breathing should be quiet, effortless, regular and of sufficient depth.

12. **a, c, d, f.** Checking the skin characteristics requires you to look at and feel the skin for four characteristics including color, moisture, temperature and capillary refill.

13. **b.** Although weak pulse, pale skin and excessive thirst may indicate shock, irritability or restlessness is often the first sign of shock.

14. **c.** When using a resuscitation mask, first assemble the mask, if necessary, by attaching the one-way valve to the mask. Next, position the mask, seal it by applying even downward pressure, open the airway and finally blow into the mask.

15. **b, a, d, c.** When performing a primary assessment on a child after sizing up the scene, check the patient for responsiveness and if no response, summon more advanced medical personnel. Next, open the airway, and check for breathing and a definite pulse. If the patient is not breathing, position the resuscitation mask and give 2 ventilations.

16. **a.** Checking the pulse involves placing two fingers on top of a major artery located close to the skin's surface and over a bony structure.

The palm, thumb or back of the hand are not used to assess pulse.

17. **c.** Patients who are stable are routinely assessed every 15 minutes. Patients who are considered unstable are reassessed every 5 minutes or more often if indicated by the patient's condition.

18. **c.** To check an infant for responsiveness, flick the underside of the foot or the top of the shoulder. Asking the parents if the infant is okay would not provide you with information about his or her LOC. Calling the infant by name would be inappropriate because although the infant may be fully aware, he or she may be unable to respond. Additionally, an infant may or may not know his or her name, depending on the age of the infant. Making a loud noise near the infant's ear may be used to evoke a response, but it would not be the most appropriate method. Additionally, the infant may have a hearing deficit that could affect the response.

19. **c.** A patient with pale, moist skin who is moving air freely in and out of the chest is breathing adequately and needs continued monitoring for changes because a patient's breathing status can change quickly. Ventilations and emergency oxygen would be used if the patient's breathing was inadequate. Clearing the airway of debris is not necessary since the patient's breathing status is adequate.

20. **a.** When positioning a resuscitation mask, place the rim of the mask between the lower lip and chin and then lower the mask until it covers the patient's mouth and nose.

SELF-ASSESSMENT: ENRICHMENT

Glasgow Coma Scale

1. **a, c, e.** The Glasgow Coma Scale uses three parameters for scoring including eye opening, verbal response and motor response.

2. **d.** For children younger than 5 years, the verbal responses must be adapted using the Pediatric Glasgow Coma Scale. You can use the standard Glasgow Coma Scale for children older than 5 years.

REVIEW OF CONCEPTS AND TERMS

Short Answer

1. The two pieces of equipment needed to measure blood pressure are a sphygmomanometer and a stethoscope.
2. The six areas addressed using the SAMPLE history are (**S**) signs and symptoms, (**A**) allergies, (**M**) medications, (**P**) pertinent past medical history, (**L**) last oral intake and (**E**) event leading up to the incident.
3. The purpose of a secondary assessment is to locate and further assess the signs and symptoms of an injury or illness.
4. The six characteristics to be assessed when gathering information about a patient's complaint following the OPQRST mnemonic include onset, provoke, quality, region/radiate, severity and time.
5. DOTS stands for **d**eformities, **o**pen injuries, **t**enderness and **s**welling.

Fill-in-the-Blank

1. Auscultation
2. respiratory rate
3. crackles
4. force
5. Palpation

Labeling

A. Performing a Physical Exam

A. 6; B. 1; C. 3; D. 8; E. 2; F. 4; G. 7; H. 5

B. Taking a Patient's Blood Pressure by Auscultation

A. 2; B. 3; C. 1; D. 5; E. 4

CASE STUDY

Scenario A

1. **d.** The chief complaint is the reason why EMS personnel were called to the scene. In this scenario, it would be that the patient "passed out" or fainted. Pale skin and the absence of chest pain

would be signs and symptoms identified as part of the SAMPLE history. The report that the patient has high blood pressure would reflect the pertinent past medical history of the SAMPLE history.

2. **c.** Although asking the patient what happened would be important to determine the chief complaint and provide evidence for the MOI or nature of the illness, you must always obtain consent before touching or providing care to a patient. Once consent is obtained, then you can gather additional information including what happened and his vital signs.

3. **b.** The "E" in the SAMPLE history refers to events leading up to the incident. In this case, it would be the patient mowing the lawn. The patient having high blood pressure correlates to the "P" or pertinent past medical history. The patient sweating profusely correlates to the "S" or signs and symptoms. The patient using medications for high blood pressure correlates with the "M" or medications.

Scenario B

1. **a.** When gaining information about the patient's chief complaint, you should use the OPQRST mnemonic. First, ask the patient what she was doing when the difficulty started because this might provide you with clues about the nature of the illness. Next, gather information about provocation (e.g., if anything makes it better), region/radiate, severity (e.g., rating the difficulty breathing) and time (e.g., the length of time the patient has been experiencing this problem).

2. **b.** As you check for the rate and quality of breathing, try to do it without the patient's knowledge because if the patient realizes that you are checking breathing, this may cause a change in breathing pattern without the patient being aware of it. Do not tell the patient that you are counting her breaths for the same reason. Each inhalation and exhalation is counted as one breath. Noisy breathing is abnormal and should not be considered an expected normal finding.

3. **c.** When auscultating a patient's blood pressure, inflate the cuff 20 mmHg beyond the approximate systolic blood pressure. In this case, inflate the cuff to 100 mmHg (80 + 20).

SELF-ASSESSMENT

1. **c.** For a trauma patient or an unresponsive medical patient, the history will likely be performed after the physical exam. For a medical patient who is responsive, the history will likely be performed first.

2. **b.** When obtaining the history from a child, position yourself at or below the child's eye level to avoid being intimidating. Do not separate the child from the parent or guardian unless absolutely necessary. A lack of response from a child to questions does not always mean that the child is unable to respond. The child may be frightened of you or the situation and may not understand the question or may not be able to speak. You need to speak clearly and slowly and include the child as well as the parent or guardian in the questions.

3. **c.** The patient's statement about drinking a glass of water is information related to "L", the last oral intake. "S" refers to signs and symptoms, findings you can see, feel, hear or smell or what the patient tells you. "M" refers to medications including prescription and over-the-counter medications, herbal remedies and recreational drugs. "E" refers to events leading up to the incident, such as what the patient was doing before and at the time of the incident.

4. **e, c, a, b, d, f.** For a responsive medical patient, you perform a secondary assessment following these steps: assessing the patient's complaints, obtaining a SAMPLE history, performing a focused medical assessment, assessing baseline vital signs, performing components of the detailed physical exam and providing emergency care.

5. **d.** When conducting the physical exam, maintain the patient's privacy by conducting the exam in an area that cannot be seen by bystanders, if possible. To access an area to be examined, cut away rather than manipulate the patient's clothing to remove it. Ask the patient questions about a particular area before examining it, and cover each area after you have examined it.

6. **b.** For a gunshot wound resulting in a fractured femur, the fractured femur would be assessed as part of the "O" of DOTS, which refers to open injuries. "D" refers to deformities, such as indentations, depressions, parts that have shifted away from their usual position or parts that are more or less rigid than normal. "T" refers to areas of tenderness even without visible injury. "S" refers to swelling involving an accumulation of blood, air or other fluid in the tissues below the skin.

7. **a.** When examining the head, the pupils should be equal in size, constrict to light and dilate on exposure to darkness. Clear fluid or blood in or around the ears, mouth and nose is abnormal and may indicate a serious head injury. The face should be symmetrical.

8. **c.** For an infant, normal respiratory rates range between 25 and 50 breaths per minute. A respiratory rate of 18 breaths per minute would be normal for an adult. A respiratory rate of 22 breaths per minute would be normal for a child between the ages of 1 and 12 years. A respiratory rate of 58 breaths per minute would be normal for a newborn up to 28 days of age.

9. **d.** When obtaining a patient's blood pressure, ensure that the cuff covers about two-thirds of the patient's upper arm and that the forearm is on a supported surface in front or to the side of the patient, not hanging down or raised above heart level. The cuff should be applied to the patient's unclothed or lightly clothed arm to prevent inaccuracies. The bladder of the cuff should be positioned with the bladder over the brachial artery.

10. **a.** The systolic blood pressure reflects the force exerted against the arteries when the heart is contracting. The diastolic blood pressure reflects the force exerted against the arteries when the heart is between contractions. When the brachial artery is occluded with compression, the sound of the pulse stops; the systolic pressure occurs when the pulse returns with release of air from the bulb. The last sound heard with the release of air from the bulb is identified as the diastolic pressure.

11. **b.** The formula for the average blood pressure for a child is $90 + (2 \times$ the age of the child in years$)$. Using this formula for this child, you would calculate the child's blood pressure to be 100 mmHg $(90 + [2 \times 5]) = 100$.

12. **d.** An ongoing assessment is completed to identify and treat any changes in the patient's condition in a timely manner and to monitor the effectiveness of interventions or care provided. The purpose of the primary assessment is to identify any life-threatening conditions. The secondary assessment is performed to locate and further assess the signs and symptoms of an injury or illness, including assessing the patient's complaints, obtaining a SAMPLE history, performing a focused medical assessment, assessing baseline vital signs, performing components of the detailed physical exam, providing emergency care and considering the need for advanced life support backup and transport.

13. **a, b.** When examining the abdomen, ask the patient if he is having any pain in the abdomen and look for any discoloration, open wounds, distention, scars or protruding organs. In addition, look at the abdomen for any pulsating and if none is present, apply slight pressure to each of the abdominal quadrants, avoiding any areas where the patient has indicated pain. Ask the patient to shrug his shoulders when examining the chest. Push in on the sides of the hips when examining the pelvis. Inspect for a protruding jugular vein when examining the neck.

14. **c.** When performing a secondary assessment for a responsive medical patient, first assess the patient's complaints, then obtain a SAMPLE history, perform a focused medical assessment, assess baseline vital signs, perform components of the detailed physical exam and finally, provide emergency care.

15. **c.** The normal pulse rate for a child between the ages of 1 and 12 years ranges from 80 to 130 bpm; therefore, a pulse rate of 90 bpm would be considered normal. A pulse rate of 60 or 75 bpm is normal for an adult. A pulse rate of 140 beats per minute would be considered abnormal.

SELF-ASSESSMENT: ENRICHMENT

Pulse Oximetry

1. **c.** A pulse oximetry reading between 91 to 94 percent indicates mild hypoxia. Readings between 95 to 100 percent are considered normal. A reading of 89 percent suggests moderate hypoxia.

2. **c.** Pulse oximetry should be taken and recorded with vital signs for stable patients at least every 15 minutes and reassessed and recorded every 5 minutes for unstable patients.

3. **a, c, d.** Factors that may reduce the reliability of the pulse oximetry reading may include shock, excessive patient movement, fingernail polish, carbon monoxide poisoning and hypothermia or other cold-related illness.

4. **b.** Although the finger is the typical site used to obtain a pulse oximetry reading, the earlobe is a recommended alternative site that can be used. The elbow or lip is not used.

Chapter 9: Communication and Documentation

REVIEW OF CONCEPTS AND TERMS

Matching

1. D; 2. E; 3. A; 4. B; 5. C

Short Answer

1. Documentation is the final element of emergency care.
2. The four key components of radio communication for an EMS system are the base station, mobile radios, portable radios and repeaters.
3. When communicating with medical control, you should provide the following information: who you are, patient characteristics, the patient's mental status, SAMPLE history, vital signs and results of your physical exam, any care you provided and the patient's response to the care, and your questions.
4. The four sections of the *prehospital care report* (PCR) are the run data, patient data, check boxes and patient narrative.
5. The run data section contains administrative information, including the time that the incident was reported, when the unit was notified, when the unit arrived and left the scene, when the unit arrived at its destination and when the transfer of care was made. It also includes information about the EMS unit number, names of the EMS crew members and their levels of certification and the address to which the unit was dispatched.

CASE STUDY

Scenario A

1. **c.** The communications center or dispatch is responsible for taking basic information from callers and dispatching the appropriate personnel. Medical control refers to directions given to EMRs by a physician when EMRs are providing care at the scene of an emergency or en-route to the receiving facility, most likely a hospital, where the patient will be transported. Other EMS personnel may arrive on the scene in response to the call, but they would not be the ones providing the initial information to the EMR.

2. **d.** When using a radio communication system, you should keep transmissions brief, organized

and to the point, omitting courtesy terms like "please" and "thank you." You also should use emergency medical frequencies only for EMS communication, speak slowly with your lips 2 to 3 inches from the microphone, and use "affirmative" and "negative" rather than "yes" and "no."

3. **a, b, e.** When communicating with the receiving facility, such as a hospital, you should give the following information: who you are (unit and role), how many patients will be arriving, patient characteristics (age, gender, chief complaint), immediate history (events leading to the injury or illness), any care that you provided and the patient's response to the care, any vital information such as the need for isolation and the *estimated time of arrival* (ETA). Questions about standing orders would be directed to medical control. The patient's SAMPLE history would not need to be included in the communication but would be documented in the PCR for review by the receiving facility on arrival.

Scenario B

1. **a.** Before doing anything, unless it is a life-threatening situation, introduce yourself to the patient. Tell the patient what your role is and what you will do. When speaking to an injured or ill person, speak slowly and clearly, and avoid using medical terms, such as fracture. Instead, use words that are easily understandable. When addressing older adults, call them by their first names only when invited to do so. Such an action shows respect. In addition, have the patient tell you about the problem. The husband may instinctively want to talk about his wife, but having the patient tell you what happened allows you to observe her ability to communicate as well as her LOC and mental status.

2. **b.** Closed-ended questions are ones to which the patient gives a yes–no or very short, specific answer. An appropriate example would be to ask the patient if she is having any pain in her arm. Asking the patient why they called for medical help, how she got out of the building and information about herself require the patient to provide more detailed or in-depth answers or descriptions.

3. **d.** To be empathetic means to listen effectively and understand, be culturally sensitive and be sensitive to the thoughts, feelings and experiences of another. Listening needs to be continuous, not sporadic.

SELF-ASSESSMENT

1. **c.** Portable radios are handheld radios that are useful when out of the vehicle. The base station is the hub of communication and should be situated in the best possible location for sending and receiving signals. Mobile radios are mounted in emergency vehicles. A mobile data terminal uses written instructions, not voice instructions, and is situated in the emergency vehicle.

2. **a, b, c, d.** *Emergency medical dispatchers* (EMDs) must gather as much information as possible regarding the emergency. They also may advise about what the callers may be able to do while awaiting your arrival. Dispatchers note the time that the call was received and the time that they dispatched emergency services. Also, they usually record all conversations and radio dispatches to establish an indisputable record of the events. The EMR typically is responsible for providing an ETA.

3. **d.** As you interview a patient or bystanders, try to let the person you are interviewing do most of the talking and do not interrupt. Be sure to word questions so that you do not provide false assurance or reassurance. Avoid giving advice or asking leading or biased questions. Avoid asking "why" questions, which can be perceived as judgmental.

4. **b.** Although the run data section of the PCR serves as a legal document, acts as an educational tool and allows billing, its primary function is to ensure quality care.

5. **d.** The patient narrative provides a description of the assessment and care provided, and it must include the SAMPLE history. The run data contains administrative information, the patient data section includes all background information on the patient and the check boxes section contains information about the patient's condition, including vital signs, chief complaint, LOC, appearance and respirations.

6. **c.** When documenting information, it is essential that the information be objective and include only the facts and observations. You should not write any subjective comments or opinions and not draw your own conclusions. The only subjective comments or opinions documented should be those of the patient. If an error of omission or commission is made, it must be highlighted in the PCR along with any steps that were made to correct the situation.

7. **c.** Vital signs are documented in the check boxes section of the PCR. Administrative information, such as the time and date of the incident, are

documented in the run data. Patient background information, such as age, gender and birth date, are documented in the patient data section. The patient narrative would include information about the assessment and care provided.

8. **a.** To facilitate communication, make eye contact to show that you are interested in what the patient is saying. Additionally, minimize distractions to promote clear communication, ensure adequate lighting and get down to the patient's eye level to avoid the patient feeling threatened.

9. **a.** Asking the daughter to tell you what happened is an open-ended question, which allows the daughter to provide as much information as possible about the situation. Telling her that her father will be fine provides false reassurance. Asking her why he was not using his cane and telling her that he needs to be watched more carefully are judgmental statements.

10. **c.** Documentation is as important as the care that you provide. Procedures for documentation are established by state regulations and may vary from state to state and from one EMS system to another. Your record is a legal document and will support what you saw, heard and did at the emergency scene should legal action occur.

11. **c.** The contents of the PCR must be kept confidential; therefore, control of the contents falls within the HIPAA. You are responsible for ensuring that the PCR is in the appropriate hands when providing care. Neither medical control nor the receiving facility controls the contents of the PCR.

12. **b.** Parts of the PCR that are most commonly falsified are vital signs and treatment. The chief complaint, time of arrival on the scene and time that the incident was reported typically are not falsified.

13. **c, d.** Patient data includes background information on the patient, such as legal name, age, home address, and billing and insurance information. The check boxes section includes information about the patient's condition, such as level of alertness, vital signs, appearance and respiratory rate. The run data section contains administrative information, such as the time that the unit arrived on the scene and the unit's number.

14. **a.** When receiving medical direction, use the echo method, that is, repeat the order word for word to ensure that you have heard and understood the order. The terms "affirmative" and "negative" should be used in any situation involving radio communication, not just communications with medical control. Asking medical control to repeat the order again would be appropriate if you did not understand the original order or if you repeated the order incorrectly back to medical control. Telling medical control that you understand would be inappropriate.

Chapter 10: Airway and Ventilation

REVIEW OF CONCEPTS AND TERMS

Matching

1. H; 2. D; 3. I; 4. G; 5. J; 6. A; 7. B; 8. F; 9. E; 10. C

Short Answer

1. Respiratory distress refers to the condition in which the patient has difficulty breathing; respiratory arrest refers to the condition in which breathing has stopped.

2. Possible reasons for difficulty breathing include inadequate amount of oxygen being taken in, a low oxygen environment, presence of poisonous gases, infection, poor circulation or other health-related issues.

3. Asthma trigger refers to a substance or situation, such as exercise, cold air, allergens or other irritants, that affect the airways and cause them to suddenly swell or narrow, leading to an asthma attack.

4. The two common methods used to open a patient's airway are the head-tilt/chin lift technique and the jaw-thrust (without head extension) maneuver.

5. The two types of airway obstruction are mechanical, such as from a foreign body, and anatomical, such as from the tongue.

6. Two techniques that are used to remove visible foreign material and fluids from the upper airway in an unconscious patient are finger sweeps and suctioning.

CASE STUDY

Scenario A

1. **c.** For an unconscious patient with visible foreign matter in the upper airway, you would use a finger sweep to remove the material. Abdominal thrusts and back blows clear an obstructed airway in conscious patients. The head-tilt/chin-lift technique would be used to open the patient's airway once the vomit was removed.

2. **c.** When giving ventilations to an adult patient, you would give 1 ventilation about every 5 seconds, with each ventilation lasting about 1 second. For a child or an infant, you would give 1 ventilation about every 3 seconds. You would recheck for breathing and a pulse after giving ventilations for approximately 2 minutes. This reassessment should last no longer than 10 seconds.

3. **a.** If the patient vomits while the EMR is providing ventilations, quickly turn the patient as a unit onto his side to keep the vomit from blocking the airway and entering the lungs. After the vomiting stops, clear the airway with finger sweeps and suction as necessary, then turn the patient onto the back and continue with ventilation. You may need to reposition the patient's head to ensure an open airway after turning him onto his back once the vomiting has stopped and the material has been cleared from the mouth. Using greater force with the vomit still in the patient's mouth could lead to aspiration of the vomit into his lungs. In addition, blowing too much air into the patient leads to gastric distention and increases the risk for vomiting.

Scenario B

1. **a, d, e, f.** Signs and symptoms associated with an asthma attack include coughing and wheezing noises; difficulty breathing; shortness of breath; rapid, shallow breathing; sweating; tightness in the chest; inability to talk without stopping for breath; bent posture with shoulders elevated and lips pursed to make breathing easier; and feelings of fear or confusion.

2. **d.** Asthma involves a sudden swelling and narrowing of the airways, usually in response to a trigger.

3. **a, c, d, e.** Common asthma triggers include dust, smoke, air pollution, exercise, plants, molds, perfume, medications (e.g., aspirin), animal dander, temperature extremes, weather changes, strong emotions and infections.

SELF-ASSESSMENT

1. **b.** When giving ventilations to an adult, you would recheck for breathing and a pulse after giving ventilations for about 2 minutes.

2. **a.** Ventilations are effective when you see the chest clearly rise. If the abdomen becomes distended, this indicates that you are blowing too much air into the patient or breathing too forcefully. A tight seal on the mask means that the mask is properly positioned. Although a properly fitting mask and breaths moving into the mask with ease enhance the chances that ventilations will be more effective, neither alone indicates that ventilations are effective.

3. **c.** The brain is the control center for breathing, directing the body to adjust the rate and depth of breaths according to the oxygen and carbon dioxide levels. The circulatory system transports oxygen-rich blood to the brain, organs, muscles and other parts of the body. The lungs contain the alveoli, which enable the exchange of oxygen and carbon dioxide between the respiratory and circulatory systems. The kidneys filter waste products. They are not involved in respiratory control.

4. **b.** When ventilations are too great or too forceful, air may enter the stomach, causing gastric distention. A blotchy skin discoloration, called mottling, indicates inadequate oxygenation, which often is caused by shock. It does not result from forceful ventilations. A neck injury would not occur with forceful ventilations. Failure of the chest to rise indicates that the airway is not open.

5. **b.** An anatomical obstruction occurs when body structures, such as the tongue, swell due to trauma, infection, asthma, emphysema, anaphylaxis or trauma to the neck. A mechanical obstruction is caused by a foreign body, such as food; fluids including saliva, blood or vomit; loose or broken dentures; and small objects, such as toy parts and balloons.

6. **b.** The normal rate of breathing for children is from 15 to 30 breaths per minute; therefore, a breathing rate of 24 breaths per minute would indicate adequate breathing. A breathing rate of 12 breaths per minute would be adequate for an adult. Breathing rates of 36 to 48 breaths per minute would be adequate for infants.

7. **d.** If a patient is conscious and has an obstructed airway, back blows, abdominal thrusts and chest thrusts have been proven to be effective in clearing an obstructed airway. Finger sweeps are used only on unconscious patients and only when you can see foreign matter in the patient's mouth.

8. **a.** The most effective response for a patient who is hyperventilating and not experiencing any life-threatening symptoms is to calm the patient, listening to his or her concerns and trying to reassure the patient while encouraging him or her to breathe slower or to breathe through pursed lips. Telling the patient to calm down would do nothing to slow the breathing. In addition, the patient may interpret this statement as uncaring. A recovery position is used to allow fluids to drain out of the mouth and to keep the airway open when a patient is breathing and is unconscious. Emergency oxygen would be given only if attempts to calm the patient and slow his or her breathing are ineffective.

9. **b.** Because it is necessary to maintain a tight seal on the mask, two rescuers should operate a BVM. With only a single rescuer, operation of a BVM is difficult and generally does not create an adequate seal to deliver oxygen to the patient.

10. **c, d, e.** Indications that breathing is inadequate include nasal flaring, deviated trachea, muscles between the ribs pulling in on inhalation, pursed-lip breathing and tripod positioning (sitting upright and leaning forward).

11. **c.** For a patient who has a mouth injury, you should provide mouth-to-nose ventilations. Mouth-to-mask ventilations are the typical method for giving ventilations. Mouth-to-mouth ventilations would be used if a resuscitation mask is not available. Mouth-to-stoma ventilations would be used for patients who have an opening in their neck used for breathing.

12. **b, a, c, e, d.** When giving ventilations to a child using a resuscitation mask, position the mask and seal it, then open the airway and blow into the mask, giving ventilations at a rate of 1 ventilation about every 3 seconds. Continue giving ventilations for about 2 minutes and then recheck for breathing and a pulse.

13. **a.** BVMs are limited in that they may interfere with the timing of chest compressions during CPR, and they require two responders to be present to ensure effectiveness. BVMs are advantageous because they can be connected to emergency oxygen. Resuscitation masks deliver only 16 percent oxygen.

14. **b.** Although saliva, the tongue and airway swelling can cause airway obstruction, in children under the age of 4, large chunks of food and small objects, such as toy parts and balloons, are the most common causes.

15. **d.** The primary advantage of mouth-to-mask ventilations when compared with mouth-to-mouth ventilations is that mouth-to-mask ventilations reduce the risk of disease transmission. Mouth-to-mask ventilations do not require less time to give. Mouth-to-mouth ventilations require pinching the nose, whereas mouth-to-mask ventilations do not. Both provide 16 percent oxygen through an exhaled breath.

SELF-ASSESSMENT: ENRICHMENT

Assessing Breath Sounds

1. **a.** To listen to the lungs in the front, identify the midclavicular lines and move down the chest, placing the stethoscope at the 2nd intercostal space, usually just above the sternal line. To listen on the side, place the stethoscope between the 4th and 5th intercostal space, approximately in line with the nipple.

2. **c.** Rhonchi are described as snoring sounds heard when listening to the lungs. Wheezing is a high-pitched whistling sound. Rales are heard as popping, clicking, bubbling or rattling sounds. Stridor is an abnormal high-pitched breath sound usually heard on inhalation, but also may be heard on exhalation.

Sellick's Maneuver (Cricoid Pressure)

1. **c.** Sellick's maneuver is used for patients who are unresponsive and/or have no gag reflex to reduce the risk of air entering the esophagus. It is not used for a patient who is responsive, one who is vomiting or begins to vomit, or one who will have a breathing tube placed by advanced-level providers.

2. **a.** When performing the Sellick's maneuver, you would ensure that the patient is in the supine or face-up position. The prone, semi-Fowler's or side-lying position would be inappropriate.

Assisting the Patient with Asthma

1. **b.** Rescue inhalers provide quick relief of symptoms during an asthmatic attack. They do not provide long-term control, allergy relief or infection control.

2. **c.** A small-volume nebulizer administers aerosolized medication as a mist over a few minutes. Asthma medication is available in liquid or tablet (pill) form for swallowing. A dry powder inhaler is a hand-held device that delivers the medication in a dry powder form.

3. **d.** After depressing the inhaler to release the medication, the patient should hold his or her breath for a count of 10.

4. **a.** Any time you assist the patient with an asthma inhaler, you need to obtain an order from medical direction through radio or phone contact or through protocols and standing orders. Once you have done this, obtain the patient's consent and help him or her to a position of comfort. Ensure that the prescription is in the patient's name and is prescribed for quick relief or acute attacks. After checking the expiration date, reading and following all instructions, shake the inhaler.

Chapter 11: Airway Management

REVIEW OF CONCEPTS AND TERMS

Fill-in-the-Blank

1. suctioning
2. airway adjunct
3. CPR breathing barrier
4. tongue
5. oropharyngeal

Labeling

A. 3; B. 4; C. 2; D. 1; E. 5

CASE STUDY

Scenario A

1. **d.** First, after positioning the infant face-down on your forearm, give 5 back blows with the heel of your hand. Then position the infant face-up and give 5 chest thrusts with two to three fingers. Continue the cycle of 5 back blows and 5 chest thrusts until the object is forced out, the infant begins to cough or breathe on her own, or she becomes unconscious.

2. **a.** During attempts to relieve the obstruction, position the infant's head lower than the chest to allow gravity to help dislodge the object.

3. **c.** When performing chest thrusts on an infant, compress the chest about 1½ inches, making a distinct attempt to dislodge the object.

Scenario B

1. **a.** Before attempting any actions, it is essential to ensure that the patient is on a firm, flat surface. Then attempt a ventilation and if there is no rise in the chest, retilt the head, and then try another ventilation. If there is no rise in the chest, then perform 30 chest compressions and look inside the mouth.

2. **c.** When giving chest compressions, keep your fingers off the chest, using the heel of one hand on the center of the chest with the other hand on top of the first hand and compressing the chest at least 2 inches. Use your body weight, not your arms, to compress the chest.

3. **b.** If you see the foreign object in a patient's mouth, remove it with your index finger by sliding it along the inside of the cheek using a hooking motion. The little finger is used for a small child or an infant in the same manner. The thumb or two fingers are not used.

SELF-ASSESSMENT

1. **a.** Manual suction devices are operated by hand and are lightweight, compact and relatively inexpensive. Mechanical suction devices are powered electrically and use either battery-powered pumps or oxygen-powered aspirators. Mechanical suction devices produce a vacuum that is powerful enough to suction substances from the throat (pharynx). If the device is not adequately charged, the vacuum will be insufficient, thus interfering with the device's ability to operate efficiently. CPR breathing barriers, such as resuscitation masks and BVMs, are used to provide positive pressure ventilations.

2. **c.** When preparing to insert an *oropharyngeal airway* (OPA), first make sure that the patient is unconscious. OPAs are used only on unconscious, unresponsive patients with no gag reflex. Airways are used to prevent—not treat—airway obstruction by the tongue. Proper size selection by measuring the distance from the earlobe to the corner of the mouth is important but this would be done once you have established that the patient is unresponsive.

3. **b.** When using mechanical or manual suction on a child, you would suction for no more than 10 seconds at a time. You would suction an adult for no more than 15 seconds at a time and an infant for no more than 5 seconds at a time. Suctioning for longer periods can starve the patient of air.

4. **d.** If a patient begins to gag as the OPA reaches the back of the throat, immediately remove the OPA, suction the airway to remove all debris, thoroughly clean the device and reinsert it only if the patient still is unconscious and does not have a gag reflex. The OPA is rotated 180 degrees as the tip approaches the mouth. Continuing to insert the airway would be inappropriate and dangerous. An OPA is inserted only into an unconscious patient, so it would be inappropriate to give the patient a sip of water. Additionally, if the patient is unconscious, it would be impossible for the patient to take a sip of water.

5. **b.** A conscious person who is clutching his or her throat is showing what is commonly called the "universal" sign of choking. Coughing may indicate an airway obstruction but could indicate another condition as well. A person with a mild or partial airway obstruction still can move some air to and from the lungs, often while wheezing and coughing forcefully. A person may be able to say that he or she is choking, but this is not always the case. Severe airway obstruction is apparent when the person cannot cough, speak, cry or breathe.

6. **c.** Abdominal thrusts may not be an effective method of care for conscious choking adults in cases where you cannot reach far enough around the patient to give effective abdominal thrusts or if the patient is obviously pregnant or known to be pregnant; therefore, back blows and chest thrusts would be appropriate. If a patient is coughing, he or she should be encouraged to continue to cough to help dislodge the object; however, if the patient is unable to cough, speak or breathe, immediate intervention is necessary.

7. **a.** An OPA is correctly placed when the flange of the device rests on the patient's lips. Resistance to the device is felt as the tip approaches the back of the patient's throat. Although gagging should not occur, absence of gagging does not indicate proper placement. The flange should not touch the patient's teeth.

8. **d.** You apply suction as you withdraw the suction tip using a sweeping motion. You should not apply suction as you insert the tip into the mouth, upon reaching the back of the mouth or when touching the tongue.

9. **c.** When performing abdominal thrusts on an adult, stand behind the patient and make a fist with one hand, placing the thumb side of the fist against the middle of the patient's abdomen, just above the navel. Then grab the fist with your other hand and give quick, upward thrusts. You could kneel behind the patient if the patient was a child, depending on his or her size.

10. **d.** Children are prone to choking on small objects as well as food. While hazardous for all children, the threat usually is greater for children younger than 4 years because they do not have a full set of teeth and cannot chew as well as older children.

11. **b.** When giving chest compressions to an unconscious adult, child or infant, compress the chest at a rate of at least 100 compressions per minute.

12. **a.** Before providing any help to this child, it is important to obtain consent from the mother to assist the child. Once consent is obtained, then encourage the child to continue coughing forcefully in an effort to dislodge the obstruction. If this is ineffective, give 5 back blows followed by 5 abdominal thrusts to attempt to dislodge the object. Lower the child to the ground only if the child became unconscious.

SELF-ASSESSMENT: ENRICHMENT

1. **b.** A *nasopharyngeal airway* (NPA), unlike an OPA, does not cause the patient to gag. An NPA can be used on a conscious responsive patient or an unconscious patient, whereas an OPA cannot be used on an unconscious patient. Both an OPA and an NPA must be measured to ensure that the correct size is used. The NPA requires lubrication for insertion, but an OPA does not.

2. **a.** When inserting an NPA, you would insert the airway with the bevel toward the septum or center of the nose. Insert an OPA with the curved end along the roof of the mouth.

3. **c, d.** An NPA is not used on a patient with suspected head trauma or a suspected skull fracture. An NPA may be used on a conscious, responsive patient or on an unconscious one for conditions such as heart attack, blunt chest trauma or penetrating abdominal injury.

Chapter 12: Emergency Oxygen

REVIEW OF CONCEPTS AND TERMS

Short Answer

1. The air that a person breathes in normally contains about 21 percent oxygen, whereas the oxygen content of the expired air in your exhaled breath is about 16 percent.
2. To administer emergency oxygen, you must have an oxygen cylinder, a pressure regulator with a flowmeter and a delivery device.
3. Oxygen cylinders have *United States Pharmacopeia* (U.S.P.) and yellow diamond labels that make them easy to recognize. In the United States, oxygen cylinders typically have green markings.
4. A pressure regulator is attached to an oxygen cylinder to reduce the delivery pressure of the oxygen to a safe level. It reduces the pressure from approximately 2000 *pounds per square inch* (psi) inside the cylinder to a safe pressure range of 30 to 70 psi.
5. A flowmeter controls the amount of oxygen administered in *liters per minute* (LPM).
6. Oxygen systems can be variable-flow rate or fixed-flow rate.

Labeling

1. Nasal cannula
2. Resuscitation mask (with oxygen inlet)
3. Non-rebreather mask
4. BVM

CASE STUDY

Scenario A

1. **c.** With a BVM, the oxygen flow rate should be set at 15 LPM or more, thereby supplying an oxygen concentration of 90 percent or higher. A nasal cannula can deliver emergency oxygen at a flow rate of 1 to 6 LPM. A resuscitation mask can deliver emergency oxygen at 6 to 15 LPM. A non-rebreather mask can deliver emergency oxygen at 10 to 15 LPM.
2. **d.** When a BVM is attached to oxygen at a flow rate of 15 LPM, the patient receives an oxygen concentration of 90 percent. A nasal cannula at a flow rate of 1 to 6 LPM delivers an oxygen concentration of 24 to 44 percent. A resuscitation mask at a flow rate of 6 to 15 LPM delivers an oxygen concentration of 25 to 55 percent.

3. **b.** To verify oxygen flow, listen for a hissing sound and feel for oxygen flow through the delivery device. The flowmeter dial should not change, but rather it should remain at the rate that is set. A pressure gauge reading below 200 psi indicates that the cylinder needs to be replaced. The O-ring should be present to ensure a tight seal between the regulator and the tank.

Scenario B

1. **a.** A nasal cannula would be inappropriate because the patient needs a device that can supply a greater concentration of oxygen than that which is supplied by a nasal cannula. A resuscitation mask, non-rebreather mask and BVM would be more appropriate for this patient because they can deliver higher concentrations of oxygen.
2. **d.** A fixed-flow-rate system typically comes with the delivery device, regulator and cylinder already connected, eliminating the need to assemble the equipment. Unfortunately, with this type of system, you often cannot adjust the flow rate to different levels.
3. **c.** The pressure gauge indicates the fullness of the cylinder. A full cylinder will show 2000 psi while a nearly empty cylinder will show about 200 psi. A reading of 1500 psi indicates that the tank is approximately three-quarters full. Subsequently, you would continue to administer emergency oxygen. The pressure gauge reading is unrelated to the flow rate. There is no need to change the cylinder immediately since it is not close to being empty. Increasing respiratory difficulty or respiratory arrest would suggest a need to prepare for assisted ventilations.

SELF-ASSESSMENT

1. **d.** Emergency oxygen would be beneficial to a child with a respiratory rate below 15 breaths per minute or above 30 breaths per minute. An adult with a respiratory rate less than 12 or more than 20 breaths per minute and an infant with a respiratory rate less than 25 or more than 50 breaths per minute also would be candidates for emergency oxygen.
2. **d.** When a cylinder reaches 200 psi, it should be replaced with a new cylinder. An oxygen cylinder is considered full at approximately 2000 psi.

Readings of 1000 psi and 500 psi indicate that the cylinder still has oxygen available for administration.

3. **a. b, e.** When working with oxygen systems, check the pressure regulator to ensure that the cylinder is not empty, handle the cylinder carefully because it is under high pressure and should not be dropped, do not lubricate any part of the oxygen system to prevent explosion, check to make sure that the pin index corresponds to the oxygen tank and hand-tighten the screw until the regulator is snug.

4. **c.** According to the *Food and Drug Administration* (FDA), emergency oxygen units are available without a prescription for first aid provided that they contain at least a 15-minute oxygen supply and that they are designed to deliver a preset flow rate of at least 6 LPM. Filling and refilling of empty or spent cylinders is strictly controlled by state and local regulations. Local protocols must always be followed.

5. **a, c, d.** A fixed-flow-rate system comes with the delivery device, regulator and cylinder already connected to each other. Therefore, to operate a fixed-flow-rate system, simply turn it on according to the manufacturer's instructions, check that oxygen is flowing and place the delivery device on the patient. Opening the cylinder valve for 1 second, attaching the regulator and opening the cylinder counterclockwise are important steps associated with a variable-flow-rate system.

6. **a.** A nasal cannula provides the lowest concentration of oxygen which ranges from 24 to 44 percent. A resuscitation mask delivers approximately 25 to 55 percent oxygen. A non-rebreather mask and BVM deliver an oxygen concentration of 90 percent or more.

7. **b.** To deliver a flow rate of 6 LPM to a nonbreathing patient, a resuscitation mask would be most appropriate to use because this device can provide oxygen at a flow rate of 6 to 15 LPM. A BVM is designed for flow rates of 15 LPM or more and can be used with breathing and nonbreathing patients. A nasal cannula can administer flow rates of 1 to 6 LPM, but this device is used for patients who are breathing. A non-rebreather mask is used with flow rates of 10 to 15 LPM for patients who are breathing.

8. **d.** An oxygen cylinder contains 100 percent oxygen.

9. **b.** A non-rebreather mask consists of a face mask with an attached oxygen reservoir bag and a one-way valve between the mask and bag to prevent the patient's exhaled air from mixing with oxygen in the reservoir bag. The reservoir bag should be about two-thirds full so that it does not deflate when the patient inhales. The patient inhales oxygen from the bag and exhaled air escapes through flutter valves on the side of the mask. A nasal cannula should not be used if the patient has a nasal injury.

10. **e.** Flow rates with a nasal cannula above 6 LPM are not commonly used because of the tendency to quickly dry out mucous membranes and cause nosebleeds and headaches.

11. **b, d.** A resuscitation mask and BVM are used to deliver emergency oxygen to patients who are not breathing. They also can be used for patients who are breathing. A nasal cannula and non-rebreather mask are used for patients who are breathing.

12. **c.** When using a variable-flow-rate system, begin by examining the cylinder to be certain that it is labeled "oxygen." Next remove the protective covering over the tank and remove the O-ring gasket if it is not built into the tank. Then open the cylinder for 1 second while it is pointed away from you. Next, examine the pressure regulator to be sure that it is labeled "oxygen," check to see that the pin index corresponds to an oxygen tank, attach the pressure regulator to the cylinder, hand tighten the screw until the regulator is snug and finally open the cylinder one full turn and listen for leaks.

13. **b.** For a patient receiving emergency oxygen with a BVM who has a respiratory rate over 30 breaths per minute, you should squeeze the bag on every second breath. If the patient's respiratory rate is less than 10 breaths per minute, squeeze the bag between each breath to supply the patient with additional oxygen.

14. **a, d.** When administering emergency oxygen, follow specific safety guidelines. These include not using oxygen around flames or sparks because it is flammable and causes fire to burn more quickly and rapidly; checking to make sure that oxygen is flowing before putting the delivery device on the patient; not using grease, oil or petroleum products to lubricate or clean the regulator because these could cause an explosion; not dragging or rolling cylinders; and not carrying a cylinder by the valve or regulator.

15. **b.** To use the blow-by technique, you, a parent or guardian holds the mask about 2 inches from the child's face, waving it slowly from side-to-side as if you are playing a game, thus allowing oxygen to pass over the face and be inhaled.

Chapter 13: Circulation and Cardiac Emergencies

REVIEW OF CONCEPTS AND TERMS

Crossword Puzzle

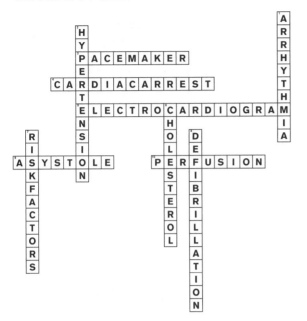

Short Answer

1. *Ventricular fibrillation* (V-fib) is the most common abnormal heart rhythm causing sudden cardiac arrest. The ventricles quiver or fibrillate without any organized rhythm. In V-fib, the electrical impulses fire at random, creating chaos and preventing the heart from pumping and circulating blood.

2. CPR is a combination of chest compressions and ventilations that circulates blood containing oxygen to the brain and other vital organs for a person whose heart and breathing have stopped.

3. Do not stop CPR except in one of these situations: another trained responder takes over, more advanced medical personnel take over for you, you see signs of life (e.g., breathing), an *automated external defibrillator* (AED) is ready to use, the scene becomes unsafe, you are presented with a valid DNR order or you are too exhausted to continue.

4. The most common conditions caused by cardiovascular disease include *coronary heart disease* (CHD), also known as *coronary artery disease* (CAD), and stroke, also called a brain attack.

5. In a healthy heart, an electrical impulse comes from a point near the top of the heart called the *sinoatrial* (SA) node. The impulse travels through the atria, the upper chambers of the heart, down to the *atrioventricular* (AV) node, near the bottom of the right atrium. From the AV node, the impulse divides into two branches, then into the right and left ventricles. These right and left branches become a network of fibers, called Purkinje fibers, which spread electrical impulses across the heart. Under normal circumstances, these impulses reach the muscular walls of the ventricles, causing the muscles to contract, which forces blood out of the heart to circulate throughout the body. The contraction of the left ventricle results in a pulse. The pauses between the pulse beats are the periods between contractions. As the left ventricle relaxes, or is at rest, blood refills the chamber and there is a pause between pulse beats.

6. The major sign of a heart attack is persistent discomfort, pressure or pain in the chest that does not go away. The pain can range from discomfort to an unbearable crushing sensation in the chest, often described as pressure, squeezing, tightness, aching or heaviness. The pain may spread to the shoulder, arm, neck, jaw, stomach or back and is not relieved by resting, changing position or taking medication.

7. The four links in the Cardiac Chain of Survival are early recognition of the emergency and early access to the EMS system, early CPR, early defibrillation and early more advanced medical care.

8. AEDs are portable electronic devices that analyze the heart's rhythm and may provide an electrical shock, known as defibrillation, which allows it to re-establish an effective rhythm. They can greatly increase the likelihood of survival if the shock is administered soon enough. AEDs monitor the heart's electrical activity through two electrodes placed on the chest. The computer determines the need for a shock by looking at the pattern, size and frequency of EKG waves. If the EKG waves resemble a shockable rhythm, the machine readies an electrical charge. When the electrical charge disrupts the irregular heartbeat, it is called defibrillation. Delivering an electrical shock with an AED disrupts all electrical activity long enough to allow the heart to develop an effective rhythm on its own.

CASE STUDY

Scenario A

1. **c.** The correct position for the hands is over the lower half of the sternum in the middle of the chest. You would place the heel of one hand on the center of the chest along the sternum and then place the other hand on top. This position allows you to perform the most effective chest compressions. The lowest point of the sternum, the xiphoid process, should be avoided because this tissue can break off and puncture underlying organs and tissues. The uppermost portion of the sternum and nipple area would not enable effective compressions.

2. **c.** When performing chest compressions on a child, you should compress the chest about 2 inches. For an infant, compress to a depth of about 1½ inches. For an adult, compress to a depth of at least 2 inches.

3. **d.** When performing chest compressions, you need to allow the chest to fully recoil after each compression before starting the next compression. This allows the chambers of the heart to refill with blood to circulate throughout the body with the next compression. The elbows should be as straight as possible with your shoulders directly over your hands. Each compression should be a straight, steady, smooth up-and-down motion without any rocking and without any pauses between compressions.

4. **b.** Since you are near a lake and the child was submerged in water for several minutes, water may be around the area where you are working and the child is most likely wet. Therefore, make sure that there are no puddles of water around you, the patient or the AED. You also should remove any wet clothing for proper pad placement and dry the patient's chest thoroughly to ensure pad adhesion. Correct pad placement is important, but if the pads are not adhered properly, the shock may be ineffective. Pediatric defibrillator pads are appropriate for infants and children up to 8 years of age or weighing less than 55 pounds; however, this child is 10 years old. It is helpful to make sure that spare batteries are available in case a low battery warning occurs, but this is not as essential as ensuring that there is no water near you or the patient or ensuring a dry chest.

Scenario B

1. **a, c, d, e.** Signs and symptoms suggesting a heart attack would include pain that is described as squeezing, pressure, tightness, aching or heaviness that radiates to the shoulder, arm, neck, jaw, stomach or back and usually is not relieved by rest, changing position or taking medication. A history of hypertension is a main risk factor for a heart attack. Difficulty breathing is another sign and may be noted if the patient sits upright and leans forward. Complaints of dizziness and pale or ashen skin, especially around the face, and heavy sweating also may be seen with a heart attack.

2. **b.** If you suspect that a patient is experiencing a heart attack, you need to take immediate action and summon more advanced medical personnel. Next, you would have the patient stop any activity and rest and loosen any tight or uncomfortable clothing. You then would continue to monitor the patient until more advanced medical personnel take over. Administer emergency oxygen, if it is available and you are authorized to administer it. If the patient suffers a cardiac arrest, then begin CPR.

3. **d.** A conscious patient who is showing early signs of a heart attack may be helped with an appropriate dose of aspirin when the signs first begin. If the patient is conscious and able to take medicine by mouth and the patient is not allergic to aspirin, does not have a stomach ulcer or stomach disease, is not taking blood thinners and has not been told by a doctor to avoid taking aspirin, then the patient may be given two chewable (162 mg) baby aspirins or one 5-gram (325 mg) adult aspirin tablet with a small amount of water. Only aspirin, not acetaminophen (Tylenol®) or ibuprofen (Motrin®) should be given.

Scenario C

1. **a.** After opening the airway, checking for breathing and a pulse and giving 2 ventilations, you would begin chest compressions. If the infant was conscious and had an airway obstruction, you would begin with 5 back blows. You would give ventilations if the patient had a pulse but was not breathing. You would only use a finger sweep if foreign material was visible in the infant's mouth.

2. **b.** To perform chest compressions on an infant, use two or three fingers placed on the center of the chest just below the nipple line. The heel of the hand is used to perform chest compressions on an adult or a child. The fist or thumbs are not used for chest compressions.

3. **c.** Since there are now two responders, the cycles of compressions and ventilations would be 15 compressions and 2 ventilations. A cycle of 30 compressions and 2 ventilations would be used for one-rescuer CPR for an adult, child and infant and two-rescuer CPR for an adult. No method of CPR ever uses just one ventilation.

SELF-ASSESSMENT

1. **a.** Atrial fibrillation is the most common type of abnormal cardiac rhythm. Sinus rhythm reflects the normal conduction of electrical impulses without any disturbances. It is a normal rhythm. *Ventricular tachycardia* (V-tach) is a less common life-threatening, abnormal heart rhythm. V-fib is the most common cause of sudden cardiac arrest.

2. **b.** When cardiac arrest occurs in children and infants, it is most often caused by airway and breathing problems. Other possible but less common causes include traumatic injuries or accidents, such as motor-vehicle collisions, drowning, poisoning, a hard blow to the chest, congenital heart disease or sudden infant death syndrome (SIDS).

3. **d.** When performing chest compressions during CPR, position yourself at the patient's side, opposite the chest. This position allows you to push straight down on the patient's sternum, making compressions more effective for the patient and less tiring for you. Being at the patient's shoulders or between the patient's legs would not allow you to provide effective chest compressions.

4. **c.** Breathing and return of a pulse indicate signs of life; therefore, you would stop CPR (compressions and ventilations) and continue to monitor the patient, ensuring that his or her airway remains open. It would be inappropriate to cancel the call for more advanced medical personnel. The patient still may require additional care and should be transported to a medical facility for evaluation. Although an AED would analyze the rhythm, there is no need to use it at this time since the patient has a pulse.

5. **a, c, e.** An AED is used when all three conditions are present: the patient is unresponsive, there is no breathing and there is no pulse.

6. **c.** If the pads risk touching each other, you should use an anterior/posterior pad placement with one pad placed in the middle of the child's chest and the other placed on the child's back, between the shoulder blades. Both pads must be used, remain intact and not touch each other.

7. **b.** The electrical impulse comes from a point near the top of the heart called the SA node. It travels through the atrium down to the AV node near the bottom of the right atrium. The right atrium receives oxygen-depleted blood from the veins of the body. The left ventricle pumps oxygen-rich blood to all parts of the body.

8. **d.** Due to a general decrease in pain perception, older adults often experience a "silent heart attack," meaning there is an absence of chest pain. The symptoms of a heart attack most commonly shown by older adults include general weakness or fatigue, aching shoulders and abdominal pain or indigestion.

9. **b.** Angina normally is a transient condition in which the patient experiences chest pain but the pain does not spread and is relieved by medicine and/or rest. Persistent chest pain that spreads to the jaw and neck and is accompanied by difficulty breathing suggests a heart attack.

10. **a.** When two rescuers are performing CPR, they should change position about every 2 minutes to reduce the possibility of rescuer fatigue.

11. **c.** When CPR is in progress with one rescuer and a second rescuer arrives, the second rescuer should confirm whether more advanced medical personnel have been summoned. If they have not, the second rescuer should do so before getting the AED or assisting with care. If more advanced medical personnel have been summoned, the second rescuer should get the AED, or if an AED is not available, the second rescuer should help perform two-rescuer CPR.

12. **d.** After a shock is delivered, a period of time is programmed into the device to allow for CPR until the next rhythm analysis begins. You should not wait for the device to re-analyze the rhythm because valuable time would be lost. If at any time you notice obvious signs of life, stop CPR, monitor the patient's condition and leave the patient in a face-up position while maintaining an open airway.

13. **b.** Although all of the questions could be helpful, it is most appropriate to obtain as much information as possible about the chest pain in the patient's own words. This would be accomplished by asking the patient to tell you how he or she feels at that moment. Asking about previous episodes of pain, the spread of the pain or the type of pain, such as crushing or squeezing, require yes-or-no answers and would not be as helpful initially as the patient's description.

14. **c.** Although women may experience chest pain or discomfort during a heart attack, they are more likely to experience some of the other warning signs, particularly shortness of breath; nausea or vomiting; stomach, back or jaw pain; or unexplained fatigue or malaise. When they do experience chest pain, women may have a greater tendency to have atypical chest pain, such as sudden, sharp but short-lived pain outside of the breastbone. As a result, women often delay telling others about their symptoms to avoid bothering or worrying them.

15. **c.** Remove any medication patches that you see on a patient's chest with your gloved hand before defibrillation and never place an AED pad directly on top of a medication patch.

SELF-ASSESSMENT: ENRICHMENT

Preventing Coronary Heart Disease

1. **c.** CHD develops slowly as deposits of cholesterol, a fatty substance, build up on the inner walls of the arteries, leading to arterial narrowing and decreased supply of oxygen-rich blood to the heart. CHD is the leading cause of death for adults in the United States and is associated with numerous risk factors, not just genetic and family history.

2. **b.** Risk factors for CHD include those that a person can change as well as those that cannot be changed. Those that cannot be changed include ethnicity, gender and family history. Diet, obesity and activity level are factors that can be changed.

3. **b, d, e.** Certain risk factors can be altered. Actions would include eating a well-balanced diet with foods that are low in cholesterol and saturated fats; avoiding fast foods, junk foods and foods that are high in animal fat; engaging in regular exercise; not smoking or stopping smoking; and ensuring control of blood cholesterol and blood pressure.

Chapter 14: Medical Emergencies

REVIEW OF CONCEPTS AND TERMS

Crossword Puzzle

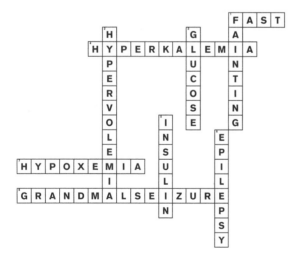

Matching

1. D; 2. F; 3. H; 4. C; 5.B; 6. E; 7. A; 8. G

Short Answer

1. There are many possible causes of altered mental status, including fever, infection, poisoning or overdose (e.g., substance abuse or misuse), blood sugar/endocrine emergencies, head injury, inadequate oxygenation or ventilation, any condition resulting in decreased blood flow or oxygen to the brain, cardiac emergencies, diabetic emergencies, shock, stroke, behavioral illness or seizures.

2. Altered mental status is one of the most common medical emergencies. It is characterized by a sudden or gradual change in a person's LOC and includes drowsiness, confusion and partial or complete loss of consciousness.

3. Generalized seizures, also called grand mal seizures or tonic-clonic seizures, are the most common type of seizure. They involve both hemispheres (halves) of the brain and usually result in loss of consciousness. The seizure activity is known as tonic-clonic, which refers to the rhythmic, tonic-clonic muscle contractions or

convulsions. This type of seizure rarely lasts for more than a few minutes.

4. Stroke is most commonly caused by a blood clot that forms or lodges in the arteries supplying blood to the brain. Another less common cause is bleeding from a ruptured artery in the brain.

5. There are two types of diabetes: in type 1 diabetes, the body produces little or no insulin; in type 2 diabetes, the body does produce insulin but either the cells do not use the insulin effectively or not enough insulin is produced.

6. The FAST mnemonic stands for Face (Ask the patient to smile. Does one side of the face droop?); Arm (Ask the patient to raise both arms. Does one arm drift downward?); Speech (Ask the person to repeat a simple sentence. Are the words slurred? Can the person repeat the sentence correctly?); and Time (Try to determine the time of onset of symptoms).

CASE STUDY

Scenario A

1. **c.** Diabetes involves a problem with the regulation of *blood glucose levels* (BGLs) in that the body produces little or no insulin or the body does not effectively use the insulin produced. Regulation of oxygen levels typically involves the lungs. The electrical activity of the brain is regulated by the neurons (nerve cells). Fluid volume is regulated by the kidneys.

2. **b.** Based on the patient's statements and history of diabetes, you would most likely suspect that the patient is experiencing hypoglycemia, or low blood glucose. There is no evidence of changes in mental status or signs of involuntary body movement, function, sensation or behavior that would suggest a seizure. Although the signs and symptoms of hypo- and hyperglycemia are similar, the fact that the patient was exercising and has not eaten in a while suggests that her blood sugar level is too low. If the patient was experiencing a *transient ischemic attack* (TIA), she would be complaining of numbness or weakness or would exhibit facial drooping or drooling, difficulty with speech, vision changes or trouble walking.

3. **b.** Since the patient's BGL most likely is low and the patient is conscious, you should give her something containing sugar, such as glucose paste, milk and most fruit juices or a non-diet soft drink, which contain sufficient amounts of sugar to help restore the BGL. Insulin administration would be inappropriate because it would lower her BGL even more. There is no need to place the patient in a supine (face-up) position because she is alert and conscious. She is talking, which indicates that her airway is open. Only if the patient should become unconscious or shows signs of airway obstruction would you need to open her airway.

Scenario B

1. **c.** Based on the description from bystanders, the patient is experiencing a generalized seizure, also called a tonic-clonic or grand mal seizure, as evidenced by reports of his "whole body shaking." With a simple partial seizure, the patient usually remains conscious and there is involuntary muscular contraction in one area of the body. Some people cannot speak or move but remember everything that occurred. With a complex partial seizure, the patient experiences a blank stare followed by random movements, such as lip smacking or chewing. The patient appears dazed, and movements are clumsy. Although rhythmic jerking of the head and limbs may occur, a febrile seizure most commonly occurs in children and is associated with a rapid increase in body temperature.

2. **a.** The report of "hearing a strange sound" reflects the aura phase, in which the patient senses something unusual. During the tonic phase, unconsciousness and muscle rigidity occur. During the clonic phase, the seizures occur. During the post-ictal phase, deep sleep with gradual recovery occurs.

3. **a.** As the seizure begins to stop, the patient most likely will be drowsy and disoriented. After the seizure stops, place the patient on his or her side, if possible, and maintain his airway. You should check to see if the patient was injured during the seizure and offer comfort and reassurance. Do not put anything into the patient's mouth or restrain him in any way during the seizure or afterwards. Having the patient sit up in a chair would be difficult because the patient is drowsy and feels a need to sleep.

4. **b.** Status epilepticus is an epileptic seizure that lasts longer than 5 minutes without any signs of slowing down. It is a true medical emergency.

SELF-ASSESSMENT

1. **c.** Fainting reflects an altered mental status in which the brain suddenly becomes deprived of its

blood supply and momentarily shuts down. Altered mental status often is characterized by a sudden or gradual change in a person's LOC and results from many different and variable causes. Children who are experiencing altered mental status may exhibit a change in behavior, personality or responsiveness beyond what is expected at their age.

2. **a, b, c, d.** Common causes of altered mental status requiring immediate medical attention include respiratory failure, deficiency in oxygen concentration in arterial blood (hypoxemia), shock, hypoglycemia, brain injury (including shaken baby syndrome), seizures, poisoning, intentional overdose, sepsis, meningitis, hyperthermia and hypothermia.

3. **b.** When the normal functions of the brain are disrupted by injury, disease, fever, infection, metabolic disturbances or conditions causing a decreased oxygen level, a seizure may occur. Elevated levels of glucose in the blood result in hyperglycemia. Disrupted blood flow to the brain results in a stroke. Abnormally low pressure results in hypotension.

4. **c.** An absence seizure, also known as a petit mal seizure, most commonly occurs in children. During an absence seizure there is a brief, sudden loss of awareness or conscious activity. There may be minimal or no movement, and the person may appear to have a blank stare. A rectal temperature over 102° F would be noted with a febrile seizure. Jerking of a body area, such as the leg, would be seen with a simple partial seizure. Drooling would be noted with a tonic-clonic seizure.

5. **a.** Protecting the patient from injury and managing the airway are your priorities when caring for a patient having a seizure. Preventing tongue biting would not be necessary because people having seizures rarely bite the tongue or cheeks with enough force to cause any significant bleeding. Airway patency is a priority; however, you should not place anything in the mouth to prevent this type of injury. Foreign bodies in the mouth may cause airway obstruction. Following, not during, the seizure, you should position the patient on the side, if possible, so that fluids (saliva, blood, vomit) can drain from the mouth. You should never put fingers into the mouth of an actively seizing patient to clear the airway. After the seizure, you need to provide maximum privacy because the patient may feel embarrassed and self-conscious.

6. **b.** The patient usually will recover from a seizure in a few minutes. If you discover that the patient has a history of medically controlled seizures, there may be no further need for medical attention; however, in cases of pregnancy, known diabetes or seizures occurring in the water, more advanced medical care should be provided.

7. **d.** With simple partial seizures, there may be involuntary, muscular contractions in one area of the body, for example, the arm, leg or face. An extremely high body temperature would be assessed in a patient with febrile seizures. A blank stare followed by random movements characterize complex partial seizures. Unconsciousness followed by muscular rigidity occurs during the tonic phase of generalized seizures.

8. **c.** Since the patient is unconscious and is hypoglycemic, you need to summon more advanced medical personnel immediately. Fruit juice or glucose tablets are used only if the patient is conscious. After giving either of these, you would recheck the BGL in 15 minutes.

9. **b.** A stroke usually is caused by a blood clot, called a thrombus or embolism, that forms or lodges in the arteries supplying blood to the brain. Another less common cause of stroke is bleeding from a ruptured artery in the brain. Known as a hemorrhagic stroke, this condition is brought on by high blood pressure or an aneurysm—a weakened area in an artery wall that balloons out and can rupture. Less commonly, a tumor or swelling from a head injury may cause a stroke by compressing an artery.

10. **c.** A TIA, often referred to as a "mini-stroke," is a temporary episode that, like a stroke, is caused by reduced blood flow to a part of the brain. Unlike a stroke, the signs and symptoms of a TIA (which are similar to a stroke) disappear within a few minutes or hours of its onset. If symptoms persist after 24 hours, the event is not considered a TIA but a stroke. The risk factors for stroke and TIA are similar to those for heart disease.

11. **a, d, e.** Signs and symptoms associated with a stroke typically include facial drooping or drooling, trouble walking and numbness of the face, arm(s) or leg(s). Speech often is affected, and the patient may complain of a sudden, severe headache.

12. **a.** When responding to an emergency call related to abdominal pain, you need to assume that the pain is serious since the patient and/or family members were concerned enough to seek emergency medical attention. Abdominal pain is felt between the chest and groin, which commonly is referred to as the stomach region or belly. There are many organs in the abdomen, so when a

patient is experiencing abdominal pain, it can originate from any one of them. Abdominal pain can be difficult to pinpoint since the pain may start from another part of the body and could result from numerous generalized infections, including the flu or strep throat. The intensity of abdominal pain does not always reflect the seriousness of the condition.

13. **a, b, c.** Patients on dialysis can experience several types of complications, including uremia (accumulation of urinary waste products in the blood), fluid overload (reduction in the body's ability to excrete fluid through urine), anemia (hemoglobin deficiency), hypertension, hyperkalemia (excess potassium in the blood) and coronary artery disease. Emergencies also can occur as complications of the dialysis itself, including hypotension, disequilibrium syndrome, hemorrhage, equipment malfunction (e.g., introducing an air embolus or other foreign body into the circulatory system) or complications from being temporarily removed from medications. More specifically, after dialysis, patients may have hypovolemia (reduced blood volume) and exhibit cold, clammy skin; poor skin turgor (elasticity); tachycardia; and hypotension. When dialysis is delayed, patients may experience hypervolemia (increased blood volume) and may have abnormal lung sounds, such as crackles; generalized edema; hypertension; or jugular venous distension.

14. **b.** To assess abdominal pain in a patient, first obtain an impression of the patient's appearance, breathing and circulation to determine the urgency of the situation; evaluate the patient's mental status, airway, adequacy of breathing and circulation; take the patient's history; and perform a hands-on physical exam noting any injury, hemorrhage, discoloration, distention, rigidity, guarding or tenderness within the four abdominal quadrants. If a life-threatening condition is noted, provide immediate treatment before continuing.

15. **c.** When assessing for stroke in a patient, you would use the FAST mnemonic, which addresses specific areas in the following order: face, arm, speech and time.

SELF-ASSESSMENT: ENRICHMENT

Basic Pharmacology

1. **a, c, d.** A drug's profile is a description of what it does, why it is or is not given to a patient and any issues that may develop as a result of taking it. It includes actions, indications, contraindications, side effects, dose and route of administration. The drug's serial number and commonly the drug's expiration date and manufacturer's name are part of the medication prescription.

2. **a.** Nitroglycerin dilates the blood vessels, allowing blood to flow more freely and thus providing more oxygen to the heart tissue. Aspirin relieves pain and also thins the blood. Oral glucose is used to elevate BGLs.

3. **a, b, d, e.** Whenever a drug is administered, from a patient's supply or from your stock, this must be documented thoroughly. You must document the reason for administration; drug name, dose, route of administration, time(s) of administration, any improvement or side effects noted, how often it was administered; and any changes in the patient's status. The manufacturer's name and address do not need to be documented.

4. **b.** Aspirin thins the blood by reducing the platelets' ability to produce a chemical that helps to form blood clots. It also reduces inflammation at the source, thereby reducing pain. Nitroglycerin dilates blood vessels, allowing blood to flow more freely, thus providing more oxygen to the heart tissue. Oral glucose acts by increasing the amount of blood glucose in the blood stream.

5. **c.** Nitroglycerin is contraindicated in patients who are exhibiting early signs of a heart attack. It is indicated for the treatment of chest pain due to angina. It is not contraindicated for patients who are taking aspirin. It is contraindicated in patients whose systolic blood pressure is below 90 mmHg.

Blood Glucose Monitoring

1. **d.** It is generally accepted that the normal range for BGLs before meals is 90 to 130 mg/dL and after meals it is less than 180 mg/dL; therefore, a value of 145 mg/dL before a meal would be considered abnormal.

2. **a.** Hypoglycemia occurs when the BGL drops below 70 mg/dL; therefore a reading of 62 mg/dL would confirm the suspicions that the patient is experiencing hypoglycemia.

REVIEW OF CONCEPTS AND TERMS

Matching

1. C; 2. B; 3. A; 4. D; 5. E

Chart Completion

STIMULANTS	HALLUCINOGENS	DEPRESSANTS	NARCOTICS	DESIGNER DRUGS
Methampheta-mine Cocaine	*Lysergic acid diethylamide* (LSD) *Phencyclidine* (PCP)	Ketamine Diazepam (Valium)	Morphine Heroin	Ecstasy MDMA

CASE STUDY

Scenario A

1. **b.** Alcohol is classified as a depressant because it affects the *central nervous system* (CNS) by decreasing physical and mental activity. Caffeine, cocaine and amphetamines are classified as stimulants. LSD, PCP, mescaline and peyote are classified as hallucinogens. Morphine, heroin and codeine are examples of narcotics.

2. **a.** Although you suspect alcohol poisoning, the patient is unresponsive, so you would need to first call for more advanced medical personnel. You then would complete your primary assessment. You also would turn the patient onto his side to clear the airway of vomit. Trying to get the patient to sit up would be inappropriate because the patient is unresponsive.

3. **c.** The poison, alcohol, entered the patient's body by way of ingestion, that is, the patient swallowed the poison. Poisoning by inhalation occurs when a person breathes in poisonous gases or fumes. An absorbed poison enters through the skin or mucous membranes in the eyes, mouth and nose. Injected poisons enter the body through bites or stings or as drugs or misused medications injected with a hypodermic needle.

4. **d.** Codeine is a natural opium derivative and is classified as a narcotic. Alcohol, benzodiazepines and barbiturates are considered depressants. LSD, PCP and mescaline are classified as hallucinogens. Cannabis products include marijuana, *tetrahydrocannabinol* (THC) and hashish.

5. **c.** Since alcohol and codeine depress the CNS, you would expect that the use of both drugs

together would heighten or exaggerate the effect of either drug alone. This is called a synergistic effect. Dependency occurs when the patient experiences a desire to continually use the drug. Tolerance occurs with the continual use of a drug and leads to a decrease in the drug's effects on the body, requiring the patient to increase the amount and frequency to achieve the desired effects. Addiction refers to the compulsive need for a substance when cessation of use would lead to mental, physical and emotional distress.

Scenario B

1. **b.** The first action would be to call the national *Poison Control Center* (PCC) hotline immediately and then follow the call taker's direction. You should not induce vomiting in this situation because drain cleaner is a corrosive substance. You should not give the child anything to eat or drink unless you are told to do so by the PCC.

2. **d.** The severity of a poisoning depends on the type and amount of the substance, the time that has elapsed since the poison entered the body, and the patient's age, size, weight and medical conditions. The patient's gender would have no impact on the severity of the poisoning.

SELF-ASSESSMENT

1. **b.** In 2007, PCCs received more than 2.4 million calls about people who had come into contact with a poison. About 90 percent (2.1 million) of these poisonings took place in the home and 50 percent (1.1 million) involved children younger than 6 years. Poisoning deaths in children younger than age 6 represented less than 3 percent of the total deaths from poisoning, whereas the 20- to 59-year-old age group represented about 73 percent of all deaths from poisoning. Due in part to child-resistant packaging and to preventive actions by parents and caregivers, there has been a decline in child poisonings. At the same time, there has been an increase in adult poisoning deaths, which is linked to an increase in both suicides and drug-related poisonings.

2. **a.** Lead is a primary source of chemical food poisoning. Botulism, *E. coli* and *Salmonella* are causes of bacterial food poisoning.

3. **a, d, e.** The symptoms of food poisoning, which can begin between 1 and 48 hours after eating contaminated food, include nausea, vomiting, abdominal pain, diarrhea, fever and dehydration. Severe cases of food poisoning can result in shock or death, particularly in children, the elderly and those with an impaired immune system. Excessive eye burning would most likely be seen with chemicals or poisons coming in contact with the eyes. Disorientation and seizures would be unlikely unless the patient developed severe food poisoning leading to extreme dehydration and shock.

4. **b.** Poisons that result from an insect sting enter the body by injection. Absorbed poisons enter the body through the skin or mucous membranes in the eyes, mouth and nose. Inhaled poisons enter the body when the person breathes in poisonous gases or fumes. Ingested poisons are poisons that are swallowed.

5. **d.** Chloroform is an example of a common inhaled poison. Poison ivy is an example of an absorbed poison. Contaminated water is an example of an ingested poison. Venom from a snake bite is an example of an injected poison.

6. **b.** Signs and symptoms of a severe allergic reaction (anaphylaxis) include weakness, nausea, dizziness, swelling of the throat or tongue, constricted airway and difficulty breathing. Itching, hives or a rash suggests a localized allergic reaction.

7. **a.** Substance misuse refers to the use of a substance for unintended purposes or for appropriate purposes but in improper amounts or doses. Substance abuse is the deliberate, persistent and excessive use of a substance without regard to health concerns or accepted medical practices.

8. **c.** Stimulants are drugs that affect the CNS by increasing physical and mental activity. They produce temporary feelings of alertness and prevent fatigue. They also suppress appetite and provide bursts of energy. Hallucinogens are substances that cause changes in mood, sensation, thought, emotion and self-awareness. Cannabis products produce feelings of elation, distorted perceptions of time and space, and impaired judgment and motor coordination. Inhalants produce mind-altering effects and depress the CNS.

9. **d.** When providing care to a patient with suspected substance abuse, it is most important to identify potential life-threatening conditions and intervene accordingly. Many of the signs and symptoms of substance abuse mimic other conditions, so you may not be able to determine that a patient has overdosed on a substance. Although it would be helpful to know the identity of the substance, care focuses on the abnormal behavior exhibited by the patient. If a patient becomes agitated or makes the scene unsafe in any way, you should retreat until the scene is safe. Restraints are used only as a last resort. Administering emergency oxygen would be appropriate if the patient was experiencing difficulty breathing.

10. **b.** A telltale sign of cannabis use is red, bloodshot eyes. Drowsiness would be seen with inhalant abuse and depressants. Mood changes and a flushed face suggest hallucinogen abuse.

11. **b, c, e.** When caring for a patient with substance misuse, always summon more advanced medical personnel. In addition, keep the patient's airway clear, and calm and reassure the patient. Applying several heavy blankets would be inappropriate because these probably would cause the patient to become overheated. Rather, you should take measures to prevent chilling and overheating. You should attempt to find out what substance was taken, how much was taken and when it was taken.

12. **a.** A patient who abuses depressants may show signs and symptoms that include drowsiness, confusion, slurred speech, slow heart and breathing rates, and poor coordination. Mood changes, flushing and hallucinations would suggest hallucinogen or designer drug abuse. Tachycardia (increased pulse), hypertension, rapid breathing, excitement, restlessness and irritability would suggest stimulant abuse.

13. **b, d, e.** Contributing factors for substance abuse include the lack of traditional family structure; peer pressure; widespread availability of substances; media glamorization of substances, especially alcohol and tobacco; and low self-esteem.

14. **d.** Not all substances that are abused are illegal. Caffeine is the most common stimulant used followed by nicotine. Ephedra, now banned by the FDA, and cocaine are other stimulants that are abused.

15. **c.** Withdrawal refers to the condition produced when a person stops using or abusing a substance to which he or she is addicted. Dependency refers to the desire to continually use the substance in order to function normally. Tolerance refers to the increase in substance amount and frequency to obtain the desired effect. Overdose refers to the use of an excessive amount of the substance.

SELF-ASSESSMENT: ENRICHMENT

Administering Activated Charcoal

1. **b.** Activated charcoal is only given if the patient is fully conscious and alert and you have been directed by medical control or the PCC. It should not be given to a patient who cannot swallow, has overdosed on cyanide, or swallowed acids or alkalis (including hydrochloric acid, bleach and ammonia).
2. **b.** Ideally, activated charcoal is administered within 1 hour of the patient swallowing the poison.
3. **c.** In general, the dosage is calculated at 1 gram of activated charcoal per kilogram of the patient's weight or 1 g/kg. For a patient weighting 75 kg, you would expect to give 75 grams of activated charcoal.

Carbon Monoxide and Cyanide Poisoning

1. **d.** The initial signs and symptoms of carbon monoxide poisoning include a dull or throbbing headache, nausea and vomiting, which can often be mistaken for something benign.

2. **a.** The only treatment for carbon monoxide poisoning at the scene is administering emergency oxygen. Blood sample testing would most likely be done at the receiving facility. There is no antidote for carbon monoxide poisoning and there is no need to clean the skin because the poison is inhaled.
3. **a, b, c.** Cyanide poisoning is generally thought of as a weapon used in terrorism or wartime. However, cyanide is found naturally in some everyday foods, such as apricot pits; in other products, such as cigarettes; and as byproducts of production, such as plastic manufacturing. Cyanide is also used in some production processes, such as making paper and textiles, developing photographs, cleaning metal and in rodent poisons.
4. **b.** Hydrogen cyanide can enter the body through inhalation or ingestion or by being absorbed into the skin or eyes. It is not injected.
5. **c.** The most likely signs and symptoms in someone who has suffered cyanide toxicity include altered mental status, abnormal pupil dilation, low respiratory rate, low systolic blood pressure with increased heart rate, metabolic acidosis (increased plasma acidity) and a large increase in lactate levels in the plasma.

Chapter 16: Environmental Emergencies

REVIEW OF CONCEPTS AND TERMS

Crossword Puzzle

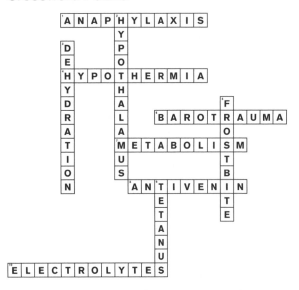

Short Answer

1. The body is cooled by radiation, convection, conduction, evaporation and respiration.

2. Factors that can increase a person's risk for heat-related illnesses include climate, exercise and activity, age, pre-existing illness and/or conditions, and drugs and/or medications.
3. The two types of cold-related emergencies are hypothermia and frostbite.
4. Human bites are common and differ from other bites because they may be more contaminated, tend to occur in higher-risk areas of the body (especially on the hands) and often receive delayed care.
5. Classic heat stroke normally is caused by environmental changes and often occurs during the summer months. Exertional heat stroke occurs when excess heat is generated through exercise and exceeds the body's ability to cool off. Exposure to factors such as high air temperature, high relative humidity and dehydration increases the risk for developing exertional heat stroke.
6. For a water rescue, the four steps to follow are reach, throw, row and then go with "go" only for those who are trained to perform deep water rescue.

CASE STUDY

Scenario A

1. **c.** Due to the weather and the patient's complaints, the most likely condition suspected would be frostbite. Although hypothermia is a possibility, it would be manifested by more generalized signs and symptoms. The patient's signs and symptoms do not suggest stroke, which would be noted by weakness of the face, arm or leg, possible speech difficulties and continued changes in the patient's LOC. The signs and symptoms also do not reflect a generalized seizure, where the patient would become rigid, and then experience sudden, uncontrollable muscular contractions (convulsions).

2. **a, b.** Signs and symptoms of frostbite include lack of feeling in the affected area, swelling and skin that appears waxy, is cold to the touch or is discolored (flushed, white, yellow or blue). In more serious cases of frostbite, blisters may form and the affected part may turn black and show signs of deep tissue damage. Impaired judgment, glassy stare and decreased LOC would support hypothermia.

3. **b.** The priority is to get the patient out of the cold. Once the patient is removed from the cold, handle the area gently because rough handling can damage the body part. You should never rub the affected area since this can cause skin damage. The scenario does not suggest any dangers other than the cold environment, so scene safety is not a problem. Reorienting the patient would be appropriate if the patient was confused, and this would be done once you get the patient out of the cold.

4. **d.** When providing care, avoid breaking any blisters to prevent further damage and possible infection. Gently warm the affected area by soaking it in warm, not hot, water (100°–105° F or 37.7°–40.5° C) until normal color returns and the body part feels warm. Loosely bandage the area with dry, sterile dressings. If the patient's fingers or toes are frostbitten, place dry, sterile gauze between them to keep them separated. If there is damage is to the feet, DO NOT allow the patient to walk.

Scenario B

1. **d.** The bite of a coral snake leaves a semicircular mark. The bite of other venomous snakes leaves one or two distinct puncture wounds, which may or may not bleed.

2. **b.** The first priority with any snake bite is to wash the wound. You would need to keep the injured area still and lower than the heart. Apply an elastic roller bandage. Checking for infection would be done at a later time. Ice is not used with snake bites.

3. **c.** You should apply an elastic roller bandage to slow the spread of venom through the lymphatic system. The roller bandage does not reduce swelling, provide support or control pain.

4. **a.** When transporting the patient, keep the injured area still and lower than the heart. The patient should be transported by stretcher or be carried. The patient should not walk unless absolutely necessary.

SELF-ASSESSMENT

1. **d.** Heat stroke is the most serious heat-related illness because the body is no longer able to cool itself. Hyperthermia is a general term that refers to overheating of the body and includes heat cramps, heat exhaustion and heat stroke. Heat cramps are painful, involuntary muscle spasms that occur during or after physical exertion in high heat, and are caused by loss of fluids and associated electrolytes from perspiration. Heat exhaustion is a more severe form of heat-related illness. Heat exhaustion results when fluid lost through perspiration is not replaced by other fluids.

2. **b, c.** Appropriate measures to prevent heat-related illnesses include wearing light-colored clothing to reflect the sun's rays; exercising for brief periods and then taking frequent rests, preferably in a cool, shaded area; avoiding exercising and activities during the hottest part of the day (usually late morning to early afternoon); drinking at least six, 8-ounce glasses of fluid daily; and avoiding beverages that contain caffeine and alcohol.

3. **c.** Early signs and symptoms of dehydration include excessive thirst, fatigue, weakness, headache, irritability, nausea, dizziness, and dry lips and mouth. Sunken eyes, a rapid pulse and decreased perspiration indicate worsening dehydration.

4. **a.** Heat loss that occurs through the head results from radiation, the transfer of heat from one object to another without physical contact. Heat loss through convection occurs when cold air moves over the skin and carries the skin's heat away. Heat loss through conduction occurs when the body is in direct contact with a substance that is cooler than the body's temperature. Heat loss through evaporation occurs with perspiration.

5. **b.** With high humidity, the body is less able to cool down through sweating. Thus, evaporation decreases as the relative humidity increases because the air contains excessive moisture. If the temperature is high, the body is not as able to lower its temperature through radiation. Conduction and convection may or may not be affected.

6. **c.** The human body usually keeps itself at a constant core (internal temperature) of 98.6° F (37° C).

7. **a.** If the body starts to become too cold, it responds by constricting (closing up) the blood vessels close to the skin so that it can keep the warmer blood near the center of the body. This helps to keep the organs warm. If this does not work, the body then begins to shiver. The shivering motion increases body heat because it is a form of movement. In a warm or hot environment, the hypothalamus detects an increase in blood temperature. Blood vessels near the skin dilate (widen), to bring more blood to the surface, which allows heat to escape.

8. **a.** Heat-related illnesses can happen to anyone, but several predisposing factors can put some people at higher risk. When exposed to the same conditions, of the individuals listed, the 75-year-old diabetic with heart disease would have the greatest risk for a heat-related illness because of age and the presence of two pre-existing health conditions (diabetes and heart disease). Each of the other individuals has only one risk factor, such as use of diuretics, working outside or caffeine intake.

9. **b.** To care for a patient with heat cramps, the most important initial action is to reduce the cramps. First, have the patient rest, then gently massage and lightly stretch the cramped muscles to ease the discomfort. In addition, encourage the patient to drink fluid, such as a commercial sports drink, milk or water, to replace what was lost to perspiration.

10. **a, c.** Signs and symptoms of heat stroke include flushed or red skin that is either dry or moist; rapid, weak pulse; shallow breathing; low blood pressure; decreasing LOC; body temperature above 104° F; and lack of sweating. Heavy sweating is associated with heat exhaustion.

11. **b, a, c, d, e.** When providing care to a patient who is known to be hypothermic, your initial priority is to move the patient into a warmer environment. You then would perform a primary assessment, call for more advanced medical personnel, remove any wet clothing and dry the patient, and begin to rewarm the patient slowly.

12. **a.** A localized skin rash would be more indicative of a localized allergic reaction than anaphylaxis. Anaphylaxis is a generalized, severe allergic reaction often manifested by difficulty breathing; wheezing or shortness of breath; chest or throat tightness; facial, neck or tongue swelling; weakness; dizziness or confusion; low blood pressure; and shock.

13. **c.** All scorpion stings are treated as medical emergencies because it is difficult to distinguish highly poisonous scorpions from non-poisonous ones. Only a few species of scorpions have a potentially fatal sting. The sting of the brown recluse spider causes tissue destruction. Although allergic reactions are possible with any bite or sting, this is not the reason for treating the situation as a medical emergency.

14. **d.** When working on a water rescue, you must consider your own safety before all else. Other considerations then would include the condition of the water and the patient and the resources that are available.

15. **a, c.** Someone who is conscious (responsive) and has no spinal injury should be removed from the water. A patient who is unresponsive, lying face-down in the water or has a neck injury should be cared for in the water.

SELF-ASSESSMENT: ENRICHMENT

Assisting with an Epinephrine Auto-Injector

1. **a.** When assisting with an auto-injector, check the expiration date on the device and do not use it if it has expired. You also should inspect the liquid to make sure that it is clear; if it is cloudy, you should not use it. If the patient already has taken a dose of epinephrine or an antihistamine, you should only administer a second dose when more

advanced medical personnel are not present and if anaphylactic symptoms persist for a few minutes. The cap on the auto-injector should be left on until it is ready to be used.

2. **b.** The auto-injector is given into the lateral (outer) aspect of the patient's thigh. It is not given in the lateral (outer) arm, abdomen or buttocks. The lateral (outer) mid-thigh area is the preferred and most often recommended intramuscular site for administering an epinephrine auto-injector. Be sure to always follow manufacturer's instructions and medical direction.

Lightning

1. **b.** Every 5 seconds between a flash of lightning and the sound of thunder equals 1 mile of distance. So the time span of 20 seconds divided by 5 seconds would indicate that the storm is 4 miles away.

2. **b.** The threat of lightning continues for a much longer period than most people realize. You should wait at least 30 minutes after the last clap of thunder before leaving a shelter.

SCUBA and Free-Diving Emergencies

1. **c.** Decompression sickness occurs when a diver ascends too quickly without sufficient time for gases to exit the body tissues and be removed from the body through exhalation. Pulmonary overinflation syndrome, also known as pulmonary overpressure syndrome, occurs because gases under pressure contract and take up less volume. The air inhaled at depth will expand during ascent as the pressure decreases and can go beyond the lungs' capacity. Nitrogen narcosis occurs at depths over 100 feet when the pressure causes nitrogen to dissolve into brain nerve membranes, causing a temporary disruption in nerve transmission.

2. **a.** If the patient is alert, he or she should be placed in the supine (face-up) position. If mental status is altered, you would place the patient in the supine (face-up) position. If a spinal injury is suspected, you would need to maintain spinal motion restriction. The prone or Fowler's position would be inappropriate.

Chapter 17: Behavioral Emergencies

REVIEW OF CONCEPTS AND TERMS

Fill-in-the-Blank

1. behavioral
2. anxiety
3. suicide
4. paranoia
5. schizophrenia
6. Females

Short Answer

1. Those in the 15- to 24-year age group are at highest risk of dying by suicide.

2. Self-mutilation, or self-injury, refers to deliberately harming one's own body through acts such as burning or cutting. It usually is not meant as an attempt to commit suicide, but is an unhealthy coping mechanism to deal with overwhelming negative emotions, such as tension, anger and frustration. The individual experiences momentary calmness and a release of tension but then quickly feels a sense of shame and guilt, in addition to a return of the negative feelings that the person was trying to avoid.

3. Sexual assault is defined as any form of sexual contact against a person's will, often by coercion, force or threat.

4. Child abuse is the physical, verbal, psychological or sexual assault of a child resulting in injury and/or emotional trauma. Child neglect is the most frequently reported type of abuse in which a parent or guardian fails to provide the necessary, age-appropriate care to a child or insufficient medical or emotional attention or respect given to a child.

5. Restraining a person without justification can give rise to a claim of assault and battery.

6. It must be assumed that any patient with a behavioral emergency has an altered mental status.

CASE STUDY

Scenario A

1. **d.** A victim of sexual assault experiences physical as well as emotional trauma; therefore, it would be essential to treat the patient with sensitivity. Although it would be important to gain as much information as possible, this would need to be done with tact and sensitivity. The patient's

clothing should be removed only to provide care, and efforts should be made to ensure that any evidence on the clothing is preserved. You should not clean the patient or offer something for the patient to use to clean him- or herself because doing so may destroy evidence.

2. **c.** Common signs and symptoms of rape include an unresponsive, dazed state; intense pain from assault and penetration; psychological and physical shock and paralysis; possible bleeding or body fluid discharge; torn or removed clothing; and nausea, vomiting, gagging or urination.

3. **b.** Any evidence you collect while treating the patient for injuries should be isolated, and each piece of evidence needs to be bagged individually in a paper bag to prevent cross-contamination. Plastic bags do not allow for air movement and cause the DNA to deteriorate due to moisture buildup. You need to follow local protocols and give the evidence to the police as soon as possible.

Scenario B

1. **a.** Other signs and symptoms associated with mania include aggressiveness, agitation and an inability to complete a task. Feelings of hopelessness and an inability to work suggest depression.

2. **b.** Bipolar disorder is characterized by a person swinging from the extreme lows of depression to the highs of mania. Schizophrenia is a severe, chronic mental illness in which the patient hears voices or feels that his or her thoughts are being controlled by others. Clinical depression is a chronic illness involving persistent feelings of being useless along with a loss of interest in regular activities, feelings of hopelessness or guilt, and unexplained sadness. A panic attack is an anxiety disorder in which the patient experiences an out-of-control feeling often accompanied by difficulty breathing and heart palpitations.

3. **c, d.** When establishing rapport, you should speak directly to the patient, maintain eye contact and tell the patient who you are and that you are there to help. Telling the patient to calm down would be inappropriate because the statement can be interpreted as threatening. You should not touch the patient without permission.

SELF-ASSESSMENT

1. **b.** A phobia typically is manifested by an exaggerated fear response. Intense feelings of sadness are associated with depression. Bizarre

behavior and an extreme increase in body temperature suggest excited delirium syndrome.

2. **b.** Patients experiencing behavioral emergencies may appear agitated or speak in a rapid or incoherent manner, or they may be subdued or withdrawn. These individuals pose a threat to themselves, their families or the community at large. It is assumed that a patient with a behavioral emergency has an altered mental status. Typically, signs and symptoms present with a rapid onset.

3. **b, c, d, e.** Possible causes of behavioral emergencies include injury, primarily head injury; physical illness; adverse effects of prescribed medications; mental illness; noncompliance with prescribed psychiatric medications; and extreme emotional distress.

4. **a.** Excited delirium syndrome is characterized by high body temperatures, increased body strength, insensitivity to pain and agitation.

5. **c.** Anxiety attacks can last any length of time, but panic attacks generally last no longer than 30 minutes.

6. **d.** Paranoia can be a side effect of any recreational drug use; however, it is particularly associated with the use of stimulants.

7. **b.** Schizophrenia is a mental illness characterized by the person hearing voices or feeling that his or her thoughts are being controlled by others. These voices or thoughts can instruct the person to do things he or she would otherwise not do. Phobia is characterized by an exaggerated fear response often related to objects or events that usually are harmless. Self-mutilation is characterized by self-injury through acts such as burning or cutting. Clinical depression is characterized by extreme feelings of sadness, hopelessness or uselessness.

8. **c.** Your primary concern as an EMR is to treat any injuries or medical conditions arising from the violence or suicide attempt and then transport the patient to a facility where he or she can receive medical and psychiatric treatment. If it is necessary to prevent the patient from harming you, him- or herself, or others, you may need to use medical restraints to transport the patient.

9. **a.** Older people are at a higher risk for suicide than the general population because depression is common in the geriatric population and it may be misdiagnosed as dementia or confusion. They do not have an increased tendency for impulsive action, nor do they experience more problems with alcohol abuse. An individual of any age may be reluctant to seek help for mental health problems due to the stigma attached to suicidal

thoughts, suicide attempts or general mental health problems.

10. **d.** Asking the question, "You're not a threat to yourself, are you?" implies the answer "No," regardless of what the patient is feeling. It makes the assumption that the patient is not a threat to him- or herself. Asking the patient how he or she is feeling, if he or she is thinking about hurting him- or herself, or if he or she has suffered any trauma recently provide direct specific information to help gain insight into the situation.

11. **a, b, d.** When sizing up the scene, identify and locate the patient before entering. You also need to identify exit or escape routes for your safety and clear the scene of any objects that could be used to injure the patient or others as soon as possible. You need to be aware that there may be more than one patient.

12. **d.** When you are involved in restraining a patient, you should place the patient in the face-up position and monitor his or her breathing regularly. You may be required to obtain police authorization before you can use restraints. Be aware of the laws regarding the use of restraints in your jurisdiction. You also should seek medical direction and approval before applying restraints and be aware of and follow local protocols involving their use.

Chapter 18: Shock

REVIEW OF CONCEPTS AND TERMS

Fill-in-the-Blank

1. hypoperfusion
2. ashen
3. hemorrhagic
4. Obstructive
5. septic

Short Answer

1. Three types of distributive shock are neurogenic/vasogenic, anaphylactic and septic shock.
2. The three conditions are a functioning heart, intact blood vessels with the ability to adjust blood flow and an adequate amount of blood circulating.
3. Psychogenic shock can occur from emotional distress.
4. Although the patient is likely to be thirsty due to the fluid loss, a patient in shock is not given any food or drink because, depending on his or her condition, surgery may be needed and it is better for the patient's stomach to be empty if that is the case.
5. Shock occurs when the circulatory system fails to provide adequate oxygenated blood to all parts of the body. It results from inadequate delivery of oxygenated blood to the body's tissues for several reasons, including severe bleeding or loss of fluid from the body, failure of the heart to pump enough oxygenated blood, abnormal dilation of the vessels or impaired blood flow to the organs and cells.

CASE STUDY

Scenario A

1. **a, c, e.** A patient in the early stages of shock would exhibit apprehension and anxiety; slightly lower than normal temperature; increased respiratory rate; slightly increased pulse; normal or slightly lower blood pressure; and pale, ashen cool skin.

2. **c.** The patient is most likely experiencing hypovolemic shock because of the possible internal blood loss secondary to the fall. Cardiogenic shock is the result of the heart being unable to supply adequate blood circulation to the vital organs, resulting in an inadequate supply of oxygen and nutrients; disease, trauma or injury to the heart causes this type of shock. Distributive shock refers to any type of shock caused by inadequate distribution of blood, either in the blood vessels or throughout the body, leading to inadequate volumes of blood returning to the heart. Obstructive shock is caused by some type of obstruction to blood flow, usually within the blood vessels, such as a pulmonary embolism, tension pneumothorax or cardiac tamponade.

3. **a.** Due to the patient's injury, an increase in the pulse rate along with a weak pulse occurs as the body's response to blood loss, either externally or internally. The pulse rate does not reflect blood glucose levels, early signs of sepsis or cardiac trauma.

4. **b.** The patient's signs and symptoms reflect the body's attempt to compensate for the effects of the injury. They are unrelated to stress and are not a

routine fear reaction. They also do not reflect recovery from the initial injury.

5. **b.** Since you are unsure of the patient's condition, keep the patient lying flat. Sitting up is inappropriate because it may cause further injury, especially if the patient's head, neck or spine is injured. A recovery position would be appropriate if the patient was unconscious and the airway needed to be maintained or you needed to leave the patient to call for help.

6. **a.** Since the patient's LOC is decreasing, you need to maintain an open airway and administer emergency oxygen if available. Then you could cover the patient to prevent chilling if this has not already been done, and keep the patient flat since you are unsure of his injuries. Immobilizing any fractures or dislocations would be appropriate if this has not been done, but immobilizing his body would be inappropriate.

SELF-ASSESSMENT

1. **b.** Metabolic shock is the result of a loss of body fluid, which can be due to severe diarrhea, vomiting or a heat-related illness. Cardiogenic shock is the result of the heart being unable to supply adequate blood circulation to the vital organs, resulting in an inadequate supply of oxygen and nutrients. Disease, trauma or injury to the heart causes this type of shock. Anaphylaxis (also referred to as anaphylactic shock) occurs as the result of exposure to an allergen. Neurogenic/vasogenic shock is caused by spinal cord or brain trauma.

2. **a.** Shock, or hypoperfusion, is a progressive condition in which the circulatory system fails to adequately circulate oxygenated blood to all parts of the body. When vital organs, such as the brain, heart and lungs, do not receive sufficient oxygenated blood, the body begins a series of responses to protect those organs. The amount of blood circulating to the less important tissues of the arms, legs and skin is reduced so that more can go to the vital organs. This reduction in blood circulation to the skin causes a person in shock to appear pale or ashen (grayish) and to feel cool.

3. **c.** Anaphylactic shock is a whole-body reaction that causes dilation of the blood vessels and constriction (closing) of the airways, which in turn causes blood to pool and difficulty breathing. The airways may close completely from inflammation. Tissue damage occurs in septic shock.

4. **a.** Your goal is to control the patient's body temperature. Cover the patient with a blanket to prevent loss of body heat. Be careful that you do not overheat the patient while trying to prevent chilling. Immersing his feet in warm water would be appropriate if the patient was experiencing frostbite. Applying cool compresses to his neck or groin would be appropriate if the patient was experiencing a heat-related illness.

5. **b.** The patient's skin becomes pale and the skin feels cool due to the reduction in circulation to the skin due to vessel constriction and as blood flow is increased to the vital organs. Shock does not damage the temperature control center, nor does it cause the heart to beat slowly. The response is not due to self-cooling measures.

6. **d.** To minimize shock, administer emergency oxygen to assist with ensuring adequate oxygenation to the blood. Estimating the amount of blood loss is helpful in determining the extent of shock, but you may not be able to do so if the bleeding is internal. The better action would be to control any bleeding, if present, and prevent further loss, if appropriate. Lay the patient flat. You should not give the patient anything to eat or drink in case the patient requires surgery.

7. **c.** Vasogenic or neurogenic shock is caused by spinal cord or brain trauma. Septic shock occurs with infection. Cardiogenic shock occurs with trauma or injury to the heart. Obstructive shock occurs with a pulmonary embolism, tension pneumothorax or cardiac tamponade.

8. **b, c, e.** Signs and symptoms that shock is progressing include dilated pupils; listlessness and confusion; decreasing blood pressure; shallow, irregular respirations; and irregular, weak, rapid pulse.

9. **b.** Hypovolemic shock is due to a severe lack of blood and fluid within the body. Hemorrhagic shock is the most common type of hypovolemic shock. It results from blood loss, either through external or internal bleeding, which causes a decrease in total blood volume. Obstructive shock is caused by an obstruction to blood flow, usually within the blood vessels, such as a pulmonary embolism, tension pneumothorax or cardiac tamponade. Distributive shock refers to any type of shock caused by inadequate distribution of blood either in the blood vessels or throughout the body, leading to inadequate volumes of blood returning to the heart. Cardiogenic shock is the result of the heart being unable to supply

adequate blood circulation to the vital organs, resulting in an inadequate supply of oxygen and nutrients. Disease, trauma or injury to the heart causes this type of shock.

10. **a.** First ensure that the patient's airway is open and clear, and then perform a primary assessment, administer emergency oxygen, if available, and provide appropriate ventilatory support. Next, take steps to control any bleeding, if present, and prevent further blood loss, if appropriate. Keep the patient lying flat. If you suspect that any bones are broken or see dislocated or damaged joints, immobilize them to prevent movement. Broken bones or dislocated or damaged joints can cause more bleeding and damage.

Chapter 19: Bleeding and Trauma

REVIEW OF CONCEPTS AND TERMS

Matching

1. C; 2. F; 3. G; 4. H; 5. A; 6. B; 7. D; 8. E

Short Answer

1. The most common cause of arterial bleeding is blunt trauma.
2. Blood from capillary bleeding is darker red than from arterial bleeding, oozes and usually clots spontaneously.
3. An occlusive dressing does not allow air and fluid to pass through.
4. A triangular bandage, when folded, can hold a dressing or splint in place on most body parts. It also can be used as a sling to provide support to an injured shoulder, arm or hand.
5. The two main pressure points are the brachial artery (inside the elbow) and the femoral artery (groin).

CASE STUDY

Scenario A

1. **d.** Venous blood flows steadily and is darker red than arterial blood. Arterial blood is bright red, spurts from the wound and will not clot or stop easily.
2. **a.** The most important action to protect yourself when caring for a patient who is bleeding is to adhere to standard precautions and use appropriate PPE, such as disposable gloves. A dressing applied to bleeding wounds should be sterile. Preventing the patient from developing signs and symptoms of shock would be a priority for providing care to the patient; however, it is not related to actions needed to protect yourself. Elevating the extremity would help to control bleeding, but this protects the patient, not you.

3. **d.** Tourniquets should *only* be used as a last resort in cases of delayed-care or delayed EMS response situations when direct pressure does not stop the bleeding or you are not able to apply direct pressure. Appropriate measures include placing a sterile gauze dressing over the wound, applying direct pressure with a gloved hand and elevating the body part above heart level.

Scenario B

1. **a, b, e.** Signs and symptoms of internal bleeding include bruising on the neck, chest, abdomen or side; nausea, vomiting or coughing up blood; patient guarding the area; rapid pulse or breathing; skin that is cool or moist or looks pale, ashen or bluish; excessive thirst; declining LOC; and a drop in blood pressure.
2. **d.** If you suspect a skull fracture, you should not try to stop the nosebleed because it may increase pressure in the brain. Instead, cover the nostrils loosely with sterile gauze. Tilting the head forward slightly and pinching the nostrils firmly together would be appropriate to stop the nosebleed if no fracture was suspected. A patient with a nosebleed never should blow his or her nose.
3. **b.** If a patient is bleeding internally, first call for more advanced medical personnel if serious internal bleeding is suspected. Then ensure the patient remains as still as possible to reduce the heart's blood output and care for shock. The bleeding is internal, not external, so applying direct pressure to the chest would be inappropriate.

SELF-ASSESSMENT

1. **d.** A sterile dressing is used on open bleeding wounds to minimize the risk of infection and contamination. Although dressings and bandages help to control bleeding and absorb drainage, the

primary reason for using *sterile* dressings is to prevent infection. Most dressings are porous and allow air to circulate to the wound to promote healing.

2. **a.** A trauma system is a system of definitive care facilities offering services within a region or community in various areas of medical expertise in order to care for injured individuals. These systems consist of many different components that provide medical services for injury prevention, prehospital care, acute care facilities and post-hospital care. The value of a trauma system is that it provides a seamless transition for patients to move between each phase of care, leading to improved patient outcomes. Trauma is the physical injury, wound or shock caused by an agent, force or mechanism. The Golden Hour refers to the time period when a severely injured patient requiring surgery has the best chance of survival.

3. **d.** A Level IV trauma setting often is a rural clinic in a remote area and generally offers patient care only until arrangement for transportation can be made. A Level I trauma facility must have the capability to deal with all levels and types of patient injury on a 24-hour basis. A Level II trauma facility is expected to be able to provide definitive care to patients, despite the type of patient injury; however, this facility sometimes may have to send a patient with more severe injuries to a Level I facility. A Level III trauma facility is found in smaller communities that do not have access to larger Level I or II medical centers. They can provide prompt assessment, resuscitation and emergency operations and arrange for transport to a Level I or II facility, as required.

4. **b.** To reduce the risk of disease transmission when controlling bleeding, always follow standard precautions, including avoiding direct or indirect contact with the patient's blood by using barriers, such as disposable gloves and protective eyewear; avoiding eating, drinking and touching your mouth, nose or eyes while providing care or before washing your hands; and always washing your hands thoroughly before and after providing care, even if you wore gloves or used other barriers.

5. **b.** Arterial bleeding is the most urgent because it is oxygenated and is pumped from the heart to supply the body with nutrients. Venous blood is the second most serious. The seriousness of external or internal bleeding depends on whether it is arterial, venous or capillary.

6. **a.** Arterial bleeding is bright red, spurts from the wound, does not clot easily and decreases in

pressure as the patient's blood pressure drops. Venous blood flows steadily, and capillary bleeding usually clots spontaneously.

7. **b.** An occlusive dressing does not allow air to pass through; it is used for sucking chest wounds and open abdominal wounds. Universal dressings or trauma dressings are used to cover very large wounds and multiple wounds in one body area. A roller bandage generally is wrapped around the body part, over a dressing, using overlapping turns until the dressing is completely covered. Elastic bandages are designed to keep continuous pressure on a body part.

8. **b.** When using a roller bandage, you should secure the end of the bandage first and then wrap the bandage around the body part using overlapping turns until the dressing is completely covered and the bandage extends several inches beyond the dressing. The fingers and toes should not be covered.

9. **b.** If blood soaks through the bandage, apply additional dressings and another bandage directly on top of the soiled ones and reapply direct pressure. Do not remove the blood-soaked ones. Elevating the body part would be appropriate if bleeding cannot be controlled by direct pressure alone.

10. **a.** If the patient is experiencing internal capillary bleeding, bruising around the wound area results, which is not serious. To reduce discomfort, apply ice or a cold pack to the area, ensuring that the cold pack does not come into direct contact with the patient's skin. Elevating the body part, applying direct pressure and maintaining pressure at a pressure point is appropriate for external bleeding.

11. **c.** Immobilization restricts movement and subsequently blood flow. Blood clotting is not affected. Pressure on a pressure point compresses the artery. A hemostatic agent removes moisture from blood and speeds up the process of clot formation.

12. **d.** For serious bleeding, apply strong direct pressure to the wound using fingertip pressure first. If the wound is large and fingertip pressure does not work, use hand pressure with gauze dressings to stop the bleeding. If direct pressure, elevation and immobilization do not control the bleeding, then apply pressure to a pressure point. Using the thumb would be inappropriate.

13. **c.** Some organs and organ systems are especially sensitive to changes in the efficiency of perfusion. The brain and spinal cord (the nervous system) are most quickly affected, lasting only about 4 to 6

minutes without constant perfusion before irreversible damage is done. The kidneys (renal system) can last up to 45 minutes without perfusion. The skeletal system can last up to 45 minutes without perfusion.

14. **d.** A tourniquet rarely is used as part of emergency care because it can do more harm than good. It should only be used as a last resort in cases of a serious emergency or in delayed-care or delayed EMS response situations when direct pressure does not stop the bleeding or you are not able to apply direct pressure. Direct pressure is used first and may be used in conjunction with elevation and immobilization. If direct pressure, elevation and immobilization do not control the severe bleeding, a pressure point is used.

SELF-ASSESSMENT: ENRICHMENT

Mechanisms of Injury—The Kinematics of Trauma

1. **b.** In a feet-first fall, injury will be less severe if the knees are bent on landing. Outstretched hands can results in wrist injuries. Hitting with the buttocks first can lead to spinal injuries. Flexing the feet on impact may lead to ankle and foot injuries.

2. **d.** Burns, crush injuries and toxic inhalation are examples of quaternary blast injuries. Primary blast injury is caused by the direct effect of blast overpressure on a patient's tissue, resulting in injury to air-filled structures, such as the lungs, ears and gastrointestinal tract. Secondary blast injury is caused when a patient is struck by flying objects. The most common secondary blast injuries include penetrating thoracic trauma, such as lacerations of the heart and major blood vessels, which often leads to death. Tertiary blast injuries are caused by individuals flying through the air and striking other objects, generally from high-energy explosions. The patient usually is very close to the explosion source when injured this way.

3. **a, b, d, e.** Injuries common to head-on collisions include face, head, neck, chest and abdominal injuries. Burns and contusions are more commonly associated with injuries related to airbag deployment.

4. **c.** Motorcycle accidents may be head-on, angular, ejection and laying the bike down. Rotational impact occurs with motor vehicles.

Chapter 20: Soft Tissue Injuries

REVIEW OF CONCEPTS AND TERMS

Matching

1. C; 2. E; 3. A; 4. F; 5. D; 6. B

Short Answer

1. The three functions of the skin include providing a protective barrier for the body, helping to regulate the body's temperature and receiving information about the environment through the nerves that run through it.

2. The two major layers of the skin are the epidermis and dermis.

3. A wound is considered closed when the soft tissue damage occurs beneath the surface of the skin, leaving the outer layer intact; this often results in internal bleeding. A wound is considered open when there is a break in the skin's outer layer; this usually results in external bleeding.

4. Burns are classified as superficial, partial thickness and full thickness.

5. The extent of a burn is commonly described using the Rule of Nines for adults. It approximates the percentage of the burned surface area of the patient. In an adult, the body surface is divided into 11 sections, each comprising approximately 9 percent of the body's skin coverage. The extent of burn in a child requires modification because the head is a proportionately larger contributor to body surface area and the upper legs contribute less. The pediatric Lund-Browder diagram reflects this difference and commonly is used for children.

Labeling

Skin Structures
A. Epidermis
B. Dermis
C. Fatty tissue
D. Muscle

CASE STUDY

Scenario A

1. **b.** An amputation involves complete severing of a body part. An avulsion involves a portion of the skin and sometimes other soft tissue being partially or completely torn away. A laceration is a cut, usually from a sharp object, resulting in jagged or smooth edges. Impalement occurs when an object is embedded in an open wound.

2. **a.** The priority is to care for the patient and control the bleeding immediately. You should have your partner retrieve the body part and care for it. Direct pressure would be applied first to control the bleeding, followed by other measures, such as immobilizing and elevating the injured body part. Pain control, although important, would be appropriate once measures for controlling the bleeding are instituted.

3. **c.** The external bleeding associated with an amputation typically is severe, although it may not be as profuse as expected. However, you still need to be alert for signs and symptoms of shock from the blood loss. Infection would be a greater concern later. Respiratory failure and cardiac arrest would be of lesser concern unless the patient developed shock and body systems begin to fail.

4. **b.** If the body part is completely severed, once it has been found, you or another responder should wrap it in sterile gauze that has been moistened in sterile saline, if available. You then should place it in a plastic bag and label it with the patient's name and the date and time when it was placed in the bag. It is important to keep the bag cool by placing it in a larger bag or a container of ice and water slurry (but not on ice alone and not on dry ice). The body part never should be placed directly into the slurry. Transfer the bag to the EMS personnel transporting the patient to the hospital.

Scenario B

1. **c.** In this situation, because the patient is on fire, you would need to extinguish the flames first. You then would perform a primary assessment, help to cool the burn and summon more advanced medical personnel.

2. **d.** Thermal burns are caused by contact with an open flame, a hot object, steam or other hot gas, or hot liquid (scalding). Chemical burns result from exposure to substances such as cleaning solutions (i.e., household bleach or oven, toilet bowl or drain cleaners), paint strippers, and lawn and garden products. Electrical burns result from exposure to an electrical source, such as a power line, malfunctioning household appliance or lightning. Radiation burns result from exposure to radiation sources, such as X-rays or the sun's rays, or they can occur as a side effect of radiation therapy.

3. **b.** Cool any burned area immediately with large amounts of cold water until the pain is relieved. You should not use ice or ice water except on small, superficial burn areas because these may cause a critical loss of body heat and could make the wound deeper. Applying petroleum jelly or other products is inappropriate because it seals in heat.

4. **d.** Using the Rule of Nines for an adult, the chest accounts for 9 percent, the abdomen accounts for 9 percent and the upper and lower back, 18 percent (each accounting for 9 percent inidividually); thus, the woman would be experiencing burns over 36 percent of her body.

5. **a.** Burns often expose sensitive nerve endings. Cover the burned area to keep out air and to help reduce pain. Use dry, sterile dressings and loosely bandage them into place. The bandage should not put pressure on the burn surface. Oil-based lubricants should not be used because they seal in heat and do not relieve pain. Antibiotic ointment may be applied to small, superficial burns if protocols permit.

SELF-ASSESSMENT

1. **d.** An injury to the soft tissue is called a wound. It can be open or closed and involve any of the skin layers, such as the epidermis, dermis or hypodermis, as well as the fatty tissue and muscle layers beneath the skin.

2. **a.** The simplest type of closed wound is a contusion. Laceration and puncture wounds are types of open wounds. A burn is a special type of soft tissue injury that may result in a closed or open wound, depending on the depth of the burn.

3. **c.** Ice is applied to a closed wound for about 20 minutes, after which time you would remove it for 20 minutes before applying the ice again. If 20 minutes cannot be tolerated, apply ice for periods of 10 minutes.

4. **b.** You should call for more advanced medical personnel if the patient complains of severe pain, the force that caused the injury seems great enough to cause serious damage, the patient cannot move the body part without pain, if the injured extremity is blue or extremely pale, or the patient shows signs and symptoms of shock. Swelling would be expected because blood and other fluids seep into the surrounding tissues.

5. **c.** Puncture wounds generally do not bleed profusely but are potentially more dangerous than other bleeding wounds because puncture wounds can become infected with microorganisms from the object as it passes through the tissues. Crush syndrome is a complication of crush injuries; it develops as the pressure is released and the tissues become reperfused with blood. Shock is less likely because puncture wounds generally do not bleed profusely. External hemorrhage would be less likely because the skin usually closes around the penetrating object; thus, external bleeding generally is not severe.

6. **b.** Your first action would be to control any bleeding by applying a sterile dressing over the wound and using direct pressure until the bleeding stops. Next, clean the wound with soap and water and, if possible, irrigate it with clean, warm running water or saline (or any source of clean water if clean running water is not available) for about 5 minutes to remove any dirt and debris. Once the bleeding has stopped, remove the dressing and apply antibiotic ointment.

7. **a.** Superficial burns involve only the top layer of skin and appear red and dry. Partial-thickness burns are red but also have blisters that may open and weep clear fluid. The burned skin may look mottled (blotchy). A full-thickness burn may look brown or black (charred) with the tissues underneath sometimes appearing white.

8. **b.** Using the Rule of Nines, the genital area accounts for 1 percent of the body surface area. The chest, back and each entire leg account for 18 percent; the head and each arm accounts for 9 percent.

9. **d.** Evidence of soot or burns around the mouth, nose or the rest of the face may be a sign that air passages or lungs have been burned, leading to possible airway closure. These findings do not necessarily suggest toxic inhalation, but should it occur, it could lead to respiratory arrest. Scarring would not be an immediate concern. Shock may occur, but finding soot around the mouth and nose would not indicate shock.

10. **a, b, c, e.** Patients should be referred to a burn unit if they have the following: partial- or full-thickness burns that cover more than 10 percent of the body surface (patients younger than 5 years or older than 60 years); partial- or full-thickness burns that cover more than 2 percent of the body surface among those in other age groups; partial- or full-thickness burns that involve the face, hands, feet, genitalia, perineum or major joints; full-thickness burns that cover more than 5 percent of the body surface in patients of any age; electrical burns, including injury caused by lightning; chemical burns; inhalation injury; and circumferential burns.

11. **c, e.** Full-thickness burns are painless, with no sensation to touch; are pearly white or charred; and also are dry and may appear leathery. Superficial partial-thickness burns are painful and reddened and blanch (turn white) when touched. Deep partial-thickness burns may or may not be painful or blanch when touched, but the hair usually is gone. Superficial burns have a painful, red area with no blisters that turns white when touched; often, the skin appears moist.

12. **c.** If an eye is burned by a chemical, flush the affected eye for at least 20 minutes or until more advanced medical personnel arrive. When flushing, you should flush the affected eye from the nose outward and downward to prevent washing the chemical into the unaffected eye. A brush is not used when flushing the eye but would be used to remove dry or powdered chemicals from the body.

13. **d.** When caring for a patient with electrical burns, scene safety is of utmost importance. First make sure that the electrical current is secured (de-energized) and is no longer passing through the patient. Then perform a primary assessment and care for any immediate life-threatening conditions. During the physical exam, look for two burn sites (entry and exit wounds). Cool any electrical burns with cold tap water as you would a thermal burn, until pain is relieved; then cover any burn injuries with a dry, sterile dressing and provide care to minimize shock.

REVIEW OF CONCEPTS AND TERMS

Matching

1. D; 2. B; 3. E; 4. C; 5. A; 6. G; 7. F

Fill-in-the Blank

1. peritoneum
2. Chest
3. blunt
4. asphyxia
5. impaled
6. acute

CASE STUDY

Scenario A

1. **b.** Although rib fracture, pneumothorax and flail chest are possible due to the MOI, the sound noted with each breath strongly indicates a sucking chest wound, which allows air to enter the chest through the wound.

2. **a.** Based on the patient's status, apply an occlusive dressing to the sucking chest wound because if this is not addressed, the patient's status will deteriorate quickly. Once this is completed, institute measures to control the bleeding, assess for signs and symptoms of shock and administer emergency oxygen, if available. Ventilations would be used if the patient's respiratory status continues to deteriorate and her respiratory rate drops or if she goes into respiratory arrest.

3. **c.** When an object is embedded or impaled, do not move or remove it unless it interferes with chest compressions; otherwise, you risk further damage. Rather, stabilize the object to prevent further damage by using bulky dressings or gauze around the object. Any clothing around the wound should be removed to allow the wound to be exposed.

Scenario B

1. **a, b, e.** The abdomen contains certain organs that are easily injured or tend to bleed profusely when injured. These include the liver, spleen and stomach. The lungs are more likely injured with trauma to the chest. The kidneys are located more toward the back of the abdomen, so they would be less likely to sustain injury in this instance.

2. **a.** Indications of a serious abdominal injury include complaints of severe pain; bruising; nausea and vomiting (possibly with blood); pale or ashen, cool, moist skin; weakness; thirst; and pain, tenderness or a tight swollen feeling in the abdomen.

3. **b.** Position the patient on his back with his knees flexed slightly to assist in relaxing the muscles of his abdomen. If moving the patient's legs causes pain or you suspect a spinal injury, then leave the legs straight. Positioning the patient on his side with his head elevated or sitting up would be inappropriate. The prone position would not be used because it would require the patient to lie on his abdomen.

4. **c.** When palpating the patient's abdomen, you would begin palpating it at the furthest point from the patient's pain and progress through all four quadrants. Beginning the palpation directly over the impact area or near or around the lower ribs could lead to increased pain and possible further injury to the underlying organs. The right lower ribs provide some protection to the liver; however, the liver is extremely delicate and can be injured easily. The left lower ribs provide some protection to the spleen. Like the liver, this organ can be easily injured. Beginning the palpation around the area of the navel would be inappropriate.

SELF-ASSESSMENT

1. **c.** Assessing and treating a patient with a genital injury requires a calm and professional approach since it can be embarrassing not only for the patient, but also for you. Using a sensitive approach to the patient's situation, such as clearing onlookers from the scene, supplying a drape for privacy and reassuring the patient, will help the process be less embarrassing. If possible, the patient should be treated by someone of the same gender.

2. **b.** Genital injuries, regardless of their location, typically are extremely painful. They can be open or closed wounds and the severity of bleeding varies. Injuries to the penis usually occur as a result of an accident or assault. Straddle injury, sexual assault and childbirth are the most common situations associated with female genital injuries.

3. **a.** The diaphragm, a large muscular partition, separates the thoracic (or chest) cavity from the abdominal cavity. The ribs are part of the chest cavity. The peritoneum is the thick membrane lining of the abdominal cavity. The sternum, or breastbone, is in the chest cavity.

4. **d.** Closed chest wounds generally are caused by blunt trauma. A fractured rib breaking through the skin, a knife wound or gunshot would result in an open chest wound.

5. **b.** Traumatic asphyxia can result from injuries that often are caused by a strong crushing mechanism or by situations in which patients have been pinned under a heavy object. A patient shot in the chest, one with broken ribs due to a fall and one with a sucking chest wound have the least risk for developing traumatic asphyxia.

6. **b, d, e.** Signs and symptoms of traumatic asphyxia include distended neck veins; subconjunctival hemorrhage; bluish discoloration of the head, tongue, lips, neck and shoulders; black eyes; and a rounded, moon-like facial appearance.

7. **c.** The patient usually will attempt to ease the pain by leaning toward the side of the fracture and pressing a hand or arm over the injured area, thereby creating an anatomical splint.

8. **a.** The first priority when caring for a patient with broken ribs is to ensure adequate breathing. A patient with fractured ribs often has shallow breathing because normal or deep breathing is painful. Adequate breathing, not the airway, is the problem with fractured ribs. Any bleeding associated with fractured ribs would most likely be internal. Covering the wound would be appropriate if the patient was experiencing an open or sucking chest wound.

9. **a.** Patients with tension pneumothorax typically are in respiratory distress with reduced breath sounds or a complete absence of breath sounds. The injured side of the chest (in this case, the right side) produces abnormal breath sounds during percussion. Because the trachea is shifted away from the side of the injury and the space between the lungs, contents are shifted away from the affected side, and decreased return of blood to the heart results. The patient will show signs of unstable blood pressure, such as abnormally low blood pressure (hypotension), which can quickly develop into complete cardiovascular collapse.

10. **b.** When applying an occlusive dressing, use a dressing that does not allow air to pass through. Secure it in place on all sides except for one, which should remain loose to prevent air from entering the wound during inhalation but allow air to exit during exhalation. Sterile gauze would allow air to enter the wound and should not be used. If appropriate material is not available, you could use a folded cloth or, as a last resort, your gloved hand to seal the wound.

11. **c.** The intestine is an abdominal organ. Protrusion of an abdominal organ through a wound is called evisceration. Flail chest is a serious chest injury in which multiple rib fractures result in a loose section of the ribs that does not move normally with the rest of the chest during breathing. A tension pneumothorax is a life-threatening injury in which the lung completely collapses and air is trapped in the pleural space. An avulsion is an injury in which a portion of the skin and sometimes other soft tissue is partially or completely torn away.

12. **b.** A blow to the scrotal area can rupture the scrotum and cause pooling of blood, which is extremely painful. First, apply an ice pack to the area to reduce swelling and pain. If the area is avulsed, wrap the avulsed skin in a sterile dressing and transport it with the patient. With an avulsion, the scrotum should be dressed with gauze that is sterilized and moistened with saline and then applied with pressure to control bleeding. A warm compress would not be used because it would increase the swelling and pain.

REVIEW OF CONCEPTS AND TERMS

Crossword Puzzle

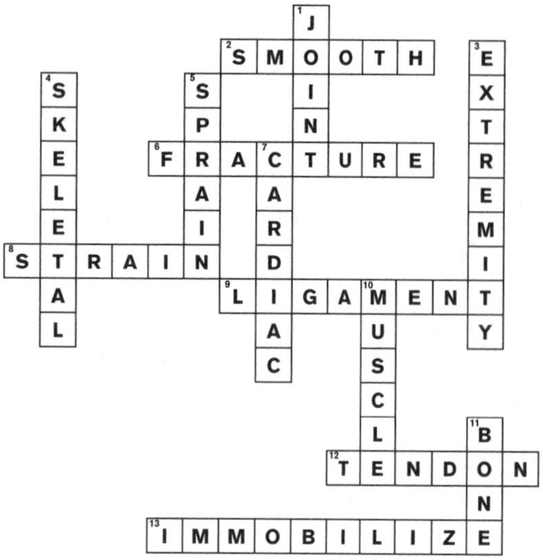

Across / Down answers (filled grid):

- SMOOTH
- FRACTURE
- STRAIN
- LIGAMENT
- TENDON
- IMMOBILIZE
- SKELETAL
- EXTREMITY
- JOINT
- SPRAIN
- CARTILAGE
- MUSCLE
- BONE

Short Answer

1. The four basic types of injuries are fractures, dislocations, strains and sprains.
2. The three basic MOIs are direct force, which causes injury at the point of impact; indirect force, which transmits energy through the body and causes injury at some distance from the original point of impact; and twisting force, or rotating force, which causes injury when one part of the body remains still while the rest of the body is twisted or turned away from it.
3. Immobilizing an injury lessens pain, prevents further damage to soft tissues, reduces the risk of serious bleeding, reduces the possibility of loss of circulation to the injured part and prevents closed injuries from becoming open injuries.
4. An anatomic splint is a splint formed by supporting an injured part of the body with an uninjured, neighboring body part.
5. The four general care measures are *rest, immobilization, cold* and *elevation* (RICE).

CASE STUDY

Scenario A

1. **a.** With any musculoskeletal injury, size-up the scene and then perform a primary assessment. Then control bleeding if necessary and if a spinal injury is suspected, stabilize the head, neck and spine and keep the patient flat. Next, clean and bandage any open wounds before splinting.
2. **a.** Before applying a splint, you need to clean and bandage the laceration. Avoid any movement to the arm, including checking for range of motion or straightening the arm. Ice would be applied for swelling, but only after cleaning and bandaging the laceration. Since there is a laceration, which could indicate an open fracture, the ice would be applied around the site.
3. **b.** The ulna and radius are the two bones that comprise the forearm. The humerus is the bone of the upper arm. The femur is the thigh bone. The tibia is one of the bones in the lower leg.
4. **d.** A rigid splint extending from the elbow to the fingertips should be applied first. A sling and binder then can be applied to support the arm against the chest. Since there is an open wound, using a vacuum splint or circumferential air splint would be inappropriate. A traction splint would be used for a fractured femur.
5. **a, b, d.** Injuries to the femur can be serious because of the risk of bleeding, which may be internal and not noticed. A broken femur causes a great deal of pain and significant swelling. The deformity of the thigh usually is quite noticeable, and the muscle often contracts (shortens) with this type of break. The leg also may be turned inward or outward.
6. **a.** After applying a splint, you would assess the patient's distal pulses, skin temperature, mobility and sensation.

Scenario B

1. **b.** Patients with a previous sprain may return to their normal activities before the injury has completely healed, increasing the risk for reinjury of the joint that was sprained. Subsequently, the joint becomes less stable and the partially healed, less-stable joint will be much more susceptible to reinjury. A previous history of a sprain does not increase the risk for fracture or bleeding. Less force would be necessary for reinjury.
2. **a.** Help the patient find a comfortable position, elevate the limb above heart level and apply ice to the area by placing a thin layer of gauze or cloth between the cold source and the skin. The injury—whether a break or sprain—should be splinted by immobilizing the entire foot and ankle. A circumferential air splint is a good

choice, but a pillow or thick blanket wrapped around the foot and ankle and secured in place also will work.

SELF-ASSESSMENT

1. **c.** Although most isolated fractures are not considered critical or life threatening, if the femur or pelvis is fractured, the patient is at serious risk of excessive blood loss, shock and death. These two bones contain many blood vessels and injury to either bone tends to cause heavy bleeding.

2. **d.** While closed fractures are more common, open fractures are more dangerous because they carry a risk of infection and severe bleeding. Dislocation and sprains may be associated with a fracture, but these pose less risk. The risk for respiratory arrest is low.

3. **d.** Some joints, such as the shoulder and fingers, are more prone to dislocation because they are relatively exposed and not as well protected by ligaments. Other joints, such as the elbow, knee and ankle, are less likely to become dislocated.

4. **b.** Soft splints include folded blankets, towels and pillows. Rigid splints can be created from cardboard boxes, rolled-up magazines, an athlete's shin guards or other items available at the scene.

5. **c.** To apply a binder, wrap the cloth around the patient and the injured part securing it against the body. Place a triangular bandage under the injured part and over the uninjured area to form a sling. Tie the ends of a sling at the side of the neck. A circumferential air splint is positioned around the injured area and then filled with air.

6. **b.** The patient's statement about having no feeling in the hand suggests that circulation to that area is compromised, requiring immediate action. Some pain is expected, but if the patient is complaining of severe pain or pain out of proportion to the visible injury, there is cause for concern. If a bone has fractured, the patient may report hearing or feeling the bone snap or break. A feeling of warmth indicates adequate circulation.

7. **b.** For a suspected elbow fracture, do not attempt to straighten or bend the elbow or change its position. Splint it with a sling and binder in the position in which you found it.

8. **c, d, e.** You would summon more advanced medical personnel if you suspect a fracture to an area other than a digit; if the injury involves severe bleeding, impairs walking or breathing, or involves the head, neck or spine; or if you see or suspect multiple injuries.

9. **d.** When splinting the femur, the distal end of each splint should extend past the bottom of the patient's foot to ensure adequate immobilization.

10. **a.** Elevating the injured part slows the flow of blood, helping to reduce swelling. It has no effect on bone alignment or healing. Pain may be reduced as swelling is controlled, but this is not the primary purpose for elevating the arm.

11. **b.** Crepitus is a grating sound or feeling when an attempt is made to move a fractured bone and is caused by the two pieces of bone rubbing against each other. Angulation refers to an abnormal alignment or angle of an injured limb when it is compared with an uninjured limb. Deformity refers to a change in the shape of a limb when an injured limb is compared with an uninjured limb. Cravat is a folded triangular bandage used to hold other splints in place.

12. **c.** Before applying any splint, obtain consent to treat the patient. Next, support the injured body part above and below the site of the injury, check for circulation and sensation beyond the injured area and then apply the splint. Immobilize the wrist and elbow when applying a rigid splint.

13. **b.** The final step when applying a sling and binder is to recheck for circulation and sensation. Before this step, you would place the triangular bandage under the injured arm and over the uninjured shoulder to form the sling, tie the ends of the sling at the side of the neck and then bind the injured body part to the chest with a folded triangular bandage.

14. **c.** When applying a splint, remove any clothing around the injured site; apply sterile dressings to open wounds, bandaging with minimal pressure; and pad the splints for comfort and allow the splint to conform to the shape of the injured body part. Make sure that you never push protruding bones below the skin.

15. **a, b, c.** A sling and binder would be used to splint the collarbone, shoulder or elbow. A rigid splint would be used to splint a forearm. A pelvic wrap is used to splint the pelvis.

SELF-ASSESSMENT: ENRICHMENT

Agricultural and Industrial Emergencies

1. **a.** When entering a confined space, always assume that it is hazardous and make sure that you have the appropriate equipment and PPE. Air testing must be done by a properly trained individual because one's senses should never be trusted. Many toxic gases and vapors cannot be

seen or smelled. An attendant must be present immediately outside of the space.

2. **b.** Before extricating a patient, it is crucial to first stabilize the equipment and turn it off. Digging a trench would be appropriate for someone trapped by a tractor. Ensuring ready access to an SCBA would be appropriate for rescuing a patient in a silo or manure storage. The reverse feature never should be used.

3. **a, b, c, d.** Required Level B equipment would include an SCBA, hooded chemical-resistant clothing, special gloves, boots with covers and a hard hat.

4. **d.** It is most important to size-up the scene and to wait to enter until it has been secured. Identifying the hazard, determining the number of victims and calling in specialized teams also are appropriate measures but not as important as sizing up the scene.

Chapter 23: Injuries to the Head, Neck and Spine

REVIEW OF CONCEPTS AND TERMS

Fill-in-the-Blank

1. skull
2. concussion
3. movement, align
4. carotid
5. *cervical collar* (C-collar)
6. spinal column
7. spinal cord

Short Answer

1. The head is easily injured because it lacks the padding of muscle and fat that are found in other areas of the body.
2. In a closed head injury, the brain is struck against the skull or receives a blow from a blunt object with the skull remaining intact. In an open head injury, there is a break in the skull or an object penetrates the skull, causing direct damage to the skull.
3. A closed head injury may be more challenging to detect because there may not be any visible damage to the skull. Although, in some cases, swelling or a depression is evident.
4. "Raccoon eyes" refers to a characteristic visible bruising around the eyes that may be seen with a head or brain injury.
5. Manual stabilization is a technique used to achieve spinal motion restriction by manually supporting the patient's head and neck in the position found without the use of any equipment.
6. Situations that may require you to remove a helmet include those in which you cannot access or assess the patient's airway and breathing, the airway is impeded and cannot be opened with the helmet on, the patient is in cardiac arrest or you cannot immobilize the spine.
7. The most common cause of death in patients with head injuries is a lack of oxygen to the brain.

CASE STUDY

Scenario A

1. **d.** You have already sized-up the scene and performed a primary assessment based on the information provided in the scenario. The patient is breathing, therefore his airway is open. Your initial action would be to stabilize his head and neck to prevent further injury.
2. **b.** Bleeding from the mouth is a highly specific sign and suggests a possible skull fracture. The abrasion on his forehead indicates an injury to the patient's face. The patient's lack of responsiveness is a general finding that could indicate any number of problems. The bystander's statement that the patient hit his head would support your suspicion, but hitting one's head is not the most likely indicator.
3. **c, d, e.** Signs and symptoms of a brain injury include high blood pressure and slowed pulse; clear fluid draining from the ears, mouth or nose; bruising behind the ears (Battle's sign); and paralysis or droopiness (often on one side of the body) or rigidity of the limbs.
4. **a.** When stabilizing the patient's head and neck, maintain the head and neck in the position found; otherwise, further injury could occur. When aligning the head and neck to place a C-collar, place your hands on each side of the patient's head and gently position it in line with the body and support it in that position. More advanced medical personnel will apply a C-collar. A patient is secured to a backboard before moving him.
5. **b.** If fluid is leaking from the ears, you should cover the area loosely with a sterile gauze dressing. Suction should not be applied to remove the fluid, nor should the ear canal be blocked or plugged with a dressing. Rather, it should be allowed to drain onto the loose sterile dressing. The patient's head should not be elevated.

Instead, maintain manual stabilization of the patient's head and neck.

Scenario B

1. **a.** Your first priority is to perform a primary assessment. If there is a problem, you can intervene immediately. Once the primary assessment is completed, you can gather additional information about what happened and take the patient's vital signs. Allow the patient to sit up only after determining that there is no injury to the head, neck or spine.

2. **b, c, d.** Signs and symptoms of a concussion include short-term confusion, headache, repeated questioning about what happened, temporary memory loss (especially for periods immediately before and after the injury), brief loss of consciousness, nausea and vomiting, speech problems and blurred vision or light sensitivity. Asymmetrical facial movements and unequal pupil size would reflect a head and brain injury.

3. **b.** Because the patient has sustained a head injury and is lethargic, you need to stabilize his head and neck with the helmet in place. Remove the helmet only if you cannot access the patient's airway and breathing, the airway is impeded and cannot be opened with the helmet on, the patient is in cardiac arrest or you cannot immobilize the spine. Placing the patient in a recovery position would be appropriate only if you did not suspect a head, neck or spinal injury. Do not elevate the patient's legs.

SELF-ASSESSMENT

1. **a.** Patients who fall from a height greater than standing height are at risk for head, neck or spinal injuries; however, a fall from 3 feet would be considered low risk for such injuries. Diving into shallow water, impacting the dashboard in a motor-vehicle collision, a motorized cycle or bicycle collision or slipping off of a two-story platform are situations that would increase a patient's risk for head, neck or spinal injuries.

2. **c.** When controlling bleeding from an open head wound, do not put direct pressure on the wound if you feel a depression, spongy area or bone fragments. Place a sterile dressing or clean cloth over the wound and gently press against the wound and the area around the wound with your hand. Elevate the head and shoulders if spinal injury is not suspected, and use a roller bandage to cover the dressing completely.

3. **d.** When providing care to a patient with a foreign object in the eye, tell the patient not to rub the eye but rather to blink several times. If the object then becomes visible on the lower eyelid, try to remove it using the corner of a sterile gauze pad, being careful never to touch the eyeball or put pressure on the eyeball. Next, gently flush the eye with sterile saline or water. If the object becomes visible on the upper eyelid, gently roll the upper eyelid back over a cotton swab and attempt to remove it with the corner of a sterile gauze pad, again being careful not to touch the eyeball.

4. **b.** If chemicals have been in contact with the patient's eyes, irrigate the eyes with clean water for at least 20 minutes.

5. **c.** If you feel any resistance when attempting to align the head and neck with the spine, stop the movement and gently maintain stabilization of the head and neck in the position in which you found them. Further movement would increase the risk of further injury. A C-collar typically is applied by more advanced medical personnel. Stabilization is necessary, even with resistance.

6. **d.** When providing care to a patient with an object embedded in the eye, do not attempt to remove the object but rather stabilize it by encircling the eye with gauze or a soft sterile cloth, being sure to avoid applying any pressure on top of the area. Styrofoam® materials are not used to shield the area because small particles can break off and get into the eye.

7. **a.** Evidence of fluid draining from the ear suggests cerebrospinal fluid leakage, indicating a skull fracture. Although a skull fracture may be associated with a scalp injury, typically you will see bleeding from the scalp ranging from minor to severe. A concussion is indicated by a temporary loss of consciousness along with confusion, headache, temporary memory loss, nausea and vomiting, speech problems and blurred vision or light sensitivity. A penetrating skull injury would result in a visible wound.

8. **b.** Bruising behind the ears is referred to as Battle's sign. Raccoon eyes refers to visible bruising around the eyes. A concussion is a temporary loss of brain function due to a blow to the head. A nosebleed is bleeding from the nose, usually from a blow from a blunt object.

9. **c.** When a tooth has been knocked out, handle the tooth by the crown, rinse it under running

water and place it in a glass of milk or, if milk is not available, place the tooth in clean water or moistened sterile gauze. If the patient is conscious and able to cooperate, rinse out the mouth with cold tap water if available. Control the bleeding by placing a rolled sterile dressing into the space left by the missing tooth. Have the patient gently bite down to maintain pressure. Ice is inappropriate. Do not attempt to reimplant the tooth. Contact a dentist or bring the tooth and the patient to an emergency care center as soon as possible.

10. **d.** Injuries to the neck or spine can damage both bone and soft tissue, including the spinal cord. It is difficult to determine the extent of damage in neck or spinal injuries, so you must always care for these types of injuries as if they are serious. The patient's ability to walk does not necessarily rule out the possibility of an injury to the bone, spine or spinal cord.

11. **b.** The priority when providing care to a patient with a suspected head injury is to establish manual stabilization to prevent further injury before doing anything else. Once this is accomplished, you then would perform a primary assessment while maintaining stabilization, maintain an open airway and control any bleeding. You also should try to engage the patient in conversation to calm the patient and prevent loss of consciousness.

12. **c, e, d, a, b.** When performing manual stabilization, call for more advanced medical personnel first and then place your hands on both sides of the patient's head. Next, gently position the patient's head in line with the body and support it in that position. Then maintain an open airway, control any external bleeding and keep the patient from getting chilled or overheated.

SELF-ASSESSMENT: ENRICHMENT

Removing Helmets and Other Equipment

1. **b.** When removing a non-athletic helmet, such as a motorcycle helmet, two rescuers need to be present.

2. **c.** Removal of a football helmet alone without removal of the athlete's shoulder pads increases the risk of cervical movement and further spinal injury. Shoulder pads would not interfere with completing a primary assessment, and ventilations could be performed even with the shoulder pads in place. Although it would be important to look for additional injuries, such as a chest injury, this would not be a reason to remove the shoulder pads.

3. **d.** To remove an athletic helmet, one responder would provide cervical stabilization while a second responder cuts away the chin strap, shoulder pad straps and jersey. This is followed by removing the internal cheek pads and deflating the helmet's air bladder system. Next, the athlete is lifted and the helmet is slid off. Once the helmet is off, the shoulder pads are immediately removed by spreading apart the front panels and pulling them around the head.

Cervical Collars and Backboarding

1. **a, c, d.** To immobilize a patient's body, you would use a backboard, straps and head immobilizer. A C-collar limits movement of the head and neck. Splints are used to immobilize a specific injured body part.

2. **c.** If the patient's head does not appear to be resting in line with the body, you may need to use some padding, such as a small folded towel, to support the head. Normally, approximately 1 inch of padding is all that is needed to keep the head in line with the body and provide comfort for the patient. Do not elevate the head more than about an inch. Once the head is resting in line with the body, a rolled blanket around the patient's head is used if a commercial head immobilizer is not available.. Crisscrossing straps is commonly used to secure the chest when a patient is placed on a backboard.

Chapter 24: Childbirth

REVIEW OF CONCEPTS AND TERMS

Matching

1. C; 2. E; 3. B; 4. G; 5. F; 6. H; 7.D; 8. A

Fill-in-the-Blank

1. cervix
2. placenta
3. amniotic fluid
4. 40
5. first
6. stabilization; one
7. Braxton Hicks
8. APGAR

CASE STUDY

Scenario A

1. **b.** True labor contractions get closer together, increase in how long they last, feel stronger as time goes on and occur at regular intervals.
2. **c.** For first-time mothers, labor typically lasts between 12 and 24 hours. Subsequent deliveries usually require less time.
3. **a.** The woman is experiencing contractions that are 5 minutes apart and lasting about 30 seconds and her water has broken. There is no evidence of crowning. Therefore, the woman is most likely in the first stage of labor, which begins with the first contraction and ends with the cervix being fully dilated. The second stage of labor begins when the cervix is completely dilated as the baby moves through the birth canal. During this stage, the mother will report feelings of enormous pressure and contractions that are more frequent and may last between 45 to 90 seconds. The third stage of labor begins with emergence of the baby's body and includes separation and delivery of the placenta. The fourth stage of labor involves the initial recovery and stabilization of the mother after childbirth.

Scenario B

1. **b.** The baby is crowning; therefore, the woman is nearing the end of the second stage of labor (expulsion). The first stage of labor begins with the first contraction until the cervix is fully dilated. The third stage of labor begins with the baby's

body emerging from the vaginal opening. The fourth stage of labor involves the initial recovery and stabilization of the mother after childbirth.

2. **b.** A prolapsed umbilical cord occurs when a loop of the umbilical cord protrudes from the vaginal opening while the baby still is in the birth canal. A breech birth is one in which the baby is delivered feet- or buttocks-first. A premature birth is one in which a baby is born before the end of 37 weeks of pregnancy. Meconium aspiration involves the baby's inhalation of meconium-stained amniotic fluid (an indication that the baby experienced a period of oxygen deprivation), which can result in complications such as a blocked airway or respiratory distress, pneumonia and infection.

3. **a.** Prompt intervention is necessary because a prolapsed cord can threaten a baby's life. As the baby moves through the birth canal, the cord will be compressed against the unborn child and the birth canal, cutting off blood flow. Without this blood flow, the baby will die from lack of oxygen within a few minutes. Aspiration leading to possible pneumonia occurs with meconium aspiration. A history of previous excess bleeding after delivery, multiple births, or a prolonged or abnormal labor would increase the woman's risk for hemorrhage leading to shock. Eclampsia occurs during pregnancy and is associated with elevated blood pressure, edema and excess protein in the urine. It is unrelated to a prolapsed cord.

4. **b.** With a prolapsed cord, you would have the woman assume a knee-chest position to help take the pressure off the cord. Massaging the lower abdomen would be appropriate if the woman was experiencing hemorrhage. Avoiding any pulling on or touching of the baby would be appropriate if the baby was in a limb presentation. Forming a "V" with a gloved index and middle finger inserted into the vagina would be appropriate to help the baby breathe with a breech birth.

SELF-ASSESSMENT

1. **b, c, d, e.** A breech birth is one in which the baby is delivered feet- or buttocks-first. It also may be an incomplete breech when the baby's foot or feet, arm or shoulder appear first. The head typically is the part of the baby delivered first with a normal delivery.

2. **a.** Implantation occurs 6 to 7 days after conception when the fertilized egg attaches to the

lining of the uterus. From there, an embryo develops. After about 8 weeks, the embryo is called a fetus. Quickening, or movement of the fetus, occurs during the second trimester.

3. **c.** During the third trimester, the mother gains the most weight as the fetus grows most rapidly. Morning sickness and placental development occur during the first trimester. Fetal movement typically is felt during the second trimester.

4. **b.** After delivery of the baby, the placenta usually separates from the wall of the uterus and exits from the birth canal, which normally occurs within 30 minutes after the delivery of the baby.

5. **c.** You can help the expectant mother cope with the discomfort and pain of labor by staying calm, firm and confident and by offering encouragement. Doing so can help reduce her fear and apprehension which, in turn, will aid in reducing her pain and discomfort. Telling the woman that she has to learn to endure the discomfort is not supportive and will only add to her fear and apprehension. You should begin by reassuring her that you are there to help. Explain what to expect as labor progresses. Suggest specific physical activities that she can do to relax, such as regulating her breathing. Ask her to breathe slowly and deeply in through the nose and out through the mouth. Ask her to focus on one object in the room while regulating her breathing.

6. **a.** Once crowning takes place, you should place a hand on the top of the baby's head and apply light pressure to allow the head to emerge slowly, not forcefully. At this point, you should tell the expectant mother to stop pushing and to concentrate on her breathing techniques. Next, check to see if the umbilical cord is looped around the baby's neck. If it is, gently slip it over the baby's head. If you cannot slip it over the head, slip it over the baby's shoulders as they emerge. The baby can slide through the loop. You then guide one shoulder out at a time without pulling on the baby.

7. **b.** When using the APGAR scoring system, the baby is assigned a number from 0 to 2 for each part of the assessment. The highest score given to each area therefore would be 2.

8. **d.** If a newborn has not made any sounds, you would stimulate a cry reflex by flicking your fingers on the soles of the feet or gently rubbing the newborn's back. Slapping the newborn's back and placing the newborn with the head lower than his or her chest would not be effective in stimulating the newborn. Suctioning the mouth and nose would help to remove secretions but would not necessarily stimulate the newborn.

9. **b.** Resuscitation of a newborn begins immediately if respirations fall to less than 30 respirations per minute or the newborn is gasping or not breathing, if the pulse is less than 100 bpm or if cyanosis (bluish skin) around the chest and abdomen persists after administering emergency oxygen.

10. **a.** About 85 percent of miscarriages or spontaneous abortions occur during the first 12 weeks of pregnancy. A miscarriage or spontaneous abortion refers to the loss of a fetus due to natural causes before about 20 weeks of pregnancy. A stillbirth or fetal death is the term for the death of a baby before delivery but after 20 weeks gestation.

11. **d.** With an ectopic pregnancy, the fertilized egg most commonly implants in one of the fallopian tubes; less commonly, it implants in the abdomen, ovary or cervix.

12. **b.** Delivery is considered imminent when the mother reports a strong urge to push; contractions are intense, occurring every 2 minutes or less and lasting 60 to 90 seconds; the woman's abdomen is very tight and hard; the mother reports a feeling of the infant's head moving down the birth canal or has a sensation like an urge to defecate; and crowning occurs. A sudden gush of fluid from the vagina, indicating that the amniotic sac has ruptured, often signals the onset of labor.

13. **d.** A newborn with an APGAR score between 1 and 3 points is severely depressed and requires emergency oxygen with BVM ventilations and CPR. A score of 4 to 6 indicates a moderately depressed newborn who requires stimulation and oxygen. A score of 7 to 10 indicates an active, vigorous newborn that is ready to receive routine care.

14. **a.** When positioning the newborn, place the newborn on his or her side with the head slightly lower than the trunk to allow secretions to drain. Newborns lose heat quickly, so it is important to dry them thoroughly and wrap them in a clean, warm towel or blanket. The nasal passages and mouth need to be clear; therefore, you would clear or suction the mouth before the nose until the airway is clear.

15. **c.** The most common complication of childbirth is persistent vaginal bleeding, known as postpartum hemorrhage. Other, less common complications include prolapsed umbilical cord, breech birth and premature birth.

SELF-ASSESSMENT: ENRICHMENT

More Complications During Pregnancy and Delivery

1. **c.** The initial and only symptom of placenta previa is painless vaginal bleeding. Abdominal pain, abdominal rigidity and uterine tenderness are associated with abruptio placenta.

2. **a.** The risk for a ruptured uterus is increased in women who have had prior cesarean sections. Advanced maternal age also is a risk factor. Risk is reduced in women with first-time pregnancies and those who have previously delivered vaginally.

3. **b.** If the fetal head emerges from the vagina and then retracts, it is considered a symptom of shoulder dystocia. This often is called the "turtle sign." Shoulder dystocia has no other recognized symptoms.

Chapter 25: Pediatrics

REVIEW OF CONCEPTS AND TERMS

Matching

1. E; 2. D; 3. C; 4. B; 5. A

Short Answer

1. The three general age groups are infant (anyone who appears to be younger than 1 year of age), child (anyone who appears to be between the ages of 1 year and about 12 years) and adult (anyone 12 years of age and older).

2. Child development is divided into five groups: infants (birth to 1 year), toddlers (1 to 3 years), preschoolers (3 to 5 years), school-age children (6 to 12 years) and adolescents (13 to 18 years).

3. The three components of the Pediatric Assessment Triangle are appearance, breathing and skin (circulation).

4. A respiratory emergency usually begins with respiratory distress, followed by respiratory failure, which then is followed by respiratory arrest if emergency interventions are not attempted or are not successful.

5. Fever is the most common cause of seizures in children. Other causes include head trauma, epilepsy or other seizure disorders, low blood glucose, poisoning, hypoxia (too low a level of oxygen), and serious infections, such as meningitis or encephalitis.

6. Child neglect is the most frequently reported type of abuse in which a parent or guardian fails to provide the necessary, age-appropriate care to a child. It involves insufficient attention given, or a lack of respect shown to a child who has a claim to that attention.

CASE STUDY

Scenario A

1. **b.** A 20-month-old child is considered a toddler. An infant is a child up to 1 year of age. A toddler is between the ages of 1 and 3 years and a preschooler is a child between the ages of 3 and 5 years. A school-age child is between 6 and 12 years of age.

2. **d.** When performing a primary assessment of the child, you would use the Pediatric Assessment Triangle and evaluate the child's appearance, breathing and skin. Vital signs would be done later.

3. **b.** Toddlers may be fearful of strangers and may not be cooperative when dealing with an unknown person. Therefore, it would be important for you to speak calmly and softly to the child while maintaining eye contact. In addition, you should try to have only one individual deal with the child to reduce his anxiety of being handled by multiple strangers. Since the child is visibly upset, it would be more appropriate to perform the exam in a toe-to-head fashion to minimize the child's anxiety and allow the child to get used to you rather than have you in his face from the start. Delaying the exam would be inappropriate because you need to gather as much information as possible about the child's condition.

Scenario B

1. **c.** The area of greatest concern is the child's skin (circulation) because a piece of the fence has cut through the child's pant leg, possibly cutting the child's skin and increasing his risk for bleeding. The child is crying and talking to his parents,

indicating that he is alert, has an open airway and is breathing.

2. **b.** The evidence of bleeding on the pant leg and blood on the ground in conjunction with the physical trauma and child's age places the child at high risk for shock. In small children, the loss of blood may be much more significant than in adolescents and adults, adding to the increased risk of shock and the speed at which it may develop. The child's airway is open and there is no evidence to suggest that an obstruction may occur. Although infection could occur, it would not be the priority at this time. There is no information about the child having a history of seizures, so this would be of least concern at the moment.

3. **b, c, d.** Signs and symptoms suggesting a problem requiring immediate intervention include increasing lethargy; cool, clammy skin; and rapid breathing. All of these would suggest that shock is developing. A strong, palpable pulse would be a normal finding. Increased crying has numerous causes, such as increased pain, fear or anxiety.

SELF-ASSESSMENT

1. **c.** Preschoolers often feel that bad things are caused by their thoughts and behaviors. They have difficulty understanding complex sentences that contain more than one idea, and their fears may seem out of proportion to the events. School-age children are more likely to cooperate with strangers.

2. **a.** Primary assessments on a conscious child should be done unobtrusively, so that the child has time to get used to you and feel less threatened. Try to carry out as many of the components of the initial evaluation by careful observation, without touching the child or infant. Approach the parents or caregivers, if possible, as the child will see you communicating with them and subsequently may feel more comfortable with your exam and treatment. If the child is upset, perform the assessment in a toe-to-head fashion, which allows the patient to get used to you rather than have you in their face from the start.

3. **b.** The Pediatric Assessment Triangle is a quick initial assessment of a child that takes between 15 and 30 seconds and provides a picture of the severity of the child's or infant's injury or illness. This is done during the scene size-up and before assessing breathing and pulse. It is the primary assessment that is completed before any other assessment, including the SAMPLE history and physical exam.

4. **d.** Although vital sign assessment can provide valuable information about a child's condition, it would not be an appropriate method to assess a child's LOC. The AVPU scale, pupil assessment and evidence of spontaneous movement are appropriate methods to evaluate a child's LOC.

5. **d.** For AED use, a patient who is between the ages of 1 and 8 or who weighs less than 55 pounds is considered a child.

6. **a, b, c.** Indicators of a partial airway obstruction in a child include alertness, drooling, frequent coughing, retractions and abnormal, high-pitched musical sounds. Loss of consciousness and cyanosis suggest a complete airway obstruction.

7. **b.** The epiglottitis is much higher in children and infants than it is in adults. Children and infants have proportionately larger tongues than do adults, they breathe at a rate two to three times faster and their breathing is shallower.

8. **b.** For the child in shock, cover him or her with a light blanket to help maintain body temperature. In addition, position the child flat on the back unless there is a risk of choking, in which you would place the patient in a recovery position. You also need to monitor the child closely for any changes in status. Ventilations are appropriate if the child is not breathing adequately or stops breathing. Back blows and chest thrusts are appropriate if the child has a foreign body obstructing the airway.

9. **c.** In a normal reaction, the pupil constricts in response to the light and then dilates again after the light is removed.

10. **c.** The child's trachea is not as long as an adult's, so any attempt to open the airway by tilting the child's head too far back will result in blocking the airway. The tongue in children is larger in relation to the space in the mouth than it is in adults, increasing the risk of the tongue blocking the trachea. Children's airways are smaller, resulting in more objects posing a choking hazard. However, this would have no effect on how far back to tilt a child's head to open the airway. Young children and infants breathe through their nose, but this would not affect maneuvers to open the airway.

11. **b.** A child with epiglottitis can move from respiratory distress to respiratory failure very quickly without emergency care. With epiglottitis, do not examine the throat using a tongue

depressor or place anything in the child's throat, as these can trigger a complete airway blockage. Additionally, keeping the child as calm as possible is vital. Children often assume the tripod position to ease breathing. This should be maintained if it is helpful to the child. You also should continue to monitor the child for additional signs associated with epiglottitis, such as drooling, difficulty swallowing, voice changes and fever.

12. **d.** Febrile seizures occur with rapidly rising or excessively high fever, higher than 103°F. Thus, a report of a temperature of 103.8°F would support that the child had a febrile seizure.

13. **a, c, d.** Although fever is the most common cause of seizures in children, other causes include head trauma, epilepsy or other seizure disorders, low blood glucose, poisoning, hypoxia and serious infections, such as meningitis or encephalitis. The common cold and respiratory distress are not associated with the development of seizures.

14. **a.** In a young child, even a minor infection can result in a rather high fever, which often is defined as a temperature higher than 103°F. If a fever is present, call for more advanced medical help at

once. Your care for a child with a high fever is to gently cool the child. Never rush cooling down a child. If the fever was caused by a febrile seizure, rapid cooling could bring on another seizure. Parents or caregivers often heavily dress children with fevers. If this is the case, remove the excess clothing or blankets and sponge the child with lukewarm water. Do *not* use an ice water bath or rubbing alcohol to cool down the body. Both of these are dangerous.

15. **c.** When caring for a child who may have been abused, your first priority is to care for the child's injuries or illness. You should not confront the parents or caregivers because this could put you and the child at risk. An abused child may be frightened, hysterical or withdrawn, often unwilling to talk about the incident in an attempt to protect the abuser or for self-protection. You should explain your concerns to the responding police officers and report your suspicions to a community or state agency. It is not your responsibility to remove the child from the abusive situation.

Chapter 26: Geriatrics and Special Needs Patients

REVIEW OF CONCEPTS AND TERMS

Matching

1. C; 2. E; 3. A; 4. B; 5. F; 6. D

Fill-in-the-Blank

1. service
2. decreased
3. Cognitive
4. Down syndrome
5. conductive
6. catastrophic reaction

CASE STUDY

Scenario A

1. **c.** The patient is most likely exhibiting a catastrophic reaction as evidenced by his screaming, shouting and throwing things. His behavior does not indicate hallucinations or the belief that things are not true, nor is he demonstrating depression (sadness or lack of

desire or interest). Sundowning typically involves restlessness, crying, pushing others away, gritting the teeth or being reluctant to enter a room or a brightly lit area.

2. **b.** You need to reassure the patient that you are not going to cause him any harm and that you will not allow him to hurt anyone. Telling the patient to stop screaming or threatening to call the police are not reassuring; in fact, they are threatening and may agitate the patient further. Asking the patient "why" is inappropriate because the patient does not understand why due to his cognitive impairment.

3. **b.** When assessing this patient, speak slowly, clearly and calmly and allow time to ensure that the patient understands what you are saying. You also should speak to the patient at his eye level and turn on the lights to make it easier for you to see the patient. Although the wife can provide valuable information, you should not focus solely on her. Involve the patient and be sure to clearly explain what you are doing.

4. **a, b, d.** Patients with Alzheimer's disease may demonstrate some common patterns, such as pacing and wandering, rummaging and hoarding,

speaking nonsense and sundowning. Abuse and intellectual impairment are not typically associated with Alzheimer's disease.

Scenario B

1. **c.** When a person is hard of hearing, you should identify yourself and speak slowly and clearly but not shout. You should position yourself so that the patient can hear you better by facing him. You also can try speaking directly into the patient's ear. Although you may need to repeat questions, repeating the same question several times may lead to frustration on everyone's part.

2. **d.** The term, "hard of hearing" is used to describe a person who has a less severe hearing loss and still is able to rely on his or her hearing for communication. Deafness describes someone who is unable to hear well enough to rely on hearing as a means of communication. There are two types: conductive, which occurs when there is a problem with the outer or middle ear, and sensorineural, which is due to a problem with the inner ear and possibly the nerve that goes from the ear to the brain.

SELF-ASSESSMENT

1. **a.** Normal age-related changes include a thickening of the heart muscle, decreased lung elasticity and slowed movement through the digestive system. Most middle-aged and older adults retain their abilities to learn, remember and solve problems.

2. **c.** In the elderly, bones become less dense over time. This is especially true in women; subsequently, this loss of bone density increases their risk for fractures. A diminished pain sensation could lead to a decreased awareness of an injury but not the risk for injury, such as a fracture. A decreased tolerance to glare could lead to an increased risk for accidents. Changes in the musculoskeletal system can lead to a more sedentary lifestyle and inactivity leading to a decline in function. But this decline in function would not be directly related to the increased risk for fractures.

3. **b.** Memory loss reflects cognitive impairment and is not considered a normal part of aging. Older adults may downplay their symptoms due to fear of institutionalization or losing their independence. Lungs become stiffer and less

elastic. This causes the airways to shrink and the chest muscles to weaken, thus decreasing the air flow into and out of the lungs and increasing their risk for breathing problems. Aging patients often have decreased sharpness of the senses, and this loss of sensory awareness brings possible risks that are unique to this age group.

4. **b.** Three visits to an emergency room over a 2-week period is suspicious and would be a clue to possible elder abuse. Other clues include a patient who is frequently left alone, has had repeated falls and is malnourished. Having a person present and providing care in the home 24 hours each day is not being left alone frequently. Weight loss due to an underlying medical condition would not suggest possible abuse. One fall in a year would not be considered repeated falling.

5. **a, b, c, d, e.** Patients with Down syndrome experience other health problems, such as heart disease, dementia, hearing loss and problems with the intestines, eyes, thyroid and skeleton.

6. **c.** A patient who is experiencing a loss of visual field cannot see as wide an area as normal unless he or she moves the eyes or turns the head. Glasses are used to adapt to a loss of visual acuity. A white cane typically is used for a patient who cannot see or has significantly reduced vision. Patients who are blind typically use other senses to compensate for their lack of sight.

7. **d.** When providing care for a patient being treated for cancer, infection control is extremely important because chemotherapy and radiation therapy affect a person's immune system. Strict hand washing guidelines and standard precautions must be taken. Although skin inspection, observation of hair loss and evaluation of the patient's vomiting are appropriate, they are not as important as adhering to strict infection control measures.

8. **c.** The most common signs and symptoms of cystic fibrosis include frequent coughing with thick sputum, salty tasting skin, dehydration, ongoing diarrhea and increased appetite with poor weight gain and growth.

9. **b.** Multiple sclerosis is a chronic disease that destroys the coating on the nerve cells in the brain and spinal cord, interfering with the nerves' ability to communicate with each other. Its symptoms usually appear and disappear over a period of years. Muscular dystrophy is a group of genetic disorders in which patients experience progressive weakness and degeneration of the muscles, primarily skeletal muscles. In later stages

of the disease, patients often develop respiratory problems, requiring assisted ventilation.

10. **a.** Patients with autism may not look directly at you, and physical touch may be disturbing to them. In addition, they may exhibit repetitive behaviors and interests and focus intently on one item for prolonged periods of time.

11. **b.** Hospice care is the care provided to a terminally ill patient in the final 6 months of life. The focus of hospice care is keeping the patient as comfortable and as pain free as possible. The emphasis is not on curing the illness but rather on providing physical, emotional, social and spiritual comfort to the dying patient. Central to the hospice way of thinking is that dying is a normal and expected part of the life cycle. Pain relief is administered without the use of needles, using oral medications, pain relieving patches and pills that can be given between the cheek and gum.

12. **b.** When caring for an elderly patient, handle the skin gently because it can tear easily. You should explain everything you are doing in a calm and slow manner. When giving ventilations, do not apply too much pressure because this could result in chest injury. You should use an oropharyngeal airway only if the patient is unconscious and unresponsive and does not have a gag reflex.

13. **a, b, c.** The National Institute of Mental Health describes several types of mental illness, including mood disorders (major depression and bipolar disorder), schizophrenia, anxiety disorders (panic disorder, *obsessive-compulsive disorder* [OCD] and post-traumatic stress disorder), eating disorders, *attention-deficit/hyperactivity disorder* (ADHD), autism and Alzheimer's disease. Down syndrome and cerebral palsy are not mental illnesses.

14. **b.** The evidence of old and new bruises on the patient suggest physical abuse. Financial exploitation, for example, using the patient's money for things other than what the patient needs, would be an example of abuse. Isolating the patient would be an example of abuse. Taking the patient to a senior center daily would allow the patient to engage in social interaction, thereby decreasing the patient's isolation. Inappropriate dress or poor hygiene would suggest abuse.

15. **a.** Autism spectrum disorders are a range of developmental disorders. Autism is at the more-severe end of the spectrum and Asperger syndrome is at the less-severe end. ADHD and Alzheimer's disease are classified as mental illnesses.

Chapter 27: EMS Support and Operations

REVIEW OF CONCEPTS AND TERMS

Fill-in-the-Blank

1. nontraditional
2. nine (9)
3. helicopter
4. audible
5. jump kit
6. packaging

Short Answer

1. An EMR may assume the traditional role (functioning within the 9-1-1 system) and the non-traditional role (functioning in less traditional settings).

2. The first phase of a typical EMS response is the preparation for the emergency call. During this time, you would prepare yourself, your equipment and your vehicle. This means ensuring that you are adequately trained and up to date with your knowledge and skills, having the basic medical equipment on hand and ensuring that any vehicles are safe and well equipped.

3. The communication center or *public safety answering point* (PSAP) has a central access number, such as 9-1-1, for ambulance, police or fire rescue personnel. Specially trained personnel, called EMDs, assist by obtaining the caller's location and information critical for dispatching the appropriate equipment and personnel. They are specially trained to help the caller care for patients until emergency personnel arrive.

4. The two main types of air medical transport are rotorcraft and fixed-wing crafts.

5. A 360-degree assessment means that you scan up and down and behind you, as well as looking forward and side to side, as you size-up the scene. Doing so allows you to more thoroughly assess the entire situation.

6. All moveable equipment in the vehicle must be secured for your safety. In the event of a motor-vehicle collision, all unsecured items have the potential of becoming life-threatening projectiles.

7. A jump kit should contain at the minimum the following items: airways (oral), suction equipment, artificial ventilation devices (resuscitation mask or BVM) and basic wound supplies (dressings and bandages).

CASE STUDY

Scenario A

1. **b.** The EMS response phase of dispatch occurs when the caller reports the accident to the communications center. Preparation for the call occurs before notifying the EMRs. The phase—en-route to the scene—involves the emergency response to the scene, including reaching the scene safely. Patient contact occurs when you arrive on the scene and size-up the scene and the situation.

2. **c.** When travelling to an emergency scene, it is extremely important to arrive there safely. Wear a safety belt and drive according to the weather conditions, which in this case involves snow and ice. Getting as much information as possible would occur when receiving the call from dispatch. Ensuring that you have the appropriate equipment available would be done as preparation before receiving any emergency call. Notifying dispatch about the need for additional emergency services would occur when you arrive on the scene and size it up.

3. **b.** Both patients were involved in a vehicle rollover, were unrestrained and have sustained multiple injuries. Subsequently, they would most likely meet the criteria for trauma alert, making air medical transport appropriate. Although it might be appropriate to use an ambulance to transport the patients, valuable time could be lost if the facility is more than 30 minutes away or if it would take longer to transport the patient to the trauma center by ambulance than by air transport. Notifying law enforcement would not be necessary unless the area needed to be cleared to allow air medical transport to land.

Scenario B

1. **a.** Although having the patient ready for transport is important in an emergency situation, choosing a safe landing zone for a helicopter is paramount. The coordinator who will be assisting with the helicopter landing should be protected with a fastened helmet, hearing and eye

protection, long sleeves and pants. Bystanders should be moved back to a minimum of 200 feet away from the site.

2. **a.** Only personnel who must approach the helicopter should be permitted within the landing zone and only after the pilot has signaled that it is safe to approach. The cessation of tail rotor movement (which is dangerous), the medical crew exiting the aircraft and the helicopter coming to a stop are not appropriate indications that it is safe to approach the aircraft. Typically, you should allow the medical crew from the aircraft to approach you instead to prevent possible injury.

SELF-ASSESSMENT

1. **c.** During phase 7, arrival at the receiving facility, the crew members give information about the scene and the patient, transferring the care of the patient to the nurses and doctors. During phase 5, the patient is transferred to the ambulance. During phase 6, en-route to the receiving facility, the patient and transport crew notify the receiving facility about the patient and their ETA. During phase 8, the EMRs return to the station and notify the communications center of their return.

2. **c.** A minimum of 10,000 square feet (100 × 100 feet) is needed for a safe landing zone.

3. **b.** Generally, air medical transport may be required for emergency calls that include a pedestrian struck at greater than 10 mph (or greater than 5 mph based on a patient's age or physical condition), a vehicle rollover with an unrestrained passenger(s), a motorcycle driver thrown at a speed greater than 20 mph, multiple injured or ill persons, a person who fell from a height greater than about 15 feet, critical stroke or cardiac patients, and critical trauma patients (if ambulance transport would exceed 30 minutes).

4. **c.** Rotorcrafts (e.g., helicopters) are used to get into areas that are not accessible to any other type of rescue craft. Their maneuverability allows them to move up as well as side to side, allowing for special rescue procedures, such as hoisting. Fixed-wing craft are used to transport over long distances, usually between medical facilities.

5. **d.** The amount of space available in a helicopter depends on the type of helicopter and its maximum takeoff and landing weights. However, the weight of the fuel load is important in calculating the weight, not just the space. When calculating space, rescuers must take into account how many patients require transport, the rescuers who must

accompany the patient(s) and any essential life-saving equipment. In calculating weight, the pilot must take into account the weight of the passengers and equipment as well as the fuel load.

6. **a.** A safe landing zone needs to be on flat land that is firm and clear of any obstacles, such as trees or utility poles, vehicles or pedestrians. An open soccer field would be most appropriate. There is no guarantee that ice on a body of water would ever be strong enough for a helicopter landing. A dry barren pasture would most likely be firm but dusty and could possibly contain loose debris, such as rocks, that could become projectiles when the helicopter takes off or lands. Powdery snow would not provide a firm surface for landing.

7. **b.** When approaching a helicopter, you should adopt a somewhat crouched over position and if there is an incline of any sort, you must approach from the lowest point and always from the side or front, never from the rear. Approaching from the side or front allows the pilot to see you and any other responders. You should not be wearing a hat of any type. Only a fastened helmet is permitted. When carrying equipment, such as an IV pole, keep it low and parallel to the ground.

8. **d.** A jump kit, at the minimum, must contain basic wound supplies, such as dressings, as well as airways (oral), suction equipment and artificial ventilation supplies. PPE, such as gloves and protective eyewear, as well as maps and a stethoscope, also are recommended.

9. **a.** You would check the jump kit during phase 1, preparation for an emergency call, thus allowing you to be ready to respond to a scene. Phase 2, dispatch, involves communication from dispatch in which information about the emergency is received and then given to the appropriate personnel for a response. Phase 3, en-route to the scene, involves getting to the scene. Phase 4, arrival at the scene and patient contact, involves approaching the scene, sizing up the scene and the situation, and ultimately beginning patient care.

10. **a, c, e.** Situations that can impact your safety include going through intersections, entering (as opposed to exiting) a highway, driving in inclement weather, listening to a vehicle's stereo (as opposed to turning if off) or other distraction in the vehicle and responding alone.

11. **c.** If you feel sleepy, you should open the vehicle's window and breathe fresh air, do 10 minutes of deep breathing or, if possible, get out of the vehicle for a few minutes. Stretching also helps. Avoid foods with caffeine and sugar, such as coffee, candy bars or gum, because they provide energy in the short term, but they cause a rebound drop in energy a few hours later.

12. **d.** When a vehicle is in contact with an electrical wire, you must consider the wire energized (live) until you know otherwise. When you arrive at the scene, you should notify the power company and establish a safety area at a point twice the length of the span of the wire. Attempt to reach and move patients only after the power company has been notified and secured any electrical current from reaching downed wires or cables. You also need to tell occupants inside the involved vehicle to remain in the vehicle.

13. **a.** While performing CPR when transporting a patient, you need to be secure and supported. However, using the stretcher for balance would be inappropriate. Rather, you should spread your feet to shoulder width to maintain a secure stance and bend your knees to lower your center of gravity. If possible, have someone help you by holding onto your belt to stabilize you. In addition, you should ask the driver to call out if any bumpy areas or severe turns are coming up so that you can brace yourself.

SELF-ASSESSMENT: ENRICHMENT

Operational Safety and Security Measures

1. **a.** The beginning of each shift should involve a briefing, either in person or through written notes, about any issues involving crew safety. Security measures, including vehicle monitoring, should have been discussed previously in training and reviewed as needed. Any retraining should be done at a separate time.

2. **b.** Under no circumstances should an ambulance or rescue vehicle be left running or unattended with the key in the ignition. All vehicles must be monitored, whether in or out of service. A vehicle no longer used for emergency or rescue purposes must be stripped of all emergency equipment, lights, sirens and markings. All use of ambulances and rescue vehicles must be tracked to avoid unauthorized use.

REVIEW OF CONCEPTS AND TERMS

Crossword Puzzle

```
              ¹E
  ²C O M P L E X A C C E S S
  R           T
  I           R
  B     S I M P L E
  B           C
  C H O C K I N G A C C E S S
  N           A
  G           T
              I
              O
              N
```

Short Answer

1. Basic extrication equipment includes crowbars, screwdrivers, chisels, hammers, pliers, work gloves and goggles, wrenches, shovels, car jacks, tire irons, knives, and ropes or chains.
2. When responding to a motor-vehicle collision or other extrication situation, EMRs should have a protective helmet with chin strap; protective eyewear; puncture- and flame-resistant outerwear (turnout gear); heavy, protective gloves; and boots with steel toes and insoles.
3. Blocking is a technique of positioning fire apparatus, such as large engines, at an angle to traffic lanes. This creates a physical barrier between the work area and traffic flowing toward the emergency scene.
4. The term "rule of thumb" states that, to be safe, position yourself far enough away from the scene that your thumb, pointing up at arm's length, covers the hazardous area from your view.
5. A vehicle is unstable if it is positioned on a tilted surface, stacked on top of another vehicle (even partly), on a slippery surface, or overturned or on its side.

CASE STUDY

Scenario A

1. **a.** When dealing with a patient who is trapped, your role is to administer the necessary care before extrication and to ensure that the patient is removed in a way that minimizes further injury. In many cases, patient care will occur simultaneously with the extrication process. As an EMR, you would not actually perform the extrication but would work closely with other rescuers to protect the patient. Specially trained extrication personnel would establish the chain of command. Law enforcement would play a major role in helping to secure the scene and control the crowd during extrication.
2. **b.** The first priority for all EMRs is to size-up the scene to ensure your safety and the safety of the patient and others. Once you have determined that the scene is safe and accessed the patient, you then would begin a primary assessment. Upon arrival on the scene, you should request assistance for additional law enforcement to help control the scene and the traffic.
3. **d.** Since the patient is trapped under plywood and a scaffold, a pneumatic tool would most likely be used to lift the plywood and scaffold off of the patient. Ropes may be helpful in pulling the material off of the patient, but this pulling action could lead to further injury. Pliers or a shovel would not be helpful in this situation.

Scenario B

1. **b.** You can assume a vehicle is unstable if it is positioned on a tilted surface; stacked on top of another vehicle, even partly; on a slippery surface; or overturned or on its side. A vehicle that is positioned on a flat or dry surface or side by side (next to) another vehicle would be considered stable.
2. **a.** To stabilize a vehicle, first put the vehicle in "park," or in gear (if a manual transmission), then set the parking brake, turn off the vehicle's ignition and remove the key. If there are no patients in the seats, move the seats back and roll down the windows, then disconnect the battery or power source.
3. **b.** As with any conventional vehicle, removing the ignition key and disconnecting the battery will disable a hybrid's high-voltage controller. However, some models may remain "live" for up to 10 minutes after the vehicle is shut off or disabled. Thus, a hybrid vehicle can remain silent and still be operational if the collision is minor and/or did not activate any of the collision sensors. Therefore, it is essential that rescuers chock or block the wheels to prevent the vehicle from moving under power or by gravity. Be

careful not to place cribbing under any high-voltage (usually *orange* in color) cabling.

4. **b.** Simple access methods include trying to open each door or the windows or having the patient unlock the doors or roll down the windows. A ratcheting cable and tool cutter would be used with complex access. Breaking the window glass would be inappropriate because it could cause injury to yourself and the patient.

5. **c.** Emergency vehicles should be placed in optimal positions for safety and for easy patient loading. Blocking is a technique of positioning fire apparatus, such as large engines, at an angle to traffic lanes. This creates a physical barrier between the work area and traffic flowing toward the emergency scene. The scene should be protected with the first-arriving apparatus and with at least one additional lane blocked off. Ambulances should park within the "shadow" created by the larger apparatus. The apparatus also should "block to the right" or "block to the left" so as not to obstruct the loading doors of ambulances. To create a safe zone, traffic cones or flares should be placed at 10- to 15-foot intervals in a radius of at least 50 feet around the scene.

SELF-ASSESSMENT

1. **d.** If a patient is pinned directly behind an undeployed air bag, both battery cables should be disconnected, following established safety protocols. Ideally, you should wait for deactivation of the system before attempting to extricate the patient. You should not mechanically cut through or displace the steering column until after deactivating the system. You also should not cut or drill into the air bag module or apply heat to the area of the steering wheel hub since an undeployed air bag will inflate if the chemicals sealed inside the air bag module reach a temperature above 350° F.

2. **b, a, d, c, f, e.** After putting the vehicle in "park" or in gear (if a manual transmission), you then would set the parking brake; turn off the vehicle's ignition and remove the key; move the seats back and roll down the windows; disconnect the battery or power source; and finally, identify and avoid hazardous vehicle safety components.

3. **a.** Cribbing is a system that creates a stable environment for the vehicle. It uses wood or supports, arranged diagonally to a vehicle's frame, to safely prop it up, creating a stable environment. Cribbing should not be used under tires because it tends to cause rolling. There should never be more than 1 or 2 inches between the cribbing and vehicle.

4. **b.** Unless you have received special training in HAZMAT handling and have the necessary equipment to do so without danger, you should not attempt to be a hero. Rather, you should stay clear of the scene, well away from the area or in the designated cold zone. Stay out of low areas where vapors and liquids may collect and stay upwind and uphill of the scene. It is common for responding ambulance crews approaching the scene to recognize a HAZMAT placard and immediately move to a safe area and summon more advanced help.

5. **b, c, d, f.** When approaching any scene, whether a motor-vehicle collision or an industrial emergency, you should be able to recognize clues that indicate the presence of HAZMATs. These include signs (placards) on vehicles or storage facilities identifying the presence of these materials, evidence of spilled liquids or solids, unusual odors, clouds of vapor and leaking containers.

6. **c.** During extrication, it is crucial to maintain cervical spinal stabilization to minimize the risk for additional patient injury. In addition, a sufficient number of personnel are needed during extrication. Often, these individuals try to move the device, not the patient, using the path of least resistance when making decisions about equipment and patient movement.

7. **d.** Chocking refers to the process of placing blocks or wedges against the wheels of a vehicle to reduce the chance of the vehicle moving. Blocking is a technique of positioning fire apparatus, such as large engines, at an angle to traffic lanes, creating a physical barrier between the work area and traffic flowing toward the emergency scene. Cribbing refers to creating a stable environment for the vehicle using wood or supports arranged diagonally to the vehicle's frame to safely prop up a vehicle. Extricating refers to the process of safely and appropriately removing a patient trapped in a vehicle or other dangerous situation.

8. **a.** The most commonly used extrication tool is the power hydraulic tool, such as the Hurst Jaws of Life® Other commonly used extrication tools include pneumatic tools, such as air bags, and manual hydraulic tools, such as a jack and tool cutters.

9. **b.** Other methods to prevent an upright vehicle from rolling include cutting the tire valves so that the car rests safely on its rims, turning the wheels toward the curb and tying the car frame to a strong anchor point, such as a guardrail, large tree or another vehicle. Letting the air out of the tires also reduces the possibility of movement.

10. **c.** The first priority for a patient who is to be extricated is to ensure that the cervical spine is stabilized. Then perform the primary assessment. Based on your assessment, administer emergency oxygen, if necessary, and/or obtain a SAMPLE history while you continuously monitor and care for the patient.

11. **b.** Air bags that have not deployed may present a hazard during extrication because the force of the deploying air bag can turn access and extrication tools into destructive missiles, which can cause serious injury to rescuers and patients. HAZMATs are not released with deployment. Air bags are found in several locations throughout a vehicle. Deployment of an air bag could lead to patient injury but not necessarily crushing of the patient's spine. Extrication will not necessarily fail if an air bag deploys.

Chapter 29: Hazardous Materials Emergencies

REVIEW OF CONCEPTS AND TERMS

Fill-in-the-Blank

1. placards
2. shipping papers
3. exclusion
4. Gross
5. *Material Safety Data Sheet* (MSDS)
6. toxicity
7. Flammability
8. higher
9. warm
10. recognition

Labeling

Safety Zones

A. Hot zone (exclusion zone)
B. Warm zone (contamination reduction zone)
C. Cold zone (support zone)

CASE STUDY

Scenario A

1. **a.** As the first person to arrive on the scene of a potential HAZMAT incident, it is your responsibility to help lay the groundwork for the rescue scene. The first step is to recognize the presence of a HAZMAT and then to contact dispatch and report specific details of the scene, including information about placard colors and numbers and any label information. Once this information is relayed, you would position yourself at a safe distance and establish a clear chain of command, including establishing safety zones. It would be inappropriate to access the patient until the scene is safe.

2. **c.** When on the scene of a HAZMAT incident, position yourself uphill and upwind of the scene and stay out of low-lying areas where vapors and liquids collect. In addition, remain at a safe distance from the scene throughout the incident.

3. **a, b, c.** Additional information can be gained about the substance in the tanker from warning signs, such as "flammable," "explosive," "corrosive" or "radioactive"; *National Fire Protection Association* (NFPA) numbers; and shipping papers. The *Emergency Response Guidebook* (although available for download) and CAMEO® are references for identifying HAZMATs and include appropriate care procedures. However, these may or may not be readily accessible at the scene.

4. **b.** The warm and hot zones can be entered only by those who have received *Occupational Safety and Health Administration* (OSHA) *Hazardous Waste Operations and Emergency Response* (HAZWOPER) training at the first responder awareness level and who are wearing appropriate PPE and an SCBA.

SELF-ASSESSMENT

1. **b.** A HAZMAT is any chemical substance or material that can pose a threat to the health, safety and property of an individual. It can include wastes, chemicals and other dangerous products, such as explosives, poisonous gases,

corrosives, radioactive materials, compressed gases, oxidizers and flammable solids and liquids, fertilizers, insecticides and pesticides. It also can include various waste products from numerous manufacturers that may be considered toxic or hazardous.

2. **b.** The degree to which a substance is poisonous refers to its toxicity. Flammability refers to the degree to which a substance may ignite. Reactivity refers to the degree to which a substance may react when exposed to other substances. Radioactivity refers to the degree to which a substance gives off radiation.

3. **c.** In preparation for a worst-case scenario developing at a HAZMAT incident, a clear chain of command must be established first. A single command officer then should be assigned to maintain control of the situation and make decisions at every stage of the rescue. Next, a system of communication that is accessible and familiar to all rescuers should be established. Finally, a receiving facility should be established that is as close as possible to the scene, is able to receive and handle the number of patients and is able to continue the required decontamination processes.

4. **d.** The shipping papers list the names, associated dangers and four-digit identification numbers of the substances. The MSDS are provided by the manufacturer and identify the substance, physical properties and any associated hazards for a given material, such as fire, explosion and health hazards.

5. **a.** With a HAZMAT incident, a clear chain of command is established with one command officer being assigned to maintain control of the situation and make decisions at every stage of the rescue. The rescue team must be aware of who is in command and when decision-making powers are transferred to another officer. The system of communication is one that is accessible and familiar to all rescuers.

6. **b.** The presence of odors such as bitter almonds, peaches, mustard, freshly cut grass, garlic or pungent or sweet odors suggest terrorism. Clues that a HAZMAT incident might involve terrorism include an incident in a well-populated area with numerous people experiencing an unidentifiable illness and animals in the area that are dead or incapacitated.

7. **d.** In the warm zone, complete decontamination takes place and life-saving emergency care, such as airway management and immobilization, occurs. In the hot zone, rescue, treatment for any life-threatening conditions and initial decontamination occur.

8. **b, c, e.** When radiation is suspected, you should immediately don an SCBA and protective clothing and seal off all openings with duct tape. Double gloves and two pairs of paper shoe covers under heavy rubber boots should be worn.

9. **b.** The longer the time, the closer the distance and the more materials to which you are exposed, the worse the situation and the more protection will be required to decrease your risk of exposure. The use of increased protective equipment would decrease your exposure risk.

10. **d.** The support zone also is called the cold zone, which is the outer perimeter. The hot zone, also called the exclusion zone, is the area where the most danger exists. The contamination reduction or warm zone is immediately outside of the hot zone.

11. **d.** In your role as an EMR who is the first on the scene of a possible HAZMAT incident, you would follow three steps: recognition, identification and determination. As the last step, you would determine if the material is responsible for the injuries or the damage at the scene. During recognition, you would acknowledge the presence of a HAZMAT and demonstrate awareness that the material could be harmful to the health of others. During identification, you would establish the material's specific identity and characteristics.

12. **a, b, c, e.** A patient may be contaminated via several routes, including topical (through the skin), respiratory (inhaled), gastrointestinal (ingested) or parenteral (*intramuscular* [IM], *intravenous* [IV] or *subcutaneous* [sub-Q]).

13. **b.** Initial, or "gross" decontamination, is performed as the person enters the warm zone. Any immediate life-threatening conditions are addressed during this stage. Soap and copious amounts of water are used and any clothing, equipment and tools must be left in the hot zone. Dilution refers to the method of reducing the concentration of a contaminant to a safe level. Absorption is the process of using material that will absorb and hold contaminants, such as corrosive and liquid chemicals. Neutralization involves chemically altering a substance to render it harmless or make it less harmful.

REVIEW OF CONCEPTS AND TERMS

Fill-in-the-Blank

1. incident commander
2. transportation
3. Communication
4. four (4)
5. *National Response Framework* (NRF)
6. triage
7. black

Short Answer

1. The *National Incident Management System* (NIMS) provides a systematic, proactive approach to guide departments and agencies at all levels of government, non-governmental organizations and the private sector to work seamlessly to prevent, protect against, respond to, recover from and mitigate the effects of incidents, regardless of cause, size, location or complexity, in order to reduce the loss of life and property and harm to the environment. It provides the template for the management of incidents.
2. The *incident command system* (ICS) is an all-hazards incident management system. It allows for effective management of emergency situations by organizing who is responsible for overall direction, the roles of other participants and the resources required.
3. Functional positions that may be required include the triage officer, who supervises the initial triage, tagging and moving of patients to designated treatment areas; the treatment officer, who sets up a treatment area and supervises medical care, ensuring triage order is maintained and changing the order if patients deteriorate and become eligible for a higher triage category; the transportation officer, who arranges for ambulances or other transport vehicles while tracking priority, identity and destination of all injured or ill people leaving the scene; the staging officer, who releases and distributes resources as needed to the incident and works to avoid transportation gridlock; and the safety officer, who maintains scene safety by identifying potential dangers and taking action to prevent them from causing injury to all involved. Other roles that may be needed include supply, mobile command/

communications, extrication, rehabilitation, morgue and logistics.
4. Examples that may be considered *multiple-casualty incidents* (MCIs) include motor-vehicle collisions and other transportation accidents, flood, fire, explosion, structure collapse, train derailment, airliner crash, HAZMAT incidents, earthquake, tornado and hurricane.
5. The METTAG™ patient identification system uses symbols rather than words to allow rescuers to quickly identify patient status. The rabbit means "urgent," the turtle means "can be delayed," the ambulance with a bold X through it means "no urgent transport is needed" and a shovel and cross symbol means "the victim is dead."
6. The four colors commonly used for triage are green, red, yellow and black.
7. The three areas assessed using START include breathing, circulation and LOC.

CASE STUDY

Scenario A

1. **b.** Since fire personnel have arrived first, one of these individuals would assume the role of the *incident commander* (IC). Upon your arrival, you would identify yourself to the IC and report to the staging officer. The staging officer then would tell you where you are most needed. The IC would be responsible for determining the number of ambulances needed.
2. **c.** Patients who are ambulatory are tagged as green. Patients requiring immediate care are tagged red. Those who may be severely injured but a delay in their treatment will not decrease their chance of survival are tagged yellow. Patients who are obviously dead or have mortal wounds are tagged black.
3. **a.** An emergency that involves children must be handled differently from an emergency with adults. The JumpSTART triage method should be used on anyone who appears to be a child, regardless of actual chronological age, but is not done on infants younger than 12 months. The Smart Tag™, METTAG™ and START systems are used with adults.
4. **a, d, e.** Patients who are tagged red require immediate care and transport to a medical facility. Patients are considered immediate care if

they are unconscious or cannot follow simple commands, require active airway management, have a respiratory rate of greater than 30, have a delayed (more than 2 seconds) capillary refill or absent radial pulse, or require bleeding control for severe hemorrhage from major blood vessels. Patients who are non-ambulatory or have incurred a spinal injury with or without spinal cord damage would be tagged yellow.

5. **d.** The safety officer maintains scene safety by identifying potential dangers and taking action to prevent them from causing injury to all involved. The treatment officer sets up a treatment area and supervises medical care, ensuring triage order is maintained and changing the order if patients deteriorate and become eligible for a higher triage category. The triage officer supervises the initial triage, tagging and moving of patients to designated treatment areas. The staging officer releases and distributes resources as needed to the incident and works to avoid transportation gridlock.

6. **d.** Patients who are tagged white are categorized as "hold" to indicate that they have minor injuries that do not require a doctor's care. Patients with life-threatening conditions are tagged red. Those who are injured but ambulatory are tagged green. Patients with severe injuries for which treatment can be delayed are tagged yellow.

Scenario B

1. **a.** In any emergency, the first responder on the scene becomes the IC. As IC, it is your responsibility to identify a scene as an MCI, assess the scene safety and determine if any action is required to secure the scene. You then are responsible for deciding what calls to make, what tasks need to be done and which tasks to assign to appropriate personnel. The rescuer who assumes the role as IC remains in that role until a more senior or experienced person arrives on the scene and assumes command, or until the incident is over.

2. **c.** The triage officer is the first person to be assigned because he or she determines the requirements for additional resources for triage, performs triage of all patients and assigns personnel and equipment to the highest priority patients. Triage is crucial because it directly impacts the survival of the patients. Once the triage officer is assigned, other roles such as

transportation, safety and staging officer can be assigned. The staging officer often is one of the first officers assigned by the IC.

3. **b.** When someone with more experience or seniority arrives on the scene, you should transfer incident command to that person, providing that person with a verbal report of all important and pertinent information, including what has been recorded. The person taking over will need to know such information as when the incident began, when you arrived on the scene, how many people are injured, how many people are acting as rescuers, any potential dangers, what has been done since the beginning of the rescue and what objectives need to be accomplished. The oncoming IC then will assign you to an area where you are needed most.

4. **c.** Patients with burns involving flame; burns occurring in a confined space; burns covering more than one body part; burns to the head, neck, feet or genitals; partial-thickness or full-thickness burns in a child or an older adult; or burns resulting from chemicals, explosions or electricity are classified as needing immediate care. The category of minor or walking wounded would apply to ambulatory patients. The category of delayed would be used for patients with severe injuries for whom a delay in treatment would not reduce their chance of survival. The category of deceased/non-salvageable is used for patients who are obviously dead or who have mortal injuries.

SELF-ASSESSMENT

1. **b.** The METTAG™ system uses symbols rather than words to identify patients. The START, Smart Tag™ and JumpSTART systems use words and colors to identify patient levels.

2. **a.** The color red signifies that the patient needs immediate or urgent care. Yellow indicates delayed care and green signifies that the patient is ambulatory and not in grave danger. Black indicates that the patient is deceased or non-salvageable.

3. **c.** Although it is highly individualized, in general, a 55-year-old man involved in a factory explosion would have the least risk for a severe stress reaction. Those that have a greater risk for severe stress reactions include children who may react strongly and experience extreme fears of further harm, elderly patients and those who already have health problems.

4. **c.** After an MCI, debriefing is a vital part of the process. It allows rescuers to go over their role in the MCI and the outcome allows for release of stress and learning opportunities for future events. Scheduling down time, having responders talk among themselves and setting clear expectations are appropriate measures to help reduce stress during the MCI.

5. **a, c, e.** To help manage and reduce stress for patients at the scene, helpful measures would include reuniting family members, limiting the amount of information that is getting out of the scene, being honest and telling patients what is happening in terms that they can understand, encouraging questions and discussions, and asking others to help if they are able to assist with tasks.

6. **d.** To effectively manage an emergency situation involving an MCI and provide care, an ICS must be established. The ICS organizes who is responsible for overall direction, the roles of other participants and the resources required. Triage is one aspect involved in the ICS. The NRF is a guide to how the nation conducts an all-hazards response. The START system is a triage system.

7. **c, d, e.** The most commonly required positions include triage officer, treatment officer, transportation officer, staging officer and safety officer. Other roles that may be needed include those for supply, extrication and logistics.

8. **c.** A large-scale MCI would involve large numbers of individuals, for example, an event in a metropolitan area. A motor-vehicle crash with two individuals, a fire involving a family of four or a building collapse affecting 10 workers would be an MCI, but the scale would be much smaller.

9. **b.** Secondary triage is performed after primary triage, usually after patients have been moved to the treatment area or are at a funnel point just before they enter the treatment area. It is not performed before transport or on arrival to the receiving facility.

10. **b.** You would tag this patient with a red tag because although the patient is breathing, the respiratory rate is high, over 30 breaths per minute, indicating that the patient needs immediate care. A person who is alert and responds appropriately to verbal stimuli is classified as delayed care and is tagged yellow. A patient who is ambulatory is not in grave danger and would be tagged green. A patient who is not breathing despite an open airway is classified as deceased/non-salvageable and is tagged black.

11. **c.** According to START principles, it should take no longer than 30 seconds per patient to do your assessment and tagging.

12. **a.** The staging officer is responsible for establishing an area suitable to park multiple units in an organized fashion. The transportation officer is responsible for communicating with receiving hospitals and for assigning patients to ambulances, helicopters and buses for transport. The treatment officer is responsible for identifying a treatment area of sufficient space with adequate ingress and egress for ambulances.

13. **d.** The METTAG™ system uses symbols rather than words to identify patient status. The rabbit means urgent care, the turtle means that care can be delayed, the ambulance with a bold X through it means no urgent transport is needed, and a shovel and cross symbol indicates that the patient is dead.

14. **a.** When using the START or JumpSTART triage system, you would determine the different levels by assessing four aspects using the acronym ARPM, which stands for ambulatory status (ability to get up and walk), respiratory status, perfusion status and mental status.

15. **a, b, d, e, f.** The SALT Mass Casualty Triage prioritizes patients into one of five categories, including immediate, expectant, delayed, minimal or dead.

Chapter 31: Response to Disasters and Terrorism

REVIEW OF CONCEPTS AND TERMS

Matching

1. E; 2. A; 3. D; 4. F; 5. C; 6. B

Fill-in-the-Blank

1. subsonic
2. five
3. natural, human-caused, biological
4. all-hazards
5. CBRNE
6. vesicants
7. A
8. Blast lung
9. Tertiary effects
10. Mark I™ kit

CASE STUDY

Scenario A

1. **c.** The report of an odor resembling "freshly cut hay" suggests the use of phosgene. Sulfur mustard can be detected by its odor of garlic, onions or horseradish. Cyanide has an odor of bitter almonds. Tabun is odorless.
2. **b.** Phosgene is a pulmonary agent; upon contact with the mucous membranes, it irritates and damages the lung tissue. There is no specific antidote; the only way to provide care is to remove the patient from the agent and resuscitate him or her. Sodium thiosulfate is an antidote for cyanide. Decontamination procedures and the use of bleach are appropriate for exposure to blister agents.
3. **b.** In a situation in which phosgene may be present, it is essential that you protect yourself by using a chemical protective mask with a charcoal canister. A HAZMAT suite or gown may or may not be necessary. Gloves most likely would be needed. A HEPA filter mask would be more appropriate for use with biological agents.

Scenario B

1. **a, d, e.** Examples of high-order explosives include TNT, C-4, Simtex, nitroglycerin, dynamite and ammonium nitrate fuel oil. Pipe bomb and gunpowder are examples of low-order explosives.

2. **a.** Primary effects of the explosion result from the impact of the over-pressurization wave on the body surface, most commonly injuring the lungs, middle ear, gastrointestinal tract, eyes and head. Tympanic membrane perforation is an example of a middle ear injury due to primary effects. Lacerations due to flying debris or a penetrating wound from a bomb fragment suggest injury due to secondary effects. Fracture of the arm from hitting the wall suggests tertiary effects since the patient is thrown by the blast wind.

3. **c.** The site of a bomb blast is a crime scene, and as an EMR, you must preserve evidence and avoid disturbing areas not directly involved in rescue activities, although your primary responsibility is to rescue living people and provide care for life-threatening injuries. Any fatalities should be left at the area where they are found with the surroundings undisturbed.

SELF-ASSESSMENT

1. **a.** Biological disasters include epidemics, pandemics and outbreaks of communicable diseases; contamination of food or water supplies by pathogens; and the use of viruses, bacteria and other pathogens for bioterrorism. A nuclear explosion or chemical exposure would be a human-caused disaster. A tornado is a natural disaster.

2. **b.** Class B biological agents/diseases pose a moderate level of risk and include brucellosis, Q fever, glanders, alphaviruses, food pathogens (e.g., *Salmonella, Shigella, E coli*), water pathogens (e.g., *Vibrio cholerae, Cryptosporidium*), ricin toxin, *staphylococcal enterotoxin B* and epsilon toxin of *Clostridium perfringens*. Hantavirus, yellow fever and tick-borne virus are examples of Class C biological agents/diseases.

3. **c.** FEMA ultimately is responsible for coordinating the response to and recovery from disasters in the United States when the disaster is large enough to overwhelm the local and state resources. The NRF was developed and introduced by FEMA as a guide for all organizations involved in disaster management as to how to respond to disasters and emergencies. NIMS is a comprehensive national framework for managing incidents; it outlines the structures for response activities for command and management and provides a consistent, nationwide response at

all levels. The ICS is a management system that allows effective incident management by bringing together facilities, equipment, personnel, procedures and communications within a single organizational structure so that everyone has an understanding of their roles and can respond effectively and efficiently.

4. **d.** ESF #1, transportation, is involved in damage and impact assessment, movement restrictions, transportation safety, restoration/recovery of transportation infrastructure, and aviation/airspace management and control. ESF #2, communications, is involved in coordination with telecommunications and information technology industries; restoration and repair of telecommunications infrastructure; protection, restoration and sustainment of cyber and information technology resources; and oversight of communications within the federal incident management and response structures. ESF#5, emergency management, is involved in the coordination of incident management and response efforts, issuance of mission assignments, resource and human capital, incident action planning and financial management. ESF #8, public health and medical services, is involved in public health, medical and mental health services and mass fatality management.

5. **a, c, d, e.** *Weapons of mass destruction* (WMDs) are classified as chemical, biological, radiological/nuclear and explosives, also known by the acronym CBRNE. Guns are not considered a WMD.

6. **c.** A blood agent attacks the body's cellular metabolism, disrupting cellular respiration. Blister agents cause the formation of blisters when they come in contact with the skin and mucous membranes. Nerve agents disrupt the chemical recovery phase that follows a neuromuscular signal. An incapacitating agent produces temporary physiological or mental effects or both, rendering individuals incapable of concerted effort in the performance of their duties.

7. **d.** Atropine is an antidote for nerve agent toxicity. Hydroxocobalamin, sodium nitrite and sodium thiosulfate are antidotes for cyanide poisoning.

8. **c.** Anthrax is a Class A biological agent/disease that is easily spread from person to person and results in a high mortality rate. Q fever, ricin toxin and brucellosis are Class B biological agents/disease with moderate morbidity rates and low mortality rates.

9. **a.** Although most biological agents are not highly contagious, a few are, so it is essential to isolate the patient, protect yourself with the proper PPE and use standard infection control procedures including a HEPA filter mask and gloves. Antibiotics may be used to treat bacterial illnesses but not to treat illness caused by a virus. Antidotes are not used with biological agents. Decontamination is used for radiological/nuclear exposure.

10. **a.** Acute radiation syndrome follows a predictable pattern that unfolds over several days or weeks after substantial exposure or catastrophic events. Specific symptoms of concern, especially after a 2- to 3-week period with nausea and vomiting, are thermal burn-like skin lesions without documented heat exposure, a tendency to bleed (nosebleeds, gingival [gum] bleeding, bruising) and hair loss. Symptom clusters, as delayed effects after radiation exposure, include headache, fatigue, weakness, partial- and full-thickness skin damage, hair loss, ulceration, anorexia, nausea, vomiting, diarrhea, reduced levels of white blood cells, bruising and infections.

11. **b.** Although identifying the weapon, assessing the patients and following appropriate protocols are important, the top priority is to ensure your own safety. Without this, the other actions would be futile.

12. **a, b.** Exposure to a small amount of liquid nerve agent would be noted by sweating and blanching of the skin and occasional muscle twitching at the site. Signs of a large amount of exposure include loss of consciousness, seizures, apnea and muscle flaccidity.

13. **c.** A patient who is unconscious and convulsing is classified as immediate. This classification would also apply to the patient if he or she was breathing with difficulty, had apnea and is possibly flaccid. A patient is classified as delayed if further medical observation, large amounts of antidotes or artificial ventilation is required after triage. A patient is classified as expectant if the patient shows the same signs as immediate but has no pulse or blood pressure and thus is not expected to survive. A patient is classified as minimal if he or she is walking, talking, breathing and whose circulation is intact.

14. **d.** The auto-injector is administered into the mid-outer thigh. It is not given in the upper arm, buttocks or abdomen.

15. **b, c.** The DuoDote™ auto-injector kit contains two drugs: atropine and *pralidoxime chloride* (2-PAM). Sodium thiosulfate is an antidote for

cyanide, a blood agent. Hydroxocobalamin also is an antidote for cyanide and is included in the Cyanokit®.

SELF-ASSESSMENT: ENRICHMENT

Preparing for a Public Health Disaster–Pandemic Flu

1. **a.** Pandemic influenza is virulent human influenza A virus that causes global outbreak of serious illness in humans. The National Strategy for Pandemic Influenza identifies responsibilities for federal, state and local governments as well as non-governmental organizations, businesses and individuals, and is built on three pillars: preparedness and communication, surveillance and detection, and response and containment. Vaccinations play a key role in controlling the flu.

2. **a, c.** Measures to help in planning for pandemic influenza include ensuring early detection; treating with antiviral medications; using infection control measures; vaccinating, treating (with antiviral medications) and isolating persons with confirmed or probable pandemic influenza; dismissing students from school and school-based activities and closing childcare programs; and using social distancing in the community for children, adolescents and adults.

Personal Preparedness

1. **b.** When assembling or restocking your kit, you should store at least 3 days' worth of food, water and supplies in an easy-to-carry preparedness kit. It is important to keep extra supplies on hand at home in case you cannot leave the affected area. In addition, you should keep your kit where it is easily accessible and remember to check your kit every 6 months and replace expired or outdated items.

2. **a, c, e.** When making a plan, you should always talk with your family, plan and learn how and when to turn off utilities, and use life-saving tools such as fire extinguishers. It is important to tell everyone where emergency information and supplies are stored and provide copies of the family's preparedness plan to each member of the family. Ensure that information always is up to date and practice evacuations, following the routes outlined in your plan. Additionally, you should choose an out-of-area contact to call in case of an emergency, telling your family and friends that this out-of-area contact is the person they all should phone to relay messages. You also should predetermine two meeting places: one right outside of the home and one outside of your neighborhood or town for when you cannot return home or must evacuate.

Chapter 32: Special Operations

REVIEW OF CONCEPTS AND TERMS

Fill-in-the-Blank

1. fifth
2. 5
3. distressed
4. litter
5. 40
6. confined

Short Answer

1. An active drowning victim is vertical in the water but has no supporting kick and is unable to move forward. The person's arms are at the sides, pressing down in an attempt to keep the mouth and nose above water to breathe. All energy is going into the struggle to breathe, and the person cannot call out for help. In contrast, a passive drowning victim is not moving and will be floating face-up or face-down on or near the surface of the water or may be submerged.

2. The three types of assists are reaching, throwing and wading assists.

3. In icy water, a person's body temperature begins to drop almost as soon as the body hits the water. The body loses heat in water 32 times faster than it does in the air. Swallowing water accelerates this cooling. As the body's core temperature drops, the metabolic rate drops. Activity in the cells comes almost to a standstill, and the person requires very little oxygen. Any oxygen left in the blood is diverted from other parts of the body to the brain and heart.

4. The reason 18 to 20 people are required to evacuate a patient over hazardous terrain is to

ensure that no one on the team becomes overtired. After a short distance, teams should rotate positions, changing sides and positions after each progression. Teams then should alternate, giving each team a chance to rest. This will ensure a safe rescue without anyone becoming exhausted and unable to complete the evacuation.

5. If you are not trained to fight fires or lack the necessary equipment, you should follow these basic guidelines: do not approach a burning vehicle; never enter a burning or smoke-filled building; if you are in a building that is on fire, always check doors before opening them (if a door is hot to the touch, do not open it); since smoke and fumes rise, stay close to the floor; and never use an elevator in a building that may be burning.

CASE STUDY

Scenario A

1. **b.** A distressed swimmer may be too tired to get to shore or to the side of the pool but is able to stay afloat and breathe and may be calling for help. The person may be floating, treading water or clinging to an object or a line for support. Someone who is trying to swim but making little or no forward progress may be in distress. A patient who is motionless and floating face-up or face-down indicates a passive drowning victim. A patient struggling to keep his or her mouth and nose above water indicates an active drowning victim.

2. **c.** With the drop in body temperature due to icy water, the metabolic rate drops. Cellular activity comes almost to a standstill, and the person requires very little oxygen. Any oxygen left in the blood is diverted from other parts of the body to the brain and heart.

3. **a.** If a person falls through the ice, it is your responsibility as a rescuer to immediately call for an ice rescue team. You should not go onto the ice to attempt a rescue because the ice may be too thin to support you. Once you have summoned the specialized team, you need to continue talking to the child, parents and brother to help calm them. If possible, you should use reaching or throwing assists to rescue the child, but you should not go into the icy water.

4. **d.** Once the child is pulled from the water, you should provide care for hypothermia because the body loses heat in icy water 32 times faster than it does in air. This cooling effect is further accelerated if the child has swallowed water. Providing care for seizures or a hemorrhage would not be the priority. Fever is highly unlikely.

Scenario B

1. **d.** There is no water in the silo, so the patient is not at risk for drowning. Below-ground areas, such as vaults, sewers, wells or cisterns, can contain water and pose a drowning risk. Silos used to store agricultural materials often are designed to limit oxygen and, therefore, present the hazard of poisonous gases caused by fermentation. The danger of engulfment by the contained product in the silo also is a possibility. Low oxygen levels in these spaces pose a significant risk, as do poisonous gases, such as carbon monoxide, hydrogen sulfide and carbon dioxide.

2. **b.** Silos used to store grain(s) are an example of a confined space, that is, any space with limited access that is not intended for continuous human occupancy. A cave-in involves the ground coming in and filling the area. The patient may be buried completely or partially. Hazardous terrain involves dangerous, rough ground that makes maneuvering difficult, such as ravines or cliffs. A special event is one that involves many people, for example, major sporting activities, concerts, large-scale conventions or national security events.

SELF-ASSESSMENT

1. **b.** Rappelling is the act of descending by sliding down a secured rope to reach a patient such as from a cliff, gorge or side of a building. Reaching and throwing are types of assists used to rescue a drowning victim. Shoring is supporting the walls of a trench to prevent a cave-in.

2. **a.** After a short distance, teams should rotate positions, changing sides and positions after each progression. Teams then should alternate, giving each team a chance to rest. This will ensure a safe rescue, without anyone becoming exhausted and unable to complete the evacuation. Time and efficiency are key, so stopping to rest would be inappropriate. Switching hands would be

ineffective in preventing you from tiring. Getting a replacement would be appropriate only as a last resort if, for some reason, you were unable to continue.

3. **b.** For a special event involving more than 25,000 people but fewer than 55,000 people, two ambulances should be readily available. One ambulance would be necessary for crowds of 5,000 to 25,000 people, while three ambulances would be required for events with over 55,000 people.

4. **d.** If the water is safe and shallow enough (not over your chest), you can wade in to reach the person. You should wear a life jacket and take something with you to extend your reach if possible such as a ring buoy, buoyant cushion, kickboard, an extra life jacket, tree branch, pole, air mattress, plastic cooler, picnic jug, paddle or water exercise belt.

5. **a.** The most appropriate method would be to attempt a reaching assist by lying down at the side of the pool and reaching out to her using your arm or leg or an object such as a pole, tree branch or towel. If this is not possible, you could attempt a throwing assist. A wading assist would not be appropriate because the water in the deep end would most likely be over your head. Your first goal is to stay safe, so rushing or jumping into the water would put you at risk for drowning, too.

6. **c.** Younger children can drown at any moment, even in as little as an inch of water. Males are four times more likely to drown than females. Most people who are drowning cannot or do not call for help. They spend their energy trying to keep the mouth and nose above the water to breathe.

7. **b.** A passive drowning victim is not moving and is floating face-up or face-down on or near the surface of the water or may be submerged. A distressed swimmer may be floating, treading water or clinging to an object or a line for support. An active drowning victim is vertical in the water, typically with his or her arms at the sides, pressing down in an attempt to keep the mouth and nose above water to breathe.

8. **d.** Throwing equipment includes heaving lines, ring buoys, throw bags or any floating object available, such as a picnic jug, small cooler, buoyant cushion, kickboard or extra life jacket. A paddle, tree branch or towel would be appropriate to use for a reaching assist.

9. **b.** The HAZMAT EMS Response Unit would be used for situations involving WMD and HAZMAT incidents to provide EMS care to patients in the warm zone (i.e., the area immediately outside of the hot zone, where most of the danger exists). The Tactical EMS Unit would be used for situations such as hostage barricades, active shooters and high-risk warrants and other situations requiring a tactical response team. The Fire Rehabilitation Unit would be used to provide rest, rehydration, nourishment and medical evaluation to members (firefighters) who are involved in extended or extreme incident scene operations. The Specialized Vehicle Response Unit would be called to support operations involving all-terrain response vehicles required for difficult-to-reach hazardous terrains.

10. **a.** This is a crime scene, so it is extremely important for you to consult with law enforcement to obtain permission to enter the crime scene, for your own safety as well as to ensure that you do not disturb crime scene evidence. Once you have permission to enter, you may find it necessary to call for more advanced medical personnel based on your assessment. You must take precautions to avoid disturbing any evidence, including the patient by moving him or removing any obstacles that are blocking access. If it is absolutely essential to move something in the interest of patient care, you must inform law enforcement and document it.

11. **b, c, d, e.** Only highly trained firefighters, who have the equipment to protect them against smoke and fire, should approach a fire. Your responsibilities would include gathering information to help the responding firefighting and EMS units. You should not allow any other individuals to approach the fire. If possible, attempt to find out about the number of possible victims who may be trapped and any possible causes. You should give this information to emergency personnel when they arrive. Since local firefighters already are present, someone from this unit would assume the IC position.

12. **d.** When involved with a crime scene, you must take precautions to avoid disturbing any evidence, including that which may be on the patient's clothing. Subsequently, you should allow bloody clothing to dry and should not cut clothing near the stab wound. Never roll clothes

into a ball or place wet or bloody clothes into a plastic bag.

13. **a, c, d.** A special event where more than 25,000 participants or spectators are expected requires an on-site treatment facility, providing protection from weather or other elements to ensure patient safety and comfort. Beds and equipment for at least four simultaneous patients must be provided for evaluation and treatment, with adequate lighting and ventilation. A special event EMS system also must have on-site communication capabilities to ensure uniform access to care for patients in need of EMS care, on-site coordination of EMS personnel activities, communication with existing community PSAP and interface with other involved public safety agencies. Receiving facilities and ambulances providing emergency transportation also must be ensured.

END-OF-UNIT EXAMS

| UNIT 1 PREPARATORY |

Directions: *Circle the letter that best answers the question.*

1. Which of the following *emergency medical services* (EMS) personnel would be responsible for preparing the patient for transport?
   a. *Emergency medical technician* (EMT)
   b. *Emergency medical responder* (EMR)
   c. Paramedics
   d. *Advanced emergency medical technician* (AEMT)

2. You are working alongside an AEMT. Which of the following would this person be allowed to do?
   a. Provide strictly basic emergency care
   b. Work to stabilize the patient
   c. Perform an in-depth physical assessment
   d. Insert an *intravenous* (IV) line

3. Which of the following best describes the EMS system in the United States today?
   a. A group of varied, informal resources
   b. Multi-tiered, nationwide system
   c. Police and fire-based response systems
   d. Private organizations and companies providing care

4. Which of the following would be a primary responsibility for you in your role as an EMR?
   a. Directing bystanders to help
   b. Ensuring the patient's safety
   c. Recording what you did
   d. Reassuring the patient

5. Which of the following would be considered a component of an effective EMS system?
   a. Certification
   b. Scope of practice
   c. Medical oversight
   d. Core content

6. While at the scene of an accident, you speak to the physician via radio to obtain permission for a procedure not included in the standing orders. This is an example of which type of medical control?
   a. Offline
   b. Indirect
   c. Protocol
   d. Direct

7. An EMR is granted the right to practice via which mechanism?
   a. Certification
   b. Licensure
   c. Local credentialing
   d. Medical direction

8. Which of the following best emphasizes the importance of the role of an EMR?
   a. EMR's actions may determine whether a seriously injured person survives.
   b. EMRs function similarly in most areas across the country.
   c. EMRs have knowledge of advanced skills and techniques.
   d. EMRs can provide care without input from a physician.

9. The following are four nationally recognized levels of EMS training. Which level is the most advanced?
   a. Paramedic
   b. EMR
   c. AEMT
   d. EMT

10. Which of the following would be addressed by the resource management component of the Technical Assistance Assessment Standard?
    a. 9-1-1 communication system
    b. Available supplies for care
    c. Specialty care centers
    d. Personnel training programs

11. A patient is lying face-down on the floor in what appears to be a puddle of urine. There is blood oozing from a cut on her forehead. When providing care to his patient, which *personal protective equipment* (PPE) would be essential to use?
    a. Disposable gloves
    b. Safety glasses
    c. *High-efficiency particulate air* (HEPA) mask
    d. Disposable gown

12. As you provide care to a patient, some of the patient's blood gets on your forearm. Which of the following would you do next?
    a. Use alcohol to clean off the blood
    b. Irrigate the area with sterile saline for 10 minutes
    c. Wash the area with a diluted bleach solution
    d. Clean the area thoroughly with soap and water

13. You are called to the home of an elderly gentleman who has been diagnosed with a terminal illness. His family states that he has an advance directive. Your assessment reveals that the patient is not breathing. Which action would be most appropriate?
    a. Ask the family if you can see the written directive
    b. Begin to resuscitate the patient
    c. Call the funeral director for the family
    d. Tell the family that there is nothing that you can do

14. Which of the following is the most effective natural defense against infection?
    a. Hand washing
    b. Intact skin
    c. Pale mucous membranes
    d. PPE

15. You are providing care to a patient who is thought to have rabies. You understand that this condition is transmitted by which method?
    a. Indirect contact
    b. Respiratory droplet transmission
    c. Direct contact
    d. Vector-borne transmission

16. When removing disposable gloves, which of the following would you do first?
    a. Pull the first glove off by pulling on each of the fingertips
    b. Slide two gloved fingers under the first glove at the wrist
    c. Remove the second glove so that the first glove ends up inside of it
    d. Pinch the palm side of the first glove near the wrist to pull it off inside out

17. Which of the following would be considered a work practice control?
    a. Providing biohazard containers
    b. Disinfecting work surfaces possibly soiled with blood or body fluids
    c. Ensuring that sharps disposal containers are available
    d. Posting signs at entrances where infectious materials may be present

18. You are preparing to clean up a spill of blood that occurred while you were providing care to a patient. You would expect to use which solution?
    a. Chlorine bleach
    b. Hydrogen peroxide
    c. Alcohol
    d. Liquid soap

19. You and several fellow EMRs had responded to a multiple casualty incident several days ago. You suspect that one of your colleagues is experiencing critical incident stress when he exhibits which of the following?
    a. Increased attention span
    b. Enhanced concentration
    c. Heightened job performance
    d. Unusually excessive silence

20. You are with the family of a patient who has suddenly died as a result of a heart attack. You would do which of the following?
    a. Encourage the family to refrain from becoming angry
    b. Provide reassurance that may or may not be accurate
    c. Remain calm and nonjudgmental
    d. Speak to them in a firm, authoritative voice

21. After a critical incident, you are to participate in debriefing. Which of the following best describes this technique?
    a. One-to-one interaction with a peer counselor
    b. Group discussion with a trained professional
    c. Short informal discussion with others
    d. Brief interaction occurring immediately after the incident

22. You are providing care to a patient at the scene of a building explosion. The patient is lying on the ground and unconscious, but breathing. He has a large laceration on his upper leg and blood can be seen spurting from the wound. Which PPE would be least appropriate to use?
    a. HEPA mask
    b. Disposable gloves
    c. Gown
    d. Face shield

23. While caring for a patient, some blood splashes into your eyes. Which of the following would you do first?
    a. Wash your face with soap and water
    b. Apply antiseptic eye drops
    c. Flush the eyes with clean water for 20 minutes
    d. Report the incident to the designated person in your agency

24. Which of the following would be a most likely route of transmission for hepatitis B?
    a. Drinking contaminated water
    b. Having sexual contact with an infected person
    c. Hugging an infected person
    d. Eating contaminated food

25. You obtain consent from a patient before touching him to prevent which of the following?
    a. Battery
    b. Abandonment
    c. Assault
    d. Negligence

26. You are providing care to an adolescent female who is a legally emancipated minor. The female has a 9-month-old infant who needs medical care. The adolescent nods her head in response to your request to care for her infant. This is an example of—
    a. Implied consent.
    b. Expressed consent.
    c. Informal consent.
    d. Parental consent.

27. Which of the following would be appropriate to do while caring for a patient who is an emancipated minor if the patient tells you that she is fine and does not want further care?
    a. Notify more advanced medical personnel to obtain further assistance
    b. Inform her that if you stop care, she cannot call the EMS system later on
    c. Honor her refusal, following local policies for such situations
    d. Tell her you are legally required to continue to provide care

28. When applying the principle of the patient's best interest, you would—
    a. Ensure that the patient remains free from harm.
    b. Help the patient regardless of what it involves.
    c. Show respect for the patient's human dignity.
    d. Provide care that focuses solely on helping the patient.

29. The following are statements that reflect the steps in obtaining consent from a patient. Which statement would you use first?
    a. "I am going to loosen your sleeve to check your arm."
    b. "My name is Jane Smith."
    c. "I notice that you have a large cut on your arm. May I help you?""
    d. "I am an emergency medical responder."

30. You arrive at the home of a patient experiencing severe difficulty breathing. The patient's spouse tells you that the patient has terminal cancer and has a *Do Not Resuscitate* (DNR) order. However, the spouse is unable to find the written document. Which of the following would you do first?
    a. Prepare to perform the usual emergency care
    b. Notify medical direction about how to proceed
    c. Call the patient's physician for verification
    d. Honor the spouse's statement and the patient's wishes

31. An EMR made an error when providing care to a patient that resulted in patient injury. Which aspect of negligence was involved?
    a. Duty to act
    b. Proximate cause
    c. Breach of duty
    d. Patient harm

32. Which of the following would you identify as the least appropriate condition that would require mandatory reporting?
    a. Child abuse
    b. Tuberculosis
    c. Gunshot wound from a robbery
    d. Epilepsy

33. The *Health Insurance Portability and Accountability Act* (HIPAA) Privacy Rule requires that identifying patient information cannot be shared with certain individuals. Which of the following would be least likely to require the patient's specific consent for sharing?
    a. Family members
    b. Media
    c. Employers
    d. Organ procurement agencies

34. A patient at the scene of a motor-vehicle crash refuses care. Which response would be most appropriate initially?
    a. Telling the patient that he needs to be checked out
    b. Respecting the patient's right to refuse care
    c. Contacting the local law enforcement agency for help
    d. Documenting the patient's refusal for care

35. Medical futility is an exception to which of the following, specifically?
    a. Living wills
    b. Health care proxy
    c. DNR orders
    d. Durable power of attorney for health care

36. A patient who appears to be mentally incompetent is seriously injured and alone. You would—
    a. Begin to treat the patient based on implied consent.
    b. Attempt to contact the patient's guardian for consent.
    c. Summon law enforcement to control the patient.
    d. Try to talk the patient into giving consent.

37. You arrive on the scene of an emergency involving a man who has fallen off a ladder while painting the outside of his two-story home. The patient is lying on his back with his upper body elevated about 45 degrees. You would describe the patient's position as which of the following?
    a. Supine
    b. Prone
    c. Fowler's
    d. Anatomical

38. Which structure would you expect to be involved if a patient's upper arm is broken?
    a. Humerus
    b. Ulna
    c. Radius
    d. Femur

39. When describing a patient's upper arm injury, you would identify it as which of the following?
    a. Lateral to the wrist
    b. Superior to the elbow
    c. Anterior to the ribs
    d. Medial to the sternum

40. You are checking the temperature of a patient and find it to be below normal. Which prefix would you use to describe this finding?
    a. Hyper-
    b. Hypo-
    c. Brady-
    d. Tachy-

41. You observe a patient straightening his leg. You identify this motion as which of the following?
    a. Extension
    b. Flexion
    c. Superior
    d. Proximal

42. A patient is placed in the supine position. You would expect to find this patient—
    a. Face-down on his stomach.
    b. Sitting up slightly.
    c. Lying flat on his back.
    d. On his back with his legs elevated.

43. Which of the following occurs during expiration?
    a. Relaxation of the diaphragm
    b. Contraction of the chest muscles
    c. Movement of ribs outward
    d. Expansion of the chest cavity

44. A patient is not breathing and does not have a pulse. This may reflect a problem with which part of the nervous system?
    a. Spinal cord
    b. Brainstem
    c. Cerebellum
    d. Cerebrum

45. You are called to the scene involving an infant who is having difficulty breathing. Which of the following would be most important for you to keep in mind about the infant's respiratory system in contrast to an adult's respiratory system?
    a. Trachea is wider but softer.
    b. Chest wall is more rigid.
    c. Infants are nose-breathers.
    d. The respiratory rate is slower.

46. A patient has jumped from a second-floor balcony in an attempt to escape a fire. The patient has landed face-up on the ground next to the building. Which emergency move would be appropriate to use for this patient?
    a. Firefighter's carry
    b. Clothes drag
    c. Ankle drag
    d. Shoulder drag

47. When preparing to move a patient, which of the following would be most important for you to do?
    a. Make sure that a stretcher is readily available
    b. Keep your knees rigidly straight
    c. Be aware of your own physical abilities
    d. Twist your back to reach the patient

48. You and your partner arrive on the scene of a commuter train fire and are providing care to a patient who is sitting on the side of the train station walkway after falling on the train tracks and sustaining several cuts to her face and arms. The patient is coughing and breathing rapidly. The patient is being prepared for transport. You would expect to place the patient in which position?
    a. Supine
    b. Upright sitting
    c. Left lateral recumbent position
    d. Modified *high arm in endangered spine* (H.A.IN.E.S)

49. You and three other responders are preparing to log roll a patient. The person at which position would direct the move?
   a. Head
   b. Shoulders
   c. Hips
   d. Opposite side

50. Which patient would you identify as most likely in need of restraint?
   a. A patient who is lying face-down and unconscious
   b. A patient who is screaming loudly in pain
   c. A patient who is violently thrashing about
   d. A patient who is difficult to arouse

51. When preparing to restrain a patient, at least how many EMRs should be available?
   a. 3
   b. 4
   c. 5
   d. 6

52. You are preparing to transport a patient who weighs 700 lbs. Which type of stretcher would be most appropriate to use?
   a. Scoop stretcher
   b. Standard wheeled stretcher
   c. Orthopedic stretcher
   d. Bariatric stretcher

53. You and your partner arrive at the home of a patient who needs to be transported to the medical facility. You plan to move the patient from the bed to the stretcher using the direct carry technique. You position the stretcher—
   a. At a right angle to the patient's bed.
   b. With the stretcher's head parallel to the bed's head.
   c. Alongside the bed with the stretcher's head at the bed's foot.
   d. At the foot of the bed, parallel to the bottom of the bed.

54. You always begin lifting a patient with your—
   a. Head facing down.
   b. Feet close together.
   c. Flexed arms relaxed.
   d. Back in locked-in position.

55. When preparing to move and lift a patient, you should—
   a. Keep the weight of the patient as far away from your body as possible.
   b. Refrain from talking with the patient who is being moved.
   c. Estimate the weight of the patient and any equipment to be used.
   d. Bend at the knees rather than at your hips and waist.

| UNIT 2 ASSESSMENT |

Directions: Circle the letter that best answers the question.

1. You are called to the scene of a motor vehicle crash on a dark, two-lane highway. The car crashed through the guardrail and landed on a slope of a small ravine. The driver is alert but complaining of pain, and there is a strong odor of gasoline in the area. Which of the following would be the most important for you to do?
   a. Get the patient out of the car.
   b. Put on PPE.
   c. Stabilize the vehicle.
   d. Ask the patient if he can move his arms.

2. You are providing care to a patient involved in a head-on motor vehicle crash. The patient was wearing a seat belt with a shoulder strap, and the front and side airbags were activated. The patient is complaining of pain in his chest and difficulty breathing. Based on the patient's *mechanism of injury* (MOI), you would least likely suspect injuries to which of the following?
   a. Chest
   b. Face
   c. Abdomen
   d. Shoulders

3. You are the first to arrive at the scene of an emergency involving four to five individuals who are engaged in a fight that started inside a local tavern and now has spilled out onto the street. Two of the individuals are lying on the sidewalk and bleeding. Broken glass and bottles are strewn all over the ground. Which of the following would be your initial action?
   a. Wait for law enforcement personnel to arrive to secure the scene.
   b. Walk quickly to the two injured individuals to provide care.
   c. Set up barriers around the scene to keep bystanders back.
   d. Notify personnel trained to deal with hazardous materials.

4. Which of the following would be least likely to affect your decision about the number of additional resources needed at the scene?
   a. Nature of the illness
   b. Number of injured persons
   c. Evidence of any hazards
   d. Number of bystanders

5. When approaching an emergency scene, which of the following would least likely suggest that hazardous materials are present?
   a. Vapor cloud
   b. Broken glass
   c. Strange odor
   d. Spilled liquid

6. You determine that a patient requires assisted ventilations. Which of the following would you expect to use when adhering to standard precautions?
   a. Mask
   b. Protective eyewear
   c. CPR breathing barrier
   d. Gown

7. When on scene, which individual is responsible for traffic control at an emergency scene?
   a. EMR
   b. Designated bystander
   c. Law enforcement personnel
   d. Driver of an emergency vehicle

8. Which vehicle would you identify as being unstable?
   a. A vehicle that has been struck and has rolled over with its two side wheels over the guardrail
   b. A vehicle that has been struck from the rear and has ended up on the shoulder of the road
   c. A vehicle that has collided head-on with a telephone pole
   d. A vehicle that has been struck from the side and now is facing oncoming traffic

9. During the primary phase of a blast injury, which body structures would least likely experience injury?
   a. Stomach
   b. Muscles
   c. Lungs
   d. Inner ears

10. Which of the following is the highest priority when responding to a call involving domestic violence?
    a. Ensuring that the suspected perpetrator is on the other side of the room when caring for the patient
    b. Waiting for law enforcement to secure the scene before attempting to enter
    c. Using yes–no questions with the patient to prevent further escalation of violence
    d. Asking questions while speaking directly to the patient and suspected perpetrator together

11. When arriving on the scene of an emergency involving a person who has fallen from a ladder, you understand that the severity of the injury increases with the height of the fall because—
    a. More objects are present to cause additional injuries.
    b. The landing is less likely to be soft and yielding.
    c. The speed of the fall increases with greater heights.
    d. The patient is more likely to fall head first.

12. When sizing up the scene of an emergency, which of the following would be most appropriate?
    a. Await the arrival of additional resource personnel.
    b. Ensure the safety of the patient above anything else.
    c. Rely on the information provided to you by dispatch.
    d. Use each of your senses to determine any hazards.

13. During your primary assessment, you assess that the patient can open her eyes when you ask her to do so. You would describe this as which of the following?
    a. The patient responds to verbal stimuli.
    b. The patient responds to painful stimuli.
    c. The patient is alert and aware of surroundings.
    d. The patient is unconscious.

14. The patient should be in which position when you assess his or her airway status?
    a. On his or her left side
    b. In the position in which you found him or her
    c. Supine, face-up
    d. Prone, face turned to the side

15. Which of the following findings would you consider abnormal?
    a. Pulse of 70 beats per minute
    b. Capillary refill of 2 seconds
    c. Respiratory rate of 18 breaths per minute
    d. Pale, cool skin

16. When approaching a patient, you would proceed in a specific manner. Which of the following would be stated or asked first?
    a. "Can you tell me what happened?"
    b. "I am an emergency medical responder here to help you."
    c. "What is your name?"
    d. "Will you let me examine you?"

17. You perform a primary assessment for which reason?
    a. To identify possible immediate threats to life
    b. To ensure scene safety
    c. To decide if you need additional resources
    d. To help determine the MOI

18. You would least expect to summon more advanced medical personnel if you assess which of the following?
    a. Persistent abdominal pressure
    b. Difficulty breathing
    c. Vomiting
    d. Seizure

19. When assessing the pulse of an infant you would place your fingers at which artery?
    a. Carotid
    b. Femoral
    c. Radial
    d. Brachial

20. While performing the head-tilt/chin-lift technique, tilt the patient's head just past neutral if the patient is a(n)—
    a. Adult.
    b. Adolescent.
    c. Child.
    d. Infant.

21. Which of the following would lead you to suspect that a conscious patient is experiencing a breathing problem?
    a. Shrill whistling sounds with breaths
    b. Quiet, effortless breaths
    c. Absent gasping with breathing
    d. Deep, regular breathing

22. When evaluating perfusion, which of the following would be least appropriate to note about the skin?
    a. Color
    b. Intactness
    c. Moisture
    d. Temperature

23. Which of the following would you expect to note first if a patient was developing shock?
    a. Irritability
    b. Weak pulse
    c. Pale skin
    d. Excessive thirst

24. A drowning patient has a pulse but is not breathing. You prepare to use a resuscitation mask to give 2 initial ventilations. Which of the following would you do first?
    a. Kneel behind or to the side of the patient's head
    b. Open the patient's airway
    c. Attach a one-way valve to the mask
    d. Seal the mask

25. After sizing up the scene, the following are steps involved with performing a primary assessment. Which of the following would you do first?
   a. Summon more advanced medical personnel
   b. Open the patient's airway
   c. Check the patient for responsiveness
   d. Give 2 ventilations

26. Which method is most appropriate to use when checking an infant for responsiveness?
   a. Clapping your hands near the infant's ear
   b. Asking the parent if the infant is okay
   c. Calling the infant by his or her name
   d. Flicking the underside of the foot

27. Your primary assessment reveals that the patient is moving air freely in and out of the chest and has pale, moist skin. Which action would be most appropriate?
   a. Providing 2 initial ventilations immediately
   b. Continuing to monitor for changes
   c. Administering emergency oxygen to the patient if available
   d. Clearing the airway of debris

28. You arrive on the scene of an emergency in which a patient had been working in his yard when his wife states that he suddenly "passed out." The patient is alert and oriented but pale and sweaty. He tells you that he takes medication for his high blood pressure. The patient reports no complaints of chest pain. When obtaining the SAMPLE history, you would identify which of the following as the chief complaint?
   a. Pale skin
   b. Absence of chest pain
   c. High blood pressure
   d. Fainting

29. You arrive at the home of a patient who is having trouble breathing. The patient's roommate tells you that the patient has a history of asthma and allergies. Which of the following questions would you ask first?
   a. "When did this difficulty first start?"
   b. "Does anything make it better or worse?"
   c. "How would you rate your difficulty breathing?"
   d. "How long have you been experiencing this problem?"

30. When obtaining the SAMPLE history from a patient, she states that she drank a glass of water about 2 hours ago. You identify this as related to which of the following of the mnemonic?
   a. S
   b. L
   c. M
   d. E

31. You perform a secondary assessment on a responsive patient. After assessing the patient's complaints and obtaining a SAMPLE history, which of the following would you do next?
   a. Perform a focused medical assessment.
   b. Assess baseline vital signs.
   c. Perform components of a detailed physical exam.
   d. Provide emergency care.

32. When performing the physical exam, which of the following is most important for you to do?
   a. Manipulate the patient's clothing to access the area to be examined.
   b. Keep the area covered while you are examining it.
   c. Ask the patient questions about the area after examining it.
   d. Conduct the exam in a location that cannot be seen by bystanders.

33. You are examining the head of a patient. Which finding would you identify as normal?
    a. Clear fluid around the ears
    b. Both pupils are equal in size
    c. Pupil constriction on exposure to darkness
    d. Facial asymmetry

34. When obtaining a patient's blood pressure, which of the following would be most appropriate?
    a. Apply the cuff over the patient's thickly clothed arm.
    b. Position the bladder of the cuff over the radial artery.
    c. Ensure that the cuff covers about two-thirds of his upper arm.
    d. Allow the patient's arm to hang down at his side.

35. You provide an ongoing assessment for which reason?
    a. To monitor changes in the patient's condition
    b. To clarify the patient's history
    c. To further assess signs and symptoms
    d. To identify life-threatening conditions

36. When examining the abdomen during the physical exam, which of the following would you do?
    a. Observe for pulsations.
    b. Have the patient shrug his or her shoulders.
    c. Push in on the sides of the hips.
    d. Inspect for a protruding jugular vein.

37. Which of the following would you do first when performing a secondary assessment for a responsive medical patient?
    a. Obtain a SAMPLE history.
    b. Perform a physical exam.
    c. Assess the patient's complaints.
    d. Assess baseline vital signs.

38. When using radio communication, which of the following is the most appropriate?
    a. Using any radio frequency available
    b. Responding by saying "yes" or "no"
    c. Speaking quickly with mouth 10 inches away from the microphone
    d. Avoiding the use of "please" and "thank you"

39. You and your partner arrive at the scene of a fire in a senior citizen apartment complex. You prepare to treat an older adult couple who have been helped across the street to a safe area. The woman is sitting upright and coughing. She is holding her left arm and grimacing. The husband is standing next to her, visibly distraught about his wife. When preparing to care for this couple, which of the following is most important for you to do?
    a. Introduce yourself to the couple.
    b. Tell the woman that she fractured her arm.
    c. Address the couple by their first names.
    d. Have the husband describe the wife's problem.

40. When interviewing a patient, which of the following would be most appropriate?
    a. Asking leading questions to get focused information
    b. Using why-type questions to gain insight
    c. Allowing the patient to do most of the talking
    d. Frequently interrupting the patient for clarification

41. The primary function of the run report is to—
    a. Serve as a legal document.
    b. Ensure high-quality care.
    c. Act as an educational tool.
    d. Allow for billing for services.

42. You would document the SAMPLE history in which section of the *prehospital care report* (PCR)?
   a. Patient narrative
   b. Patient data
   c. Check boxes
   d. Run data

43. When providing care to a patient experiencing a medical emergency, which of the following would be the least effective in facilitating communication?
   a. Being on the same eye level with the patient
   b. Minimizing distractions
   c. Ensuring adequate lighting
   d. Avoiding eye contact

44. You are interviewing the daughter of an older adult patient who has fallen and hit his head. Which of the following is most appropriate to say?
   a. "Can you tell me what happened?"
   b. "I'm sure your father will be fine."
   c. "Why was he walking without his cane?"
   d. "He really should be watched more carefully."

45. You are documenting information in the patient data section of the PCR. Which of the following would you include?
   a. Level of alertness
   b. Respiratory rate
   c. Age
   d. Time of arrival on scene

46. You are communicating with medical control and receive an order for a specific treatment that you are qualified to perform. Which of the following is most appropriate when receiving the order?
   a. Tell medical control, "Affirmative."
   b. Repeat the order word for word.
   c. Have medical control repeat the order again.
   d. Tell medical control that you understand the order.

| UNIT 3 AIRWAY |

Directions: *Circle the letter that best answers the question.*

1. Which technique would you use to clear an unconscious patient's mouth of vomit?
   a. Abdominal thrusts
   b. Back blows
   c. Head-tilt/chin-lift
   d. Finger sweep

2. You determine that the patient is not breathing but has a pulse. You prepare to give ventilations using a resuscitation mask, giving 1 ventilation about every—
   a. 1 second.
   b. 3 seconds.
   c. 5 seconds.
   d. 10 seconds.

3. As you are providing ventilations, a patient vomits. Which of the following would you do first?
   a. Turn the patient as a unit onto his side.
   b. Clear the airway of the vomit immediately.
   c. Reposition the patient's head to reopen the airway.
   d. Use greater force when ventilating to bypass the vomit.

4. When giving ventilations to an adult, you would give the ventilations for how long before rechecking for breathing and a pulse?
   a. 1 minute
   b. 2 minutes
   c. 3 minutes
   d. 4 minutes

5. Which of the following indicates that your ventilations are effective?
   a. The mask is sealed tightly.
   b. The abdomen becomes distended.
   c. The chest clearly rises.
   d. Your breaths move easily into the mask.

6. Which structure is responsible for controlling the rate and depth of breathing based on oxygen and carbon dioxide levels in the body?
   a. Heart
   b. Lungs
   c. Kidneys
   d. Brain

7. You determine that a child is breathing adequately based on which breathing rate?
   a. 12 breaths per minute
   b. 26 breaths per minute
   c. 38 breaths per minute
   d. 48 breaths per minute

8. When using a *bag-valve-mask resuscitator* (BVM), how many rescuers should be present to ensure effectiveness?
   a. 1
   b. 2
   c. 3
   d. 4

9. Which of the following would lead you to suspect that a patient's breathing is adequate?
   a. Midline trachea
   b. Rib muscles pulling in on inhalation
   c. Pursed-lip breathing
   d. Tripod positioning

10. You are caring for a patient who is not breathing and who has a significant injury to his mouth. Which method is most appropriate to use to give ventilations?
    a. Mouth-to-mouth
    b. Mouth-to-mask
    c. Mouth-to-nose
    d. Mouth-to-stoma

11. Mouth-to-mask ventilations are advantageous over mouth-to-mouth ventilations because mouth-to-mask ventilations—
    a. Require less time to give.
    b. Reduce the risk of disease transmission.
    c. Deliver a higher percentage of oxygen.
    d. Necessitate pinching the nose for a seal.

12. You arrive at the home of a 6-month-old girl who is struggling to breathe and is cyanotic. You suspect that the infant's airway is obstructed because you do not see the chest rising or falling or hear or feel any air going in and out of her mouth and nose. Which of the following would you do first?
    a. Give 2 slow ventilations.
    b. Tilt the head back.
    c. Give 5 back blows.
    d. Perform 5 chest thrusts.

13. When performing chest thrusts on an infant, you would compress the chest to a depth of about—
    a. ¼ inch.
    b. ½ inch.
    c. 1½ inches.
    d. 2 inches.

14. You arrive at a restaurant in response to a call that a man was choking on some food. The patient is now unconscious. Which of the following should you do first?
    a. Ensure that the patient is on a firm, flat surface.
    b. Attempt to ventilate the patient.
    c. Give 5 chest compressions.
    d. Look inside the patient's mouth.

15. Which of the following is the most important assessment to make when preparing to insert an *oropharyngeal airway* (OPA)?
    a. Evidence of airway obstruction
    b. Presence of a gag reflex
    c. Unresponsiveness
    d. Distance from the earlobe to the mouth

16. When preparing to suction a child using a mechanical suction device, you would limit each suction attempt to no more than—
    a. 5 seconds.
    b. 10 seconds.
    c. 15 seconds.
    d. 20 seconds.

17. You are inserting an OPA into an adult. As you reach the back of the patient's throat, he begins to gag. Which of the following would you do next?
    a. Immediately remove the airway.
    b. Give the patient a sip of water.
    c. Continue to insert the airway.
    d. Rotate the airway 90 degrees.

18. Which situation would require you to use back blows followed by chest thrusts for an adult?
    a. The patient is thin and frail.
    b. The patient is pregnant.
    c. The patient is coughing.
    d. The patient is unconscious.

19. You determine that an OPA is properly placed by which of the following?
    a. The flange is resting on the patient's lips.
    b. Resistance to the device is felt.
    c. No gagging occurs.
    d. The edge touches the patient's teeth.

20. You are using a mechanical suction device. You would apply the suction—
    a. As you insert the tip into the mouth.
    b. Upon reaching the back of the mouth.
    c. As you withdraw the suction tip.
    d. When touching the back of the tongue.

21. You arrive at a playground in response to a call that a child is choking. The 8-year-old child is responsive and coughing. His mother is standing next to him. Which of the following would you do first?
    a. Obtain consent from the mother to help the child.
    b. Encourage the child to continue coughing forcefully.
    c. Give 5 back blows followed by 5 abdominal thrusts.
    d. Lower the child to a flat, firm surface on the ground.

22. You are using a BVM to ventilate the patient, and you attach emergency oxygen to it. You would expect to set the oxygen flowmeter to which setting?
    a. 5 *liters per minute* (LPM)
    b. 10 LPM
    c. 15 LPM
    d. 20 LPM

23. When administering emergency oxygen, which of the following would you use to verify the oxygen flow?
    a. Movement of the flowmeter dial
    b. Absence of the O-ring gasket
    c. Pressure gauge reading 190 *pounds per square inch* (psi)
    d. Audible hissing sound through the device

24. You decide that a patient experiencing difficulty breathing requires emergency oxygen. The patient is pale and anxious and is breathing through his mouth at a rate of 28 breaths per minute. Which delivery device would be least appropriate for this patient?
    a. Nasal cannula
    b. Resuscitation mask
    c. Non-rebreather mask
    d. BVM

25. You determine that a child breathing at which respiratory rate would benefit from emergency oxygen?
    a. 16 breaths per minute
    b. 20 breaths per minute
    c. 26 breaths per minute
    d. 38 breaths per minute

26. When working with emergency oxygen systems, which of the following would be least appropriate?
    a. Checking the pressure regulator
    b. Handling the cylinder carefully
    c. Lubricating the connections
    d. Hand-tightening the screw to ensure a snug regulator

27. When administering emergency oxygen by a fixed-flow-rate system, which of the following would be appropriate?
    a. Turning on the system
    b. Opening the cylinder valve for 1 second
    c. Attaching the regulator
    d. Opening the cylinder counterclockwise one full turn

28. A patient who is not breathing is to receive emergency oxygen at 6 LPM. Which delivery device is most appropriate?
    a. BVM
    b. Resuscitation mask
    c. Nasal cannula
    d. Non-rebreather mask

29. You are using a non-rebreather mask to administer emergency oxygen. Which of the following is most important to keep in mind?
    a. The patient exhales into the reservoir bag.
    b. The device is inappropriate for a patient with a nasal injury.
    c. The reservoir bag should be about two-thirds full.
    d. Several valves control the flow of oxygen in and out of the mask.

30. A patient is receiving emergency oxygen via nasal cannula. Which flow rate would be least appropriate to use with this device?
    a. 2 LPM
    b. 4 LPM
    c. 6 LPM
    d. 8 LPM

31. When preparing to administer emergency oxygen using a variable-flow-rate system, which of the following would you do first?
    a. Inspect the cylinder label for an indication that it contains oxygen.
    b. Check the pressure regulator for the label "oxygen."
    c. Open the cylinder valve after removing the O-ring gasket.
    d. Open the cylinder counterclockwise for one full turn.

| UNIT 4 CIRCULATION |

Directions: *Circle the letter that best answers the question.*

1. You are preparing to perform chest compressions on a 10-year-old boy. Where do you place your hands to be most effective?
   a. Uppermost portion of the sternum
   b. Directly over the nipple area
   c. Atop the xiphoid process at the lower sternum
   d. In the middle of the chest

2. You would compress a child's chest to which depth?
   a. About 1 inch
   b. About 1½ inches
   c. About 2 inches
   d. About 2½ inches

3. You are performing CPR on an 11-year-old child who has been pulled from a pond after being submerged for several minutes. An *automated external defibrillator* (AED) becomes available, and you prepare to use it. Which of the following is the most important for you to do before using the AED on this child?
   a. Correctly placing the pads on the child's chest
   b. Ensuring that the child is not lying in a puddle of water
   c. Using pediatric defibrillation pads if available
   d. Checking to see if spare batteries are included

4. You obtain a SAMPLE history from a patient. Which of the following would least likely suggest that the patient is experiencing a heart attack?
   a. The pain is described as squeezing, unrelieved by rest.
   b. The pain does not radiate.
   c. The patient is sitting up and leaning forward.
   e. The patient complains of feeling dizzy.

5. Which of the following would you do first if you suspect that a patient is having a heart attack?
   a. Get the patient to stop any activity and rest
   b. Closely monitor the patient's vital signs
   c. Summon more advanced medical personnel
   d. Begin CPR

6. You are providing care to a 6 month old at the scene of an apartment fire. You open the infant's airway and find that she is not breathing. After immediately giving 2 ventilations that are effective, which action would you do next?
   a. Begin chest compressions.
   b. Deliver 5 back blows.
   c. Check for a brachial pulse.
   d. Do a finger sweep.

7. You are on the scene of an emergency and are giving CPR to the patient. Another EMR arrives on the scene to assist you. The cycle of compressions and ventilations that you would perform is—
   a. 30 compressions and 2 ventilations.
   b. 15 compressions and 1 ventilation.
   c. 15 compressions and 2 ventilations.
   d. 30 compressions and 1 ventilation.

8. You are the only EMR present and are performing CPR. Where would you position yourself to give chest compressions?
   a. At the patient's head
   b. On the patient's side at the chest
   c. Even with the patient's shoulders
   d. Between the patient's legs

9. You have been performing CPR on a patient and the patient begins to breathe. You also note a pulse. Which action is most appropriate?
   a. Cancel the call for more advanced medical personnel.
   b. Stop chest compressions but continue ventilations.
   c. Continue to monitor the patient while maintaining an open airway.
   d. Obtain an AED to check the heart rhythm.

10. Which condition would be a least likely indication for using an AED?
    a. Absence of a pulse
    b. Obstructed airway
    c. No evidence of the chest rising and falling
    d. Lack of responsiveness

11. You are called to a patient's home because the patient is complaining of chest pain. Which of the following would lead you to suspect that the patient is most likely experiencing angina?
    a. Pain spreading to the jaw and neck
    b. Pain accompanied by difficulty breathing
    c. Pain that is persistent
    d. Pain that eases with resting

12. You and another EMR are performing two-rescuer CPR. You would expect to switch positions approximately every—
    a. 2 minutes.
    b. 4 minutes.
    c. 6 minutes.
    d. 8 minutes.

13. You arrive on the scene where another EMR is performing CPR on a patient. Which of the following would you do first?
    a. Call for a position change at the end of the last compression cycle.
    b. Confirm if more advanced medical personnel have been called.
    c. Immediately begin giving ventilations to the patient.
    d. Obtain an AED, if available.

14. An AED has delivered a shock to the patient. Which of the following would you do next?
    a. Wait for the device to re-analyze the heart rhythm.
    b. Continue to monitor the patient's condition.
    c. Begin performing CPR for about 2 minutes.
    d. Place the patient in a face-up position while maintaining an open airway.

15. You are preparing to apply AED pads to a patient's chest when you notice a smoking cessation patch on the patient's upper chest area. Which action would be most appropriate?
    a. Place the pads directly over the medication patch.
    b. Move the medication patch to another area on the body.
    c. Apply the pads to a chest area away from the patch.
    d. Remove the medication patch with a gloved hand.

| UNIT 5 MEDICAL EMERGENCIES |

Directions: *Circle the letter that best answers the question.*

1. You arrive at the scene of an emergency involving a patient who is wearing a medical identification bracelet stating that the patient has diabetes. You understand that diabetes involves a problem with regulation of which of the following?
   a. Fluid volume
   b. Blood glucose levels
   c. Brain electrical activity
   d. Oxygen levels

2. While providing care to a female patient who is conscious and talking, you suspect that the patient is experiencing hypoglycemia. Which of the following would you do?
   a. Have the patient give herself a dose of insulin.
   b. Place the patient in a supine (face-up) position.
   c. Offer the patient fruit juice or a non-diet soft drink.
   d. Use the head-tilt/chin-lift technique to open her airway.

3. Upon arriving at the scene of an emergency, several bystanders tell you that the patient suddenly fell to the floor and "his body started to shake all over." You suspect which type of seizure?
   a. Generalized seizure
   b. Febrile seizure
   c. Simple partial seizure
   d. Complex partial seizure

4. You would assess the patient as having status epilepticus if the seizure shows no signs of slowing down and lasts longer than—
   a. 10 minutes.
   b. 8 minutes.
   c. 5 minutes.
   d. 2 minutes.

5. Which of the following is the underlying mechanism involved with seizures?
   a. Blood pressure that drops to abnormally low levels
   b. Disruption in blood flow to the brain
   c. Insulin levels that are extremely elevated.
   d. Disruption in the brain's normal electrical activity

6. A patient is experiencing tonic-clonic seizures. What is the priority when caring for this patient?
   a. Maintaining privacy
   b. Preventing tongue biting
   c. Protecting the patient from injury
   d. Clearing the airway

7. A patient has a history of seizures. Which situation would least likely require you to summon more advanced medical personnel?
   a. A patient who is currently pregnant.
   b. A patient whose seizure occurred while swimming
   c. A patient who has seizures that are medically controlled.
   d. A patient who is known to have diabetes.

8. A patient is hypoglycemic and unconscious. Which of the following would you do?
   a. Crush 2 to 5 glucose tablets, placing them under his or her tongue.
   b. Pour a small amount of non-diet soda on his or her lips.
   c. Summon more advanced medical personnel.
   d. Give the patient 4 ounces of fruit juice through a straw.

9. You arrive at the home of a 65-year-old man in response to a 9-1-1 call from his wife saying that he is having a stroke. The patient is conscious. Which of the following would you least likely expect to find with your SAMPLE history and physical exam?
   a. Facial drooping
   b. Clear speech
   c. Trouble walking
   d. Facial numbness

10. You are responding to an emergency call in which the patient is experiencing abdominal pain. Which of the following is most important to note?
    a. The patient is most likely experiencing a problem in the digestive system.
    b. The pain is serious enough to cause concern to the patient and/or others.
    c. The pain is originating from the area involving the stomach.
    d. The intensity of the pain will reveal the severity of the situation.

11. You are called to the home of a patient with renal failure who is receiving dialysis at his home. When assessing this patient, which of the following would you least likely identify as a possible complication?
    a. Hypotension
    b. Air embolism
    c. Hypervolemia
    d. Bradycardia

12. You are called to the scene of an emergency and you suspect that a patient has poisoning. You understand that alcohol is classified as which of the following?
    a. Narcotic
    b. Hallucinogen
    c. Depressant
    d. Stimulant

13. While caring for a patient at the scene, you find a bottle of prescription medication next to him. The label reads codeine. You would identify this drug as which of the following?
    a. Depressant
    b. Hallucinogen
    c. Narcotic
    d. Cannabis product

14. Which of the following would you identify as least likely to affect the severity of the poisoning in a child?
    a. Amount of substance ingested
    b. Child's weight
    c. Child's sex
    d. Time elapsed since ingesting the poison

15. When reading an article about the statistics related to poisoning in the United States, which of the following would you expect to find?
    a. A decrease in suicides has led to a decrease in adult poisoning deaths.
    b. The number of child poisonings has been gradually increasing.
    c. The death rate is highest in the 6- to 10-year-old age group.
    d. The majority of poisonings take place in the home.

16. Which of the following would be the least likely source of bacterial food poisoning?
    a. Botulism
    b. Lead
    c. *E. coli*
    d. *Salmonella*

17. You are called to the scene of an emergency involving several family members who may be experiencing food poisoning. Which signs and symptoms would you expect to find?
    a. Vomiting
    b. Excessive eye burning
    c. Disorientation
    d. Seizures

18. A child is stung by a wasp and experiences a reaction. This reaction is in response to a poison that has entered the body by which mechanism?
    a. Absorption
    b. Inhalation
    c. Injection
    d. Ingestion

19. Which of the following would you identify as an inhaled poison?
    a. Poison ivy
    b. Contaminated water
    c. Chloroform
    d. Snake venom

20. When providing care to a patient with suspected substance abuse, which of the following is most important?
    a. Identifying potential life-threatening conditions
    b. Determining which substance is involved
    c. Administering emergency oxygen, if available
    d. Restraining the patient if he or she becomes aggressive

21. You suspect that a patient is experiencing hallucinogen abuse. Which of the following would you most likely find?
    a. Drowsiness
    b. Bloodshot eyes
    c. Mood change
    d. Pale face

22. Which of the following would be least appropriate when caring for a patient with substance misuse?
    a. Applying several heavy blankets to prevent chilling
    b. Maintaining an open airway
    c. Providing reassurance in a calm voice
    d. Summoning more advanced medical personnel

23. You would suspect cocaine abuse in a patient exhibiting which of the following?
    a. Drowsiness, slurred speech and confusion
    b. Mood changes, flushing and hallucinations
    c. Tachycardia, hypertension and rapid breathing
    d. Excitement, restlessness and irritability

24. Which of the following would least likely be a possible contributing factor for substance abuse?
    a. Traditional family structure
    b. Peer pressure
    c. Media glamorization
    d. Low self-esteem

25. You arrive on the scene of an emergency involving an elderly woman who was found sitting on the front steps of her house. She tells you that she accidently locked herself outside the house. She has been outside for the past several hours in 20-degree temperatures and snow. She states, "My feet feel like they are numb." You would suspect which of the following as most likely?
    a. Hypothermia
    b. Frostbite
    c. Stroke
    d. Generalized seizure

26. A patient tells you that he was bitten by a coral snake. You inspect the bite wound and expect to find which of the following?
    a. A star-like distribution of marks at the opening.
    b. A distinct single puncture wound.
    c. A semicircular mark.
    d. A rectangular pattern of marks.

27. Which action is most appropriate when providing care to a patient who is experiencing frostbite?
    a. Gently warm the affected area in hot water.
    b. Bandage the affected area tightly with a clean dressing.
    c. Avoid breaking any blisters that have formed.
    d. Keep the toes secured closely together.

28. Which of the following would be the least appropriate to do to prevent heat-related illnesses?
    a. Wearing light-colored clothing when outdoors
    b. Exercising for brief periods with frequent rests
    c. Avoiding activities during the late morning to afternoon
    d. Increasing the intake of caffeinated fluids

29. You suspect that a patient under your care is experiencing late signs of dehydration. Which of the following would you expect to find?
    a. Sunken eyes
    b. Fatigue
    c. Excessive thirst
    d. Headache

30. Which mechanism for cooling the body is most affected by high humidity?
    a. Evaporation
    b. Radiation
    c. Conduction
    d. Convection

31. Which individual would have the greatest risk for experiencing a heat-related illness based on predisposing factors?
    a. A 28-year-old woman who drinks coffee throughout the day
    b. A 35-year-old construction worker working outside
    c. A 45-year-old woman taking a diuretic agent
    d. An 80-year-old patient with heart disease and diabetes

32. You are called to the high school football practice facility where one of the athletes who has been practicing is complaining of dizziness and a throbbing headache. The weather is extremely hot and humid. You examine the athlete and suspect heat exhaustion based on which of the following?
    a. Flushed, dry skin
    b. Rapid, weak pulse
    c. Decreasing *level of consciousness* (LOC)
    d. Heavy sweating

33. You are providing care for a patient with hypothermia. Which of the following would you do first?
    a. Perform a primary assessment.
    b. Move the patient to a warmer environment.
    c. Call for more advanced medical personnel.
    d. Remove any wet clothing.

34. An adolescent who has been stung by a wasp begins to exhibit signs and symptoms of anaphylaxis. Which of the following would you least likely expect to find during the assessment?
    a. Localized skin rash
    b. Wheezing
    c. Chest tightness
    d. Facial swelling
    e. Low blood pressure

35. Which of the following would be the priority consideration before entering the water for a water rescue?
    a. Condition of the water
    b. Personal safety
    c. Resources available
    d. Patient's condition

36. A patient requires a water rescue. Which of the following is an appropriate indication for removing the patient from the water to provide care?
    a. The patient is unresponsive.
    b. The patient is face-down in the water.
    c. The patient has a neck injury.
    d. The patient is conscious.

37. You arrive at the scene of an emergency involving a woman who has been raped. She is upset but quiet and controlled. Her husband is nearby and visibly angry and upset. Which of the following would be most important for you to do?
    a. Offer the patient something to clean herself up.
    b. Demonstrate sensitivity when interacting with the patient.
    c. Obtain as much information from the patient as possible.
    d. Remove the patient's clothing to inspect for injuries.

38. When assessing a victim of rape, which of the following would you expect to assess?
    a. Lack of pain due to numbing
    b. Psychological but not physical shock
    c. Intact clothing
    d. A dazed, almost emotionally paralyzed state

39. You suspect that a young woman at an emergency scene to which you have been called is experiencing mania. You understand that mania is characteristic of which disorder?
    a. Bipolar disorder
    b. Clinical depression
    c. Schizophrenia
    d. Panic attack

40. Which of the following would you least likely identify as a cause of a behavioral emergency?
    a. Abdominal injury
    b. Physical illness
    c. Adverse effects of prescribed medications
    d. Mental illness

41. A patient is experiencing excited delirium syndrome. What would you expect to find?
    a. Decreased body strength
    b. High body temperature
    c. Increased pain sensitivity
    d. Relaxed demeanor

42. You are attempting to provide care to a patient experiencing paranoia when a friend mentions that the patient uses recreational drugs. You would suspect which drug group as being most likely involved?
    a. Narcotics
    b. Depressants
    c. Stimulants
    d. Inhalants

43. A patient has attempted suicide. Which of the following would be the priority in your role as an EMR?
   a. Getting the patient to the medical facility
   b. Using medical restraints for transporting
   c. Obtaining immediate on-site psychiatric care
   d. Treating any injuries related to the attempt

44. When assessing a patient who is at risk for suicide, which question is least appropriate to ask?
   a. "You're not a threat to yourself, are you?"
   b. "Are you thinking of hurting yourself?"
   c. "Have you suffered any trauma recently?"
   d. "How are you feeling?"

45. Which of the following is least appropriate when sizing up the scene for safety?
   a. Identifying the patient before entering the scene
   b. Identifying possible escape routes as necessary
   c. Leaving any objects as they are on the scene
   d. Looking for signs of more than one patient

| UNIT 6 TRAUMA EMERGENCIES |

1. Which of the following would lead you to suspect that a patient may be in the early stages of shock?
   a. Apprehension
   b. Elevated body temperature
   c. Elevated blood pressure
   d. Decreased respiratory rate

2. You are assessing the pulse rate of a patient who has fallen about 10 feet from a ladder. Before landing on a cement floor, his abdomen struck the edge of a metal shelf protruding from the side of the wall. You find that his pulse rate is 120 beats per minute and weak. You would interpret this to indicate which of the following?
   a. Early signs of sepsis
   b. Low blood glucose levels
   c. Internal blood loss
   d. Cardiac trauma

3. You are providing care to a patient who has fallen off a two-story scaffold onto the ground. While checking the patient's vital signs, you notice that his skin is moist, cool and a little pale. He is alert but complains of feeling light-headed. Which of the following does this best reflect?
   a. A normal stress reaction to injury
   b. Recovery from the initial injury
   c. A routine fear reaction
   d. The body's attempt to compensate for the injury

4. You suspect that a patient under your care is experiencing internal bleeding. While waiting for more advanced medical personnel to arrive, his condition continues to deteriorate. His breathing rate is fast, his pulse is fast and weak, and now he is responsive only to painful stimuli. Which of the following would you do first?
   a. Cover him to prevent chilling.
   b. Maintain an open airway.
   c. Elevate his head and chest.
   d. Immobilize his body.

5. Which of the following occurs with shock?
   a. Blood flow to vital organs is shunted.
   b. Blood vessels fail to constrict.
   c. Flow of oxygenated blood to the skin increases.
   d. Airway obstruction leads to respiratory failure.

6. In septic shock, which of the following occurs?
   a. Airways dilate.
   b. Blood vessels constrict.
   c. Blood pools.
   d. Tissues are damaged.

7. Which measure would be the most helpful to minimize shock?
   a. Covering the patient with a blanket
   b. Removing any excess patient clothing
   c. Immersing the feet in warm water
   d. Applying cool compresses to the neck and groin

8. A patient experiences a spinal cord injury. You would be alert for which type of shock?
   a. Obstructive
   b. Vasogenic
   c. Cardiogenic
   d. Septic

9. You are providing care to a patient who has been stabbed. He is bleeding profusely and develops signs and symptoms of shock. You would identify this type of shock as—
   a. Obstructive
   b. Distributive
   c. Hypovolemic
   d. Cardiogenic

10. When caring for a patient in shock, which of the following would be the priority?
    a. Controlling any visible bleeding
    b. Ensuring the patient's airway is open
    c. Immobilizing any fractures
    d. Elevating the lower extremities

11. You are providing care to a patient who is bleeding from a deep cut in his leg. You identify that the bleeding is venous because it—
    a. Flows steadily.
    b. Fails to clot easily.
    c. Spurts from the wound.
    d. Is bright red.

12. When implementing measures to control a patient's arterial bleeding, which of the following would be considered least appropriate?
    a. Applying direct pressure with your hand
    b. Using a tourniquet to stop the bleeding
    c. Placing a sterile gauze pressure dressing over the wound
    d. Elevating the patient's leg above heart level

13. You are assessing a patient involved in a motor-vehicle collision and suspect that he is bleeding internally. Which of the following would lead you to that suspicion?
    a. Rapid breathing
    b. Bounding pulse
    d. Warm, pink skin
    e. Coughing up mucous

14. You suspect that a patient who was involved in a head-on collision may have a skull fracture because he hit his head on the dashboard and is complaining of a headache. His nose is bleeding. Which of the following actions would be the most appropriate when caring for the patient's nosebleed?
    a. Tilt his head forward slightly.
    b. Pinch his nostrils firmly together.
    c. Cover the nostrils loosely with sterile gauze.
    d. Have the patient blow his nose.

15. A facility in a small community that offers assessment, resuscitation and emergency operations and arranges emergency transport to a large medical trauma center describes which trauma system level?
    a. I
    b. II
    c. III
    d. IV

16. Which of the following characteristics of blood denote capillary bleeding?
    a. Bright red color
    b. Steady flow
    c. Spontaneous clotting
    d. An increase in pressure corresponding to a decrease in blood pressure

17. Assessment reveals that a patient has a sucking chest wound. Which type of dressing would you use?
    a. Universal dressing
    b. Elastic bandage
    c. Roller bandage
    d. Occlusive dressing

18. While providing care to a patient with an open bleeding wound, you notice that blood has soaked through a dressing and bandage. You would—
    a. Reapply a new bandage, leaving the dressings in place.
    b. Apply additional dressings and another bandage.
    c. Elevate the body part above heart level.
    d. Reapply direct pressure to the site over the soiled dressings.

19. Immobilizing a limb while maintaining direct pressure for bleeding is done to—
    a. Slow blood clotting.
    b. Compress the artery.
    c. Restrict blood flow.
    d. Remove moisture from the blood.

20. You apply fingertip pressure to control bleeding but you find that it is ineffective in controlling the bleeding from a large wound. You would then apply pressure using—
    a. Your thumb.
    b. Your hand.
    c. A pressure point.
    d. Your knuckles

21. When caring for a conscious patient with a nosebleed, which action would you do first?
    a. Tilt the patient's head and upper body slightly forward.
    b. Have the patient assume a sitting position.
    c. Pinch the nostrils together firmly.
    d. Hold the pressure on the nostrils for 5 to 10 minutes.

22. You and your partner are called to the scene of an emergency in which a patient's arm has been completely severed at the middle of the forearm. This situation involves which of the following?
    a. Amputation
    b. Avulsion
    c. Impalement
    d. Laceration

23. Which of the following is the top priority when dealing with a completely severed body part?
    a. Caring for the severed body part
    b. Minimizing the patient's pain
    c. Immobilizing the arm
    d. Controlling the bleeding

24. You arrive at the scene of an emergency involving a patient who has lost a portion of his finger while attempting to repair his lawn mower. The portion of the finger is no longer attached but is found in the grass nearby. Which of the following is appropriate to do when caring for the severed finger?
    a. Put the finger into a brown paper bag just as it is.
    b. Wrap the finger in sterile saline-moistened gauze.
    c. Put the finger in a container of ice.
    d. Pour ice cold water onto the finger continuously.

25. You arrive on the scene of an apartment fire and suddenly a young man runs screaming from the building with his clothes on fire. Which of the following would you do first?
    a. Cool the burn area.
    b. Perform a primary assessment.
    c. Summon more advanced medical personnel.
    d. Extinguish the flames.

26. Which of the following would be most appropriate to use to cool a burn?
    a. Ice applied directly to the burned area
    b. Petroleum jelly liberally applied to the burned area
    c. Large amounts of cold running water
    d. Alternating warm and cool compresses on the burned area

27. You apply ice to a closed wound injury, removing it after which amount of time?
    a. 5 minutes
    b. 15 minutes
    c. 20 minutes
    d. 25 minutes

28. You are providing care for a small superficial laceration on a patient's arm. Your first action would be to—
    a. Irrigate the wound with clear, warm running water.
    b. Control the bleeding.
    c. Clean the wound with soap and water.
    d. Apply antibiotic ointment.

29. You determine that a patient has a superficial burn based on which findings?
    a. Mottling
    b. Blistering
    c. Red and dry skin
    d. Blackened skin

30. While assessing a burn patient, you notice soot around the mouth and nose. You would be alert for which of the following?
    a. Airway closure
    b. Scarring
    c. Shock
    d. Toxic inhalation

31. You would least likely expect a patient experiencing which type of burn to be referred to a burn unit?
    a. Chemical burns
    b. Electrical burns
    c. Circumferential burns
    d. Superficial burns

32. A patient has sustained a chemical burn to the eye. When flushing the eye, you would—
    a. Use cold tap water.
    b. Continue to flush the eye for about 20 minutes.
    c. Position the head so that water flows toward the nose.
    d. Use a brush to facilitate removing the chemical.

33. Which of the following is a priority when providing care for a patient with an electrical burn?
    a. Performing a primary assessment
    b. Cooling the burn
    c. Ensuring the current is de-energized.
    d. Evaluating entry and exit sites

34. You are called to the scene of an industrial incident in which an employee was struck in the chest with a gas cylinder that exploded on impact. The patient is lying on the floor, gasping but alert. His lips are blue, and the front of his shirt is torn and soaked with blood. You notice a strange "swooshing" sound every time the patient breathes. Which of the following would you most likely suspect?
    a. Pneumothorax
    b. Flail chest
    c. Rib fracture
    d. Sucking chest wound

35. You are assessing a patient whose leg was cut by a steel rod when he fell off of a construction scaffold. As you complete your physical exam, you find a small piece of a steel rod sticking out of his other leg. Which of the following would you do?
    a. Immediately remove the protruding object.
    b. Press the surrounding clothing around the object.
    c. Stabilize the object with gauze at its current position.
    d. Wiggle the object to evaluate its depth of penetration.

36. A patient was hit in the abdomen with a baseball bat. Based on the location of the injury, which organ is least susceptible to injury?
    a. Liver
    b. Spleen
    c. Kidneys
    d. Stomach

37. When assessing a patient who was struck in the abdomen with a wooden beam, you would palpate the abdomen, beginning the assessment at which location?
    a. Directly at the point of impact of the beam
    b. From the furthest point away from the patient's pain
    c. Around the area of the navel (belly button)
    d. Around the lower ribs on both sides

38. Which of the following is the least appropriate when caring for a male patient with a genital injury?
    a. Have a male EMR provide the care.
    b. Ensure that bystanders are moved far back from the scene.
    c. Provide a drape to maintain the patient's privacy.
    d. Remove all of the patient's clothing to view the injury.

39. Which of the following is the least likely cause of an open chest wound?
    a. Fractured rib breaking through the skin
    b. Knife wound
    c. Gunshot
    d. Blunt trauma

40. Which of the following would you least expect to find in a patient with traumatic asphyxia?
    a. Flattened neck veins
    b. Subconjunctival hemorrhage
    c. Black eyes
    d. Moon-like face

41. You suspect a patient has a tension pneumothorax on the right based on which findings?
    a. Increased breath sounds on the right
    b. Tracheal shifting to the left
    c. Severe hypertension
    d. Abnormal percussion sounds on the left

42. When applying an occlusive dressing to a sucking chest wound, which of the following would be appropriate?
    a. Use sterile gauze dressings and tape.
    b. Cover the dressing with a disposable glove.
    c. Tape the dressing on three of the four sides.
    d. Use a clean folded cloth for a dressing.

43. Your physical exam of a patient leads you to suspect an evisceration based on which finding?
    a. A loose rib section that does not move normally with the rest of the chest
    b. Crackling sound of the tissues under the skin
    c. Abdominal organs protruding through a wound
    d. Partial tearing away of a portion of skin and soft tissue

44. You are preparing to care for a patient's forearm that you suspect is fractured. The forearm has a bloody laceration near a visible deformity. Which of the following would you do before applying the splint?
    a. Apply ice directly to the site.
    b. Check for range of motion.
    c. Bandage the laceration.
    d. Straighten the arm.

45. Which type of splint is most appropriate to use for a patient with a fractured forearm?
    a. Rigid
    b. Traction
    c. Circumferential air
    d. Sling

46. Which of the following would you least expect if a patient with a thigh injury has a fractured femur?
    a. Turning in of the leg
    b. Swelling
    c. Muscle relaxation
    d. Significant pain

47. A fracture to which of the following bones places the patient at highest risk for shock?
    a. Ulna
    b. Pelvis
    c. Tibia
    d. Radius

48. Which body part is at highest risk for a dislocation?
    a. Finger
    b. Knee
    c. Ankle
    d. Elbow

49. When applying a rigid splint, which of the following is inappropriate to use?
    a. Cardboard box
    b. Pillow
    c. Rolled-up magazine
    d. Shin guard

50. You are providing care to a patient with a suspected musculoskeletal injury. Which statement would help to confirm your suspicions?
    a. "I'm not having pain when I move my arm."
    b. "I can move my hand and fingers easily."
    c. "My wrist doesn't feel cold."
    d. "I have no feeling in my hand."

51. For which of the following would you least expect to summon more advanced medical personnel?
    a. Suspected fracture of the toe
    b. Inability to walk
    c. Open femur fracture
    d. Suspicion of multiple injuries

52. A patient with a musculoskeletal injury asks you why you are elevating his arm. Which response is most accurate?
    a. "It helps to keep the bones aligned."
    b. "It helps to reduce the swelling."
    c. "It makes the pain less noticeable."
    d. "It promotes healing."

53. You are preparing to apply a splint to a patient's forearm. Which of the following would you do first?
    a. Check for circulation and sensation beyond the injured area.
    b. Support the injured part above and below the injury.
    c. Obtain the patient's consent for treatment.
    d. Immobilize the wrist and elbow.

54. Which of the following is the final step when applying a sling and binder?
    a. Tying the ends of the sling at the side of the neck
    b. Positioning the triangular bandage
    c. Binding the injured body part to the chest
    d. Checking for circulation and sensation

55. When using a splint, which of the following is an appropriate action?
    a. Push any protruding bones back below the skin.
    b. Avoid padding splints to prevent further deformities.
    c. Apply sterile dressings over open wounds.
    d. Keep clothing intact around the injured site.

56. A patient's co-worker tells you that the patient fell off of the roof of a two-story home and landed on his back, possibly hitting his head on the ground. You suspect a possible skull fracture is most likely based on which finding?
    a. Abrasion on the forehead
    b. Lack of responsiveness
    c. Bleeding from the mouth
    d. The co-worker's statement

57. Which of the following would you interpret as least indicative of a brain injury in a patient who has sustained a head injury?
    a. Hypotension
    b. Slowed pulse
    c. Clear fluid draining from the nose
    d. Bruising behind the ear

58. You suspect that a patient has a concussion. Which of the following would least likely support your suspicion?
    a. Asymmetrical facial movements
    b. Inability to recall what happened
    c. Headache
    d. Confusion

59. A 9-year-old boy playing youth football collided with another boy, helmet to shoulder pads, and was knocked to the ground, losing consciousness for approximately 3 minutes. The boy is lethargic but responds to verbal stimuli. Which of the following is the most appropriate when providing care to this patient?
    a. Remove his helmet to assess his head more closely.
    b. Stabilize his head and neck with the helmet in place.
    c. Place the patient in the prone position.
    d. Elevate the patient's legs about 12 inches.

60. Which patient would you identify as having the lowest risk for sustaining a head, neck or spinal injury?
    a. A person who fell off of a 2-foot step stool
    b. A person who dove into 4 feet of water in a swimming pool
    c. A passenger in a car who hit the dashboard in a motor-vehicle collision
    d. A person who slipped off of a two-story platform

61. Which of the following is appropriate to do when caring for a patient who has a foreign body in the eye?
    a. Telling the patient to rub his eye
    b. Touching the eyeball directly with a gloved finger
    c. Using the corner of a sterile gauze pad to remove the visible object
    d. Ensuring that the patient refrains from blinking

62. You feel resistance when attempting to align a patient's head and neck. Which of the following should you do next?
    a. Apply a *cervical collar* (C-collar) instead.
    b. Continue to move the head to align it with the neck.
    c. Avoid further attempts to stabilize the head and neck.
    d. Stabilize the patient's head and neck in the position found.

63. Which of the following is appropriate to do when providing care to a patient who has a piece of metal embedded in his eyeball from an industrial incident?
    a. Encircle the eye with gauze dressing to stabilize the object.
    b. Secure a Styrofoam® cup over the embedded object.
    c. Apply a sterile dressing over top of the object.
    d. Remove the object immediately to prevent permanent damage.

64. When assessing a patient with a closed head injury, you notice fluid leaking from the patient's ear leading you to suspect a—
    a. Scalp injury.
    b. Skull fracture.
    c. Concussion.
    d. Penetrating skull injury.

65. You are assessing a patient with a suspected head injury and observe bruising behind the ears. You would identify this as which of the following?
    a. Raccoon eyes
    b. Concussion
    c. Battle's sign
    d. Nosebleed

66. When dealing with any injury to the neck or spine, you must always—
    a. Treat the underlying cause.
    b. Consider it to be a serious injury.
    c. Rule out injury to the neck or spine if the patient can walk.
    d. Establish the certainty of the injury.

67. Which of the following is the priority when providing care to a patient with a head injury?
    a. Performing a primary assessment
    b. Establishing manual stabilization
    c. Controlling any bleeding
    d. Encouraging the patient to talk to you

| UNIT 7 SPECIAL POPULATIONS |

Directions: *Circle the letter that best answers the question.*

1. When assessing a pregnant patient, you determine that the patient is in labor when she reports that the contractions are—
   a. Lasting about the same length.
   b. Occurring sporadically.
   c. Getting closer together.
   d. Alternating between mild and strong.

2. You arrive at the scene of an emergency involving a pregnant woman in labor. The woman tells you that her water broke and that she is having contractions approximately every 5 minutes, with each contraction lasting about 30 seconds. The baby's head is not crowning. You determine that the patient is in which stage of labor?
   a. First stage
   b. Second stage
   c. Third stage
   d. Fourth stage

3. Upon arrival at the home of a pregnant woman in labor, you assess her and find that the baby's head is crowning. You also observe a small loop of rope-like tissue protruding from her vaginal opening. You interpret your findings to suggest which of the following?
   a. Premature birth
   b. Breech birth
   c. Prolapsed umbilical cord
   d. Meconium aspiration

4. Which of the following would you least expect to see at the opening of the birth canal if the woman was experiencing a breech birth?
   a. Head
   b. Buttocks
   c. Foot
   d. Shoulder

5. When providing care to a woman who is in her third trimester of pregnancy, which of the following would you identify as occurring during this time?
   a. Morning sickness
   b. Majority of weight gain
   c. Placental development
   d. Fetal movement

6. You are assisting a pregnant woman who is in labor to cope with the discomfort and pain. Which of the following is the least effective?
   a. Encouraging her to breathe slowly and deeply
   b. Asking her to focus on an object to help her breathing
   c. Providing her with explanations about what is happening
   d. Telling her that she has to learn to endure the discomfort

7. You are assisting a pregnant woman with delivery and the baby is crowning. Which of the following would you do next?
   a. Place a hand on top of the baby's head and apply light pressure.
   b. Check for looping of the umbilical cord around the baby's neck.
   c. Tell the mother to stop pushing and concentrate on her breathing.
   d. Guide one shoulder out at a time without pulling on the baby.

8. A newborn has just been born and has not yet made any sounds. Which method is most appropriate to stimulate breathing and the cry reflex in a newborn?
   a. Bending the newborn's feet firmly backward
   b. Placing the newborn in a head-down position
   c. Mechanically suctioning the mouth and nose
   d. Gently rubbing the newborn's back

9. Which of the following would indicate the need to begin resuscitation of the newborn?
   a. A respiratory rate less than 30 respirations per minute
   b. A pulse greater than 100 *beats per minute* (bpm)
   c. A pink body with bluish limbs
   d. No gasping movements

10. Which of the following would lead you to suspect that delivery is imminent?
    a. Strong contractions occurring every 3 to 4 minutes
    b. The absence of crowning at the vaginal opening
    c. The woman's report of a strong urge to push
    d. A sudden gush of fluid from the vagina

11. You would expect to stimulate and administer emergency oxygen to a newborn with which APGAR score?
    a. 3
    b. 5
    c. 7
    d. 9

12. You are called to an emergency involving a 15-month-old child who was a passenger in a motor vehicle that collided head-on with a tree. You would identify this child as being at which developmental stage?
    a. Infant
    b. Toddler
    c. Preschooler
    d. School age

13. Which of the following is of least importance when completing your primary assessment of a child involved in an emergency situation?
    a. Appearance
    b. Breathing
    c. Vital signs
    d. Skin

14. You are called to the scene of an emergency in which a 3 year old fell off of a wooden backyard fence. A piece of the fence has cut through the child's upper pant leg and is protruding. There is blood on the child's clothing and the ground. The child is crying loudly. Which of the following is of greatest concern to you?
    a. Airway
    b. Breathing
    c. LOC
    d. Skin

15. While caring for a child involved in an emergency, which of the following would be the least likely to indicate the need for immediate intervention?
    a. Strong, palpable pulse
    b. Increasing lethargy
    c. Cool, clammy skin
    d. Rapid breathing

16. You are providing care to an injured preschooler. Which of the following is the most important to keep in mind?
    a. Preschoolers can understand complex sentences.
    b. Preschoolers may feel that they caused the injury.
    c. Preschoolers' fears correspond to the severity of the injury.
    d. Preschoolers readily cooperate with strangers.

17. When using the Pediatric Assessment Triangle, you would complete this assessment—
    a. After checking the patient's breathing and pulse
    b. After obtaining the SAMPLE history
    c. During the scene size-up
    d. Before beginning the physical exam

18. You would consider which patient to be a child when using an *automated external defibrillator* (AED)?
    a. 6-year-old girl
    b. 9-year-old boy
    c. 12-year-old girl
    d. 14-year-old boy

19. You are to provide care to a child who is having difficulty breathing. Which of the following would lead you to suspect that the child has a complete airway obstruction?
    a. Drooling
    b. Frequent coughing
    c. Retractions
    d. Cyanosis

20. Which of the following is the most appropriate when caring for a child who is developing shock?
    a. Positioning the child flat on his or her back.
    b. Covering the child with a several heavy blankets
    c. Administering ventilations immediately
    d. Using back blows and abdominal thrusts

21. When attempting to open the airway of a child, you do not tilt the head as far back as that for an adult because—
    a. The smaller tongue will fall back more easily.
    b. The shorter trachea will become blocked due to the bending.
    c. Breathing through the nose will become the major way to inhale.
    d. The smaller airway will become obstructed more readily.

22. Which of the following is the least likely to cause a seizure?
    a. Head trauma
    b. Hypoxia
    c. Low blood glucose
    d. Respiratory distress

23. You arrive on the scene and suspect that the patient, a child, is a victim of child abuse. Which of the following is most appropriate to do first?
    a. Confront the caregivers about the child's injuries.
    b. Obtain a thorough history of events from the child.
    c. Provide care for the child's injuries.
    d. Remove the child from the abusive situation.

24. You arrive at the home of an elderly couple where the patient, a woman, has been diagnosed with Alzheimer's disease. The husband states that his wife suddenly started screaming and shouting and tried to throw a lamp at him. You suspect that the patient is experiencing which of the following?
    a. Hallucinations
    b. Depression
    c. Sundowning
    d. Catastrophic reaction

25. You are interviewing the family of a patient with Alzheimer's disease. Which of the following behaviors would the family be least likely to report?
    a. Pacing
    b. Rummaging
    c. Intellectual impairment
    d. Nonsensical speaking

26. When dealing with a patient who is hard of hearing, which of the following is the most important?
    a. Using a loud shouting voice when talking to the patient during the interview
    b. Repeating the same question several times before allowing the patient to answer
    c. Approaching the patient from behind rather than the front
    d. Speaking slowly and clearly to the patient when interacting with him

27. Which of the following would you identify as a normal change related to aging?
    a. Thinning of the heart muscle
    b. Decreased lung elasticity
    c. Increased movement through the digestive system
    d. Loss of the ability to learn

28. When communicating with a patient who has a history of Alzheimer's disease and is experiencing a catastrophic reaction, which statement is most appropriate?
    a. "I'm not going to hurt you in any way."
    b. "You have to stop screaming, or else."
    c. "If you don't behave, I'm going to call the police."
    d. "Why are you acting so horribly?"

29. Older women are at increased risk of fractures because their—
    a. Pain sensation is diminished.
    b. Tolerance to glare is reduced.
    c. Bones become less dense.
    d. Level of activity declines.

30. You are talking with other EMRs in your unit about the elderly population that you service. Which statement by a colleague indicates a lack of knowledge about this age group?
    a. "Older people might not really tell you how sick they feel."
    b. "They have a much greater risk for breathing problems."
    c. "You need to expect that they have trouble remembering things."
    d. "Older adults experience sensory changes that put them at risk."

31. Which of the following patients may be a victim of possible elder abuse?
    a. A patient who has been to the emergency room three times in 2 weeks
    b. A patient who has someone providing care in the home 24 hours a day
    c. A patient who has lost weight due to an underlying medical problem
    d. A patient who has experienced one fall in the last 12 months.

32. You are caring for an elderly patient who has a loss of visual field. Which of the following would you most likely observe?
    a. The need to wear glasses to see
    b. The need to turn his head to see
    c. The use of a white cane
    d. The use of other senses to compensate

33. Which of the following would you expect to assess in a patient with cystic fibrosis?
   a. Dehydration
   b. Constipation
   c. Sporadic coughing
   d. Loss of appetite

34. Which of the following best reflects the focus of hospice care?
   a. The goal is to cure the patient using advanced medical technologies.
   b. Care is provided to terminally ill patients in the final 12 months of life.
   c. The emphasis is on providing comfort, not cure, to the patient and family.
   d. Pain relief is provided through medication administered through needles.

35. Which of the following is the most appropriate to keep in mind when caring for an elderly patient?
   a. Provide quick, short explanations about what you are doing.
   b. Use an oropharyngeal airway for the responsive patient.
   c. Apply additional pressure when administering ventilations.
   d. Handle the patient's skin gently to prevent tearing.

36. Which of the following is considered a type of elder abuse?
   a. Family member uses the patient's money to purchase the patient's medications.
   b. Caregiver takes the patient to a senior center daily.
   c. Patient has numerous old and new bruises on his inner arms.
   d. Patient is clean and dressed appropriately for the weather.

| UNIT 8 EMS OPERATIONS |

Directions: Circle the letter that best answers the question.

1. Which phase of the EMS response is occurring when a caller reports the accident?
   a. Preparation for the emergency call
   b. Patient contact
   c. En-route to the scene
   d. Dispatch

2. When travelling to the scene of an emergency, which of the following is a priority?
   a. Observing appropriate driving behavior for the weather conditions
   b. Ensuring that you have the appropriate equipment readily available
   c. Getting as much information from the *emergency medical dispatcher* (EMD) as possible
   d. Notifying dispatch about the need for additional emergency services

3. Air medical transport has been summoned. Which of the following is the most important in preparing for the helicopter's arrival?
   a. Moving bystanders back at least 20 feet
   b. Applying ear and eye protection to the patient
   c. Having the patient ready for transport
   d. Ensuring a safe landing zone

4. During which phase of the EMS response would the crew members notify the receiving facility about the patient and the *estimated time of arrival* (ETA)?
   a. Phase 5
   b. Phase 6
   c. Phase 7
   d. Phase 8

5. Which situation would be appropriate for requesting air medical transport?
   a. Pedestrian struck by a speeding car
   b. Head-on motor-vehicle collision
   c. Patient with a fracture of the leg
   d. Patient who fell from a height of 5 feet

6. Which site is the most appropriate landing zone?
   a. Dry, barren pasture
   b. Frozen lake
   c. Open soccer field
   d. Field with powdery snow

7. When approaching a helicopter for transporting a patient, which of the following would be most appropriate?
   a. Approaching the helicopter from the back
   b. Carrying an *intravenous* (IV) pole at a 90-degree angle to the ground
   c. Wearing a hat on your head
   d. Maintaining a somewhat crouched posture

8. Which of the following supplies would be mandatory to include in a jump kit?
   a. Maps
   b. Protective eyewear
   c. Wound dressings
   d. Stethoscope

9. Which situation would least likely be considered a high-risk situation impacting safety during an emergency response?
   a. Going through an intersection
   b. Exiting from a highway
   c. Driving in inclement weather
   d. Responding alone

10. You arrive at the scene of a motor-vehicle collision involving a car that has struck an electrical pole. An electrical wire has fallen across the car and onto the ground. Which action would be most appropriate?
    a. Telling the occupants of the vehicle to get out of the car immediately
    b. Moving the wire off the car onto the ground
    c. Notifying the power company to cut off the power
    d. Setting up a safety area at least 500 feet from the car

11. When arriving at the scene of an emergency involving a patient who is trapped, which of the following is your primary role as an EMR?
    a. Establishing a chain of command
    b. Extricating the patient
    c. Providing care to the patient
    d. Ensuring crowd control

12. Which type of equipment would you most likely expect to use during extrication of a patient who is trapped under construction materials and a scaffold?
    a. Ropes
    b. Pliers
    c. Shovel
    d. Pneumatic tool

13. You would identify a vehicle as unstable if it is positioned—
    a. On a flat surface.
    b. On a dry surface.
    c. On its side.
    d. Side-by-side with the other vehicle.

14. When using a simple access method, you would—
    a. Try opening the door.
    b. Remove the car roof with a tool cutter.
    c. Break the window glass.
    d. Use a ratcheting cable.

15. Emergency vehicles, including fire apparatus and ambulances, arrive on the scene. Which of the following is the most appropriate?
    a. Ambulances parked on the outside of the fire engines
    b. Traffic cones placed at 25 feet intervals
    c. Large fire apparatus positioned at an angle to the traffic lane
    d. A safety zone radius of at least 100 feet around the scene

16. When using cribbing to provide further vehicle stabilization, you would make sure that there is no more than how much distance between the cribbing and the vehicle?
    a. 8 inches
    b. 6 inches
    c. 4 inches
    d. 2 inches

17. Which of the following least likely suggests that *hazardous material* (HAZMAT) is involved?
    a. Fire
    b. Vapor cloud
    c. Leaking container
    d. Spilled liquid

18. You need to keep in mind which of the following when providing care to a patient throughout the extrication process?
    a. Move the patient, not the device.
    b. Use the path of greatest resistance.
    c. Maintain cervical spinal stabilization.
    d. Use the least number of personnel possible.

19. To ensure that an upright vehicle does not roll, which of the following would be inappropriate?
    a. Turning the wheels toward the curb
    b. Cutting the tires' valve stems
    c. Overinflating the tires
    d. Tying the car frame to a large tree

20. You gained access to a patient who is to be extricated and begin to provide care. Which of the following is the priority?
    a. Assessing the patient's breathing and pulse
    b. Ensuring that the neck and back are stabilized
    c. Administering emergency oxygen
    d. Obtaining a SAMPLE history

21. You are the first person to arrive at an emergency scene, and you suspect a potential HAZMAT incident. Which of the following would you do first?
    a. Contact dispatch to inform them of your findings
    b. Establish a clear chain of command
    c. Create safety zones
    d. Access the patient

22. Which of the following would be important when on the scene of a HAZMAT incident?
    a. Staying out of higher areas of elevation
    b. Remaining downwind of the scene
    c. Moving closer to the scene as time goes on
    d. Keeping yourself uphill and upwind of the scene

23. To be able to enter the warm zone established by the HAZMAT team, which of the following would be least appropriate?
    a. *Occupational Safety and Health Administration* (OSHA) training at the first responder awareness level
    b. *Personal protective equipment* (PPE)
    c. Double gloves applied over work gloves
    d. Positive-pressure *self-contained breathing apparatus* (SCBA)

24. Which information would you be likely to find on the *Material Safety Data Sheets* (MSDS) for a HAZMAT?
    a. Physical properties of the substance
    b. Name of the substance
    c. Dangers associated with the substance
    d. Four-digit identification number

25. When establishing a clear chain of command during a HAZMAT incident, which of the following is most accurate?
    a. The communication system is based on each rescue team's preference.
    b. One command officer is responsible for decision making throughout the rescue.
    c. Each rescue team has a command officer that communicates with other team commanders.
    d. Individual rescue team members are able to choose to work with certain other members.

26. Which of the following activities occur in the hot zone?
    a. Airway management
    b. Immobilization
    c. Complete decontamination
    d. Rescue

27. You suspect possible radiation exposure. Which of the following would be the least appropriate?
    a. Donning a positive-pressure SCBA
    b. Sealing off all openings in protective clothing with duct tape
    c. Applying triple gloves to your hands
    d. Wearing two pairs of paper shoe covers under heavy rubber boots

28. In your role as an EMR who is first on the scene of a possible HAZMAT incident, your last step would be to—
    a. Determine if the material is responsible for injuries at the scene.
    b. Show awareness of the impact of the material to safety.
    c. Identify the specific material and its characteristics.
    d. Recognize the presence of a HAZMAT.

29. Contamination by a HAZMAT would be the least likely by which route?
    a. Respiratory
    b. Gastrointestinal
    c. Topical
    d. Neurological

30. You are assisting with decontamination efforts in which the patient is being cleaned with large amounts of soap and water after his clothing was removed and left in the hot zone. Which type of decontamination is being done?
    a. Dilution
    b. Absorption
    c. Initial
    d. Neutralization

31. You arrive at the scene of a *multiple casualty incident* (MCI) involving an apartment building fire and numerous patients with burns. Fire personnel are on the scene. Which of the following would you do first?
    a. Assume the role of the incident commander.
    b. Begin providing care to the patients.
    c. Identify yourself to the incident commander.
    d. Determine the number of ambulances needed.

32. You are assisting with triage and identify patients who are able to walk with which colored tag?
    a. Red
    b. Green
    c. Yellow
    d. Black

33. One of the patients you are assisting with is a child. Which triage system would be most appropriate to use?
    a. Smart Tag™
    b. JumpSTART
    c. START
    d. METTAG™

34. An individual alerts you and other responders to potential dangers that might cause injury. This person is functioning in which role?
    a. Safety officer
    b. Triage officer
    c. Staging officer
    d. Treatment officer

35. Several patients at a fire scene have burns involving several body parts. You would expect these patients to be triaged as—
    a. Minor.
    b. Delayed.
    c. Immediate.
    d. Deceased/non-salvageable.

36. You are working with the triage officer and identifying patients' status using symbols. Which triage system are you using?
    a. METTAG™
    b. START system
    c. Smart Tag™
    d. JumpSTART

37. Which patient would you least expect to be at increased risk for severe stress reactions?
    a. An 8-year-old child involved in a bus accident
    b. An 84-year-old woman involved in a house fire
    c. A 50-year-old man involved in a factory explosion
    d. An ill 45-year-old woman involved in a train derailment

38. Which of the following is a priority to help reduce responder stress after an MCI?
    a. Allowing for down time
    b. Encouraging the EMRs to talk among themselves
    c. Ensuring clear expectations
    d. Having a debriefing

39. Which of the following is essential to manage the emergency situation and provide care in an MCI?
    a. Triage
    b. *Incident command system* (ICS)
    c. START system
    d. *National Response Framework* (NRF)

40. The transportation officer is responsible for which of the following?
    a. Designating an organized parking area for multiple rescue units
    b. Communicating with the receiving hospitals about incoming patients
    c. Identifying a treatment area that is of sufficient size
    d. Creating an area where ambulances can enter and leave adequately

41. When using the JumpSTART triage system, which parameter would you assess first?
    a. Mental status
    b. Perfusion status
    c. Respiratory status
    d. Ambulatory status

42. A worker at the scene of an explosion states that he noticed the strange "garlic-like" smell just after the explosion. Which of the following would you suspect?
    a. Sulfur mustard
    b. Cyanide
    c. Phosgene
    d. Tabun

43. Which of the following is the most important for you to use to protect yourself when dealing with an emergency involving phosphogene?
    a. HAZMAT suit
    b. Disposable gown, gloves and mask
    c. Chemical protective mask with charcoal canister
    d. *High-efficiency particulate air* (HEPA) filter mask

44. When providing care to the patients who were involved in an explosion at a shopping mall due to a high-order explosive, which of the following is the most important for you to remember?
    a. Any fatalities need to be removed from the area.
    b. The site of a bomb blast is considered a crime scene.
    c. The primary responsibility is to evacuate ambulatory patients.
    d. Evidence of the blast is collected simultaneously as you provide care.

45. Which of the following is considered a biological disaster?
    a. Tornado
    b. Nuclear explosion
    c. Chemical exposure
    d. Lake contamination with *E. coli*

46. Which of the following is ultimately responsible for coordinating the response to and recovery from large-scale disasters in the United States?
    a. NRF
    b. *Federal Emergency Management Agency* (FEMA)
    c. *National Incident Management System* (NIMS)
    d. ICS

47. Which *emergency support function* (ESF) would address damage and impact assessment?
    a. Transportation
    b. Emergency management
    c. Public health and medical services
    d. Communications

48. A patient exposed to a nerve agent is to receive an antidote. Which agent would be most appropriate to administer?
    a. Hydroxocobalamin
    b. Sodium nitrite
    c. Atropine
    d. Sodium thiosulfate

49. Which of the following is the priority when providing care to patients exposed to biological agents?
    a. Providing required antibiotics
    b. Using exposure control procedures
    c. Administering an antidote
    d. Decontaminating the patient

50. You first suspect that a patient is developing acute radiation syndrome when he exhibits which of the following?
    a. Gingival bleeding and bruising
    b. Headache and hair loss
    c. Nausea and vomiting
    d. Anorexia and partial thickness skin damage

51. You and several other EMRs are working with patients exposed to a nerve agent. One of the EMRs begins showing signs of exposure. You report this to medical direction and receive authorization to administer a nerve agent auto-injector kit. You prepare to administer the auto-injector into which site?
    a. Mid-outer thigh
    b. Buttocks
    c. Hip
    d. Outer upper arm

52. Which finding would support your assessment that a patient is a distressed swimmer?
    a. The patient is floating face-down.
    b. The patient is motionless.
    c. The patient is struggling to keep his or her mouth and nose above water.
    d. The patient is able to stay afloat.

53. You arrive at the scene of an emergency in which a patient has fallen through the ice into a pond. Several bystanders have gathered. Which of the following should you do first?
    a. Call dispatch to summon an ice rescue team.
    b. Go onto the ice to rescue the patient.
    c. Attempt to calm the bystanders.
    d. Use the wading assist to reach the patient.

54. A worker has fallen into tall cylindrical silo that is used to house agricultural materials. The patient would be at lowest risk for which of the following?
   a. Engulfment by the grain in the silo
   b. Potential for drowning
   c. Possible exposure to poisonous gases
   d. Lowered oxygen levels within the silo

55. You are part of a team that is evacuating a patient over hazardous terrain. After traveling a short distance you would expect to—
   a. Stop to rest.
   b. Switch hands.
   c. Rotate positions.
   d. Get a replacement.

56. You arrive on the scene and see a woman struggling in the water at the deep end of a swimming pool. Which method would be the most appropriate to use to rescue her and pull her to the side of the pool?
   a. Lie down at the side of the pool and try reaching her with your arm.
   b. Call for help and wade toward the deep end to grab her.
   c. Remove your shoes and jump into the pool to pull her to safety.
   d. Enter the water and extend your hand or foot to her.

57. Which of the following would lead you to suspect that a patient in the water is a drowning victim who is passive?
   a. The arms are at the person's side.
   b. The person is actively treading water.
   c. The person is floating face-up or face-down.
   d. The body is positioned vertically.

58. Which of the following special operations units would be involved in an emergency involving *weapons of mass destruction* (WMDs)?
   a. Tactical EMS Unit
   b. Specialized Vehicle Response Unit
   c. Fire Rehabilitation Unit
   d. HAZMAT EMS Response Unit

59. You are responding to the scene of a shooting involving a grocery store robbery. One of the cashiers has been shot in the abdomen, and the suspect has been apprehended. When providing care to the cashier, which of the following would you do first?
   a. Call for additional advanced medical personnel.
   b. Check with law enforcement for permission to enter the scene.
   c. Move the patient to another area to provide care.
   d. Remove any obstacles that are blocking access to the patient.

60. You arrive on the scene of an office building fire where local firefighters are present. Which action would be the least appropriate?
   a. Assuming the role of the incident commander
   b. Gathering information to help the fire units
   c. Keeping a adequate distance away from the fire
   d. Obtaining information about possible number of victims
   e. Asking about the possible cause of the fire

61. You are working as part of team at a special event that is expected to draw about 35,000 people. Which of the following would least likely be required?
   a. An on-site treatment facility
   b. Beds for at least eight simultaneous patients
   c. Communication capabilities at the site
   d. On-site coordination of EMS activities

END-OF-UNIT
EXAM ANSWER KEYS

| UNIT 1 PREPARATORY |

1. **a.** The *emergency medical technician* (EMT) takes over the care from the *emergency medical responders* (EMRs) and works on stabilizing and preparing the patient for transport. The EMR has the basic knowledge and skills needed to provide emergency care to people who are injured or who have become ill. EMRs are certified to provide care until a more highly trained professional—such as an EMT—arrives. *Advanced emergency medical technicians* (AEMTs) receive more training than EMTs, which allows them to insert *intravenous* (IV) lines, administer medications, perform advanced airway procedures and set up and assess *electrocardiograms* (ECGs or EKGs). Paramedics have more in-depth training than AEMTs, including more knowledge about performing physical exams. They also may perform more invasive procedures than any other prehospital care provider.

2. **d.** An AEMT is allowed to insert IVs, administer medications, perform advanced airway procedures and set up and assess electrocardiograms (ECGs or EKGs). EMRs are allowed to provide basic emergency care. An EMT takes over the care from EMRs and works on stabilizing and preparing the patient for transport. Paramedics have more in-depth training and would be capable of performing more in-depth physical exams.

3. **b.** In 1973, the Emergency Medical Services Act created a multi-tiered, nationwide system of emergency care with standardized training within the system. Firefighters were the first group to be trained in CPR and basic first aid. Police, fire and private systems make up the different types of emergency medical services (EMS) systems available in this multi-tiered formal, nationwide system.

4. **b.** A primary responsibility is to ensure the safety of yourself and that of the patient. Directing bystanders to help, recording what you did and reassuring the patient are secondary responsibilities.

5. **c.** Medical oversight or medical direction, in which a physician acts as the medical director, is one of the 10 components of an effective EMS system. Certification, scope of practice and core content are components of the Education Agenda.

6. **d.** Other procedures that are not covered by standing orders require EMRs to speak directly with the physician via mobile phone, radio or telephone. This kind of medical direction is called direct medical control or online medical direction. The use of standing orders is called indirect medical control or offline medical direction. Protocols are standardized procedures to be followed when providing care and are not a type of medical control.

7. **b.** Licensure is the acknowledgement that the bearer has the permission to practice in the licensing state. Certification ensures that the EMR maintains a high degree of proficiency by upgrading knowledge, skills and ability, but it does not grant the EMR the right to practice. Local credentialing involves meeting specific local requirements to maintain employment or obtain certain protocols so that he or she may practice, but it does not grant the right to practice. Medical direction is the process by which a physician directs the care provided by out-of-hospital providers.

8. **a.** As the first trained professional on the scene, your actions as an EMR often are critical, determining whether a seriously injured or ill person survives. EMRs require medical direction for providing care. EMRs have the basic knowledge and skills needed to provide emergency care to people who are injured or who have become ill. The role of the EMR can vary depending on the state and location of practice.

9. **a.** The paramedic is the most advanced level of EMS training. The EMR is the basic level of training followed by EMT and then AEMT.

10. **b.** Resource management includes planning for adequate numbers of trained personnel along with the equipment necessary to provide emergency care including vehicles for transportation and the tools and supplies necessary to provide care. A 9-1-1 communication system would be addressed under the communications component. Specialty care centers would be addressed under the facilities component. Personnel training programs is an aspect of the human resources and training component.

11. **a.** Although safety glasses, masks and disposable gowns may be appropriate in certain situations, disposable gloves would be most important to use in this situation to prevent disease transmission that may occur with exposure to the patient's blood and urine. Safety glasses would be appropriate if there was a potential for splashing; a *high-efficiency particulate air* (HEPA) mask would be appropriate if there was a risk of inhaling potential infectious particles. A CPR breathing barrier, such as a resuscitation mask, might be appropriate if the patient required CPR or ventilations. A gown would be appropriate if a large amount of blood or body fluids was present.

12. **d.** You should wash the contaminated area thoroughly with soap and water. Alcohol is not used. Irrigating the area with sterile saline for 20 minutes would be appropriate if the blood had splashed into the eyes. A diluted bleach solution is used to clean up spills, such as on surfaces or in vehicles.

13. **a.** In situations involving advance directives, you should honor the wishes of the patient if they are expressed in writing. Therefore, asking to see the written directive would be appropriate. In addition, since state and local laws vary, you should summon more advanced medical personnel immediately to provide care. If there is doubt about the validity of the directive, then you should attempt to resuscitate the patient. Telling the family that there is nothing that you can do is uncaring. Rather, you should provide support and remain calm and nonjudgmental.

14. **b.** The body has a series of natural defenses that prevent germs from entering the body and causing infection. Intact skin is the body's most effective natural defense. Mucous membranes are another natural defense but they are less effective than intact skin at keeping pathogens out of the body. Hand washing and the use of *personal protective equipment* (PPE) are effective means for preventing disease transmission, but they are not natural defenses.

15. **d.** Rabies is transmitted via the bite of an infected animal and is an example of vector-borne transmission. Indirect contact can occur when a person touches an object that contains the blood or other body fluids of an infected person and that infected blood or other body fluid enters the body through a correct entry site. Direct contact occurs when infected blood or body fluids from one person enters another person's body at a correct entry site. Respiratory droplet transmission occurs when a person inhales droplets propelled from an infected person's cough or sneezed from within a few feet.

16. **d.** When removing disposable gloves, you should pinch the palm side of the first glove near the wrist and carefully pull the glove so that it is inside out. While holding this glove in the palm of the gloved hand, you would slip two fingers under the glove at the wrist of the remaining gloved hand, pulling it off, inside out, so that the first glove ends up inside the glove just removed. At no time during the removal should bare skin come in contact with the outside of either glove.

17. **b.** Work practice controls reduce the likelihood of exposure by changing the way a task is carried out. Disinfecting work surfaces that are possibly soiled with blood or body fluids would be an example. Ensuring that sharps disposal containers and biohazard containers are readily available and posting signs at entrances where there may be infectious materials are examples of engineering controls, measures that isolate or remove a hazard from the workplace.

18. **a.** When a spill occurs, the area should be flooded with a fresh disinfectant solution, most commonly 1½ cups of liquid chlorine bleach to 1 gallon of water (one part bleach per 9 parts water or a 10 percent solution). Other commercial disinfectant/antimicrobial solutions are available and may be used. However, alcohol, hydrogen peroxide and soap would not be appropriate.

19. **d.** Signs and symptoms of critical incident stress include uncharacteristic, excessive humor or silence, confusion, guilt, poor concentration, decreased attention span, inability to do his or her job well, denial, depression, anger, a change in interactions with others, increased or decreased eating and any other unusual behavior.

20. **c.** When dealing with the family of a patient who has died suddenly, you should listen empathetically and remain calm and nonjudgmental, allow them to express their rage, anger and despair, speak in a gentle tone of voice and not give false reassurance.

21. **b.** Debriefing usually takes place in a group setting within a controlled environment with a trained professional. Defusing is a less formal, less structured interaction that usually occurs within the first few hours after an event and lasts 30 to 45 minutes. It is done on a one-to-one basis between the responder and a peer counselor.

22. **a.** A HEPA mask would be inappropriate because it would provide no protection from the patient's blood. It would be appropriate if a respiratory illness was suspected. In addition to disposable gloves, you should wear a gown to protect your clothing and a face shield to protect yourself from splashing.

23. **c.** If the eyes are involved in an exposure, you should irrigate the eyes with clean water, saline or a sterile irrigant for 20 minutes. Other areas that are exposed, such as the skin, should be washed with soap and water. Antiseptic eye drops would not be appropriate. Reporting the incident to the designated person in your agency is important but the eyes need to be flushed first.

24. **b.** Hepatitis B, a bloodborne pathogen, is spread by sexual contact through infected body fluids. It is not spread by contaminated food or water or by casual contact, such as hugging an infected person.

25. **a.** Touching a patient without first obtaining that patient's consent could be considered battery. Abandonment refers to the stoppage or cessation of care once is it started. Your obligation for care ends when more advanced medical personnel take over. However, if you stop your care before that point without a valid reason, you could be legally responsible for abandonment. Assault is a threat or an attempt to inflict harm on someone with the patient feeling threatened with bodily harm. Negligence refers to a failure to follow a reasonable standard of care thereby causing or contributing to injury or damage to another. It can involve acting wrongly or failing to act at all.

26. **b.** Expressed consent is given verbally or through a gesture. Implied consent is consent that is obtained from patients who are unable to give expressed consent, recognizing that the patient would give informed consent for care if he or she was able to do so. Informal consent is not a type of consent. Parental consent, which would most likely be expressed consent, would be obtained if the patient was considered a minor.

27. **c.** Although you are legally responsible for continuing to provide care once initiated, patients with decision-making capacity who are of legal age have a right to refuse care at any time during this period. You should honor her refusal and follow local policies for refusal of care. You also should remind the patient that she can call EMS personnel again if the situation changes or if she changes her mind. In addition, you should try to convince the patient that care is needed and notify medical direction and local EMS personnel.

28. **c.** To act in the patient's best interest refers to providing competent care with compassion and respect for human dignity, implying that the care provided serves the integrity of the patient's physical well-being while at the same time respecting the patient's choices and self-determination. The principle of do no harm means that people who intervene to help others must do their best to ensure that their actions will not harm the patient or patients. The principle of acting in good faith means to act in such a way that the goal is first and foremost to help the patient and that all actions serve that purpose.

29. **b.** When obtaining consent, you should first identify yourself to the patient ("My name is Jane Smith.") and then give your level of training ("I am an emergency medical responder here to help you."). Next you should explain what you observe ("I notice that you have a large cut on your arm. May I help you?") and then explain what you plan to do ("I'm going to loosen your sleeve to check your arm.").

30. **a.** In the out-of-hospital setting, unless you are provided with written documentation (or unless your state laws and regulations allow acceptance of oral verification [which most states' laws do not]) or if there is any doubt as to whether a *Do Not Resuscitate* (DNR) order is valid or in effect, care should proceed as it would in the absence of a DNR order. You need to be aware of the DNR laws in your state. Notifying medical direction is important in order to inform them of the situation but not for direction about how to proceed.

Calling the physician for verification would not be appropriate at this time. Although you would want to honor the spouse's statement and patient's wishes, you need to be presented with a valid written DNR order.

31. **c.** Breach of duty occurred with the error in providing care. The duty to act is the obligation to respond to emergency calls and to provide emergency care. Proximate cause refers to the injury that resulted from the breach of duty. Patient harm is the end result of the EMR's actions.

32. **d.** Epilepsy is not a condition that requires mandatory reporting. Mandatory reporting must be done in cases of abuse and violence, such as child abuse and gunshot wound from a crime, as well as in cases of certain infectious diseases, such as tuberculosis, HIV infections and AIDS and hepatitis B.

33. **d.** According to the *Health Insurance Portability and Accountability Act* (HIPAA), you cannot relay any identifying information about the patient to anyone without the patient's specific consent. This includes the media, employers, colleagues, other family members or co-workers. Health information may be disclosed to public health authorities in cases of mandatory reporting, such as for abuse, neglect or domestic violence, and organ procurement agencies for the purposes of facilitating a transplant.

34. **b.** All patients have the right to refuse care, and as an EMR you must honor the patient's refusal. In addition, you should follow local policies for refusal of care, tell the patient what treatment is needed and why, trying to convince them but not arguing with them. You also should remind the person that they can call EMS if the situation changes or if they change their minds. Finally, you should notify local EMS personnel and medical direction according to local protocols and document the patient's refusal according to local policy.

35. **c.** Medical futility is an exception to the need for written proof of a DNR order and providing care. It is not involved with living wills or durable power of attorney for health care documents. It is unrelated to a health care proxy, the person named in a durable power of attorney for health care to make medical decisions.

36. **a.** A mentally incompetent person who is seriously injured falls under implied consent when a parent or guardian is not present. You should attempt to verify if there is a guardian present with the legal right to consent to treatment, but the priority here is to provide care to the patient. Law enforcement personnel may be necessary to help notify or contact the guardian while you provide care. Trying to talk the patient into giving consent is inappropriate because his consent would be invalid.

37. **c.** The patient is in the Fowler's position because he is lying on his back with his upper body elevated 45 to 60 degrees. In the supine position, the patient is lying face-up on his or her back. The prone position would indicate that the patient is lying face-down on his or her stomach. The anatomical position is the position used as the basis for all medical terms that refer to the body; it is used to describe the position when the patient stands with the body erect and arms down at the sides, palms facing forward.

38. **a.** The humerus is the bone in the upper arm. The radius and ulna are bones in the forearm. The femur is the bone in the upper lower extremity.

39. **b.** The injured part is the patient's upper arm, which would be toward the patient's head, which is above, or superior to, the elbow. Lateral to the wrist would indicate an injury away from the midline of the body or in this situation away from the wrist. Anterior to the ribs would indicate that the injury is toward the front of the body or in front of the chest. Medial to the sternum would indicate that the injury was closer to the midline of the body.

40. **b.** Hypo- is the prefix used to describe a less than normal finding, such as temperature. Hyper- indicates something that is excessive, above, over or beyond. Brady- means slow or dull. Tachy- indicates fast, swift, rapid or accelerated.

41. **a.** Extension refers to a straightening movement. Flexion describes a bending movement. Superior does not describe a movement but rather describes any part toward the patient's head. Proximal does not describe movement; it refers to any part close to the trunk.

42. **c.** In the supine position, the patient is lying face-up on his or her back. The Fowler's position is one in which the patient is lying on his or her back with the upper body elevated at a 45- to 60-degree angle. In the prone position, the patient is lying face-down on his or her stomach.

43. **a.** During expiration, the diaphragm relaxes and moves up. During inspiration, the chest muscles contract, moving the ribs outward and upward and allowing the chest cavity to expand.

44. **b.** The brainstem is the control center for several vital functions, including respiration, cardiac

function and vasomotor control. The spinal cord consists mainly of nerve cells and carries information from the body to the brain. The cerebellum is responsible for coordinating movement and balance. The cerebrum is the largest and outermost structure.

45. **c.** Children, especially infants, are nose breathers, increasing the ease at which the airway can become blocked. The trachea is narrower and softer than an adult's trachea. The chest wall is softer, and infants breathe faster.

46. **b.** For a patient with a suspected head, neck or spinal injury, only the clothes drag move would be appropriate to use. The firefighter's carry, ankle drag and shoulder drag can be used if there is no suspected head, neck or spinal injury.

47. **c.** When preparing to move any patient, you need to be aware of your own physical abilities to prevent injury to yourself. Although having a stretcher is helpful, it is not the most important factor. Your knees should be bent, and your back should be in the locked-in position.

48. **b.** The patient should be allowed to assume a position of comfort, which in this case would most likely be an upright sitting position due to her breathing difficulties. The supine position would be appropriate if the patient was not breathing rapidly or coughing. The left lateral recumbent position would be used if the patient were pregnant or had abdominal pain. The modified *high arm in endangered spine* (H.A.IN.E.S) recovery position is used if you are alone and have to leave the person (e.g., to call for help), or you cannot maintain an open and clear airway because of fluids or vomit.

49. **a.** The responder positioned at the head will be the lead for the move and will stabilize the head and neck during the move. The second responder stands at the patient's shoulders and upper back area. The third responder stands at the patient's hips. The fourth responder stands on the opposite side to position the backboard.

50. **c.** If a patient is aggressive or violent and in need of emergency care, he or she may need to be restrained. However, restraints are used only when the patient presents a danger to him- or herself or to others. A patient who is violently thrashing about poses a threat to the EMR and to him- or herself. A patient who is unconscious, screaming loudly in pain or who is difficult to arouse is not violent or aggressive and does not pose a danger to him- or herself or to others.

51. **c.** When preparing to restrain a patient, you will need at least four responders trained in the use of restraints plus an additional EMR who can advise the patient about what is taking place.

52. **d.** A bariatric stretcher is designed to accommodate a weight of up to 1600 pounds and would be appropriate for this patient. A scoop or orthopedic stretcher is intended for patients who weigh up to 300 pounds and is designed to be assembled and disassembled around the patient. A standard wheeled stretcher is most commonly used when moving patients from a situation in which transport by ambulance for more advanced medical care is required.

53. **a.** When performing the direct carry, you would position the stretcher at a right angle to the bed with the head of the stretcher at the foot of the bed and two responders placed beside the bed on the same side as the stretcher. The stretcher is not positioned with the stretcher's head parallel to the head of the bed, alongside the bed with the stretcher's head at the bed's foot or at the foot of the bed, parallel to the bottom of the bed.

54. **d.** When beginning to lift a patient, you should always begin your lift facing the patient and with your back in a locked-in position. Your legs should be shoulder-width apart, head up, back straight and shoulders square. Your arms should be locked.

55. **c.** To minimize injury, you should estimate the total weight to be lifted or carried including the weight of any equipment to be used in addition to the patient. You should communicate clearly and frequently with your partner, patient and other responders. When carrying the patient, you should keep the weight as close to your body as possible and bend and flex at the hips and knees rather than your waist.

56. **a.** The supine position is used when assessing an unconscious patient, when a patient needs CPR or assisted ventilation or when a patient has a suspected head, neck or spinal injury. A patient with difficulty breathing may be more comfortable sitting up and is normally transported in a sitting-up position of comfort. A patient with abdominal pain will be more comfortable lying on the side with the knees drawn up. A patient with vomiting should be allowed to remain in whatever position is most comfortable for that patient.

| UNIT 2 ASSESSMENT |

1. **c.** In this situation, the vehicle is tilted and considered unstable. Therefore, it would be most important to stabilize the vehicle because any movement of the vehicle during patient care or extrication can prove dangerous or even fatal to the patient and rescue personnel. Once the vehicle is stabilized and the scene is safe, other measures may be done, including putting on PPE, gathering information about the patient's injuries and attempting to remove the patient from the vehicle.

2. **b.** The patient was involved in a head-on crash while wearing his seatbelt with a shoulder strap. The seatbelt prevents head and facial injuries. However, it can cause injuries to the shoulder, chest and abdomen. The patient's complaints of pain in the chest and difficulty breathing support the suspicion that these areas may be injured.

3. **a.** If you arrive at the scene of violence or a crime, you should not try to reach a patient until you are sure that the scene is safe. Law enforcement personnel must make it secure. Once the scene is secured, then you can walk quickly to the patient to demonstrate calmness. It may be necessary to set up a barrier around the scene but only after law enforcement has made the scene secure. There is no evidence of hazardous materials, so notifying hazardous materials personnel is unnecessary.

4. **d.** The number of resources will depend on whether there are any hazards at the scene, the number of injured or ill persons and the mechanism of injury or nature of the illness. The number of bystanders would not impact your decision about the need for additional resources.

5. **b.** Hazardous materials are any chemical substances or materials that can pose a threat to the health, safety and property of an individual. Clues suggesting the presence of hazardous materials include clouds of vapor, spilled liquids or solids, unusual odors, leaking containers, bottles or glass cylinders, and signs (placards) on vehicles, storage facilities or railroad cars. Broken glass would not be considered a hazardous material.

6. **c.** As part of standard precautions, CPR breathing barriers, such as resuscitation masks and *bag-valve-mask resuscitators (*BVMs), would be used when providing ventilations to a patient. Masks block potentially infectious body fluids from reaching your face. However, they would interfere with your ability to provide ventilations.

Protective eyewear is used to protect the eyes from debris, heat and body fluids. They would not protect you from exposure to blood and body fluids that may occur with ventilations. Gowns provide protection from fluids that may be splashed onto the clothing or skin.

7. **c.** The responsibility for directing traffic at an emergency scene lies with law enforcement. However, if the police have not yet arrived, the EMR may need to manage this task. In some situations, the EMR may need to designate another individual, such as a bystander, to assist in this area.

8. **a.** A vehicle is unstable if it is positioned on a tilted surface or on its side. The vehicle that has rolled over with its two side wheels over the guardrail is unstable because the vehicle is on its side and tilted. A vehicle that is on the shoulder of the road, has collided with a telephone pole or is facing oncoming traffic is on a flat surface. Consequently, the risk that a vehicle in any of these situations would move is minimal.

9. **b.** In the primary phase of a blast injury, energy is released during the explosion, sending a wave of pressure expanding outward from the center of the blast. Individuals hit by this pressure can experience injury to any body part that is air-filled, especially the lungs, stomach, intestines and inner ears. Blunt or penetrating injuries are common during the secondary phase of a blast injury, causing injury to the skin. Bones and muscles may be injured during the secondary phase as debris is blown outward and strikes the person and also during the tertiary phase as the person is knocked to the ground or hit by another object by the force of the explosion.

10. **b.** In a domestic disturbance, you should not approach the scene until law enforcement personnel have arrived and secured it. Once inside, you must be continually aware of your surroundings and take nothing for granted. Speak directly to the patient and ask open-ended questions that allow the patient to talk. If possible, separate yourself and the patient from the suspected perpetrator.

11. **c.** The severity of injuries caused by falls is determined by the distance the patient fell because the speed of the fall increases when the person falls from a greater height. The height has no effect on landing or vice versa. Objects may or may not be present to slow the fall or cause

additional injury. Height and the direction of the fall, such as head first, are unrelated.

12. **d.** In an emergency, use each of your senses to size-up the scene. The priority is safety, but personal safety comes before patient safety. If you determine that the scene is safe, you do not need to wait for additional personnel to arrive. Information provided by dispatch, although helpful, is likely to be incomplete and may not be entirely accurate.

13. **a.** Using the mnemonic AVPU, you would describe this patient as responding to verbal stimuli, that is, the patient reacts to sounds, such as your voice. A patient who is alert and aware of his or her surroundings is able to acknowledge your presence and respond to your questions. A patient who does not respond to verbal stimuli or commands but does respond when someone inflicts pain, such as pinching the skin above the collarbone, is described as responding to painful stimuli. A patient who does not respond to any stimuli is described as being unconscious or unresponsive to stimuli.

14. **c.** To assess a patient's airway status, you would assess the patient in the supine position, face-up so that you can see the chest rising and falling. This observation would be difficult in the side-lying position and impossible if the patient was lying prone. Turning the patient's head to the side when prone could lead to further injury, especially if the patient has a head, neck or spinal injury.

15. **d.** Pale skin is not a normal finding and typically reflects low body temperature, blood loss, shock or poor blood flow to a body part. Cool skin may indicate low body temperature or shock. A pulse rate of 70 beats per minute, capillary refill of 2 seconds and a respiratory rate of 18 breaths per minute are normal findings.

16. **b.** When approaching a patient, speak to the patient, first identifying yourself as a rescuer and saying that you are there to help the patient. Then obtain consent from the patient before beginning the primary assessment and providing care. Next, ask the patient about what happened and additional questions, such as "What is your name?" and "Where are you?", to form an idea about the patient's *level of consciousness* (LOC).

17. **a.** The primary assessment is used to quickly identify those conditions that represent an immediate threat to a patient's life. Ensuring scene safety, determining the *mechanism of injury* (MOI) and deciding which additional resources are needed all are components of sizing up the scene.

18. **c.** As a general rule, you should summon more advanced medical personnel for prolonged chest pain, difficulty breathing, seizures, for vomiting blood and persistent abdominal pain or pressure. Vomiting in general would not necessarily require you to summon more advanced medical personnel.

19. **d.** For an infant who is conscious or unconscious, check the brachial artery located in the inside of the upper arm, midway between the shoulder and elbow for a pulse. For adults and children, check the radial pulse on the thumb side of the patient's wrist. If the adult or child is unconscious, check the carotid pulse located in the neck. The femoral pulse is located in the groin area and is not typically used to assess pulse.

20. **c.** When performing the head-tilt/chin-lift technique, tilt the head slightly past neutral if the patient is a child. Tilt the head further back for an adult or adolescent. Tilt the head to the neutral position for an infant.

21. **a.** Indicators that a patient is having difficulty breathing include shrill whistling sounds, grunting and gasping with breaths. Breathing should be quiet, effortless, regular and of sufficient depth.

22. **b.** Intactness of the skin does not help in evaluating perfusion. Evaluation of perfusion requires you to look at and feel the skin for four characteristics including color, moisture, temperature and capillary refill.

23. **a.** Although weak pulse, pale skin and excessive thirst may indicate shock, irritability or restlessness often is the first sign of shock.

24. **c.** When using a resuscitation mask, first assemble the mask, if necessary, by attaching the one-way valve to the mask. Next, position the mask, seal it, open the airway and finally blow into the mask.

25. **c.** When performing a primary assessment after sizing up the scene, check the patient for responsiveness and if no response occurs, summon more advanced medical personnel. Next, open the airway and check for breathing and a pulse. Lastly, scan for severe bleeding.

26. **d.** To check an infant for responsiveness, flick the underside of the foot or the top of the shoulder. Asking the parents if the infant is okay would not provide you with information about his or her LOC. Calling the infant by name would be inappropriate because although the infant may be fully aware, he or she may be unable to respond.

Additionally, an infant may or may not know his or her name, depending on the age of the infant. Making a loud noise near the infant's ear may be used to evoke a response but it would not be the most appropriate method. Additionally, the infant may have a hearing deficit that could affect the response.

27. **b.** A patient with pale, moist, pink skin who is moving air freely in and out of the chest is breathing adequately and needs continued monitoring for changes because a patient's breathing status can change quickly. Ventilations and emergency oxygen would be used if the patient's breathing was inadequate. Clearing the airway of debris is not necessary since the patient's breathing status is adequate.

28. **d.** The chief complaint is the reason why EMS personnel were called to the scene. For this patient, it would be that he fainted or "passed out." Pale skin and the absence of chest pain would be signs and symptoms identified as part of the SAMPLE history. The report that the patient has high blood pressure would reflect the pertinent past medical history of the SAMPLE history.

29. **a.** When gaining information about the patient's chief complaint, you should use the OPQRST mnemonic. First, ask the patient what she was doing when the difficulty started because this might provide you with clues about the nature of the illness. Next, gather information about provocation (e.g., if anything makes it better), region/radiate, severity (e.g., rating the difficulty breathing) and time (e.g., the length of time the patient has been experiencing this problem).

30. **b.** The patient's statement about drinking a glass of water is information related to "L," the last oral intake. "S" refers to signs and symptoms, findings you can see, feel, hear or smell or what the patient tells you. "M" refers to medications including prescription and over-the-counter medications, herbal remedies and recreational drugs. "E" refers to events leading up to the incident, such as what the patient was doing before and at the time of the incident.

31. **a.** For a responsive medical patient, you perform a secondary assessment. After assessing the patient's complaints and obtaining a SAMPLE history, you would perform a focused medical assessment. Then you would assess baseline vital signs, perform components of the detailed physical exam and provide emergency care.

32. **d.** When conducting the physical exam, maintain the patient's privacy by conducting the exam in an area that cannot be seen by bystanders, if possible. To access an area to be examined, cut away rather than manipulate the patient's clothing to remove it. Ask the patient questions about a particular area before examining it, and cover each area after you have examined it.

33. **b.** When examining the head, both pupils should be equal in size, constrict to light and dilate on exposure to darkness. Clear fluid or blood in or around the ears, mouth and nose is abnormal and may indicate a serious head injury. The face should be symmetrical.

34. **c.** When obtaining a patient's blood pressure, ensure that the cuff covers about two-thirds of the patient's upper arm and that the forearm is on a supported surface in front or to the side of the patient, not hanging down or raised above heart level. The cuff should be applied to the patient's unclothed or lightly clothed arm to prevent inaccuracies. The bladder of the cuff should be positioned with the bladder over the brachial artery.

35. **a.** An ongoing assessment is completed to identify and treat any changes in the patient's condition in a timely manner and to monitor the effectiveness of interventions or care provided. The purpose of the primary assessment is to identify any life-threatening conditions. The secondary assessment is performed to locate and further assess the signs and symptoms of an injury or illness, including assessing the patient's complaints, obtaining a SAMPLE history, performing a focused medical assessment, assessing baseline vital signs, performing components of the detailed physical exam, providing emergency care and considering the need for advanced life support backup and transport.

36. **a.** When examining the abdomen, ask the patient if he or she is having any pain in the abdomen and look for any discoloration, open wounds, distention, scars or protruding organs. In addition, look at the abdomen for any pulsating and if none is present, apply slight pressure to each of the abdominal quadrants, avoiding any areas where the patient has indicated pain. Ask the patient to shrug his or her shoulders when examining the chest. Push in on the sides of the hips when examining the pelvis. Inspect for a protruding jugular vein when examining the neck.

37. **c.** When performing a secondary assessment for a responsive medical patient, first assess the patient's complaints, then obtain a SAMPLE history, perform a focused medical assessment, assess baseline vital signs, perform components of

the detailed physical exam and finally, provide emergency care.

38. **c.** When using a radio communication system, you should keep transmissions brief, organized and to the point, omitting courtesy terms like "please" and "thank you." You also should use emergency medical frequencies only for EMS communication, speak slowly with your lips 2 to 3 inches from the microphone, and use "affirmative" and "negative" rather than "yes" and "no."

39. **a.** Before doing anything, unless it is a life-threatening situation, introduce yourself to the patient. Tell the patient what your role is and what you will do. When speaking to an injured or ill person, speak slowly and clearly, and avoid using medical terms, such as "fracture." Instead, use words that are easily understandable. When addressing older adults, call them by their first names only when invited to do so. Such an action shows respect. In addition, have the patient tell you about the problem. The husband may instinctively want to talk about his wife, but having the patient tell you what happened allows you to observe her ability to communicate as well as her LOC and mental status.

40. **c.** As you interview a patient or bystanders, try to let the person you are interviewing do most of the talking and do not interrupt. Be sure to word questions so that you do not provide false assurance or reassurance. Avoid giving advice or asking leading or biased questions. Avoid asking "why" questions, which can be perceived as judgmental.

41. **b.** Although the run data section of the *prehospital care report* (PCR) serves as a legal document, acts as an educational tool and allows billing, its primary function is to ensure quality care.

42. **a.** The patient narrative provides a description of the assessment and care provided and it must include the SAMPLE history. The run data contains administrative information, the patient data section includes all background information on the patient and the check boxes section contains information about the patient's condition, including vital signs, chief complaint, LOC, appearance and respirations.

43. **d.** To facilitate communication, make eye contact to show that you are interested in what the patient is saying. Additionally, minimize distractions to promote clear communication, ensure adequate lighting and get down to the patient's eye level to avoid the patient feeling threatened.

44. **a.** Asking the daughter to tell you what happened is an open-ended question, which allows the daughter to provide as much information as possible about the situation. Telling her that her father will be fine provides false reassurance. Asking her why he was not using his cane and telling her that he needs to be watched more carefully are judgmental statements.

45. **c.** Patient data includes background information on the patient, such as legal name, age, home address, and billing and insurance information. The check boxes section includes information about the patient's condition, such as level of alertness, vital signs, appearance and respiratory rate. The run data section contains administrative information, such as the time that the unit arrived on the scene and the unit's number.

46. **b.** When receiving medical direction, use the echo method, that is, repeat the order word for word to ensure that you have heard and understood the order. The terms "affirmative" and "negative" should be used in any situation involving radio communication, not just communications with medical control. Asking medical control to repeat the order again would be appropriate if you did not understand the original order or if you repeated the order incorrectly back to medical control. Telling medical control that you understand would be inappropriate.

| UNIT 3 AIRWAY |

1. **d.** For an unconscious patient with visible foreign matter in the upper airway, you would use a finger sweep to remove the material. Abdominal thrusts and back blows clear an obstructed airway in conscious patients. The head-tilt/chin-lift technique would be used to open the patient's airway, once the vomit was removed.

2. **c.** When giving ventilations to an adult patient, you would give 1 ventilation about every 5 seconds, with each ventilation lasting about 1 second. For a child or an infant, you would give 1 ventilation about every 3 seconds. You would recheck for breathing and a pulse after giving ventilations for approximately 2 minutes. This reassessment should last no longer than 10 seconds.

3. **a.** If the patient vomits while providing ventilations, quickly turn the patient as a unit onto his side to keep the vomit from blocking the airway and entering the lungs. After the vomiting stops, clear the airway with finger sweeps and suction as necessary, then turn the patient onto the back and continue with ventilation. You may need to reposition the patient's head to ensure an open airway after turning him or her onto the back once the vomiting has stopped and the material has been cleared from the mouth. Using greater force with the vomit still in the patient's mouth could lead to aspiration of the vomit into the lungs. In addition, blowing too much air into the patient leads to gastric distention and increases the risk for vomiting.

4. **b.** When giving ventilations to an adult, you would recheck for breathing and a pulse after giving ventilations for about 2 minutes.

5. **c.** Ventilations are effective when you see the chest clearly rise. If the abdomen becomes distended, it indicates that you are blowing too much air into the patient. A tight seal on the mask means that the mask is properly positioned. Although a properly fitting mask and breaths moving into the mask with ease enhance the chances that ventilations will be more effective, neither alone indicates that ventilations are effective.

6. **d.** The brain is the control center for breathing, directing the body to adjust the rate and depth of breaths according to the oxygen and carbon dioxide levels. The circulatory system transports oxygen-rich blood to the brain, organs, muscles and other parts of the body. The lungs contain the alveoli, which enable the exchange of oxygen and carbon dioxide between the respiratory and circulatory systems. The kidneys filter waste products. They are not involved in respiratory control.

7. **b.** The normal rate of breathing for children is from 15 to 30 breaths per minute; therefore, a breathing rate of 26 breaths per minute would indicate adequate breathing. A breathing rate of 12 breaths per minute would be adequate for an adult. Breathing rates of 38 to 48 breaths per minute would be adequate for infants.

8. **b.** Because it is necessary to maintain a tight seal on the mask, two rescuers should operate a BVM. With only a single rescuer, operation of a BVM is difficult and generally does not create an adequate seal to deliver emergency oxygen to the patient.

9. **a.** A midline trachea is the normal position and indicates that breathing is adequate. Indications that breathing is inadequate include nasal flaring, deviated trachea, muscles between the ribs pulling inward on inhalation, pursed lips breathing and tripod positioning (sitting upright and leaning forward).

10. **c.** For a patient who has a mouth injury, you should provide mouth-to-nose ventilations. Mouth-to-mask ventilations are the typical method for giving ventilations. Mouth-to-mouth ventilations would be used if a resuscitation mask is not available. Mouth-to-stoma ventilations would be used for patients who have an opening in their neck used for breathing.

11. **b.** The primary advantage of mouth-to-mask ventilations when compared with mouth-to-mouth ventilations is that mouth-to-mask ventilations reduce the risk of disease transmission. Mouth-to-mask ventilations do not require less time to give. Mouth-to-mouth ventilations require pinching the nose, whereas mouth-to-mask ventilations do not. Both provide 16 percent oxygen through an exhaled breath.

12. **c.** First, after positioning the infant face-down on your forearm, give 5 back blows with the heel of your hand. Then position the infant face-up and give 5 chest thrusts with two to three fingers. Continue the cycle of 5 back blows and 5 chest thrusts until the object is forced out, the infant begins to cough or breathe on her own or she becomes unconscious.

13. **c.** When performing chest thrusts on an infant, compress the chest about 1½ inches, making a distinct attempt to dislodge the object.

14. **a.** Before attempting any actions, it is essential to ensure that the patient is on a firm, flat surface. Then attempt a ventilation and if there is no rise in the chest, retilt the head and try another ventilation. If there is no rise in the chest, then perform 30 chest compressions and look inside the mouth.

15. **c.** When preparing to insert an *oropharyngeal airway* (OPA), first make sure that the patient is unconscious. OPAs are used only on unconscious, unresponsive patients with no gag reflex. Airways are used to prevent, not treat, airway obstruction by the tongue. Selecting the proper size by measuring the distance from the earlobe to the corner of the mouth is important, but this would be done once you have established that the patient is unresponsive.

16. **b.** When using mechanical or manual suction on a child, you would suction for no more than 10 seconds at a time. You would suction an adult for no more than 15 seconds at a time and an infant for no more than 5 seconds at a time. Suctioning for longer periods can starve the patient of air.

17. **a.** If a patient begins to gag as the OPA reaches the back of the throat, immediately remove the OPA, suction the airway to remove all debris, thoroughly clean the device and reinsert it only if the patient still is unconscious and does not have a gag reflex. The OPA is rotated 180 degrees as the tip approaches the mouth. Continuing to insert the airway would be inappropriate and dangerous. An OPA is inserted only into a patient who is unconscious, so it would be inappropriate to give the patient a sip of water. Additionally, if the patient is unconscious, it would be impossible for the patient to take a sip of water.

18. **b.** Back blows followed by chest thrusts would be appropriate in cases where you cannot reach far enough around the patient to give effective abdominal thrusts or if the patient is obviously pregnant or known to be pregnant. Abdominal thrusts would be appropriate to use on a thin, frail patient since you should have no difficulty reaching around the patient. Chests thrusts alone would be used for a patient who is unconscious. A patient who cannot speak requires immediate intervention with back blows and abdominal thrusts.

19. **a.** An OPA is correctly placed when the flange of the device rests on the patient's lips. Resistance to the device is felt as the tip approaches the back of the patient's throat. Although gagging should not occur, absence of gagging does not indicate proper placement. The flange should not touch the patient's teeth.

20. **c.** You apply suction as you withdraw the suction tip using a sweeping motion. You should not apply suction as you insert the tip into the mouth, upon reaching the back of the mouth or when touching the tongue.

21. **a.** Before providing any help to this child, it is important to obtain consent from the mother to assist the child. Once consent is obtained, then encourage the child to continue coughing forcefully in an effort to dislodge the obstruction. If this is ineffective, give 5 back blows followed by 5 abdominal thrusts to attempt to dislodge the object. Lower the child to the ground only if the child became unconscious.

22. **c.** With a BVM, the oxygen flow rate should be set at 15 *liters per minute* (LPM) or more, thereby supplying an oxygen concentration of 90 percent or higher. A nasal cannula can deliver emergency oxygen at a flow rate of 1 to 6 LPM. A resuscitation mask can deliver emergency oxygen at 6 to 15 LPM. A non-rebreather mask can deliver emergency oxygen at 10 to 15 LPM.

23. **d.** To verify oxygen flow, listen for a hissing sound and feel for oxygen flow through the delivery device. The flowmeter dial should not change, but rather it should remain at the rate that is set. A pressure gauge reading below 200 *pounds per square inch* (psi) indicates that the cylinder needs to be replaced. The O-ring should be present to ensure a tight seal between the regulator and the tank.

24. **a.** A nasal cannula would be inappropriate because the patient needs a device that can supply a greater concentration of oxygen than that which is supplied by a nasal cannula. A resuscitation mask, non-rebreather mask or a BVM would be more appropriate for this patient because they are used with patients who are breathing and they can deliver higher concentrations of oxygen.

25. **d.** Emergency oxygen would be beneficial to a child with a respiratory rate below 15 breaths per minute or above 30 breaths per minute. An adult with a respiratory rate less than 12 or more than 20 breaths per minute and an infant with a respiratory rate less than 25 or more than 50 breaths per minute also would be candidates for emergency oxygen.

26. **c.** When working with oxygen systems, check the pressure regulator to ensure that the cylinder is not empty, handle the cylinder carefully because it is under high pressure and should not be dropped,

do not lubricate any part of the oxygen system to prevent explosion, check to make sure that the pin index corresponds to the oxygen tank and hand-tighten the screw until the regulator is snug.

27. **a.** A fixed-flow-rate system comes with the delivery device, regulator and cylinder already connected to each other. Therefore, to operate a fixed-flow-rate system, simply turn it on according to the manufacturer's instructions, check that oxygen is flowing and place the delivery device on the patient. Opening the cylinder valve for 1 second, attaching the regulator and opening the cylinder counterclockwise are important steps associated with a variable-flow-rate system.

28. **b.** To deliver a flow rate of 6 LPM to a non-breathing patient, a resuscitation mask would be most appropriate to use because this device can provide emergency oxygen at a flow rate of 6 to 15 LPM. A BVM is designed for flow rates of 15 LPM or more and can be used with breathing and nonbreathing patients. A nasal cannula can administer flow rates of 1 to 6 LPM, but this device is used for patients who are breathing. A non-rebreather mask is used with flow rates of 10 to 15 LPM for patients who are breathing.

29. **c.** A non-rebreather mask consists of a face mask with an attached oxygen reservoir bag and a one-way valve between the mask and bag to prevent the patient's exhaled air from mixing with oxygen in the reservoir bag. The reservoir bag should be about two-thirds full so that it does not deflate when the patient inhales. The patient inhales oxygen from the bag and exhaled air escapes through flutter valves on the side of the mask. A nasal cannula should not be used if the patient has a nasal injury.

30. **d.** A nasal cannula is used to administer emergency oxygen at flow rates between 1 and 6 LPM. Flow rates higher than that are not used because of the tendency to quickly dry out the mucous membranes and cause nosebleeds and headaches.

31. **a.** When using a variable-flow-rate system, begin by examining the cylinder to be certain that it is labeled "oxygen." Next remove the protective covering over the tank and remove the O-ring gasket if it is not built into the tank. Then open the cylinder for 1 second while it is pointed away from you. Next, examine the pressure regulator to be sure that it is labeled "oxygen," check to see that the pin index corresponds to an oxygen tank, attach the pressure regulator to the cylinder, hand tighten the screw until the regulator is snug and finally open the cylinder one full turn and listen for leaks.

| UNIT 4 CIRCULATION |

1. **d.** The correct position for the hands is over the lower half of the sternum in the middle of the chest. You would place the heel of one hand on the center of the chest along the sternum and then place the other hand on top. This position allows you to perform the most effective chest compressions. The lowest point of the sternum, the xiphoid process, should be avoided because this tissue can break off and puncture underlying organs and tissues. The uppermost portion of the sternum and nipple area would not provide effective compressions.

2. **c.** When performing chest compressions on a child, you should compress the chest about 2 inches. For an infant, compress to a depth of about 1½ inches. For an adult, compress to a depth of at least 2 inches.

3. **b.** Since you are near water (the pond) and the child was submerged in water for several minutes, water may be around the area where you are working and the child is most likely wet. Therefore, make sure that there are no puddles of water around you, the patient or the *automated external defibrillator* (AED) to prevent conduction of the shock to you or bystanders. You also should remove any wet clothing for proper pad placement and dry the patient's chest thoroughly to ensure pad adhesion. Correct pad placement is important, but if the pads are not adhered properly, the shock may be ineffective. Pediatric defibrillator pads are appropriate for children and infants up to 8 years of age or weighing less than 55 pounds; however, this child is 11 years old. It is helpful to make sure that spare batteries are available in case a low battery warning occurs, but this is not as essential as ensuring that there is no water near you or the patient or ensuring a dry chest.

4. **b.** Signs and symptoms suggesting a heart attack include pain that is described as squeezing, pressure, tightness, aching or heaviness that radiates to the shoulder, arm, neck, jaw, stomach or back that usually is not relieved by rest, changing position or taking medication. A history of hypertension is a main risk factor for a heart attack. Difficulty breathing is another sign and may be noted as the patient sits upright and leans forward. Complaints of dizziness and pale or ashen skin, especially around the face, and heavy sweating also may be seen with a heart attack.

5. **c.** If you suspect that a patient is experiencing a heart attack, you need to take immediate action and summon more advanced medical personnel. Next, you would have the patient stop any activity and rest, and you would loosen any tight or uncomfortable clothing. You then would continue to monitor the patient until more advanced medical personnel take over. Administer emergency oxygen, if it is available and you are authorized to administer it. If the patient experiences a cardiac arrest, begin CPR.

6. **c.** After opening the airway, checking for breathing and a pulse, and giving 2 ventilations, you would check the infant for a pulse at the brachial artery. If there is no pulse, then you would begin chest compressions. If the airway was obstructed so that you are not seeing the chest rise and fall with the ventilations, you then would attempt to relieve the obstruction with 30 chest compressions followed by looking in the mouth for an object. You would use a finger sweep only if foreign material was visible in the infant's mouth.

7. **c.** Since there are now two responders, the cycles of compressions and ventilations would be 15 compressions and 2 ventilations. A cycle of 30 compressions and 2 ventilations would be used for one-rescuer CPR for an adult, child and infant and for two-rescuer CPR for an adult. No method of CPR uses just one ventilation.

8. **b.** When performing chest compressions during CPR, position yourself at the patient's side opposite the chest. This position allows you to push straight down on the patient's sternum, making compressions more effective for the patient and less tiring for you. Being at the patient's shoulders or between the patient's legs would not allow you to provide effective chest compressions.

9. **c.** Breathing and return of a pulse indicate signs of life; therefore, you would stop CPR (compressions and ventilations) and continue to monitor the patient, ensuring that his or her airway remains open. It would be inappropriate to cancel the call for more advanced medical personnel. The patient still may require additional care and should be transported to a medical facility for evaluation. Although an AED would analyze the rhythm, there is no need to use it at this time since the patient has a pulse.

10. **b.** An AED is used when all three conditions are present: the patient is unconscious, there is no breathing and there is no pulse. An obstructed airway is not an indication for using an AED.

11. **d.** Angina normally is a transient condition in which the patient experiences chest pain but the pain does not spread and is relieved by medicine and/or rest. Persistent chest pain that spreads to the jaw and neck and is accompanied by difficulty breathing suggests a heart attack.

12. **a.** When two rescuers are performing CPR, they should change position about every 2 minutes to reduce the possibility of rescuer fatigue.

13. **b.** When CPR is in progress with one rescuer and a second rescuer arrives, the second rescuer should confirm whether more advanced medical personnel have been summoned. If they have not, the second rescuer should do so before getting the AED or assisting with care. If more advanced medical personnel have been summoned, the second rescuer should get the AED, or if an AED is not available, the second rescuer should help perform two-rescuer CPR.

14. **c.** After a shock is delivered, a period of time is programmed into the device to allow for CPR until the next rhythm analysis begins. You should not wait for the device to re-analyze the rhythm because valuable time would be lost. If at any time you notice obvious signs of life, stop CPR, monitor the patient's condition and leave the patient in a face-up position while maintaining an open airway.

15. **d.** Remove any medication patches that you see on a patient's chest with your gloved hand before defibrillation and never place an AED pad directly on top of a medication patch.

| UNIT 5 MEDICAL EMERGENCIES |

1. **b.** Diabetes involves a problem with regulation of blood glucose levels in that the body produces little or no insulin or does not use the insulin produced. Fluid volume is regulated by the kidneys. The electrical activity of the brain is regulated by the neurons (nerve cells). Regulation of oxygen levels typically involves the lungs.

2. **c.** Hypoglycemia refers to a low blood glucose level. Since the patient is conscious, you should give her something with sugar in it, such as glucose paste, milk and most fruit juices or a non-diet soft drink, which contain sufficient amounts of sugar to help restore the blood glucose level. Insulin administration would be inappropriate because it would lower her blood glucose level even more. There is no need to place the patient in a supine (face-up) position because she is alert and conscious. She is talking, which indicates that her airway is open. Only if the patient becomes unconscious or shows signs of airway obstruction would you need to open her airway.

3. **a.** Based on the description from bystanders, the patient is experiencing a generalized seizure, also called a tonic-clonic or grand mal seizure, as evidenced by reports of his body shaking all over. Although rhythmic jerking of the head and limbs may occur, a febrile seizure usually occurs in children and is associated with a rapid increase in body temperature. With a simple partial seizure, the patient usually remains conscious and there is involuntary muscular contraction in one area of the body. Some people cannot speak or move but remember everything that occurred. With a complex partial seizure, the patient experiences a blank stare followed by random movements such as lip smacking or chewing. The patient appears dazed and movements are clumsy.

4. **c.** Status epilepticus is an epileptic seizure that lasts longer than 5 minutes without any signs of slowing down. It is a true medical emergency.

5. **d.** When the normal functions of the brain are disrupted by injury, disease, fever, infection, metabolic disturbances or conditions causing a decreased oxygen level, a seizure may occur. Hypotension results from low blood pressure levels. Disrupted blood flow to the brain results in a stroke. An elevated insulin level results in hypoglycemia.

6. **c.** Protecting the patient from injury and managing the airway are your priorities when caring for a patient having a seizure. Preventing tongue biting would not be necessary because people having seizures rarely bite the tongue or cheeks with enough force to cause any significant bleeding. An open airway is a priority; however, you should not place anything in the mouth to prevent this type of injury. Foreign bodies in the mouth may cause airway obstruction. Following, not during, the seizure, you should position the patient on the side, if possible, so that fluids (saliva, blood, vomit) can drain from the mouth. You should never put fingers into the mouth of an actively seizing patient to clear the airway. After the seizure, you need to provide maximum privacy because the patient may feel embarrassed and self-conscious.

7. **c.** The patient will usually recover from a seizure in a few minutes. If you discover that the patient has a history of medically controlled seizures, there may be no further need for medical attention; however, in cases of pregnancy, known diabetes or seizures occurring in the water, more advanced medical care should be provided.

8. **c.** Since the patient is hypoglycemic and unconscious, you need to summon more advanced medical personnel immediately. Fruit juice, non-diet soda or glucose tablets are used only if the patient is conscious and can ingest them. After giving either of these, you then would recheck the blood glucose level (BGL) in 15 minutes.

9. **c.** Signs and symptoms associated with a stroke typically include facial drooping or drooling, trouble walking and numbness of the face, arm(s) or leg(s). Speech often is affected, and the patient may complain of a sudden, severe headache.

10. **b.** When responding to an emergency call related to abdominal pain, you need to assume that the pain is serious since the patient and/or family members were concerned enough to seek emergency medical attention. Abdominal pain is felt between the chest and groin, which commonly is referred to as the stomach region or belly. There are many organs in the abdomen, so when a patient is suffering from abdominal pain, it can originate from any one of them. Abdominal pain can be difficult to pinpoint since the pain may start from somewhere else and could be a result of any number of generalized infections, including the flu or strep throat. The intensity of abdominal pain does not always reflect the seriousness of the condition.

11. **d.** Patients on dialysis can experience several types of complications, including uremia (accumulation of urinary waste products in the

blood), fluid overload (reduction in the body's ability to excrete fluid through urine), anemia (hemoglobin deficiency), hypertension, hyperkalemia (excess potassium in the blood) and coronary artery disease. Emergencies also can occur as complications of the dialysis itself, including hypotension, disequilibrium syndrome, hemorrhage, equipment malfunction (e.g., introducing an air embolus or other foreign body into the circulatory system) or complications from being temporarily removed from medications. More specifically, after dialysis, patients may have hypovolemia (reduced blood volume) and exhibit cold, clammy skin; poor skin turgor (elasticity); tachycardia; and hypotension. When dialysis is delayed, patients may experience hypervolemia (increased blood volume) and may have abnormal lung sounds, such as crackles; generalized edema; hypertension; or jugular venous distension.

12. **a.** Alcohol is classified as a depressant because it affects the *central nervous system* (CNS) by decreasing physical and mental activity. Caffeine, cocaine and amphetamines are classified as stimulants. *Lysergic acid diethylamide* (LSD), *phencyclidine* (PCP), mescaline and peyote are classified as hallucinogens. Morphine, heroin and codeine are examples of narcotics.

13. **c.** Codeine is a natural opium derivative and is classified as a narcotic. Alcohol, benzodiazepines and barbiturates are considered depressants. LSD, PCP and mescaline are classified as hallucinogens. Cannabis products include marijuana, *tetrahydro-cannabinol* (THC) and hashish.

14. **c.** The severity of a poisoning depends on the type and amount of the substance, the time that has elapsed since the poison entered the body, and the patient's age, size, weight and medical conditions. The patient's sex would have no impact on the severity of the poisoning.

15. **d.** In 2007, *Poison Control Centers* (PCCs) received more than 2.4 million calls about people who had come into contact with a poison. About 90 percent (2.1 million) of these poisonings took place in the home, and 50 percent (1.1 million) involved children younger than 6 years. Poisoning deaths in children younger than age 6 represented less than 3 percent of the total deaths from poisoning, whereas the 20- to 59-year-old age group represented about 73 percent of all deaths from poisoning. Due in part to child-resistant packaging and preventive actions by parents and caregivers, there has been a decline in child poisonings. At the same time, there has been an increase in adult poisoning deaths, which is linked to an increase in both suicides and drug-related poisonings.

16. **b.** Lead is a primary source of chemical food poisoning. Botulism, E. coli and Salmonella are causes of bacterial food poisoning.

17. **a.** The symptoms of food poisoning, which can begin between 1 and 48 hours after eating contaminated food, include nausea, vomiting, abdominal pain, diarrhea, fever and dehydration. Severe cases of food poisoning can result in shock or death, particularly in children, the elderly and those with an impaired immune system. Excessive eye burning would most likely be seen with chemicals or poisons coming in contact with the eyes. Disorientation and seizures would be unlikely unless the patient developed severe food poisoning leading to extreme dehydration and shock.

18. **c.** Poisons that result from an insect sting enter the body by injection. Absorbed poisons enter the body through the skin or mucous membranes in the eyes, mouth and nose. Inhaled poisons enter the body when the person breathes in poisonous gases or fumes. Ingested poisons are poisons that are swallowed.

19. **c.** Chloroform is an example of a common inhaled poison. Poison ivy is an example of an absorbed poison. Contaminated water is an example of an ingested poison. Snake venom is an example of an injected poison.

20. **a.** When providing care to a patient with suspected substance abuse, it is most important to identify potential life-threatening conditions and intervene accordingly. Many of the signs and symptoms of substance abuse mimic other conditions, so you may not be able to determine that a patient has overdosed on a substance. Although it would be helpful to know the identity of the substance, care focuses on the abnormal behavior exhibited by the patient. If a patient becomes agitated or makes the scene unsafe in any way, you should retreat until the scene is safe. Restraints are used only as a last resort. Administering emergency oxygen would be appropriate if the patient was experiencing difficulty breathing.

21. **c.** Mood changes and a flushed face suggest hallucinogen abuse. A telltale sign of cannabis use is red, bloodshot eyes. Drowsiness would be seen with inhalant abuse and depressants.

22. **a.** When caring for a patient with substance misuse, always summon more advanced medical personnel. In addition, keep the patient's airway

clear, and calm and reassure the patient. Applying several heavy blankets would be inappropriate because these probably would cause the patient to become overheated. Rather, you should take measures to prevent chilling and overheating. You should attempt to find out what substance was taken, how much was taken and when it was taken.

23. **d.** A patient who abuses cocaine may show signs and symptoms of stimulant abuse. These would include tachycardia (increased pulse), hypertension, rapid breathing, excitement, restlessness and irritability. Patients who abuse depressants may show signs and symptoms that include drowsiness, confusion, slurred speech, slow heart and breathing rates, and poor coordination. Mood changes, flushing and hallucinations would suggest hallucinogen or designer drug abuse.

24. **a.** Contributing factors for substance abuse include the lack of traditional family structure; peer pressure; widespread availability of substances; media glamorization of substances, especially alcohol and tobacco; and low self-esteem.

25. **d.** Due to the weather and the patient's complaints, the most likely condition suspected would be frostbite. Although hypothermia is a possibility, it would be manifested by more generalized signs and symptoms. The patient's signs and symptoms do not suggest stroke, which would be noted by weakness of the face, arm or leg, possible speech difficulties and continued changes in the patient's LOC. The signs and symptoms do not reflect a generalized seizure, where the patient would be exhibiting rhythmic jerking, tonic-clonic muscular contractions.

26. **c.** The bite of a coral snake leaves a semicircular mark. The bite of other venomous snakes leaves one or two distinct puncture wounds, which may or may not bleed.

27. **c.** When providing care to a patient with frostbite, avoid breaking any blisters to prevent further damage and possible infection. Gently warm the affected area by soaking it in warm—not hot—water (100°–105° F or 37.7°–40.5° C) until normal color returns and the body part feels warm. Loosely bandage the area with dry, sterile dressings. If the patient's fingers or toes are frostbitten, place dry, sterile gauze between them to keep them separated. If there is damage is to the feet, *do not* allow the patient to walk.

28. **d.** Appropriate measures to prevent heat-related illnesses include wearing light-colored clothing to reflect the sun's rays; exercising for brief periods and then taking frequent rests, preferably in a cool, shaded area; avoiding exercising and activities during the hottest part of the day (usually late morning to early afternoon); drinking at least six, 8-ounce glasses of fluid daily; and avoiding beverages that contain caffeine and alcohol.

29 **a.** Early signs and symptoms of dehydration include excessive thirst, fatigue, weakness, headache, irritability, nausea, dizziness, and dry lips and mouth. Sunken eyes, a rapid pulse and decreased perspiration indicate worsening dehydration.

30. **a.** With high humidity, the body is less able to cool down through sweating. Evaporation decreases as the relative humidity increases because the air contains excessive moisture. If the temperature is high, the body is not as able to lower its temperature through radiation. Conduction and convection may or may not be affected.

31. **d.** Of the individuals listed, the 80-year-old patient with diabetes and heart disease would have the greatest risk for a heat-related illness because of age and the presence of two pre-existing health conditions (diabetes and heart disease). Each of the other individuals has only one risk factor, such as use of diuretics, working outside or caffeine intake.

32. **d.** Heavy sweating is associated with heat exhaustion. Heat stroke would be suggested by flushed or red skin that is either dry or moist; rapid, weak pulse; shallow breathing; low blood pressure; decreasing LOC; body temperature above 104° F; and lack of sweating.

33. **a.** When providing care to a patient with hypothermia, your initial priority is to move the patient into a warmer environment. You then would perform a primary assessment, call for more advanced medical personnel, remove any wet clothing and dry the patient, and begin to rewarm the patient slowly.

34. **a.** A localized skin rash would be more indicative of a localized allergic reaction than anaphylaxis. Anaphylaxis is a generalized, severe allergic reaction often manifested by difficulty breathing; wheezing or shortness of breath; chest or throat tightness; facial, neck or tongue swelling; weakness; dizziness or confusion; low blood pressure; and shock.

35. **b.** When working on a water rescue, you must consider your own safety before all else. Other considerations then would include the condition of the water and the patient and the resources that are available.

36. **d.** Someone who is conscious (responsive) and has no spinal injury should be removed from the water. A patient who is unresponsive, lying face-down in the water or has a neck injury should be cared for in the water.

37. **b.** A victim of sexual assault experiences physical as well as emotional trauma; therefore, it would be essential to treat the patient with sensitivity. Although it would be important to gain as much information as possible, this would need to be done with tact and sensitivity. The patient's clothing should be removed only to provide care and efforts should be made to ensure that any evidence on the clothing is preserved. You should not clean the patient because doing so may destroy evidence.

38. **d.** Common signs and symptoms of rape include an unresponsive, dazed state; intense pain from assault and penetration; psychological and physical shock and paralysis; possible bleeding or body fluid discharge; torn or removed clothing; and nausea, vomiting, gagging or urination.

39. **c.** Bipolar disorder is characterized by a person swinging from the extreme lows of depression to the highs of mania. Schizophrenia is a severe, chronic mental illness in which the patient hears voices or feels that his or her thoughts are being controlled by others. Clinical depression is a chronic illness involving persistent feelings of being useless along with a loss of interest in regular activities, feelings of hopelessness or guilt and unexplained sadness. A panic attack is an anxiety disorder in which the patient experiences an out-of-control feeling often accompanied by difficulty breathing and heart palpitations.

40. **a.** Abdominal injuries would be the least likely cause of a behavioral emergency. Possible causes of behavioral emergencies include injury, primarily head injury; physical illness; adverse effects of prescribed medications; mental illness; noncompliance with prescribed psychiatric medications; and extreme emotional distress.

41. **b.** Excited delirium syndrome is characterized by high body temperature, increased body strength, insensitivity to pain and agitation.

42. **c.** Paranoia can be a side effect of any recreational drug use; however, it is particularly associated with the use of stimulants.

43. **d.** Your primary concern as an EMR is to treat any injuries or medical conditions arising from the violence or suicide attempt, and then transport the patient to a facility where he or she can receive medical and psychiatric treatment. If it is necessary to prevent the patient from harming you, him- or herself, or others, you may need to use medical restraints to transport the patient.

44. **a.** Asking the question, "You're not a threat to yourself, are you?" implies the answer "no" regardless of what the patient is feeling. It makes the assumption that the patient is not a threat to him- or herself. Asking the patient how he or she is feeling, if he or she is thinking about hurting him- or herself, or if he or she has suffered any trauma recently provides direct specific information to help gain insight into the situation.

45. **c.** When sizing up the scene, identify and locate the patient before entering. You also need to identify exit or escape routes for your safety and clear the scene of any objects that could be used to injure the patient or others as soon as possible. You need to be aware that there may be more than one patient.

| UNIT 6 TRAUMA EMERGENCIES |

1. **a.** A patient in the early stages of shock would exhibit apprehension and anxiety, slightly lower-than-normal temperature, increased respiratory rate, slightly increased pulse, normal or slightly lower blood pressure and pale, ashen, cool skin.

2. **c.** Because the patient hit the metal shelf and then landed on a cement floor when he fell, you would expect to see an increase in the pulse rate along with a weak pulse since this is the body's response to blood loss, either externally or internally. The pulse rate does not reflect blood glucose levels, early signs of sepsis or cardiac trauma.

3. **d.** The patient's signs and symptoms reflect the body's attempt to compensate for the effects of the injury. They are unrelated to stress and are not a common reaction to fear. Also, they do not reflect recovery from the initial injury.

4. **b.** Since the patient's LOC is decreasing, you need to maintain an open airway and administer emergency oxygen, if available. You then could cover the patient to prevent chilling if this has not already been done, and keep the patient flat if you are unsure of his injuries. Immobilizing any fractures or dislocations would be appropriate if this has not been done, but immobilizing his body would be inappropriate.

5. **a.** Shock, or hypoperfusion, is a progressive condition in which the circulatory system fails to adequately circulate oxygenated blood to all parts of the body. When vital organs, such as the brain, heart and lungs, do not receive sufficient oxygenated blood, the body begins a series of responses to protect those organs. The amount of blood circulating to the less important tissues of the arms, legs and skin is reduced so that more can go to the vital organs. This reduction in blood circulation to the skin causes a person in shock to appear pale or ashen (grayish) and to feel cool to the touch.

6. **d.** Tissue damage occurs in septic shock. Anaphylactic shock is a whole-body reaction that causes dilation of the blood vessels and constriction (closing) of the airways, which in turn causes blood to pool and results in difficulty breathing. The airways may close completely from inflammation.

7. **a.** Your goal is to control the patient's body temperature. Cover the patient with a blanket to prevent loss of body heat. Be careful that you do not overheat the patient while trying to prevent chilling. Immersing his feet in warm water would

be appropriate if the patient was experiencing frostbite. Applying cool compresses to his neck or groin would be appropriate if the patient was experiencing a heat-related illness.

8. **b.** Vasogenic or neurogenic shock is caused by spinal cord or brain trauma. Septic shock occurs with infection. Cardiogenic shock occurs with disease, trauma or injury to the heart. Obstructive shock occurs with a pulmonary embolism, tension pneumothorax or cardiac tamponade.

9. **c.** Hypovolemic shock is caused by a severe lack of blood and fluid within the body. Hemorrhagic shock is the most common type of hypovolemic shock. It results from blood loss, either through external or internal bleeding, which causes a decrease in total blood volume. Obstructive shock is caused by some type of obstruction to blood flow, usually within the blood vessels, such as a pulmonary embolism, tension pneumothorax or cardiac tamponade. Distributive shock refers to any type of shock caused by inadequate distribution of blood either in the blood vessels or throughout the body, leading to inadequate volumes of blood returning to the heart. Cardiogenic shock is the result of the heart being unable to supply adequate blood circulation to the vital organs, resulting in an inadequate supply of oxygen and nutrients. Disease, trauma or injury to the heart causes this type of shock.

10. **b.** The priority when caring for a patient in shock is to ensure that the patient's airway is open and clear. You then would perform a primary assessment, administer emergency oxygen, if available, and provide appropriate ventilatory support. Next, take steps to control bleeding and prevent further blood loss, if appropriate. If you are unsure of the patient's condition or are concerned about possible internal injuries, keep the patient lying flat If you suspect that any bones are broken or see dislocated or damaged joints, immobilize them to prevent movement. Broken bones or dislocated or damaged joints can cause more bleeding and damage.

11. **a.** Venous blood flows steadily and is darker red than arterial blood. Arterial blood is bright red, spurts from the wound and will not clot or stop easily.

12. **b.** Tourniquets should *only* be used as a last resort in cases of delayed-care or delayed EMS response situations when direct pressure does not stop the bleeding or you are not able to apply direct pressure. Appropriate measures include applying

direct pressure with a gloved hand, elevating the body part above heart level and placing a sterile gauze pressure dressing over the wound.

13. **a.** Signs and symptoms of internal bleeding include bruising on the neck, chest, abdomen or side; nausea, vomiting or coughing up blood; patient guarding the area; rapid pulse or breathing; skin that is cool or moist or looks pale, ashen or bluish; excessive thirst; declining LOC; and a drop in blood pressure.

14. **c.** If you suspect a skull fracture, you should not try to stop the nosebleed because it may increase pressure in the brain. Instead cover the nostrils loosely with sterile gauze. Tilting the head forward slightly and pinching the nostrils firmly together would be appropriate to stop the nosebleed if no fracture was suspected. A patient with a nosebleed should never blow his nose.

15. **c.** A Level III trauma facility is found in smaller communities that do not have access to larger Level I or Level II medical centers. They can provide prompt assessment, resuscitation and emergency operations and arrange for transport to a Level I or II facility as required. A Level IV trauma setting often is a rural clinic in a remote area and generally offers patient care only until arrangement for transportation can be made. A Level I trauma facility must have the capability to deal with all levels and types of patient injury on a 24-hour basis. A Level II trauma facility is expected to be able to provide definitive care to patients, despite the type of patient injury; however, this type of facility sometimes may have to send a patient with more severe injuries to a Level I facility.

16. **c.** Capillary bleeding usually clots spontaneously. Arterial bleeding is bright red, spurts from the wound, will not clot easily and decreases in pressure as the patient's blood pressure drops. Venous blood flows steadily.

17. **d.** An occlusive dressing does not allow air to pass through; it is used for sucking chest wounds and open abdominal wounds. Universal dressings or trauma dressings are used to cover very large wounds and multiple wounds in one body area. A roller bandage generally is wrapped around the body part, over a dressing, using overlapping turns until the dressing is completely covered. Elastic bandages are designed to keep continuous pressure on a body part.

18. **a.** If blood soaks through the bandage, apply additional dressings and another bandage directly on top of the soiled ones and reapply direct pressure. Do not remove the blood-soaked ones.

Elevating the body part would be appropriate if there is bleeding that is uncontrolled by direct pressure alone.

19. **c.** Immobilization restricts movement and subsequently blood flow. Blood clotting is not affected. Applying pressure to a pressure point compresses the artery. A hemostatic agent is a substance that removes moisture from blood and speeds up the process of clot formation.

20. **b.** For serious bleeding, apply strong direct pressure to the wound using fingertip pressure first. If the wound is large and fingertip pressure does not work, use hand pressure with gauze dressings to stop the bleeding. If direct pressure, elevation and immobilization do not control the bleeding, then apply pressure to a pressure point. Using the knuckles or thumb would be inappropriate.

21. **b.** To care for a nosebleed you should ensure that the conscious patient is sitting in an upright position; tilt the patient's head and upper body forward slightly, if possible, to prevent swallowing or choking on the blood; and then pinch the patient's nostrils together firmly for about 5 to 10 minutes to slow down the blood flow.

22. **a.** An amputation involves complete severing of a body part. An avulsion involves a portion of the skin and sometimes other soft tissue being partially or completely torn away. Impalement occurs when an object is embedded in an open wound. A laceration is a cut, usually from a sharp object, resulting in jagged or smooth edges.

23. **d.** The priority is to care for the patient and control the bleeding immediately. You should have your partner retrieve the severed body part and care for it. Direct pressure would be applied first to control the bleeding, followed by other measures, such as immobilizing and elevating the injured body part. Pain control, although important, would be appropriate once measures for controlling the bleeding are instituted.

24. **b.** If the body part is completely severed, once it has been found, you or another responder should wrap it in sterile gauze that has been moistened in sterile saline, if available. You then should place it in a plastic bag and label it with the patient's name and the date and time when it was placed in the bag. It is important to keep the bag cool by placing it in a larger bag or a container of ice and water slurry (but not on ice alone and not on dry ice). The body part should never be placed directly into the water slurry. Transfer the bag to the EMS personnel transporting the patient to the hospital.

25. **d.** In this situation, because the patient is on fire, you need to extinguish the flames first. You then would perform a primary assessment, help to cool the burn and summon more advanced medical personnel.

26. **c.** Cool any burned area immediately with large amounts of cold water until the pain is relieved. You should not use ice or ice water except on small, superficial burn areas because these may result in loss of critical body heat and could make the wound deeper. Applying petroleum jelly or other products is inappropriate because it seals in heat.

27. **c.** Ice is applied to a closed wound for about 20 minutes, after which time you would remove it for 20 minutes before applying the ice again. If 20 minutes cannot be tolerated, apply ice for periods of 10 minutes.

28. **b.** Your first action would be to control any bleeding by applying a sterile dressing over the wound and using direct pressure until the bleeding stops. Next, clean the wound with soap and water and, if possible, irrigate it with clean, warm running water or saline (or any source of clean water if clean running water is not available) for about 5 minutes to remove any dirt and debris. Once the bleeding has stopped, remove the dressing and apply antibiotic ointment.

29. **c.** Superficial burns involve only the top layer of skin and appear red and dry. Partial-thickness burns are red but also have blisters that may open and weep clear fluid. The burned skin may look mottled (blotchy). A full-thickness burn may look brown or black (charred) with the tissues underneath sometimes appearing white.

30. **a.** Evidence of soot or burns around the mouth, nose or the rest of the face may be a sign that air passages or lungs have been burned, leading to possible airway closure. These findings do not necessarily suggest toxic inhalation, but should it occur, it could lead to respiratory arrest. Scarring would not be an immediate concern at this time. Shock may occur, but finding soot around the mouth and nose would not indicate shock.

31. **d.** Patients should be referred to a burn unit if they have the following: partial- or full-thickness burns that cover more than 10 percent of the body surface (patients younger than about 5 years or older than about 60 years); partial- or full-thickness burns that cover more than 2 percent of the body surface among those in other age groups; partial- or full-thickness burns that involve the face, hands, feet, genitalia, perineum or major joints; full-thickness burns that cover more than 5 percent of the body surface in patients of any age; electrical burns, including injury caused by lightning; chemical burns; inhalation injury; and circumferential burns.

32. **b.** If an eye is burned by a chemical, flush the affected eye for at least 20 minutes or until more advanced medical personnel arrive. When flushing, you should flush the affected eye from the nose outward and downward to prevent washing the chemical into the unaffected eye. A brush is not used when flushing the eye but would be used to remove dry or powdered chemicals from the body.

33. **c.** When caring for a patient with electrical burns, scene safety is of utmost importance. First make sure that the electrical current is secured (de-energized) and is no longer passing through the patient. Then perform a primary assessment and care for any immediate life-threatening conditions. During the physical exam, look for two burn sites (entry and exit wounds). Cool any electrical burns with cold tap water, as you would a thermal burn, until pain is relieved; then cover any burn injuries with a dry, sterile dressing and provide care to minimize shock.

34. **d.** Although rib fracture, pneumothorax and flail chest are possible due to the MOI, the sound noted with each breath strongly indicates a sucking chest wound, which allows air to enter the chest through the wound.

35. **c.** When an object is embedded or impaled in a body part, do not move or remove it unless it interferes with chest compressions; otherwise, you risk causing further damage. Rather, stabilize the object to prevent further damage by using bulky dressings or gauze around the object. Any clothing around the wound should be removed to allow the wound to be exposed.

36. **c.** The abdomen contains certain organs that are easily injured or tend to bleed profusely when injured. These include the liver, spleen and stomach. The kidneys are located more toward the back of the abdomen, so they would be less likely to sustain injury in this instance.

37. **b.** When palpating the patient's abdomen, palpate it at the furthest point from the patient's pain. Palpating directly over the impact area or near or around the lower ribs could lead to increased pain and possible further injury to the underlying organs. The right lower ribs provide some protection to the liver; however, the liver is extremely delicate and can be injured easily. The left lower ribs provide some protection to the spleen. Like the liver, this organ can be easily injured. Palpating around the area of the navel would be inappropriate.

38. **d.** Assessing and treating a patient with a genital injury requires a calm and professional approach since it can be embarrassing not only for the patient, but also for you. Using a sensitive approach to the patient's situation, such as clearing onlookers from the scene, supplying a drape for privacy, removing only the clothing necessary to assess the injury and reassuring the patient, will help the process be less embarrassing. If possible, the patient should be treated by someone of the same gender.

39. **d.** Closed chest wounds generally are caused by blunt trauma. A fractured rib breaking through the skin, a knife wound or gunshot would result in an open chest wound.

40. **a.** Signs and symptoms of traumatic asphyxia include distended neck veins; subconjunctival hemorrhage; bluish discoloration of the head, tongue, lips, neck and shoulders; black eyes; and a rounded, moon-like facial appearance.

41. **b.** Patients with tension pneumothorax typically are in respiratory distress with reduced breath sounds or a complete absence of breath sounds. The injured side of the chest (in this case, the right side) produces abnormal breath sounds during percussion. Because the trachea is shifted away from the side of the injury and the space between the lungs, contents are shifted away from the affected side, resulting in a decreased return of blood to the heart. The patient will show signs of unstable blood pressure, such as abnormally low blood pressure (hypotension), which can quickly develop into complete cardiovascular collapse.

42. **c.** When applying an occlusive dressing, use a dressing that does not allow air to pass through. Secure it in place on all sides except for one, which should remain loose, preventing air from entering the wound during inhalation but allowing air to exit during exhalation. Sterile gauze would allow air to enter the wound and should not be used. If appropriate material is not available, you could use a folded cloth or, as a last resort, your gloved hand to seal the wound.

43. **c.** Protrusion of an abdominal organ through a wound is called evisceration. Flail chest is a serious chest injury in which multiple rib fractures result in a loose section of the ribs that does not move normally with the rest of the chest during breathing. Subcutaneous emphysema is the collection of air under the skin that has a crackling sound. An avulsion is an injury in which a portion of the skin and sometimes other soft tissue is partially or completely torn away.

44. **a.** Before applying a splint, you need to clean and bandage the laceration. Avoid any movement to the arm, including checking for range of motion or straightening the arm. Ice would be applied for swelling but only after cleaning and bandaging the laceration. Since there is a laceration that could indicate an open fracture, ice would be applied around the site.

45. **a.** A rigid splint extending from the elbow to the fingertips should be applied first. A sling and binder then can be applied to support the arm against the chest. Since there is an open wound, it would be inappropriate to use a circumferential air splint, extending from the elbow past the fingertips. A traction splint would be used for a fractured femur.

46. **c.** Injuries to the femur can be serious because of the risk of bleeding, which may be internal and go unnoticed. A broken femur causes significant pain and swelling. The deformity of the thigh usually is noticeable, and the muscle often contracts (shortens) with this type of break. The leg also may be turned inward or outward.

47. **b.** Although most isolated fractures are not considered critical or life threatening, if the femur or pelvis is fractured, the patient is at serious risk of excessive blood loss, shock and death. These two bones contain many blood vessels, and injury to either bone tends to cause heavy bleeding.

48. **a.** Some joints, such as the shoulder and fingers, are more prone to dislocation because they are relatively exposed and not as well protected by ligaments. Other joints, such as the elbow, knee and ankle, are less likely to become dislocated.

49. **b.** Soft splints can be created from folded blankets, towels and pillows. Rigid splints can be created from cardboard boxes, rolled-up magazines, an athlete's shin guards or other items available at the scene.

50. **d.** The patient's statement about having no feeling in the hand suggests that circulation to that area is compromised, requiring immediate action. Some pain is expected, but if the patient is complaining of severe pain or pain out of proportion to the visible injury, there is cause for concern. The ability to move the body part, such as the hand and fingers, indicates normal function. A feeling of warmth indicates adequate circulation. If the patient stated that his wrist felt cold, there would be cause for concern.

51. **a.** You would summon more advanced medical personnel if you suspect a fracture to an area other than a digit; if the injury involves severe

bleeding or impairs walking or breathing or involves the head, neck or spine; or if you see or suspect multiple injuries. A suspected toe fracture would not require summoning more advanced medical personnel.

52. **b.** Elevating the injured part slows the flow of blood, helping to reduce swelling. It has no effect on bone alignment or healing. Pain may be reduced as swelling is controlled, but this is not the primary purpose for elevating the arm.

53. **c.** Before applying any splint, obtain consent to treat the patient. Next, support the injured body part above and below the site of the injury, check for circulation and sensation beyond the injured area and then apply the splint. Immobilize the wrist and elbow when applying a rigid splint.

54. **d.** The final step when applying a sling and binder is to recheck for circulation and sensation. Before this step, you would place the triangular bandage under the injured arm and over the uninjured shoulder to form the sling, tie the ends of the sling at the side of the neck and then bind the injured body part to the chest with a folded triangular bandage.

55. **c.** When applying a splint, remove any clothing around the injured site; apply sterile dressings to open wounds, bandaging with minimal pressure; and pad the splints for comfort and to allow the splint to conform to the shape of the injured body part. Make sure that you never push protruding bones below the skin.

56. **c.** Bleeding from the mouth is a highly specific sign and suggests a possible skull fracture. The abrasion on his forehead indicates an injury to the patient's face. The patient's lack of responsiveness is a general finding that could indicate any number of problems. The bystander's statement that the patient hit his head would support your suspicion, but hitting one's head is not the most likely indicator.

57. **a.** Signs and symptoms of a brain injury include high blood pressure and slowed pulse; clear fluid draining from the ears, mouth or nose; bruising behind the ears (Battle's sign); and paralysis or droopiness (often on one side of the body) or rigidity of the limbs.

58. **a.** Asymmetrical facial movements would reflect a head and brain injury. Signs and symptoms of a concussion include short-term confusion, headache, repeated questioning about what happened, temporary memory loss (especially for periods immediately before and after the injury), brief loss of consciousness, nausea and vomiting, speech problems and blurred vision or light sensitivity.

59. **b.** Because the patient has sustained a head injury and is lethargic, you need to stabilize his head and neck with the helmet in place. Remove the helmet only if you cannot access the patient's airway and breathing, the airway is impeded and cannot be opened with the helmet on, the patient is in cardiac arrest or you cannot immobilize the spine. Elevating the patient's legs about 12 inches would not be appropriate. You would lay the patient flat if the patient was exhibiting signs and symptoms of shock.

60. **a.** Patients who fall from a height greater than standing height are at risk for head, neck or spinal injuries; however, a fall from 2 feet would be considered low risk for such injuries. Diving into shallow water, impacting the dashboard in a motor-vehicle collision or slipping off a two-story platform are situations that would increase a patient's risk for head, neck or spinal injuries.

61. **c.** When providing care to a patient with a foreign object in the eye, tell the patient not to rub the eye but rather to blink several times. If the object then becomes visible on the lower eyelid, try to remove it using the corner of a sterile gauze pad, being careful never to touch the eyeball or put pressure on the eyeball. Next, gently flush the eye with sterile saline or water. If the object becomes visible on the upper eyelid, gently roll the upper eyelid back over a cotton swab and attempt to remove it with the corner of a sterile gauze pad, again being careful not to touch the eyeball.

62. **d.** If you feel any resistance when attempting to align the head and neck with the spine, stop the movement and gently maintain stabilization of the head and neck in the position in which you found them. Further movement would increase the risk of further injury. A *cervical collar* (C-collar) typically is applied by more advanced medical personnel. Stabilization is necessary, even with resistance.

63. **a.** When providing care to a patient with an object embedded in the eye, do not attempt to remove the object but rather stabilize it by encircling the eye with gauze or a soft sterile cloth, being sure to avoid applying any pressure on top of the area. Styrofoam® materials are not used to shield the area because small particles can break off and get into the eye.

64. **b.** Evidence of fluid draining from the ear suggests cerebrospinal fluid leakage, indicating a skull fracture. Although a skull fracture may be associated with a scalp injury, typically you will see bleeding from the scalp ranging from minor to severe. A concussion is indicated by a temporary loss of consciousness along with confusion,

headache, temporary memory loss, nausea and vomiting, speech problems and blurred vision or light sensitivity. A penetrating skull injury would result in a visible wound.

65. **c.** Bruising behind the ears is referred to as Battle's sign. Raccoon eyes refers to visible bruising around the eyes. A concussion is a temporary loss of brain function due to a blow to the head. A nosebleed is bleeding from the nose, usually from a blow from a blunt object.

66. **b.** Injuries to the neck or spine can damage both bone and soft tissue, including the spinal cord. It is difficult to determine the extent of damage in neck or spinal injuries, so you must always care for these types of injuries as if they are serious. The patient's ability to walk does not necessarily rule out the possibility of an injury to the bone, spine or spinal cord.

67. **b.** The priority when providing care to a patient with a suspected head injury is to establish manual stabilization to prevent further injury before doing anything else. Once this is accomplished, you then would perform a primary assessment while maintaining stabilization, maintain an open airway and control any bleeding. You also should try to engage the patient in conversation to calm the patient and prevent loss of consciousness.

1. **c.** As time goes on, true labor contractions occur closer together, increase in duration, feel stronger and occur at regular intervals.

2. **a.** The woman is experiencing contractions that are 5 minutes apart and lasting about 30 seconds and her water has broken. There is no evidence of crowning. Therefore, the woman is most likely in the first stage of labor, which begins with the first contraction and ends with the cervix being fully dilated. The second stage of labor begins when the cervix is completely dilated as the baby moves through the birth canal. During this stage, the mother will report feelings of enormous pressure and contractions that are more frequent and may last between 45 to 90 seconds. The third stage of labor begins with emergence of the baby's body and includes separation and delivery of the placenta. The fourth stage of labor involves the initial recovery and stabilization of the mother after childbirth.

3. **c.** A prolapsed umbilical cord occurs when a loop of the umbilical cord protrudes from the vaginal opening while the baby still is in the birth canal. A breech birth is one in which the baby is delivered feet- or buttocks-first. A premature birth is one in which a baby is born before the end of 37 weeks of pregnancy. Meconium aspiration involves the baby's inhalation of meconium-stained amniotic fluid (an indication that the baby experienced a period of oxygen deprivation), which can result in complications such as a blocked airway or respiratory distress, pneumonia and infection.

4. **a.** A breech birth is one in which the baby is delivered feet or buttocks first. It also may be an incomplete breech when the baby's foot or feet, arm or shoulder appear first. The head typically is the part of the baby delivered first with a normal delivery.

5. **b.** During the third trimester, the mother gains the most weight because the fetus grows the most rapidly. Morning sickness and placental development occur during the first trimester. Fetal movement typically is felt during the second trimester.

6. **d.** You can help the expectant mother cope with the discomfort and pain of labor by staying calm, firm and confident and by offering encouragement. Doing so can help reduce her fear and apprehension which, in turn, will aid in reducing her pain and discomfort. Telling the woman that she has to learn to endure the discomfort is not supportive and will only add to her fear and apprehension. You should begin by reassuring her that you are there to help. Explain what to expect as labor progresses. Suggest specific physical activities that she can do to relax, such as regulating her breathing. Ask her to breathe slowly and deeply in through the nose and out through the mouth. Ask her to focus on one object in the room while regulating her breathing.

7. **a.** Once crowning takes place, you should place a hand on the top of the baby's head and apply light pressure to allow the head to emerge slowly, not forcefully. At this point, you should tell the expectant mother to stop pushing and to concentrate on her breathing techniques. Next, check to see if the umbilical cord is looped around the baby's neck. If it is, gently slip it over the baby's head. If you cannot slip it over the head, slip it over the baby's shoulders as they emerge. The baby can slide through the loop. You then guide one shoulder out at a time without pulling on the baby.

8. **d.** If a newborn has not made any sounds, you would stimulate a cry reflex by flicking your fingers on the soles of the feet or gently rubbing the newborn's back. Bending the newborn's feet firmly backward and placing the newborn in a head-down position would not be effective in stimulating the newborn. Suctioning the mouth and nose would help to remove secretions but would not necessarily stimulate the newborn.

9. **a.** Resuscitation of a newborn begins immediately if respirations fall to less than 30 respirations per minute or the newborn is gasping or not breathing, if the pulse is less than 100 *beats per minute* (bpm) or if cyanosis (bluish skin) around the chest and abdomen persists after administering emergency oxygen.

10. **c.** Delivery is considered imminent when the mother reports a strong urge to push; contractions are intense, occurring every 2 minutes or less and lasting 60 to 90 seconds; the woman's abdomen is very tight and hard; the mother reports a feeling of the infant's head moving down the birth canal or has a sensation like an urge to defecate; and crowning occurs. A sudden gush of fluid from the vagina, indicating that the amniotic sac has ruptured, often signals the onset of labor.

11. **d.** A score between 1 and 3 points indicates a severely depressed newborn who requires emergency oxygen with BVM ventilations and CPR. A newborn with an APGAR score of 4 to 6

indicates a moderately depressed newborn that requires stimulation and emergency oxygen. A score of 7 to 10 indicates an active, vigorous newborn that is ready to receive routine care.

12. **b.** A 15-month-old child is considered a toddler. An infant is a child up to 1 year of age. A toddler is between the ages of 1 and 3 years and a preschooler is a child between the ages of 3 and 5 years. A school-aged child is between 6 and 12 years of age.

13. **c.** When performing a primary assessment of the child, you would use the Pediatric Assessment Triangle and evaluate the child's appearance, breathing and skin. Vital signs would be done later.

14. **d.** The area of greatest concern is the child's skin (circulation) because a piece of the fence has cut through the child's upper pant leg, also possibly cutting the child's skin and increasing his risk for bleeding. The child is crying and talking to his parents, indicating that he is alert, has an open airway and is breathing.

15. **a.** A strong, palpable pulse would be a normal finding. Signs and symptoms suggesting a problem requiring immediate intervention include increasing lethargy; cool, clammy skin; and rapid breathing. All of these would suggest that shock is developing.

16. **b.** Preschoolers often feel that bad things are caused by their thoughts and behaviors. They have difficulty understanding complex sentences that contain more than one idea, and their fears may seem out of proportion to the events. School-aged children are more likely to cooperate with strangers.

17. **c.** The Pediatric Assessment Triangle is a primary assessment of a child that takes between 15 and 30 seconds and provides a picture of the severity of the child's or infant's injury or illness. This is done during the scene size-up and before assessing the breathing and pulse. It is the primary assessment that is completed before any other assessment, including the SAMPLE history and physical exam.

18. **a.** For AED use, a patient who is between the ages of 1 and 8 or who weighs less than 55 pounds is considered a child.

19. **d.** Loss of consciousness and cyanosis suggest a complete airway obstruction. Alertness, drooling, frequent coughing, retractions and abnormal, high-pitched musical sounds are indicators of a partial airway obstruction.

20. **a.** For the child in shock, position the child flat on the back unless there is a risk of choking, in which case you would place the patient in a recovery position. In addition, cover him or her with a light blanket to help maintain body temperature. You also need to monitor the child closely for any changes in status. Ventilations are appropriate if the child is not breathing adequately or stops breathing. Back blows and abdominal thrusts are appropriate if the child has a foreign body obstructing the airway.

21. **b.** The child's trachea is not as long as an adult's, so any attempt to open the airway by tilting the child's head too far back will result in blocking the airway. The tongue in children is larger in relation to the space in the mouth than it is in adults, increasing the risk of the tongue blocking the trachea. Children's airways are smaller, resulting in more objects posing a choking hazard; however, this would have no effect on how far back to tilt a child's head to open the airway. Young children and infants breathe through their nose, but this would not affect maneuvers to open the airway.

22. **d.** Although fever is the most common cause of seizures in children, other causes include head trauma, epilepsy or other seizure disorders, low blood glucose, poisoning, hypoxia and serious infections, such as meningitis or encephalitis. The common cold and respiratory distress are not associated with the development of seizures.

23. **c.** When caring for a child who may have been abused, your first priority is to care for the child's injuries or illness. You should not confront the parents or caregivers because this could put you and the child at risk. An abused child may be frightened, hysterical or withdrawn, often unwilling to talk about the incident in an attempt to protect the abuser or for self-protection. You should explain your concerns to the responding police officers and report your suspicions to a community or state agency. It is not your responsibility to remove the child from the abusive situation.

24. **d.** The patient is most likely exhibiting a catastrophic reaction as evidenced by her screaming, shouting and throwing things. Her behavior does not indicate hallucinations or the belief that things are not true, nor is she demonstrating depression (sadness or lack of desire or interest). Sundowning typically involves restlessness, crying, pushing others away, gritting the teeth or being reluctant to enter a room or a brightly lit area.

25. **c.** Intellectual impairment is not typically associated with Alzheimer's disease. Patients with Alzheimer's disease may demonstrate some

common patterns, such as pacing and wandering, rummaging and hoarding, speaking nonsense and sundowning.

26. **d.** When a person is hard of hearing, you should identify yourself and speak slowly and clearly but not shout. You should position yourself so that the patient can hear you better by facing him or her. You also can try speaking directly into the patient's ear. Although you may need to repeat questions, repeating the same question several times may lead to frustration on everyone's part.

27. **b.** Normal age-related changes include a thickening of the heart muscle, decreased lung elasticity and slowed movement through the digestive system. Most middle-aged and older adults retain their abilities to learn, remember and solve problems.

28. **a.** You need to reassure the patient that you are not going to cause him or her any harm and that you will not allow him or her to hurt anyone. Telling the patient to stop screaming or threatening to call the police is not reassuring; in fact, doing so is threatening and may agitate the patient further. Asking the patient "why" is inappropriate because the patient does not understand why due to cognitive impairment.

29. **c.** In the elderly, bones become less dense over time. This is especially true in women, and subsequently, this loss of bone density increases their risk for fractures. A diminished pain sensation could lead to a decreased awareness of an injury but not the risk for injury, such as a fracture. A decreased tolerance to glare could lead to an increased risk for accidents. Changes in the musculoskeletal system can lead to a more sedentary lifestyle and inactivity, leading to a decline in function. But this decline in function would not be directly related to the increased risk for fractures.

30. **c.** Memory loss reflects cognitive impairment and is not considered a normal part of aging. Older adults may downplay their symptoms due to fear of institutionalization or losing their independence. Lungs become stiffer and less elastic. This causes the airways to shrink and the chest muscles to weaken, thus decreasing the air flow into and out of the lungs and increasing their risk for breathing problems. Aging patients often have decreased sharpness of the senses, and this loss of sensory awareness brings possible risks that are unique to this age group.

31. **a.** Three visits to an emergency room over a 2-week period is suspicious and would be a clue to possible elder abuse. Other clues include a patient who is frequently left alone, has had repeated falls and is malnourished. Having a person present and providing care in the home 24 hours each day is not being left alone frequently. Weight loss due to an underlying medical condition would not suggest possible abuse. One fall in a year would not be considered repeated falling.

32. **b.** A patient who is experiencing a loss of visual field cannot see as wide an area as normal unless he or she moves the eyes or turns the head. Glasses are used to adapt to a loss of visual acuity. A white cane typically is used for a patient who cannot see or has significantly reduced vision. Patients who are blind typically use other senses to compensate for their lack of sight.

33. **a.** The most common signs and symptoms of cystic fibrosis include frequent coughing with thick sputum, salty-tasting skin, dehydration, ongoing diarrhea and increased appetite with poor weight gain and growth.

34. **c.** Hospice care is the care provided to a terminally ill patient in the final 6 months of life. The focus of hospice care is keeping the patient as comfortable and as pain free as possible. The emphasis is not on curing the illness but rather on providing physical, emotional, social and spiritual comfort to the dying patient. Central to the hospice way of thinking is that dying is a normal and expected part of the life cycle. Pain relief is administered without the use of needles, using oral medications, pain relieving patches and pills that can be given between the cheek and gum.

35. **d.** When caring for an elderly patient, handle the skin gently because it can tear easily. You should explain everything you are doing in a calm and slow manner. When giving ventilations, do not apply too much pressure because this could result in chest injury. You should use an oropharyngeal airway only if the patient is unconscious and unresponsive and does not have a gag reflex.

36. **c.** The evidence of old and new bruises on the patient suggests physical abuse. Financial exploitation, for example, using the patient's money for things other than what the patient needs, would be an example of abuse. Isolating the patient would be an example of abuse. Taking the patient to a senior center daily would allow the patient to engage in social interaction, thereby decreasing the patient's isolation. Inappropriate dress or poor hygiene would suggest abuse.

| UNIT 8 EMS OPERATIONS |

1. **d.** The EMS response phase of dispatch occurs when the caller reports the accident to the communications center. Preparation for the call occurs before notifying the EMRs. The en-route to the scene phase involves the emergency response to the scene, including reaching the scene safely. Patient contact occurs when you arrive on the scene and size-up the scene and the situation.

2. **a.** When travelling to an emergency scene, it is extremely important to arrive there safely. Wear a safety belt and drive according to the weather conditions. Getting as much information as possible would occur when receiving the call from dispatch. Ensuring that you have the appropriate equipment available would be done as preparation before receiving any emergency call. Notifying dispatch about the need for additional emergency services would occur when you arrive on the scene and size it up.

3. **d.** Although having the patient ready for transport is important in an emergency situation, choosing a safe landing zone for a helicopter is paramount. The coordinator who will be assisting with the helicopter landing should be protected with a fastened helmet, hearing and eye protection, long sleeves and pants. Bystanders should be moved back to a minimum of 200 feet away from the site.

4. **b.** During phase 6, en-route to the receiving facility, the patient and transport crew notify the receiving facility about the patient and their *estimated time of arrival* (ETA). During phase 5, the patient is transferred to the ambulance. During phase 7, arrival at the receiving facility, the crew members give information about the scene and the patient, transferring the care of the patient to the nurses and doctors. During phase 8, the EMRs return to the station and notify the communications center of their return.

5. **a.** Generally, air medical transport may be required for emergency calls that include a pedestrian struck at greater than 10 mph (or greater than 5 mph based on a patient's age or physical condition), a vehicle rollover with an unrestrained passenger(s), a motorcycle driver thrown at a speed greater than 20 mph, multiple injured or ill persons, a fall from a height greater than about 15 feet, critical stroke or cardiac patients, and critical trauma patients (if ambulance transport would exceed 30 minutes).

6. **c.** A safe landing zone needs to be on flat land that is firm and clear of any obstacles, such as trees or utility poles, vehicles or pedestrians. An open soccer field would be most appropriate. There is no guarantee that ice on a body of water would ever be strong enough for a helicopter landing. A dry barren pasture would most likely be firm but dusty and possibly contain loose debris, such as rocks, that could be projectiles when the helicopter takes off or lands. Powdery snow would not provide a firm surface for landing.

7. **d.** When approaching a helicopter, you should adopt a somewhat crouched over position and if there is an incline of any sort, you must approach from the lowest point and always from the side or front, never from the rear. Approaching from the side or front allows the pilot to see you and any other responders. You should not be wearing a hat of any type. Only a fastened helmet is permitted. When carrying equipment, such as an *intravenous* (IV) pole, keep it low and parallel to the ground.

8. **c.** A jump kit, at the minimum, must contain basic wound supplies, such as dressings, as well as airways (oral), suction equipment and artificial ventilation supplies. PPE, such as gloves and protective eyewear, as well as maps and a stethoscope, among other supplies, also are recommended.

9. **b.** Situations that can impact your safety include going through intersections, entering—not exiting—a highway, driving in inclement weather, listening to a vehicle's stereo or other distraction in the vehicle and responding alone.

10. **c.** When a vehicle is in contact with an electrical wire, you must consider the wire energized (live) until you know otherwise. When you arrive at the scene, you should notify the power company and establish a safety area at a point twice the length of the span of the wire. Attempt to reach and move patients only after the power company has been notified and secured any electrical current from reaching downed wires or cables. You also need to tell occupants inside the involved vehicle to remain in the vehicle.

11. **c.** When dealing with a patient who is trapped, your role is to administer the necessary care before extrication and to ensure that the patient is removed in a way that minimizes further injury. In many cases, patient care will occur simultaneously with the extrication process. As an EMR, you would not actually perform the extrication but would work closely with other rescuers to protect the patient. Specially trained extrication personnel would establish the chain of

command. Law enforcement would play a major role in helping to secure the scene and control the crowd during extrication.

12. **d.** For a patient who is trapped under plywood and a scaffold, a pneumatic tool would most likely be used to lift the plywood and scaffold off of the patient. Ropes may be helpful in pulling the material off of the patient, but this pulling action could lead to further injury. Pliers or a shovel would not be helpful in this situation.

13. **c.** You can assume a vehicle is unstable if it is positioned on a tilted surface; stacked on top of another vehicle, even partly; on a slippery surface; or overturned or on its side. A vehicle that is positioned on a flat or dry surface or side by side (next to) another vehicle would be considered stable.

14. **a.** Simple access methods include trying to open each door or the windows or having the patient unlock the doors or roll down the windows. A ratcheting cable and tool cutter would be used with complex access. Breaking the window glass would be inappropriate because it could cause injury to yourself and the patient.

15. **c.** Emergency vehicles should be placed in optimal positions for safety and for easy patient loading. Blocking is a technique of positioning fire apparatus, such as large engines, at an angle to traffic lanes. This creates a physical barrier between the work area and traffic flowing toward the emergency scene. The scene should be protected with the first-arriving apparatus and with at least one additional lane blocked off. Ambulances should park within the "shadow" created by the larger apparatus. The apparatus also should "block to the right" or "block to the left" so as not to obstruct the loading doors of ambulances. To create a safe zone, traffic cones or flares should be placed at 10- to 15-foot intervals in a radius of at least 50 feet around the scene.

16. **d.** Cribbing is a system that creates a stable environment for the vehicle. It uses wood or supports, arranged diagonally to a vehicle's frame, to safely prop it up, creating a stable environment. Cribbing should not be used under tires because it tends to cause rolling. There should never be more than 1 or 2 inches between the cribbing and vehicle.

17. **a.** When approaching any scene, whether a motor-vehicle collision or an industrial emergency, you should be able to recognize clues that indicate the presence of *hazardous materials* (HAZMATs). These include signs (placards) on vehicles or storage facilities identifying the presence of these materials, evidence of spilled liquids or solids, unusual odors, clouds of vapor and leaking containers. Fire would not necessarily suggest a HAZMAT.

18. **c.** During extrication, it is crucial to maintain cervical spinal stabilization to minimize the risk for additional patient injury. In addition, a sufficient number of personnel are needed during extrication. Often, these individuals try to move the device not the patient, using the path of least resistance when making decisions about equipment and patient movement.

19. **c.** Methods to prevent an upright vehicle from rolling include cutting the tire valves so that the car rests safely on its rims, turning the wheels toward the curb and tying the car frame to a strong anchor point, such as a guardrail, large tree or another vehicle. Letting the air out of the tires also reduces the possibility of movement.

20. **b.** The first priority for a patient who is to be extricated is to ensure that the cervical spine is stabilized. Then perform the primary assessment and evaluate the patient's breathing and pulse. Based on your assessment, administer emergency oxygen, if necessary, and/or obtain a SAMPLE history while you continuously monitor and care for the patient.

21. **a.** As the first person to arrive on the scene of a potential HAZMAT incident, it is your responsibility to help lay the groundwork for the rescue scene. The first step is to recognize the presence of a HAZMAT and then to contact dispatch and report specific details of the scene, including information about placard colors and numbers and any label information. Once this information is relayed, you would position yourself at a safe distance and establish a clear chain of command, including establishing safety zones. It would be inappropriate to access the patient before the scene is safe.

22. **d.** When on the scene of a HAZMAT incident, position yourself uphill and upwind of the scene and stay out of low lying areas where vapors and liquids collect. In addition, remain at a safe distance from the scene throughout the incident.

23. **c.** The warm and hot zones can be entered only by those who have received *Occupational Safety and Health Administration* (OSHA) *Hazardous Waste Operations and Emergency Response* (HAZWOPER) training at the first responder awareness level and who are wearing appropriate PPE and a *self-contained breathing apparatus* (SCBA).

24. **a.** The *Material Safety Data Sheets* (MSDS) are provided by the manufacturer and identify the

substance, physical properties and any associated hazards for a given material, such as fire, explosion and health hazards. The shipping papers list the names, associated dangers and four-digit identification numbers of the substances.

25. **b.** With a HAZMAT incident, a clear chain of command is established with one command officer being assigned to maintain control of the situation and make decisions at every stage of the rescue. The rescue team must be aware of who is in command, as well as if and when decision-making powers are transferred to another officer. The system of communication is one that is accessible and familiar to all rescuers.

26. **d.** In the hot zone, rescue, treatment for any conditions that are life-threatening and initial decontamination occur. In the warm zone, complete decontamination takes place and life-saving emergency care, such as airway management and immobilization, occurs.

27. **c.** When radiation is suspected, you should immediately don a SCBA and protective clothing and seal off all openings with duct tape. Double gloves and two pairs of paper shoe covers under heavy rubber boots should be worn.

28. **a.** In your role as an EMR who is the first on the scene of a possible HAZMAT incident, you would follow three steps: recognition, identification and determination. As the last step, you would determine if the material is responsible for the injuries or the damage at the scene. During recognition, you would acknowledge the presence of a HAZMAT and demonstrate awareness that the material could be harmful to the health of others. During identification, you would establish the material's specific identity and characteristics.

29. **d.** A patient does not experience contamination by the neurologic route. Rather, he or she may have been contaminated via several possible routes, including topical (through the skin), respiratory (inhaled), gastrointestinal (ingested) or parenteral (*intramuscular* [IM], *intravenous* [IV] or *subcutaneous* [sub-Q]).

30. **c.** Initial, or "gross" decontamination, is performed as the person enters the warm zone. Any immediate life-threatening conditions are addressed during this stage. Soap and copious amounts of water are used, and any clothing, equipment and tools must be left in the hot zone. Dilution refers to the method of reducing the concentration of a contaminant to a safe level. Absorption is the process of using material that will absorb and hold contaminants, such as corrosive and liquid chemicals. Neutralization involves chemically altering a substance to render it harmless or make it less harmful.

31. **c.** Since fire personnel have arrived first, one of these individuals would assume the role of the *incident commander* (IC). Upon your arrival, you would identify yourself to the IC and report to the staging officer. The staging officer would then tell you where you are most needed. The IC would be responsible for determining the number of ambulances needed.

32. **b.** Patients who are ambulatory are tagged as green. Patients requiring immediate care are tagged red. Those who may be severely injured but a delay in their treatment will not decrease their chance of survival are tagged yellow. Patients who are obviously dead or have have mortal wounds are tagged black.

33. **b.** An emergency that involves children must be handled differently from the way you would an emergency with adults. The JumpSTART triage method should be used on anyone who appears to be a child, regardless of actual chronological age, but is not performed on infants younger than 12 months. The Smart Tag™, METTAG™ and START systems are used with adults.

34. **d.** The safety officer maintains scene safety by identifying potential dangers and taking action to prevent them from causing injury to all involved. The treatment officer sets up a treatment area and supervises medical care, ensuring triage order is maintained and changing the order if patients deteriorate and become eligible for a higher triage category. The triage officer supervises the initial triage, tagging and moving of patients to designated treatment areas. The staging officer releases and distributes resources as needed to the incident and works to avoid transportation gridlock.

35. **c.** Patients with burns involving flame; burns occurring in a confined space; burns covering more than one body part; burns to the head, neck, feet or genitals; partial-thickness or full-thickness burns in a child or an older adult; or burns resulting from chemicals, explosions or electricity are classified as needing immediate care. The category of minor or walking wounded would apply to ambulatory patients. The category of delayed would be used for patients with severe injuries for whom a delay in treatment would not reduce their chance of survival. The category of deceased/non-salvageable is used for patients who are obviously dead or who have mortal injuries.

36. **a.** The METTAG™ system uses symbols rather than words to identify patients. The START, Smart Tag™ and JumpSTART systems use words and colors to identify patient levels.

37. **c.** Although it is highly individualized, in general, a 50-year-old man involved in a factory explosion would have the least risk for a severe stress reaction. Those that have a greater risk for severe stress reactions include children who may react strongly and experience extreme fears of further harm, elderly patients and those who already have health problems.

38. **d.** After a *multiple casualty incident* (MCI), debriefing is a vital part of the process. It allows rescuers to go over their role in the MCI and the outcome allows for release of stress and learning opportunities for future events. Scheduling down time, having responders talk amongst themselves and setting clear expectations are appropriate measures to help reduce stress during the MCI.

39. **b.** To effectively manage an emergency situation involving an MCI and provide care, an *incident command system* (ICS) must be established. The ICS organizes who is responsible for overall direction, the roles of other participants and the resources required. Triage is one aspect involved in the ICS. The *National Response Framework* (NRF) is a guide to how the nation conducts an all-hazards response. The START system is a triage system.

40. **b.** The transportation officer is responsible for communicating with receiving hospitals and for assigning patients to ambulances, helicopters and buses for transport. The staging officer is responsible for establishing an area suitable to park multiple units in an organized fashion. The treatment officer is responsible for identifying a treatment area of sufficient space with adequate ingress and egress for ambulances.

41. **d.** When using the JumpSTART triage system, you would first assess the ambulatory status (the ability to get up and walk). With JumpSTART, the acronym ARPM is used to order the systems that need to be assessed: ambulatory status, respiratory status, perfusion status and mental status.

42. **a.** The report of an odor resembling "garlic, onions, or horseradish" suggests the presence of sulfur mustard. The odor of freshly cut hay suggests the presence of phosgene. Cyanide has an odor of bitter almonds. Tabun is odorless.

43. **c.** In a situation in which phosgene may be present, it is essential that you protect yourself by using a chemical protective mask with a charcoal canister. A HAZMAT suit or gown may or may not be necessary. Gloves would most likely be needed. A *high-efficiency particulate air* (HEPA) filter mask would be more appropriate for an emergency involving biological agents.

44. **c.** The site of a bomb blast is a crime scene and as an EMR, you must preserve evidence and avoid disturbing areas not directly involved in rescue activities, although your primary responsibility is to rescue living people and provide care for life-threatening injuries. Any fatalities should be left at the area where they are found with the surroundings undisturbed.

45. **d.** Biological disasters include epidemics, pandemics and outbreaks of communicable diseases; contamination of food or water supplies by pathogens such as E.coli; and the use of viruses, bacteria and other pathogens for bioterrorism. A nuclear explosion or chemical exposure would be a human-caused disaster. A tornado is a natural disaster.

46. **b.** The *Federal Emergency Management Agency* (FEMA) is ultimately responsible for coordinating the response to and recovery from disasters in the United States when the disaster is large enough to overwhelm the local and state resources. The NRF was developed and introduced by FEMA as a guide for all organizations involved in disaster management as to how to respond to disasters and emergencies. The *National Incident Management System* (NIMS) is a comprehensive national framework for managing incidents; it outlines the structures for response activities for command and management and provides a consistent, nationwide response at all levels. The ICS is a management system that allows effective incident management by bringing together facilities, equipment, personnel, procedures and communications within a single organizational structure so that everyone has an understanding of their roles and can respond effectively and efficiently.

47. **a.** *Emergency support function* (ESF) #1, transportation, is involved in damage and impact assessment, movement restrictions, transportation safety, restoration/recovery of transportation infrastructure, and aviation/airspace management and control. ESF #2, communications, is involved in coordination with telecommunications and information technology industries; restoration and repair of telecommunications infrastructure; protection, restoration and sustainment of cyber and information technology resources; and oversight of communications within the federal incident management and response structures. ESF #5,

emergency management, is involved in the coordination of incident management and response efforts, issuance of mission assignments, resource and human capital, incident action planning and financial management. ESF #8, public health and medical services, is involved in public health, medical and mental health services and mass fatality management.

48. **c.** Atropine is an antidote for nerve agent toxicity. Hydroxocobalamin, sodium nitrite and sodium thiosulfate are antidotes for cyanide poisoning.

49. **b.** Although most biological agents are not highly contagious, a few are, so it is essential to isolate the patient, protect yourself with the proper PPE and use standard infection control procedures including a HEPA filter mask and gloves. Antibiotics may be used to treat bacterial illnesses but not to treat illness caused by a virus. Antidotes are not used with biological agents. Decontamination is used for radiological/nuclear exposure.

50. **c.** Acute radiation syndrome follows a predictable pattern that unfolds over several days or weeks after substantial exposure or a catastrophic event. Specific symptoms of concern, especially following a 2- to 3-week period with nausea and vomiting, are thermal burn-like skin lesions without documented heat exposure, a tendency to bleed (nosebleed, gingival [gum] bleeding, bruising) and hair loss. Symptom clusters, as delayed effects after radiation exposure, include headache, fatigue, weakness, partial and full thickness skin damage, hair loss, ulceration, anorexia, nausea, vomiting, diarrhea, reduced levels of white blood cells, bruising and infections.

51. **a.** The auto-injector is administered into the mid-outer thigh. It is not given in the upper arm, buttocks or abdomen.

52. **d.** A distressed swimmer may be too tired to get to shore or to the side of the pool but is able to stay afloat and breathe and may be calling for help. The person may be floating, treading water or clinging to an object or a line for support. Someone who is trying to swim but making little or no forward progress may be in distress. A patient who is motionless and floating face-up or face-down indicates a passive drowning victim. A patient struggling to keep his mouth and nose above water indicates an active drowning victim.

53. **a.** If a person falls through the ice, it is your responsibility as a rescuer to immediately call for an ice rescue team. You should not go onto the ice to attempt a rescue because the ice may be too thin to support you. Once you have summoned the specialized team, you need to continue talking to the patient to help calm him. If possible, you should use reaching or throwing assists to rescue the patient, but you should not go into the icy water.

54. **d.** There is no water in the silo, so the patient is not at risk for drowning. Below-ground areas, such as vaults, sewers, wells or cisterns, can contain water and pose a drowning risk. Silos used to store agricultural materials are often designed to limit oxygen and, therefore, present the hazard of poisonous gases caused by fermentation. The danger of engulfment by the contained product in the silo also is a possibility. Low oxygen levels in these spaces pose a significant risk, as do poisonous gases, such as carbon monoxide, hydrogen sulfide and carbon dioxide.

55. **c.** After a short distance, teams should rotate positions, changing sides and positions after each progression. Teams then should alternate, giving each team a chance to rest. This will ensure a safe rescue, without anyone becoming exhausted and unable to complete the evacuation. Time and efficiency are key, so stopping to rest would be inappropriate. Switching hands would be ineffective in preventing you from tiring. Getting a replacement would be appropriate only as a last resort if, for some reason, you were unable to continue.

56. **a.** The most appropriate method would be to attempt a reaching assist by lying down at the side of the pool and reaching out to her using your arm or leg or an object such as a pole, tree branch or towel. If this is not possible, you could attempt a throwing assist. A wading assist would not be appropriate because the water in the deep end would most likely be over your head. Your first goal is to stay safe, so rushing or jumping into the water would put you at risk for drowning, too.

57. **c.** A passive drowning victim is not moving and is floating face-up or face-down on or near the surface of the water or may be submerged. A distressed swimmer may be floating, treading water or clinging to an object or a line for support. An active drowning victim is vertical in the water, typically with his or her arms at the sides, pressing down in an attempt to keep the mouth and nose above water to breathe.

58. **d.** The HAZMAT EMS Response Unit would be used for situations involving *weapons of mass destruction* (WMDs) and HAZMAT incidents to provide EMS care to patients in the warm zone (i.e., the area immediately outside of the hot zone,

where most of the danger exists). The Tactical EMS Unit would be used for situations such as hostage barricades, active shooters, high-risk warrants and other situations requiring a tactical response team. The Fire Rehabilitation Unit would be used to provide rest, rehydration, nourishment and medical evaluation to members (firefighters) who are involved in extended or extreme incident scene operations. The Specialized Vehicle Response Unit would be called to support operations involving all-terrain response vehicles required for difficult-to-reach hazardous terrains.

59. **b.** This is a crime scene, so it is extremely important for you to consult with law enforcement to obtain permission to enter the crime scene, for your own safety as well as to ensure that you do not disturb crime scene evidence. Once you have permission to enter, you may find it necessary to call for more advanced medical personnel based on your assessment. You must take precautions to avoid disturbing any evidence, including the patient by moving him or removing any obstacles that are blocking access. If it is absolutely essential to move something in the interest of patient care, you must inform law enforcement and document it.

60. **a.** Since local firefighters already are present, someone from this unit would assume the IC

position. Only highly trained firefighters, who have the equipment to protect them against smoke and fire, should approach a fire. Your responsibilities would include gathering information to help the responding firefighting and EMS units. You should not allow any other individuals to approach the fire. If possible, attempt to find out about the number of possible victims who may be trapped and any possible causes. You should give this information to emergency personnel when they arrive.

61. **b.** A special event where more than 25,000 participants or spectators are expected requires an on-site treatment facility, providing protection from weather or other elements to ensure patient safety and comfort. Beds and equipment for at least four simultaneous patients must be provided for evaluation and treatment, with adequate lighting and ventilation. A special event EMS system also must have on-site communication capabilities to ensure uniform access to care for patients in need of EMS care, on-site coordination of EMS personnel activities, communication with existing community *public safety answering points* (PSAPs) and interface with other involved public safety agencies. Receiving facilities and ambulances providing emergency transportation also must be ensured.

COURSE REVIEW EXAM

Directions: *Circle the letter that best answers the question.*

1. You try to reposition a piece of equipment but you find that this is not possible. You reach for the equipment with the understanding that you should reach no more than which distance in front of your body?
   a. 10 inches
   b. 15 inches
   c. 20 inches
   d. 25 inches

2. You know that your right leg is weaker than your left leg. Which technique would be the most appropriate for you to use when moving a patient?
   a. Power grip
   b. Squat lift
   c. Power lift
   d. Log rolling

3. A patient was involved in a motor-vehicle crash in which he experienced an injury to the liver and spleen. Which body cavity would you identify as being affected?
   a. Spinal
   b. Abdominal
   c. Cranial
   d. Thoracic

4. You would most likely expect to begin resuscitation efforts if you identified which of the following?
   a. Absence of pulse
   b. Rigor mortis
   c. Dependent lividity
   d. Body decomposition

5. You and a fellow *emergency medical responder* (EMR) had responded to a *multiple-casualty incident* (MCI) several days ago. Which of the following would lead you to suspect that your colleague is experiencing critical incident stress?
   a. Increased attention span
   b. Enhanced concentration
   c. Heightened job performance
   d. Unusually excessive silence

6. Scope of practice is best described as—
   a. The range of duties and skills an EMR is allowed and expected to perform.
   b. Credentialing that occurs at the local level.
   c. Protocols issued by the medical director.
   d. Permission to practice in a particular state.

7. Which of the following is the most effective natural defense against infection?
   a. Mucous membranes
   b. Hand washing
   c. Intact skin
   d. *Personal protective equipment* (PPE)

8. Which of the following would you do when placing a patient in a modified *high arm in endangered spine* (H.A.IN.E.S.) recovery position?
   a. Bend the leg up that is farthest from you.
   b. Place the patient's farther arm over his or her chest.
   c. Kneel at the patient's head.
   d. Turn the patient's head, then the patient's back.

9. You describe the elbow as being superior to which of the following?
   a. Neck
   b. Wrist
   c. Head
   d. Shoulder

10. When using the clothes drag technique, you would be moving in which direction?
    a. To the right
    b. To the left
    c. Forward
    d. Backward

11. Which individual would be the least likely to act as an EMR?
    a. Camp leader
    b. Athletic trainer
    c. Lifeguard
    d. Paramedic

12. You are the first to arrive at the scene of a motor-vehicle collision involving a car that hit a utility pole head-on. The car is overturned, and several wires are down on the ground. Which of the following would be the priority?
    a. Gaining access to the patient
    b. Providing care to the patient
    c. Ensuring the safety of the scene
    d. Recording your actions

13. After providing care to a patient, you are preparing to remove your disposable gloves. Which action would you perform?
    a. Slide two gloved fingers under the first glove at the wrist.
    b. Pull the first glove off by pulling on the fingertips.
    c. Pinch the outside of the second glove with bare fingers.
    d. Remove the second glove so that the first glove ends up inside of it.

14. You are with the family of a patient who has suddenly died as a result of a heart attack. Which of the following would be the most appropriate action?
    a. Remain calm and nonjudgmental.
    b. Provide reassurance that may or may not be accurate.
    c. Speak to them in a firm, authoritative voice.
    d. Encourage the family to refrain from becoming angry.

15. During a presentation for career day at a local high school, a participant asks you about the types of characteristics needed by an EMR. Which of the following would you be least likely to include in your response?
    a. Able to control personal fears
    b. Ability to remain inflexible
    c. Compassion
    d. Ability to stay current

16. Which of the following would best exemplify direct contact transmission?
    a. Getting bitten by a infected mosquito
    b. Touching a work surface soiled with a patient's body fluid
    c. Inhaling air and particles from a patient who sneezed nearby
    d. Patient's blood entering a cut on the responder's hand

17. You determine that an infant needs chest compressions. Which of the following would you use to perform chest compressions?
    a. The heel of your hand
    b. Thumb side of your fist
    c. Two fingers of one hand
    d. Both thumbs

18. After which age would you commonly ask for consent from the patient as opposed to the parent or guardian?
    a. 12 years
    b. 14 years
    c. 16 years
    d. 18 years

19. After performing several cycles of CPR, a patient begins to breathe and a pulse is noted. Which action is the most appropriate?
    a. Cancel the call for more advanced medical personnel.
    b. Stop chest compressions but continue ventilations.
    c. Continue to monitor the patient while maintaining an open airway.
    d. Obtain an *automated external defibrillator* (AED) to check the heart rhythm.

20. You arrive at the scene of an emergency in which a patient has fallen off of a ladder and the ladder hit the patient's ribs. Which body cavity would you suspect to be injured?
    a. Abdominal
    b. Thoracic
    c. Pelvic
    d. Cranial

21. You are called to a patient's home because the patient is complaining of chest pain. Which of the following would lead you to suspect that the patient is experiencing a heart attack?
    a. Pain spreading to the jaw and neck
    b. Pain that eases with resting
    c. Pain that is relieved with medication
    d. Pain without difficulty breathing

22. You are providing care to a patient who is bleeding from a puncture wound. You understand that which blood component is involved in helping to stop the bleeding?
    a. Red blood cells
    b. White blood cells
    c. Platelets
    d. Plasma

23. You are using the squat lift to move a patient. Which of the following is an appropriate action?
    a. Stand with feet parallel and even.
    b. Lead with your shoulders.
    c. Place the right leg in front of the left leg.
    d. Lift your upper body before your hips.

24. You arrive at the home of a patient experiencing severe difficulty breathing. The patient's spouse tells you that the patient has terminal cancer and has a *Do Not Resuscitate* (DNR) order. The spouse shows you the written document, which you determine to be valid. Which of the following would you do?
    a. Notify medical direction about how to proceed.
    b. Prepare to perform the usual emergency care.
    c. Call the patient's physician for verification.
    d. Honor the spouse's statement and the patient's wishes.

25. You are using an AED and it has delivered a shock to the patient. Which of the following would you do next?
    a. Wait for the device to re-analyze the heart rhythm.
    b. Continue to monitor the patient's condition.
    c. Begin performing CPR for about 2 minutes.
    d. Place the patient in a face-up position while maintaining an open airway.

26. Which of the following would lead you to suspect that a patient's breathing is adequate?
    a. Lack of nasal flaring
    b. Deviated trachea
    c. Rib muscles pulling in on inhalation
    d. Pursed-lip breathing

27. Which structure attaches muscle to bone?
    a. Ligament
    b. Tendon
    c. Patella
    d. Coccyx

28. You are assisting with transporting a patient to a helicopter. You determine that it is safe to approach the aircraft when—
    a. The helicopter comes to a stop.
    b. The tail rotors have stopped spinning.
    c. The medical crew begins exiting the craft.
    d. The pilot signals that it is safe.

29. A patient is conscious and experiencing an obstructed airway. Which of the following would be the least appropriate to use?
    a. Back blows
    b. Chest thrusts
    c. Finger sweeps
    d. Abdominal thrusts

30. A patient is trapped from the waist down under several large pieces of plywood and a scaffold. You are assisting in extrication. Which type of equipment would you most likely expect to use during extrication?
    a. Ropes
    b. Pneumatic tool
    c. Shovel
    d. Pliers

31. While providing care to a patient, more advanced medical personnel arrive. You inform them about the patient's condition and history, based on the understanding that this action is appropriate because it does not violate the patient's—
    a. Consent.
    b. Advance directive.
    c. Confidentiality.
    d. Competence.

32. The following are four nationally recognized levels of *emergency medical services* (EMS) training. Which level is the most basic level?
    a. Paramedic
    b. EMR
    c. *Advanced emergency medical technician* (AEMT)
    d. *Emergency medical technician* (EMT)

33. You are applying AED pads to a child and notice that the pads may touch each other. Which action is the most appropriate?
    a. Cut one of the pads in half, using a half of the pad instead of the whole.
    b. Use just one pad instead of both pads.
    c. Use both pads on the chest, overlapping the edges of the pads.
    d. Put one pad on the chest and the other on the back between the shoulder blades.

34. When using a complex access to assist in extricating a patient, you would—
    a. Use a ratcheting cable.
    b. Try opening the door.
    c. Break the window glass.
    d. Have the patient roll down the window.

35. You are giving ventilations to a patient. Which of the following might indicate that you are using too much force?
    a. The patient is developing a blotchy skin discoloration.
    b. The stomach is becoming distended.
    c. The patient is showing signs of a neck injury.
    d. The chest is failing to rise.

36. You are working to stabilize a hybrid vehicle. Which of the following would you need to keep in mind?
    a. Removing the ignition key is sufficient to stabilize the vehicle.
    b. Cribbing should be placed under the high-voltage cables.
    c. The vehicle still can be operational even if silent.
    d. Chocking the wheels should be avoided.

37. You are using a resuscitation mask to give ventilations to a child. Which of the following would you do first?
    a. Open the airway.
    b. Seal the mask.
    c. Blow into the mask at a rate of 1 ventilation about every 3 seconds
    d. Give ventilations for 2 minutes.

38. Which of the following is least likely to be considered a high-risk situation impacting safety during an emergency response?
    a. Going through an intersection
    b. Exiting from a highway
    c. Driving in inclement weather
    d. Responding alone

39. You arrive on the scene of an emergency in which an adult patient is unconscious and has an airway obstruction. You determine the need for chest compressions. Which of the following is the most important for you to do when performing chest compressions on the patient?
    a. Compress the chest about 1 inch.
    b. Use your arms to compress the chest.
    c. Keep your fingers off of the chest.
    d. Place your fist in the center of the chest.

40. Emergency vehicles, including fire apparatus and ambulances, arrive on the scene of an emergency of a motor-vehicle collision involving three vehicles. Which of the following is the most appropriate?
   a. Traffic cones are placed at 25-foot intervals.
   b. Ambulances park on the outside of the fire engines.
   c. A safety zone radius of at least 100 feet is created around the scene.
   d. Large fire apparatus is positioned at an angle to the traffic lane.

41. You are preparing to use an *oropharyngeal airway* (OPA). Which of the following would be the most important to assess first?
   a. Unresponsiveness
   b. Evidence of airway obstruction
   c. Presence of a gag reflex
   d. Distance from the earlobe to the mouth

42. You are performing chest compressions on an adult. You would compress the patient's chest to which depth?
   a. About 1 inch
   b. About 1½ inches
   c. At least 2 inches
   d. About 2½ inches

43. You are using chocking with a vehicle. Which of the following would you do?
   a. Place blocks or wedges against the wheels of a vehicle.
   b. Position large vehicles at an angle to traffic lanes.
   c. Use wood or supports diagonally to the vehicle's frame.
   d. Remove a patient who is trapped in a vehicle.

44. You suspect that a patient is showing early signs of a heart attack. Your local protocol allows you to administer medication to the patient. After asking the patient about the use of medications, you determine that it is safe to administer it. You would administer which of the following?
   a. One chewable baby aspirin
   b. A single dose of acetaminophen (Tylenol®)
   c. One 5-grain adult aspirin tablet
   d. Two tablets of ibuprofen (Motrin®)

45. A patient is receiving emergency oxygen via a *bag-valve-mask resuscitator* (BVM) at a flow rate of 15 *liters per minute* (LPM). You would expect that this patient is receiving which percentage of oxygen?
   a. 24 percent
   b. 30 percent
   c. 55 percent
   d. 90 percent

46. You are the first to arrive at the scene of a tanker truck crash. As you near the scene, you notice a sign on the rear door of the truck indicating the presence of *hazardous materials* (HAZMATs). Which of the following would be the least helpful at the scene in gaining additional information about the substance in the tanker?
   a. Warning signs
   b. *National Fire Protection Association* (NFPA) numbers
   c. Shipping papers
   d. *Emergency Response Guidebook*

47. When performing one-rescuer CPR, the cycle of compressions and ventilations that you would perform is—
   a. 30 compressions and 2 ventilations.
   b. 15 compressions and 1 ventilation.
   c. 15 compressions and 2 ventilations.
   d. 30 compressions and 1 ventilation.

48. While administering emergency oxygen to a patient, you notice that the pressure gauge reads 1200 *pounds per square inch* (psi). Which action would be the most appropriate?
   a. Increase the flow rate.
   b. Continue administering emergency oxygen.
   c. Change the cylinder immediately.
   d. Prepare to provide assisted ventilations.

49. Which color for triage would indicate that the patient requires urgent care?
   a. Green
   b. Yellow
   c. Red
   d. Black

50. You are providing care at an MCI. Which of the following is least appropriate in helping to manage and reduce stress of the patient and those around them?
   a. Reuniting family members
   b. Providing information to the media
   c. Explaining events simply and honestly
   d. Having others available who are able to assist with tasks

51. You are providing care to a woman in labor and suspect that the umbilical cord has prolapsed. You promptly intervene because you understand that—
   a. The mother is at high risk for hemorrhage and shock.
   b. The baby may aspirate amniotic fluid, which could lead to pneumonia.
   c. The blood flow to the baby can be cut off as the baby moves through the birth canal.
   d. The mother may experience a seizure because she has developed eclampsia.

52. You are providing care to a 3½- year-old child who was a passenger in a vehicle involved in a collision. You would identify this child as being at which developmental stage?
   a. Infant
   b. Toddler
   c. Preschooler
   d. School age

53. When giving ventilations to an adult, you would give the ventilations for how long before rechecking for breathing and a pulse?
   a. 1 minute
   b. 2 minutes
   c. 3 minutes
   d. 4 minutes

54. Which of the following would you identify as a normal change related to aging?
   a. Thinning of the heart muscle
   b. Increased lung elasticity
   c. Slowed movement through the digestive system
   d. Loss of the ability to learn

55. You arrive at the scene of an emergency involving a patient who suddenly developed difficulty breathing. The patient, who is pale and anxious, has a respiratory rate of 36 breaths per minute and is breathing through his mouth. You determine the need to administer emergency oxygen. Which delivery device would be the least appropriate for this patient?
   a. Nasal cannula
   b. Resuscitation mask
   c. Non-rebreather mask
   d. BVM

56. You are called to the home of a patient who is receiving chemotherapy and radiation therapy as treatment for cancer. When providing care for this patient, which of the following is the most important?
    a. Inspecting the skin for rashes
    b. Evaluating the severity of vomiting
    c. Noting the degree of hair loss
    d. Observing standard precautions

57. A patient requires air medical transport via helicopter. When calculating the amount of weight for the helicopter, which of the following would need to be considered?
    a. Number of patients to be transported
    b. Rescuers accompanying the patient(s)
    c. Weight of the fuel load
    d. Life-saving equipment needed

58. When administering emergency oxygen, which of the following would be the most important?
    a. Avoiding the use of oxygen around sparks or flames
    b. Using petroleum products to clean the regulator
    c. Rolling the cylinder when you need to move it
    d. Using the valve or pressure regulator to carry the cylinder

59. You are checking the jump kit. This occurs during which phase of the EMS response?
    a. Phase 1
    b. Phase 2
    c. Phase 3
    d. Phase 4

60. You are providing care to a patient with multiple sclerosis. Which of the following would you need to keep in mind?
    a. This disorder is a progressive genetic disorder.
    b. The condition primarily affects skeletal muscles.
    c. Its symptoms appear and disappear over a period of years.
    d. Eventually, the patient will require assisted ventilation.

61. You arrive at an emergency scene involving a 6-month-old girl who is struggling to breathe and is cyanotic. You hear very high-pitched wheezes but do not see any rise and fall of the chest or hear or feel any air going in and out at the mouth and nose. She is conscious but not crying. You suspect an obstructed airway and attempt to relieve the obstruction. You would position the baby's head—
    a. To the right or left side.
    b. Parallel with the body.
    c. Higher than the waist.
    d. Lower than the chest.

62. You are providing emergency care to an older adult man with Alzheimer's disease. The patient's wife called 9-1-1 because he started throwing things and screaming at her. You suspect that the patient is experiencing a catastrophic reaction. When assessing this patient, which of the following would you need to do?
    a. Deal solely with the wife because the patient is confused.
    b. Speak to the patient at eye level to show your interest.
    c. Turn off the lights in the room to prevent distractions.
    d. Avoid long explanations of what you are doing to prevent overstimulation.

63. You are administering emergency oxygen to a patient and want to ensure that the highest concentration of oxygen is being delivered. Which device would you be least likely to use?
   a. Non-rebreather mask
   b. Resuscitation mask
   c. Nasal cannula
   d. BVM

64. You are providing CPR to a patient while he is being transported in an ambulance. Which of the following is the most appropriate?
   a. Stand freely using the stretcher for balance.
   b. Spread your feet to shoulder width for stability.
   c. Keep your knees locked to steady yourself.
   d. Have a partner hold you at the shoulders to prevent falling.

65. You are administering emergency oxygen to a patient and determine that the oxygen is flowing by which of the following?
   a. Movement of the flowmeter dial
   b. Audible hissing sound through the device
   c. Pressure gauge reading 150 psi
   d. Absence of the O-ring gasket

66. When giving abdominal thrusts to an adult, which of the following would be appropriate to do?
   a. Kneel behind the patient.
   b. Use slow downward movements.
   c. Use the heel of your hand.
   d. Place a fist just above the navel.

67. You are providing care to a patient who is bleeding from a stab wound. You would identify this as which of the following?
   a. Blunt trauma
   b. Penetrating injury
   c. Contusion
   d. Hematoma

68. You arrive on the scene of an emergency involving a HAZMAT. Which of the following is the most appropriate?
   a. Staying in a low-lying area
   b. Approaching the area quickly
   c. Staying upwind of the scene
   d. Going to the designated hot zone

69. You are providing emergency care to a patient who tells you that he is hard of hearing. You understand that the patient's hearing problem differs from deafness in that—
   a. The patient can rely on his hearing for communication.
   b. There is a problem with the nerve that transmits sound.
   c. The patient had difficulty hearing high-frequency sounds.
   d. The patient has a problem in his middle ear.

70. You arrive at the scene of an emergency. Which of the following would you do first?
   a. Ensure patient safety.
   b. Decide on necessary additional resources.
   c. Determine the *mechanism of injury* (MOI).
   d. Ensure personal safety.

71. You arrive at a family's home in response to a call that a child has a high fever. The child's temperature is 103.4°F. Which of the following would you do first?
    a. Begin attempts to rapidly cool the child's body.
    b. Call for assistance from more advanced medical personnel.
    c. Apply extra blankets and clothing to prevent chilling.
    d. Apply rubbing alcohol to the child's body to promote evaporation.

72. You arrive at the home of a pregnant woman who is in her second trimester. Which of the following would you consider to be typical in the second trimester?
    a. Morning sickness
    b. Placental development
    c. Majority of weight gain
    d. Fetal movement

73. You arrive at the home of a patient in response to a 9-1-1 call by his wife. On arrival you observe that the patient is in the tripod position. You would suspect which of the following?
    a. Abdominal pain
    b. Fracture
    c. Difficulty breathing
    d. Stroke

74. Assessment of a patient reveals the following information. Which finding would you consider abnormal?
    a. Pale, cool skin
    b. Capillary refill of 2 seconds
    c. Respiratory rate of 18 breaths per minute
    d. Pulse of 70 *beats per minute* (bpm)

75. You are assessing a 65-year-old man who has fallen on the sidewalk. The man is talking and complaining of severe pain in his left upper leg, which has a small open wound that is oozing blood. Which of the following would be least likely based on your assessment?
    a. The patient has an open airway.
    b. The patient lacks a pulse.
    c. The patient is conscious.
    d. The patient is breathing adequately.

76. You are assessing the rate and quality of breathing for a young woman with a history of asthma and allergies. Which of the following is the most appropriate for you to do?
    a. Tell the patient that you are going to count how fast she is breathing.
    b. Check her respiratory rate and quality without her knowing you are doing so.
    c. Count each inhalation and exhalation as 2 breaths.
    d. Understand that noisy breathing is an expected, normal finding with this patient.

77. You are assisting with decontamination efforts in which the HAZMAT is being chemically altered to render it less harmful. Which type of decontamination is being done?
    a. Dilution
    b. Gross
    c. Absorption
    d. Neutralization

78. You have just assisted in the delivery of a newborn. You would expect the placenta to be delivered within which time frame?
    a. 5 minutes
    b. 15 minutes
    c. 30 minutes
    d. 45 minutes

79. You perform a secondary assessment on a responsive patient. After assessing the patient's complaints, which of the following would you do next?
   a. Perform a focused medical assessment.
   b. Assess baseline vital signs.
   c. Obtain a SAMPLE history.
   d. Perform components of a detailed physical exam.

80. While involved in caring for patients at an MCI, you notice that one of the patients is tagged white. You interpret this as an indication that the patient has—
   a. Life-threatening injuries needing attention.
   b. Minor injuries not needing a doctor's care.
   c. Severe injuries that could wait for treatment.
   d. Some injuries but is ambulatory.

81. When obtaining a patient's blood pressure, which of the following would be least appropriate?
   a. Apply the cuff over the patient's thickly clothed arm.
   b. Position the bladder of the cuff over the brachial artery.
   c. Support the patient's arm at heart level in front of his body.
   d. Ensure that the cuff covers about two-thirds of his upper arm.

82. You were the first to arrive at the scene of an MCI. Approximately 10 minutes later, a more experienced EMR arrives on the scene. Which of the following would be the most appropriate?
   a. Assign the EMR specific patient care tasks to be completed.
   b. Transfer command to the EMR after giving a verbal report.
   c. Have the EMR assume responsibility for traffic control.
   d. Tell the EMR to set up a staging area for patient treatment.

83. Which finding would correlate with the "P" in the SAMPLE history?
   a. The patient having high blood pressure
   b. The patient mowing the lawn
   c. The patient sweating profusely
   d. The patient using medications for high blood pressure

84. You are assisting a pregnant woman who is in labor to cope with the discomfort and pain. Which of the following is the most effective?
   a. Encouraging her to breathe rapidly and shallowly
   b. Asking her to focus on an object to help her breathing
   c. Telling her that she has to learn to endure the discomfort
   d. Informing her that everything will be okay

85. You are preparing to transport a patient involved in a motor-vehicle collision to the hospital. Which information would you least likely include in your communication with the hospital?
   a. The care provided to the patient and his response
   b. The personal characteristics of the patient
   c. The patient's SAMPLE history
   d. The *estimated time of arrival* (ETA)

86. You have assisted in the delivery of a newborn. Which of the following would lead you to begin resuscitation of a newborn?
   a. A respiratory rate less than 30 respirations per minute
   b. A pulse rate greater than 100 bpm
   c. A pink body with bluish limbs
   d. No gasping movements

87. You are reviewing a copy of a *pre-hospital care report* (PCR). Where would you expect to find the patient's birth date documented?
    a. Run data
    b. Patient data
    c. Check boxes
    d. Patient narrative

88. You are using the START system to assess an adult patient. You find the patient is breathing at a rate of 42 breaths per minute. You would tag this person with which color?
    a. Yellow
    b. Red
    c. Green
    d. Black

89. You are communicating with medical control and receive an order for a specific treatment that you are qualified to perform. Which of the following is the most appropriate when receiving the order?
    a. Have medical control repeat the order again.
    b. Tell medical control, "Affirmative."
    c. Repeat the order word for word.
    d. Tell medical control that you understand the order.

90. You arrive at the scene of an emergency involving a pregnant woman who is in labor. Which of the following would lead you to suspect that delivery is imminent?
    a. Strong contractions occurring every 5 to 6 minutes
    b. The woman's report of a mild need to bear down
    c. Crowning noted at the vaginal opening
    d. A sudden gush of fluid from the vagina

91. When assessing a child's *level of consciousness* (LOC), which of the following is the least appropriate to use?
    a. AVPU scale
    b. Evidence of spontaneous movement
    c. Vital signs
    d. Pupil assessment

92. Upon arrival at a scene involving a multiple-vehicle accident on a snowy and icy rural highway with two cars and a pickup truck, you observe that the truck is overturned on the side of the road and one of the cars has rolled over and landed in a shallow gulley. The driver and passenger of the car in the gulley are unresponsive with multiple injuries. Neither was wearing a shoulder restraint or seat belt. The pickup driver is responsive but unable to get out of the car. You determine that the driver and the passenger of the car in the gulley need to be transported to a trauma facility. Which of the following is the most appropriate?
    a. Contacting dispatch to summon an additional emergency vehicle for transport
    b. Making a request for air medical transport to the trauma center
    c. Getting both patients ready for transport by ambulance
    d. Notifying law enforcement to clear the roadway for transport

93. When assessing an injured child who is conscious, which of the following is the most appropriate?
    a. Use as much careful observation as possible to carry out the primary assessment.
    b. Use touch to convey a warm and caring attitude to the child.
    c. Refrain from interacting with the parents when gathering information.
    d. Perform a head-to-toe assessment for a child who is agitated.

94. You put an unstable vehicle, which contains no passengers, in "park." Which of the following would you do next?
    a. Turn off the ignition.
    b. Set the parking brake.
    c. Move the seats back.
    d. Remove the key.

95. A toddler who is injured is alert and crying. As you prepare to examine the child, he begins to scream and push you away. Which action is the most appropriate?
    a. Ask another EMR to perform the exam.
    b. Delay the physical exam until more advanced medical personnel arrive.
    c. Speak softly and calmly to the child, maintaining eye contact.
    d. Proceed with the exam in a head-to-toe manner.

96. Which of the following would you identify as a Class B biological agent/disease?
    a. Q fever
    b. Yellow fever
    c. Hantavirus
    d. Tick-borne virus

97. You arrive at a swim club in response to a call that a swimmer has been injured. A 15-year-old boy is lying on his right side beside the pool and is not moving. Your priority is to—
    a. Open the patient's airway.
    b. Check his breathing and pulse.
    c. Assess his LOC.
    d. Begin to provide ventilations.

98. You check a patient's pulse and count the number of beats occurring in 30 seconds and find it to be 40. You would determine the pulse rate to be how many beats per minute?
    a. 60
    b. 80
    c. 100
    d. 120

99. You arrive on the scene of an emergency involving a human-caused disaster. Which of the following might this be?
    a. Flu pandemic
    b. Contamination of water supply
    c. Chemical exposure
    d. Hurricane

100. You arrive at the home of a 5-year-old child who has fallen off of a wooden fence. A piece of the fence is protruding from the child's leg, which is bleeding. The child is crying and talking to his parents. Which assessment finding would be of least concern?
    a. Strong, palpable pulse
    b. Increasing lethargy
    c. Cool, clammy skin
    d. Rapid breathing

101. You need to open an unresponsive patient's mouth to clear the airway of fluids. Which of the following would you use?
    a. Head-tilt/chin-lift method
    b. Jaw-thrust (without head extension) maneuver
    c. Cross-finger technique
    d. Neck hyperextension

102. You are called to an emergency involving a pregnant woman who thinks that she is in labor. When assessing this patient, you determine that the patient is in labor when she reports that her contractions are—
    a. Occurring sporadically.
    b. Lasting about the same length.
    c. Alternating between mild and strong.
    d. Getting closer together.

103. You would anticipate a high mortality rate if patients were exposed to which of the following biological agents/diseases?
    a. Q fever
    b. Anthrax
    c. Ricin toxin
    d. Brucellosis

104. When using a resuscitation mask, you would place the rim of the mask between which of the following?
    a. The upper and lower lips
    b. The nose and mouth
    c. The lower lip and chin
    d. The bridge of the nose and lower jaw

105. You are working with the triage officer to classify patients who have been exposed to a nerve agent in vapor form. The patient you are assessing is unconscious and convulsing. You would classify this patient as—
    a. Immediate.
    b. Expectant.
    c. Delayed.
    d. Minimal.

106. You are documenting information in the PCR with the understanding that control of the contents of a PCR falls within the—
    a. Responsibility of the medical control.
    b. *Health Insurance Portability and Accountability Act* (HIPAA).
    c. State in which the EMS system is located.
    d. Facility to which the patient is transported.

107. Which of the following is the least appropriate when providing care to a child with epiglottitis?
    a. Keeping the child calm
    b. Encouraging the tripod position
    c. Examining the throat
    d. Monitoring for voice changes

108. During a high-angle rescue, the team uses a secured rope to approach a patient. This is called—
    a. Rappelling.
    b. Reaching.
    c. Shoring.
    d. Throwing.

109. A patient is hypoglycemic and unconscious. Which of the following would you do?
    a. Give the patient 4 ounces of fruit juice through a straw.
    b. Crush two to five glucose tablets, placing them under his tongue.
    c. Summon more advanced medical personnel.
    d. Contact medical control for an order to administer insulin.

110. Which type of shock is associated with a trauma to spinal cord?
    a. Cardiogenic
    b. Metabolic
    c. Anaphylactic
    d. Vasogenic

111. A child who has fallen through the ice has been removed from the water after 10 minutes. You would most likely expect to provide care for which of the following?
    a. Seizures
    b. Hypothermia
    c. Hemorrhage
    d. Fever

112. Upon arriving at the home of a 65-year-old man in response to a 9-1-1 call from his wife saying that he is having a stroke, you assess that the patient is conscious. Which of the following would you assess first?
    a. Face
    b. Speech
    c. Arm
    d. Time of onset

113. You are preparing to use the wading assist to reach a swimmer because you have determined that the water is safe and no higher than your—
    a. Ankles.
    b. Knees.
    c. Waist.
    d. Chest.

114. Which of the following would lead you to suspect that your measures to minimize shock are effective?
    a. Increase in blood pressure
    b. Dilated pupils
    c. Listlessness
    d. Irregular, rapid pulse

115. You are providing care to a patient with suspected drug intoxication. Which of the following would suggest depressant abuse?
    a. Drowsiness
    b. Bloodshot eyes
    c. Mood change
    d. Flushed face

116. You arrive on the scene of a fire in an office building where local firefighters are present. Which of the following would you do first?
    a. Assume the role of the *incident commander* (IC).
    b. Gather information to help the fire units.
    c. Prevent others from approaching the fire.
    d. Obtain information about the number of possible victims.

117. You are called to a high school soccer facility where one of the athletes who had been practicing is complaining of dizziness and a throbbing headache. The weather is extremely hot and humid. You assess the patient and suspect that he had a heat stroke. Which of the following would you be most likely to discover?
    a. Flushed, dry skin
    b. Rapid, bounding pulse
    c. Elevated blood pressure
    d. Body temperature of 102°F

118. You arrive at the scene of an emergency in which a patient has sustained an injury to his upper arm with some of his skin and soft tissue partially torn away. You would identify this situation as a(n)—
    a. Avulsion
    b. Amputation
    c. Laceration
    d. Impalement

119. You are called to an emergency scene in which an adolescent was swimming in the local river and now is in trouble. Which of the following would lead you to identify the patient as a drowning victim who is passive?
    a. The arms are at the person's side.
    b. The person is floating face-up or face-down.
    c. The person is treading water.
    d. The person has a vertical body position.

120. You arrive at the scene of a explosion at a government factory. Several of the employees are experiencing severe respiratory distress. A bystander reports that there was a strange smell immediately after the explosion, stating that it smelled like "freshly cut hay." Which of the following would be the most appropriate?
    a. Administer an antidote such as sodium thiosulfate.
    b. Use bleach to clean the exposed area.
    c. Initiate decontamination procedures to remove the agent.
    d. Begin resuscitative measures.

121. You would suspect designer drug abuse in a patient exhibiting which of the following?
    a. Drowsiness, slurred speech and confusion
    b. Mood changes, flushing and hallucinations
    c. Tachycardia, hypertension and rapid breathing
    d. Excitement, restlessness and irritability

122. Which *emergency support function* (ESF) would address coordination of incident management and response efforts?
    a. Public health and medical services
    b. Communications
    c. Emergency management
    d. Transportation

123. When caring for a patient in shock, which of the following would you do first?
    a. Control any visible bleeding.
    b. Ensure the patient's airway is open.
    c. Immobilize any fractures.
    d. Elevate the lower extremities.

124. You arrive at the scene of an emergency involving a patient who has had a grand mal seizure. His friend tells you that the patient told him he "heard a strange sound" just before the seizure occurred. You interpret this information as indicating which phase?
    a. Post-ictal
    b. Tonic
    c. Clonic
    d. Aura

125. A child's parents have called 9-1-1 because the child is complaining of severe abdominal pain. When assessing the child, which of the following would be the priority?
    a. Obtaining a general impression of the child's appearance
    b. Checking the child's mental status, breathing and pulse
    c. Gathering a SAMPLE history from the child and parents
    d. Performing a physical examination using a hands-on approach

126. Which of the following would you identify as an absorbed poison?
    a. Poison ivy
    b. Contaminated water
    c. Snake bite venom
    d. Chloroform

127. A patient receives a puncture wound of his left leg. You would anticipate that this patient is at greatest risk for which of the following?
    a. Crush syndrome
    b. Shock
    c. Internal organ rupture
    d. Infection

128. While triaging, you tag a person yellow based on which finding?
    a. Unconsciousness
    b. Evidence of a spinal injury
    c. Capillary refill greater than 2 seconds
    d. Absent radial pulse

129. You are inspecting a patient's burn and determine it is a deep partial-thickness burn based on which of the following?
    a. Absence of sensation to touch
    b. Reddened area that blanches (whitens) on touch
    c. Dry, leathery appearance
    d. Absence of hair

130. Which of the following would you need to do first for a patient experiencing a sucking chest wound?
    a. Apply an occlusive dressing.
    b. Control the bleeding.
    c. Assess for signs of shock.
    d. Begin ventilations.

131. While you are obtaining a SAMPLE history from a patient who abuses alcohol, he tells you that he has not used the drug in the last 10 hours. You would be alert for signs of—
    a. Dependency.
    b. Withdrawal.
    c. Tolerance.
    d. Overdose.

132. You are providing care to a patient with a genital injury. Which of the following would you need to keep in mind?
    a. Most often the injury is an open wound.
    b. Extreme pain usually is noted.
    c. Profuse bleeding is commonly seen.
    d. The injury typically is the result of sexual assault.

133. You arrive at the scene of an emergency involving a 60-year-old woman who accidently locked herself out of her home while getting the mail. She has been outside in 15-degree weather for the past several hours and now is exhibiting signs of frostbite in her feet. Which of the following is your priority?
    a. Ensuring scene safety
    b. Reorienting the patient
    c. Getting the patient out of the cold
    d. Rubbing the patient's feet vigorously

134. Which of the following activities would be the least likely to occur in the hot zone?
    a. Rescue
    b. Treatment of life-threatening conditions
    c. Initial decontamination
    d. Immobilization

135. Which patient would be at greatest risk for traumatic asphyxia?
    a. A patient who was shot in the chest
    b. A patient with broken ribs caused by a fall
    c. A patient trapped under a collapsed concrete wall
    d. A patient with a sucking chest wound

136. You arrive at a rural camping site in response to a call about a camper being bitten by a snake on his lower leg. Which of the following would be the priority?
    a. Check for infection.
    b. Wash the wound.
    c. Elevate the leg.
    d. Apply ice to the area.

137. When arriving on the scene of an incident potentially involving *weapons of mass destruction* (WMDs), which of the following would you do first?
    a. Identify the weapon.
    b. Assess the patients.
    c. Ensure personal safety.
    d. Follow appropriate protocols.

138. When providing care to a woman who is a victim of sexual assault, which of the following would you do with any evidence collected?
    a. Place wet clothing in a plastic bag.
    b. Give any evidence to law enforcement after the patient is transported.
    c. Allow any wet clothing to dry first.
    d. Bag each piece of evidence individually.

139. A patient is experiencing excited delirium syndrome. Which of the following would you least likely find upon assessing the patient?
    a. Low body temperature
    b. Decreased body strength
    c. Decreased pain sensitivity
    d. Relaxed demeanor

140. You need to provide manual stabilization for a patient who is lying on his back. Which of the following would you do first?
    a. Control any external bleeding.
    b. Summon more advanced medical personnel.
    c. Position the head in line with the body.
    d. Place your hands on both sides of the patient's head.

141. You arrive at the scene of an emergency in which you suspect that the patient is experiencing mania. When approaching the patient, which of the following is most appropriate to establish rapport?
    a. Telling the patient to calm down
    b. Touching the patient on the shoulder
    c. Speaking directly to the patient
    d. Avoiding eye contact as much as possible

142. A *transient ischemic attack* (TIA) differs from a stroke in that a TIA—
    a. Lasts for a short duration.
    b. Has a different cause.
    c. Has more symptoms.
    d. Has a slower onset.

143. A patient incurred a facial injury in which a tooth was knocked out. Upon finding the tooth, which of the following is the most appropriate action?
    a. Attempting to replace the tooth in the patient's mouth
    b. Handling the tooth by its root
    c. Rinsing the tooth gently under running water
    d. Placing the tooth on ice for transport

144. Older adults are at a higher risk for suicide than the general population for which reason?
    a. Depression, common in this age group, often is misdiagnosed.
    b. This age group is more reluctant to seek help for mental health problems.
    c. Older adults commonly experience more problems with alcohol abuse.
    d. Older adults have an increased tendency for impulsive actions.

145. A patient requires a water rescue. Which of the following would indicate the need to remove the patient from the water to provide care?
    a. The patient is conscious.
    b. The patient is face-down in the water.
    c. The patient has a spinal injury.
    d. The patient has a neck injury.

146. When controlling bleeding from an open head wound, you would avoid which of the following?
    a. Elevating the head and shoulders if there is no spinal injury
    b. Applying direct pressure to a spongy area
    c. Pressing a sterile dressing gently over the wound
    d. Using a roller bandage to cover the dressing

147. A patient has a piece of glass embedded in his eyeball from an industrial incident. Which of the following would be most appropriate to do?
    a. Remove the object immediately to prevent permanent damage.
    b. Secure a Styrofoam® cup over the embedded object.
    c. Apply a sterile dressing over top of the object.
    d. Encircle the eye with gauze dressing to stabilize the object.

148. While assessing a patient's injury, you attempt to move the fractured part and hear a grating sound. You would identify this as which of the following?
    a. Angulation
    b. Cravat
    c. Crepitus
    d. Deformity

149. You are called to a scene in which a patient was stung by a jellyfish. You suspect that the patient is experiencing anaphylaxis based on which of the following?
    a. Itching
    b. Tongue swelling
    c. Hives
    d. Rash

150. When applying a binder, which of the following would you do?
    a. Place a triangular bandage under the injury and over the uninjured part.
    b. Tie the ends at the side of the patient's neck.
    c. Wrap a piece of cloth around the patient and the injured body part to hold it secure.
    d. Position the bandage around the injured area and fill it with air.

151. You are providing care to a patient with a heat cramp. Which action would be the priority?
    a. Having the patient rest
    b. Massaging the area gently
    c. Stretching the area lightly
    d. Giving the patient water to drink

152. You suspect that a patient has a fractured elbow. You would immobilize the arm—
    a. After extending the arm.
    b. As you correct any deformity
    c. In the position in which you found it.
    d. After correcting the deformity.

153. Which of the following would lead you to suspect that a patient has a serious abdominal injury?
    a. Complaints of vague pain
    b. Complaints of thirst
    c. Absence of bruising
    d. Pink, dry skin

154. While assessing a burn patient, you notice soot around the mouth and nose. Your priority would be—
    a. Emergency oxygen administration
    b. Skin protection
    c. Fluid loss
    d. Airway patency

155. You are providing care to a patient with a closed extremity wound. You summon more advanced medical care based on which of the following?
    a. The wounded part is pink, warm and dry.
    b. The patient can move it with little pain.
    c. The patient says the pain is intolerable.
    d. There is some swelling of the area.

156. Which type of agent attacks the body's cellular metabolism?
    a. Blister agent
    b. Blood agent
    c. Nerve agent
    d. Incapacitating agent

157. You arrive at the scene of an emergency involving a construction worker who has fallen off of a two-story scaffold, landing on his back. You find the man unconscious but breathing. One of his co-workers tells you that he hit his head when he landed. The patient's head is turned to the right side. Your first action would be to—
    a. Size-up the scene.
    b. Perform a primary assessment.
    c. Open his airway.
    d. Stabilize the head and neck.

158. While assessing a patient for injuries, which statement would lead you to suspect that he has sustained a musculoskeletal injury?
    a. "I'm not having much pain now."
    b. "My hand feels pretty warm."
    c. "I've dislocated my finger before."
    d. "My fingers are numb and tingling."

159. A patient experiences internal capillary bleeding of the upper arm. Which action is the most appropriate?
    a. Apply a cold pack to the area.
    b. Elevate the body part above heart level.
    c. Apply direct pressure to the site.
    d. Maintain pressure at a pressure point.

160. You are providing care to a patient with suspected fractured ribs on the right side. The patient says, "The the pain eases somewhat when I lean—
    a. Forward toward my knees."
    b. Toward my right side."
    c. Away from my right side."
    d. Slightly backwards."

COURSE REVIEW
EXAM ANSWER KEY

1. **c.** If you cannot reposition an object or patient to reduce the risk of injury, you should reach no more than 20 inches in front of your body.

2. **b.** The squat lift is an alternative to the power lift and is especially useful if one of your legs or arms is weaker than the other. The power grip always is recommended because it allows for maximum stability and strength from your hands. The power lift would be appropriate to use when both legs or arms are of equal strength. Log rolling usually is used for patients with suspected spinal injury and ideally requires four people working in tandem.

3. **b.** The abdominal cavity is located in the trunk below the ribs and contains the organs of digestion and excretion, such as the liver and spleen. The thoracic cavity or chest cavity is located in the trunk between the diaphragm and the neck and contains the heart and lungs. The spinal cavity extends from the bottom of the skull to the lower back and contains the brain stem and spinal cord. The cranial cavity is located in the head and contains the brain.

4. **a.** Absence of a pulse indicates the need for resuscitation. Rigor mortis, dependent lividity and body decomposition are signs of obvious death, indicating that resuscitative efforts may not be required.

5. **d.** Signs and symptoms of critical incident stress include uncharacteristic, excessive humor or silence, confusion, guilt, poor concentration, decreased attention span, inability to do his or her job well, denial, depression, anger, a change in interactions with others, increased or decreased eating and any other unusual behavior.

6. **a.** Scope of practice refers to the range of duties and skills that an *emergency medical responder* (EMR) is allowed and expected to perform. Certification refers to the credentialing that occurs at the local level. Standing orders are protocols issued by the medical director. Licensure is the permission to practice in a particular state.

7. **c.** The body has a series of natural defenses that prevent germs from entering and causing infection. Intact skin is the body's most effective natural defense. Mucous membranes are another natural defense, but they are less effective than intact skin at keeping pathogens out of the body. Hand washing and the use of *personal protective equipment* (PPE) are effective means of preventing infection transmission, but they are not natural defenses.

8. **a.** When placing a patient in the modified *high arm in endangered spine* (H.A.IN.E.S.) recovery position, you would kneel at the patient's side; reach across the body and lift the arm farthest from you up next to the head with the person's palm facing up; take the person's arm closest to you and place it next to his or her side; grasp the leg farthest from you and bend it up; using your hand that is closest to the person's head, cup the base of the skull in the palm of your hand and carefully slide your forearm under the person's shoulder closest to you; place your other hand under the arm and hip closest to you; using a smooth motion, roll the person away from you by lifting with your hand and forearm, making sure the person's head remains in contact with the extended arm and be sure to support the head and neck with your hand; stop all movement when the person is on his or her side; bend the knee closest to you and place it on top of the other knee so that both knees are in a bent position; and make sure the arm on top is in line with the upper body.

9. **b.** The elbow would be superior to the wrist but inferior to the head, neck and shoulders.

10. **d.** The clothes drag is done with the EMR moving backward. The firefighter's drag, firefighter's carry and pack-strap carry are done moving forward. None of the moving techniques involve the EMR moving to the right or left.

11. **c.** A paramedic, the highest level of training for an *emergency medical services* (EMS) responder, has more in-depth training than an *advanced emergency medical technician* (AEMT), *emergency medical technician* (EMT), or EMR. Lifeguards, athletic trainers and camp leaders may be EMRs.

12. **c.** The first priority would be to ensure the safety of the scene, which might entail summoning more advanced medical personnel to assist with the scene. Once the scene is safe, then gaining access to the patient and providing care would be important. Recording your actions is important but not the priority at this time.

13. **d.** When removing disposable gloves, you should pinch the palm side of the first glove near the wrist and carefully pull the glove so that it is inside out. While holding this glove in the palm of the gloved hand, you would slip two fingers under the glove at the wrist of the remaining gloved hand, pulling it off, inside out, so that the first glove ends up inside the glove just removed. At no time during the removal should bare skin come in contact with the outside of either glove.

14. **a.** When dealing with the family of a patient who has died suddenly, it is most important for you to listen empathetically and remain calm and nonjudgmental; allow them to express their rage, anger and despair; speak in a gentle tone of voice; and avoid giving false reassurance.

15. **b.** An EMR needs to be flexible, maintain a caring and professional attitude by showing compassion and providing reassurance. An EMR also needs to be able to control his or her fears and keep his or her knowledge and skills up to date.

16. **d.** Direct contact transmission occurs when infected blood or body fluid from one person enters another person's body, such as infected blood or body fluid entering the other person's body through a cut in the skin. Touching a soiled work surface would be an example of indirect contact transmission. Inhalation of air and particles from a person's sneeze is an example of droplet transmission. Being bitten by an infected mosquito is an example of vector-borne transmission.

17. **c.** To perform chest compressions on an infant, use two or three fingers placed on the center of the chest just below the nipple line. The heel of the hand is used to perform chest compressions on an adult or a child. The fist or thumbs are not used for chest compressions.

18. **d.** Although it may vary by state, a minor usually is considered anyone younger than 18 years. In such cases, permission to give care must be obtained from a parent or guardian.

19. **c.** Breathing and return of a pulse indicate signs of life; therefore, you would stop CPR (compressions and ventilations) and continue to monitor the patient, ensuring that his or her airway remains open. It would be inappropriate to cancel the call for more advanced medical personnel. The patient still may require additional care and should be transported to a medical facility for evaluation. Although an *automated external defibrillator* (AED) would analyze the rhythm, there is no need to use it at this time since the patient has a pulse.

20. **b.** The ribs are part of the chest cavity, which is located in the trunk between the diaphragm and the neck and contains the lungs and heart. The pelvic cavity is located in the pelvis and is the lowest part of the trunk, containing the bladder, rectum and internal female reproductive organs. The abdominal cavity is located in the trunk below the ribs, between the diaphragm and the pelvis. It contains the organs of digestion and excretion, including the liver, gallbladder, spleen, pancreas, kidneys, stomach and intestines. The cranial cavity is located in the head and contains the brain.

21. **a.** Persistent chest pain that spreads to the jaw and neck and is accompanied by difficulty breathing suggests a heart attack. Angina normally is a transient condition in which the patient experiences chest pain but the pain does not spread and is relieved by medicine and/or rest.

22. **c.** Platelets are a solid component of blood used by the body to form blood clots when there is bleeding. Red blood cells carry oxygen to the cells of the body and take carbon dioxide away. White blood cells are part of the body's immune system and help to defend the body against infection. Plasma is the straw-colored or clear liquid component of the blood that carries the blood cells and nutrients to the tissues, as well as waste products away from the tissues to the organs involved in excretion.

23. **d.** To perform the squat lift, you should stand with your weaker leg slightly forward, keeping the foot on the weaker side flat on the ground throughout the lift sequence. You should lead with your head, lifting your upper body before your hips.

24. **b.** In the out-of-hospital setting, unless you are provided with written documentation (or unless your state laws and regulations allow acceptance of oral verification [which most states' laws do not]) or if there is any doubt as to whether a *Do Not Resuscitate* (DNR) order is valid or in effect, care should proceed as it would in the absence of a DNR order. However, in this case, the spouse has shown you a valid written DNR order and as such, you should honor the spouse's statement and the patient's wishes. You need to be aware of the DNR laws in your state. It would be important to notify medical direction to inform them of the situation, but not to inquire about how to proceed. Calling the physician for verification would not be appropriate at this time.

25. **c.** After a shock is delivered, a period of time is programmed into the device to allow for CPR until the next rhythm analysis begins. You should not wait for the device to re-analyze the rhythm because valuable time would be lost. If at any time you notice obvious signs of life, stop CPR, monitor the patient's condition and leave the patient in a face-up position while maintaining an open airway.

26. **a.** Indications that breathing is adequate include lack of nasal flaring. A deviated trachea, muscles between the ribs pulling in on inhalation, pursed lips breathing, and tripod positioning (sitting upright and leaning forward) indicate inadequate breathing.

27. **b.** Tendons attach muscle to bone. Strong tough bands called ligaments hold the bones of a joint together. The patella is the kneecap. The coccyx is the tailbone.

28. **d.** Only personnel who must approach the helicopter should be permitted within the landing zone and only after the pilot has signaled that it is safe to approach. The cessation of tail rotor movement (which is dangerous), the medical crew exiting the aircraft and the helicopter coming to a stop are not appropriate indications that it is safe to approach the aircraft. Typically, you should allow the medical crew from the aircraft to approach you instead to prevent possible injury.

29. **c.** If a patient is conscious and has an obstructed airway, back blows, abdominal thrusts and chest thrusts have been proven to be effective in clearing an obstructed airway. Finger sweeps are used only on unconscious patients and only when you can see foreign matter in the patient's mouth.

30. **b.** Since the patient is trapped under plywood and a scaffold, a pneumatic tool most likely would be used to lift the plywood and scaffold off of the patient. Ropes may be helpful in pulling the material off of the patient, but this pulling action could lead to further injury. Pliers or a shovel would not be helpful in this situation.

31. **c.** Information about a patient is considered private and confidential and is not shared with others except in certain cases, such as providing information to more advanced medical personnel who will take over care, for mandatory reporting or in certain legal circumstance.

32. **b.** The most basic level of EMS training is the EMR. The paramedic is the most advanced level of training.

33. **d.** If the pads risk touching each other, you should use an anterior/posterior pad placement with one pad placed in the middle of the child's chest and the other placed on the child's back, between the shoulder blades. Both pads must be used, should remain intact and should not touch each other.

34. **a.** Complex access methods include a ratcheting cable and tool cutter. Simple access methods include trying to open each door or the windows or having the patient unlock the doors or roll down the windows. Breaking the window glass would be inappropriate because it could cause injury to yourself and the patient.

35. **b.** When ventilations are too great or too forceful, air may enter the stomach, causing gastric distention. A blotchy skin discoloration, called mottling, indicates inadequate oxygenation, often caused by shock; it does not result from forceful ventilations. A neck injury would not occur with forceful ventilations; however, the patient may have a neck injury, depending on the mechanism of the injury. Failure of the chest to rise indicates that the airway is not open.

36. **c.** As with any conventional vehicle, removing the ignition key and disconnecting the battery will disable a hybrid's high-voltage controller. However, some models may remain "live" for up to 10 minutes after the vehicle is shut off or disabled. Thus, a hybrid vehicle can remain silent and still be operational if the collision is

minor and/or did not activate any of the collision sensors. Therefore, it is essential that rescuers chock or block the wheels to prevent the vehicle from moving under power or by gravity. Be careful not to place cribbing under any high-voltage (usually *orange* in color) cabling.

37. **b.** When giving ventilations to a child using a resuscitation mask, you would position the mask and seal it, then open the airway and blow into the mask, giving ventilations at a rate of 1 ventilation about every 3 seconds, continue giving ventilations for about 2 minutes and then recheck for breathing and a pulse.

38. **b.** Exiting from a highway would not be considered a high-risk situation. Situations that can impact your safety and thus be considered high risk include going through intersections, entering a highway, driving in inclement weather, listening to a vehicle's stereo or other distraction in the vehicle and responding alone.

39. **c.** When giving chest compressions, keep your fingers off the chest, using the heel of one hand on the center of the chest with the other hand on top of the first hand and compressing the chest at least 2 inches for an adult. Use your body weight, not your arms, to compress the chest.

40. **d.** Emergency vehicles should be placed in optimal positions for safety and for easy patient loading. Blocking is a technique of positioning fire apparatus, such as large engines, at an angle to traffic lanes. This creates a physical barrier between the work area and traffic flowing toward the emergency scene. The scene should be protected with the first-arriving apparatus and with at least one additional lane blocked off. Ambulances should park within the "shadow" created by the larger apparatus. The apparatus also should "block to the right" or "block to the left" so as not to obstruct the loading doors of ambulances. To create a safe zone, traffic cones or flares should be placed at 10- to 15-foot intervals in a radius of at least 50 feet around the scene.

41. **a.** When preparing to insert an *oropharyngeal airway* (OPA), first make sure that the patient is unconscious. OPAs are used only on unconscious, unresponsive patients with no gag reflex. Airways are used to prevent, not treat, airway obstruction by the tongue. Selecting the proper size by measuring the distance from the earlobe to the corner of the mouth is important, but this would be done once you have established that the patient is unresponsive.

42. **c.** For an adult, you would compress to a depth of at least 2 inches. When performing chest compressions on a child, you should compress the chest about 2 inches. For an infant, compress to a depth of about 1½ inches.

43. **a.** Chocking refers to the process of placing blocks or wedges against the wheels of a vehicle to reduce the chance of the vehicle moving. Blocking is a technique of positioning fire apparatus, such as large engines, at an angle to traffic lanes, creating a physical barrier between the work area and traffic flowing toward the emergency scene. Cribbing refers to creating a stable environment for the vehicle using wood or supports arranged diagonally to a vehicle's frame, to safely prop it up, creating a stable environment. Extricating refers to the process of safely and appropriately removing a patient trapped in a vehicle or other dangerous situation.

44. **c.** A conscious patient who is showing early signs of a heart attack may be helped with an appropriate dose of aspirin when the signs first begin. If the patient is conscious and able to take medicine by mouth, and if the patient is not allergic to aspirin, does not have a stomach ulcer or stomach disease, is not taking blood thinners and has not been told by a doctor to avoid taking aspirin, the patient may be given two chewable (162 mg) baby aspirins or one 5-gram (325 mg) adult aspirin tablet with a small amount of water. Only aspirin, not acetaminophen (Tylenol®) or ibuprofen (Motrin®) should be given.

45. **d.** When a *bag-valve-mask resuscitator* (BVM) is attached to emergency oxygen at a flow rate of 15 *liters per minute* (LPM), the patient receives an oxygen concentration of 90 percent. A nasal cannula at a flow rate of 1 to 6 LPM delivers an oxygen concentration of 24 to 44 percent. A resuscitation mask at a flow rate of 6 to 15 LPM delivers an oxygen concentration of 25 to 55 percent.

46. **d.** Additional information can be gained about the substance in the tanker from warning signs, such as "flammable," "explosive," "corrosive" or "radioactive"; *National Fire Protection Association* (NFPA) numbers; and shipping papers. The *Emergency Response Guidebook* (although available for download) is a reference for identifying hazardous materials and includes appropriate care procedures; however, this may or may not be readily accessible at the scene.

47. **a.** A cycle of 30 compressions and 2 ventilations would be used for one-rescuer CPR for an adult, child and infant and two-rescuer CPR for an adult. Two-rescuer CPR

for a child or infant would use a cycle of 15 compressions and 2 ventilations. No method of CPR ever uses just 1 ventilation.

48. **b.** The pressure gauge indicates the fullness of the cylinder. A full cylinder will show 2000 psi, whereas a nearly empty cylinder will show about 200 psi. A reading of 1200 psi indicates that the tank is over one-half full. Subsequently, you would continue to administer emergency oxygen. The pressure gauge reading is unrelated to the flow rate. There is no need to change the cylinder immediately since it is not close to being empty. Increasing respiratory difficulty or respiratory arrest would suggest a need to prepare for assisted ventilations.

49. **c.** The color red signifies that the patient needs immediate or urgent care. Yellow indicates delayed care, and green signifies that the patient is ambulatory and not in grave danger. Black indicates that the patient is deceased or non-salvageable.

50. **b.** To manage and reduce patients' stress at the scene, helpful measures would include reuniting family members, limiting the amount of information that is getting out of the scene, being honest and telling patients what is happening in terms that they can understand, encouraging questions and discussions, and asking others to help if they are able to assist with tasks.

51. **c.** Prompt intervention is necessary because a prolapsed cord can threaten a baby's life. As the baby moves through the birth canal, the cord will be compressed against the unborn child and the birth canal, cutting off blood flow. Without this blood flow, the baby will die within a few minutes from lack of oxygen. Aspiration leading to possible pneumonia occurs with meconium aspiration. A history of previous excess bleeding after delivery, multiple births, or a prolonged or abnormal labor would increase the woman's risk for hemorrhage leading to shock. Eclampsia occurs during pregnancy and is associated with elevated blood pressure, edema and excess protein in the urine. It is unrelated to a prolapsed cord.

52. **c.** A 3½-year-old child is considered a preschooler. An infant is a child up to 1 year of age. A toddler is between the ages of 1 and 3 years and a preschooler is a child between the ages of 3 and 5 years. A school-age child is between 6 and 12 years of age.

53. **b.** When giving ventilations to an adult, you would recheck for breathing and a pulse after giving ventilations for about 2 minutes.

54. **c.** Normal age-related changes include a thickening of the heart muscle, decreased lung elasticity and slowed movement through the digestive system. Most middle-aged and older adults retain their abilities to learn, remember and solve problems.

55. **a.** A nasal cannula would be inappropriate because the patient needs a device that can supply a greater concentration of oxygen than that which is supplied by a nasal cannula. A resuscitation mask, non-rebreather mask or a BVM would be more appropriate for this patient because they are used with patients who are breathing and they can deliver higher concentrations of oxygen.

56. **d.** When providing care for a patient being treated for cancer, infection control is extremely important because chemotherapy and radiation therapy affect a person's immune system. Strict hand-washing guidelines and standard precautions must be taken. Although inspecting the skin, observing any hair loss and evaluating the patient's vomiting may be appropriate depending on the situation, they are not as important as adhering to strict infection control measures.

57. **c.** In calculating weight, the pilot must take into account the weight of the passengers and equipment as well as the fuel load. The amount of space available in a helicopter depends on the type of helicopter and its maximum takeoff and landing weights. However, the weight of the fuel load is important in calculating the weight, not just the space. When calculating space, rescuers must take into account how many patients require transport, the rescuers who must accompany the patient(s) and any essential life-saving equipment.

58. **a.** When administering emergency oxygen, follow specific safety guidelines. The person administering the emergency oxygen should not use the oxygen around flames or sparks because it is flammable and causes fire to burn more quickly and rapidly; should not use grease, oil or petroleum products to lubricate or clean the regulator because these could cause an explosion; should not drag or roll the cylinders; and should not carry a cylinder by the valve or regulator.

59. **a.** You would check the jump kit during phase 1, preparation for an emergency call, thus allowing you to be ready to respond to a scene. Phase 2, dispatch, involves communication from dispatch in which information about the emergency is received and then given to the

appropriate personnel for a response. Phase 3, en-route to the scene, involves getting to the scene. Phase 4, arrival at the scene and patient contact, involves approaching the scene, sizing up the scene and the situation, and ultimately beginning patient care.

60. **b.** Multiple sclerosis is a chronic disease that destroys the coating on the nerve cells in the brain and spinal cord interfering with the nerves' ability to communicate with each other. Its symptoms usually appear and disappear over a period of years. Muscular dystrophy is a group of genetic disorders in which patients experience progressive weakness and degeneration of the muscles, primarily skeletal muscles. In later stages of the disease, patients often develop respiratory problems requiring assisted ventilation.

61. **d.** During attempts to relieve the baby's airway obstruction, you would position the infant's head lower than the chest to facilitate drainage of air and fluid and passage of the obstruction.

62. **b.** When assessing this patient, speak slowly, clearly and calmly and allow sufficient time to ensure that the patient understands what you are saying. You also should speak to the patient at his eye level and turn on the lights to make it easier for you to see the patient. Although the wife can provide valuable information, you should not focus solely on her. Involve the patient and be sure to clearly explain what you are doing.

63. **c.** A nasal cannula provides the lowest concentration of oxygen, which ranges from 24 to 44 percent. A resuscitation mask delivers approximately 25 to 55 percent oxygen. A non-rebreather mask and BVM deliver an oxygen concentration of 90 percent or more.

64. **b.** While performing CPR when transporting a patient, you need to be secure and supported. You should spread your feet to shoulder width to maintain a secure stance and bend your knees to lower your center of gravity. Using the stretcher for balance would be inappropriate. If possible, have someone help you by holding onto your belt to stabilize you. In addition, you should ask the driver to call out if any bumpy areas or severe turns are coming up so that you can brace yourself.

65. **b.** To verify oxygen flow, listen for a hissing sound and feel for oxygen flow through the delivery device. The flowmeter dial should not change but should remain at the rate that is set. A pressure gauge reading below 200 *pounds per square inch* (psi) indicates that the cylinder needs to be replaced.

The O-ring should be present to ensure a tight seal between the regulator and the tank.

66. **d.** When performing abdominal thrusts on an adult, stand behind the patient and make a fist with one hand, placing the thumb side of the fist against the middle of the patient's abdomen, just above the navel. Next grab the fist with your other hand and give quick, upward thrusts. You could kneel behind the patient if the patient was a child, depending on his or her size.

67. **b.** Penetrating injury occurs when the patient is hit by or falls onto something that penetrates or cuts through the skin, causing an open wound and bleeding. Blunt trauma occurs when someone falls against or is struck by an object with no sharp edges or points, often resulting in closed wounds, such as a contusion or a hematoma.

68. **c.** Unless you have received special training in handling *hazardous materials* (HAZMATs) and have the necessary equipment to do so without danger, you should not attempt to be a hero. Rather, you should stay clear of the scene, well away from the area or in the designated cold zone. Stay out of low areas where vapors and liquids may collect and stay upwind and uphill of the scene. It is common for responding ambulance crews approaching the scene to recognize a HAZMAT placard and immediately move to a safe area and summon more advanced help.

69. **a.** The term, "hard of hearing" is used to describe a person whose hearing is somewhat impaired but who still can rely on his or her hearing for communication. Deafness describes someone who is unable to hear well enough to rely on hearing as a means of communication. There are two types: conductive, which occurs when there is a problem with the outer or middle ear, and sensorineural, which is due to a problem with the inner ear and possibly the nerve that goes from the ear to the brain.

70. **d.** The first step is to ensure your personal safety. Once this is done, then you need to ensure the patient's safety. Next, you would determine the *mechanism of injury* (MOI) and decide what additional resources are needed to keep you and the patient safe or to provide care.

71. **b.** In a young child, even a minor infection can result in a rather high fever, which often is defined as a temperature higher than 103°F. If a fever is present, call for more advanced medical help at once. Your care for a child with a high fever is to gently cool the child. Never rush

cooling down a child. If the fever was caused a febrile seizure, rapid cooling could bring on another seizure. Parents or caregivers often heavily dress children with fevers. If this is the case, remove the excess clothing or blankets and sponge the child with lukewarm water. Do *not* use an ice water bath or rubbing alcohol to cool down the body. Both of these are dangerous.

72. **d.** Fetal movement typically is felt during the second trimester. During the third trimester, the mother gains the most weight as the fetus grows most rapidly. Morning sickness and placental development occur during the first trimester.

73. **c.** Patients with chest pain or difficulty breathing often lean forward while sitting in what is called a tripod position. A patient with abdominal pain often will pull his or her knees up toward the chest while lying down or sitting with his or her back against a hard surface. Inability to move a body part, such as an arm or leg, pain with movement or deformity, might suggest a fracture. Loss of bladder or bowel control can indicate that the patient had a stroke.

74. **a.** Pale skin is not a normal finding and typically reflects low body temperature, blood loss, shock or poor blood flow to a body part. Cool skin may indicate low body temperature or shock. A pulse rate of 70 *beats per minute* (bpm), capillary refill of 2 seconds and a respiratory rate of 18 breaths per minute are normal findings.

75. **b.** A patient who can speak or cry is conscious, has an open airway, is breathing and has a pulse; therefore, the patient does not lack a pulse.

76. **b.** As you check for the rate and quality of breathing, try to do so without the patient's knowledge; otherwise, the patient may consciously or subconsciously change her breathing pattern. Likewise, you would not want to tell the patient that you are counting her breaths. Each inhalation and exhalation is counted as one breath. Noisy breathing is abnormal and should not be considered an expected, normal finding.

77. **d.** Neutralization involves chemically altering a substance to render it harmless or make it less harmful. Dilution refers to the method of reducing the concentration of a contaminant to a safe level. Initial, or "gross," decontamination is performed as the person enters the warm zone. Any immediate life-threatening conditions are addressed during this stage. Soap and copious amounts of water are used, and any clothing, equipment and tools must be left in the hot zone. Absorption is the process of using a material to soak up and hold contaminants, such as corrosive and liquid chemicals.

78. **c.** After delivery of a baby, the placenta usually separates from the wall of the uterus and exits via the birth canal; this process normally occurs within 30 minutes of the delivery of the baby.

79. **c.** When performing a secondary assessment on a responsive medical patient, after you have assessed the patient's complaints, the next step would be to obtain a SAMPLE history. You then would perform a focused medical assessment, assess baseline vital signs, and perform components of the detailed physical exam.

80. **b.** Patients who are tagged white are categorized as "hold" to indicate that they have minor injuries that do not require a doctor's care. Patients with life-threatening conditions are tagged red. Those who are injured but ambulatory are tagged green. Patients with severe injuries for which treatment can be delayed are tagged yellow.

81. **a.** When obtaining a patient's blood pressure, ensure that the cuff covers about two-thirds of the patient's upper arm and that the forearm is on a supported surface in front or to the side of the patient, not hanging down or raised above heart level. The cuff should be applied to the patient's unclothed or lightly clothed arm to prevent inaccuracies. The bladder of the cuff should be positioned with the bladder over the brachial artery.

82. **b.** When someone with more experience or seniority arrives on the scene, you should transfer incident command to that person, providing that person with a verbal report of all important and pertinent information, including what has been recorded. The person taking over will need to know information such as when the incident began, when you arrived on the scene, how many people are injured, how many people are acting as rescuers, any potential dangers, what has been done since the beginning of the rescue and objectives that need to be accomplished. The oncoming *incident commander* (IC) then will assign you to an area where you are needed most.

83. **a.** The patient having high blood pressure correlates with the "P" in the SAMPLE history, or pertinent past medical history. The patient mowing the lawn would correlate with the "E," or the events leading up to the incident. The patient sweating profusely correlates with the "S," or signs and symptoms. The patient using medications for high blood pressure correlates with the "M," or medications.

84. **b.** You can help the expectant mother to cope with the discomfort and pain of labor by staying calm, firm and confident and by offering encouragement. Doing so can help reduce her fear and apprehension which, in turn, will aid in reducing her pain and discomfort. Ask her to focus on one object in the room while regulating her breathing. Telling the woman that everything will be okay is inappropriate because it does not address the needs of the woman and provides false reassurance. Telling the woman that she has to learn to endure the discomfort is not supportive and will only add to her fear and apprehension. You should begin by reassuring her that you are there to help. Explain what to expect as labor progresses. Suggest specific physical activities that she can do to relax, such as regulating her breathing. Ask her to breathe slowly and deeply in through the nose and out through the mouth.

85. **c.** The patient's SAMPLE history would not need to be included in the communication but would be documented in the *pre-hospital care report* (PCR) for review by the receiving facility on arrival. When communicating with the receiving facility, such as a hospital, you should give the following information: who you are (unit and role), how many patients will be arriving, patient characteristics (age, gender, chief complaint), immediate history (events leading to the injury or illness), any care you provided and the patient's response to the care, any vital information such as the need for isolation and the *estimated time of arrival* (ETA).

86. **a.** Resuscitation of a newborn begins immediately if respirations fall to less than 30 respirations per minute or the newborn is gasping or not breathing, if the pulse is less than 100 bpm or if cyanosis (bluish skin) around the chest and abdomen persists after administering emergency oxygen.

87. **b.** Patient background information, such as age, gender and birth date, are documented in the patient data section. Vital signs are documented in the check boxes section of the PCR. Administrative information, such as the time and date of the incident, are documented in the run data. The patient narrative would include information about the assessment and care provided.

88. **b.** You would tag this patient with a red tag because the patient's respiratory rate is high, over 30 breaths per minute, indicating that the patient needs immediate care. A person who is alert and responds appropriately to verbal stimuli is classified as delayed care and is tagged yellow. A patient who is ambulatory is not in grave danger and would be tagged green. A patient who is not breathing despite an open airway is classified as deceased/non-salvageable and is tagged black.

89. **c.** When you receive medical direction, use the echo method, that is, repeat the order word for word to ensure that you have heard and understood the order. The terms "affirmative" and "negative" should be used in any situation involving radio communication, not just communicating with medical control. Asking medical control to repeat the order again would be appropriate if you did not understand the original order or if you repeated the order incorrectly back to medical control. Telling medical control that you understand would be inappropriate.

90. **c.** Delivery is considered imminent when the mother reports a strong urge to push; contractions are intense, occurring every 2 minutes or less and lasting 60 to 90 seconds; the woman's abdomen is very tight and hard; the mother reports a feeling of the infant's head moving down the birth canal or has a sensation like an urge to defecate; and crowning occurs. A sudden gush of fluid from the vagina, indicating that the amniotic sac has ruptured, often signals the onset of labor.

91. **c.** Although vital sign assessment can provide valuable information about a child's condition, it would not be an appropriate method to assess a child's *level of consciousness* (LOC). The AVPU scale, pupil assessment and evidence of spontaneous movement are appropriate methods to evaluate a child's LOC.

92. **b.** Both patients were involved in a vehicle rollover, were unrestrained and have sustained multiple injuries. Subsequently, they would most likely meet the criteria for trauma alert, making air medical transport appropriate. Although it might be appropriate to use an ambulance to transport the patients, valuable time could be lost if the facility is more than 30 minutes away or if it would take longer to transport the patient to the trauma center by ambulance than by air transport. Notifying law enforcement would not be necessary unless the area needed to be cleared to allow air medical transport to land.

93. **a.** Primary assessments on a conscious child should be done unobtrusively, so that the child has time to get used to you and feels less threatened. Try to carry out as many of the

components of the initial evaluation by careful observation, without touching the child or infant. Approach the parents or caregivers, if possible, since the child will see you communicating with them and subsequently may feel more comfortable with your exam and treatment. If the child is upset, perform the assessment from toe to head, which allows the patient to get used to you rather than having your face in the child's from the start.

94. **b.** After putting the vehicle in "park" or in gear (if a manual transmission), you then would set the parking brake; turn off the vehicle's ignition and remove the key; move the seats back and roll down the windows; disconnect the battery or power source; and finally, identify and avoid hazardous vehicle safety components.

95. **c.** Toddlers may be fearful of strangers and may not be cooperative when dealing with an unknown person. Therefore, it would be important for you to speak calmly and softly to the child while maintaining eye contact. In addition, you should try to have only one individual deal with the child to reduce his anxiety of being handled by multiple strangers. Since the child is visibly upset, it would be more appropriate to perform the exam toe to head to minimize the child's anxiety and allow the child to get used to you rather than have you in his face from the start. Delaying the exam would be inappropriate because you need to gather as much information as possible about the child's condition.

96. **a.** Class B biological agents/diseases pose a moderate level of risk and include brucellosis, Q fever, glanders, alphaviruses, food pathogens (e.g., *Salmonella, Shigella, E coli*), water pathogens (e.g., *Vibrio cholerae, Cryptosporidium*), ricin toxin, *staphylococcal enterotoxin B* and epsilon toxin of *Clostridium perfringens*. Hantavirus, yellow fever and tick-borne virus are examples of Class C biological agents/ diseases.

97. **c.** The priority is to determine the patient's LOC. You then would summon more advanced medical personnel, if necessary. Next you would open the patient's airway and check for breathing and a pulse. For a drowning victim, for victims who have collapsed due to a respiratory cause, or for a child or an infant who you did not see collapse, you would give 2 ventilations. Lastly, you would check for severe bleeding.

98. **b.** When counting the pulse over 30 seconds, take the number of beats obtained (in this case,

20) and multiply it by 2 to arrive at a pulse rate of 80 beats per minute. If you counted the number of beats over 15 seconds, then you would multiply that number by 4.

99. **c.** A nuclear explosion or chemical exposure would be a human-caused disaster. Biological disasters include epidemics, pandemics and outbreaks of communicable diseases; contamination of food or water supplies by pathogens; and the use of viruses, bacteria and other pathogens for bioterrorism. A hurricane is a natural disaster.

100. **a.** A strong, palpable pulse would be a normal finding and not a concern. However, signs and symptoms suggesting a problem requiring immediate intervention include increasing lethargy; cool, clammy skin; and rapid breathing. All of these would suggest that shock is developing.

101. **c.** If you need to open the mouth to clear the airway of fluids, use the cross-finger technique. The head-tilt/chin-lift method and jaw-thrust (without head extension) maneuver are techniques for opening the airway. Neck hyperextension is not used.

102. **d.** True labor contractions get closer together, increase in how long they last, feel stronger as time goes on and occur at regular intervals.

103. **b.** Anthrax is a Class A biological agent/disease that is easily spread from person to person and results in a high mortality rate. Q fever, ricin toxin and brucellosis are Class B biological agents/diseases with moderate morbidity rates and low mortality rates.

104. **c.** When positioning a resuscitation mask, you would place the rim of the mask between the lower lip and chin and then lower the mask until it covers the patient's mouth and nose.

105. **a.** A patient who is unconscious and convulsing is classified as immediate. This classification also would apply to the patient if he or she was breathing with difficulty, had apnea and was possibly flaccid. A patient is classified as delayed if further medical observation, large amounts of antidotes or artificial ventilation is required after triage. A patient is classified as expectant if the patient shows the same signs as immediate but has no pulse or blood pressure and thus is not expected to survive. A patient is classified as minimal if he or she is walking, talking, breathing and whose circulation is intact.

106. **b.** The contents of the PCR must be kept confidential and, therefore, control of the contents falls within the *Health Insurance Portability*

and *Accountability Act* (HIPAA). You are responsible to ensure that the PCR is in the appropriate hands when providing care. Neither medical control nor the receiving facility controls the contents of the PCR.

107. **c.** A child with epiglottitis can move from respiratory distress to respiratory failure very quickly without emergency care. With epiglottitis, do not examine the throat using a tongue depressor or place anything in the child's throat since doing so can trigger a complete airway blockage. Additionally, keeping the child as calm as possible is vital. Children often assume the tripod position to ease breathing. This should be maintained if it is helpful to the child. You also should continue to monitor the child for additional signs associated with epiglottitis, such as drooling, difficulty swallowing, voice changes and fever.

108. **a.** Rappelling is the act of descending by sliding down a secured rope to reach a patient, such as from a cliff, gorge or side of a building. Reaching and throwing are types of assists used to rescue a drowning victim. Shoring is supporting the walls of a trench to prevent a cave-in.

109. **c.** Since the patient is hypoglycemic (low blood glucose level) and unconscious, you need to summon more advanced medical personnel immediately. Fruit juice or glucose tablets are used only if the patient is conscious. Giving insulin would further lower the patient's blood glucose level.

110. **d.** Neurogenic/vasogenic shock is caused by trauma to the spinal cord or brain. Cardiogenic shock is the result of the heart being unable to supply adequate blood circulation to the vital organs, resulting in an inadequate supply of oxygen and nutrients. Disease, trauma or injury to the heart causes this type of shock. Metabolic shock results from a loss of body fluid, which can be due to severe diarrhea, vomiting or a heat-related illness. Anaphylaxis (also referred to as anaphylactic shock) occurs as the result of exposure to an allergen.

111. **b.** Once the child is pulled from the water, you should provide care for hypothermia because the body loses heat in icy water 32 times faster than it does in air. This cooling effect is further accelerated if the child has swallowed water. Providing care for seizures or a hemorrhage would not be the priority. Fever is highly unlikely.

112. **a.** When assessing a patient for a stroke, you would use the FAST mnemonic, which addresses specific areas in the following order: face, arm, speech and time.

113. **d.** If the water is safe and shallow enough, not over your chest, you can wade into the water to reach the person. You should wear a life jacket and, if possible, take something with you to extend your reach, such as a ring buoy, buoyant cushion, kickboard, extra life jacket, tree branch, pole, air mattress, cooler, picnic jug, paddle or water exercise belt.

114. **a.** Evidence of an increase in blood pressure suggests that shock is not progressing and measures to minimize have been effective. If shock were progressing, the patient would exhibit a decrease in blood pressure, dilated pupils; listlessness and confusion; shallow, irregular respirations; and irregular, weak, rapid pulse.

115. **a.** Drowsiness would be seen with inhalant abuse and depressants. A telltale sign of cannabis use is red, bloodshot eyes. Mood changes and a flushed face suggest hallucinogen abuse.

116. **b.** Your first responsibility would be to gather information to help the responding firefighting and EMS units. Subsequently, you would prevent any other individuals from approaching the fire. If possible, attempt to find out about the number of possible victims who may be trapped and any possible causes. You should give this information to emergency personnel when they arrive. Only highly trained firefighters, who have the equipment to protect them against smoke and fire should approach a fire. Since local firefighters already are present, someone from this unit would assume the *incident commander* (IC) position.

117. **a.** Signs and symptoms of heat stroke include flushed or red skin that is either dry or moist; rapid, weak pulse; shallow breathing; low blood pressure; decreasing LOC; body temperature above 104° F; and lack of sweating.

118. **a.** An avulsion involves a portion of the skin and sometimes other soft tissue being partially or completely torn away. An amputation involves complete severing of a body part. A laceration is a cut, usually from a sharp object, resulting in jagged or smooth edges. Impalement occurs when an object is embedded in an open wound.

119. **b.** A drowning victim who is passive is not moving and may be floating face-up or face-down on or near the surface of the water, or the victim may be submerged. A distressed swimmer may be floating, treading water or clinging to an object or a line for support. A drowning victim who is active is vertical in the water, typically

with his or her arms at the sides, pressing down in an attempt to keep the mouth and nose above water to breathe.

120. **d.** The odor of "freshly cut hay" suggests the use of phosgene, a pulmonary agent, which when in contact with the mucous membranes, irritates and damages the lung tissue. There is no specific antidote; the only way to provide care is to remove the patient from the agent and resuscitate him or her. Sodium thiosulfate is an antidote for cyanide. Decontamination procedures and the use of bleach are appropriate for exposure to blister agents.

121. **b.** Mood changes, flushing and hallucinations would suggest hallucinogen or designer drug abuse. A patient who abuses depressants may show signs and symptoms that include drowsiness, confusion, slurred speech, slow heart and breathing rates, and poor coordination. Tachycardia (increased pulse), hypertension, rapid breathing, excitement, restlessness and irritability suggest stimulant abuse.

122. **c.** *Emergency support function* (ESF) #5, emergency management, involves the coordination of incident management and response efforts, issuance of mission assignments, resource and human capital, incident action planning and financial management. ESF #1, transportation, involves damage and impact assessment, movement restrictions, transportation safety, restoration/recovery of transportation infrastructure, and aviation/airspace management and control. ESF #2, communications, involves coordination with telecommunications and information technology industries; restoration and repair of telecommunications infrastructure; protection, restoration and sustainment of cyber and information technology resources; and oversight of communications within the federal incident management and response structures. ESF # 8, public health and medical services, involves public health, medical and mental health services and mass fatality management.

123. **b.** First ensure that the patient's airway is open and clear, and then perform a primary assessment, administer emergency oxygen, if available, and provide appropriate ventilatory support. Next, take steps to control any bleeding, if present, and prevent further blood loss, if appropriate. If you are unsure of the patient's condition or are concerned about possible internal injuries, keep the patient lying flat. If you suspect that any bones are broken or see dislocated or damaged joints,

immobilize them to prevent movement. Broken bones or dislocated or damaged joints can cause more bleeding and damage.

124. **d.** The report of "hearing a strange sound" reflects the aura phase in which the patient senses something unusual. During the tonic phase, unconsciousness and muscle rigidity occur. During the clonic phase, the seizures occur. During the post-ictal phase, deep sleep with gradual recovery occurs.

125. **a.** To assess abdominal pain in a child, your priority is to first obtain an impression of the child's appearance, breathing and circulation to determine urgency of the situation. You then would evaluate the child's mental status, airway, adequacy of breathing and circulation. Next, you would take the child's history and perform a hands-on physical exam noting any injury, hemorrhage, discoloration, distention, rigidity, guarding or tenderness within the four abdominal quadrants. If a life-threatening condition is noted, provide immediate treatment before continuing.

126. **a.** Poison ivy is an example of an absorbed poison. Chloroform is an example of a common inhaled poison. Contaminated water is an example of an ingested poison. Venom from a snake bite is an example of an injected poison.

127. **d.** Puncture wounds generally do not bleed profusely but are potentially more dangerous than other bleeding wounds because puncture wounds can become infected with microorganisms from the object as it passes through the tissues. Crush syndrome is a complication of crush injuries; it develops as the pressure is released and the tissues become reperfused with blood. Shock is less likely because puncture wounds generally do not bleed profusely. External hemorrhage would be less likely because the skin usually closes around the penetrating object; thus, external bleeding generally is not severe.

128. **b.** Patients who are non-ambulatory or have incurred a spinal injury with or without spinal cord damage would be tagged yellow. Patients who are tagged red require immediate care and transport to a medical facility. Patients are considered immediate if they are unconscious or cannot follow simple commands, require active airway management, have a respiratory rate of greater than 30, have a delayed (more than 2 seconds) capillary refill or absent radial pulse, or require bleeding control for severe hemorrhage from major blood vessels.

129. **d.** Full-thickness burns are painless, with no sensation to touch; are pearly white or charred; and also are dry and may appear leathery. Superficial partial-thickness burns are painful and reddened and blanch (turn white) when touched. Deep partial-thickness burns may or may not be painful or blanch when touched, but the hair usually is gone. Superficial burns have a painful, red area with no blisters and turn white when touched; often, the skin appears moist.

130. **a.** Based on the patient's status, apply an occlusive dressing to the sucking chest wound because if this is not addressed, the patient's status will deteriorate quickly. Once this is completed, institute measures to control the bleeding, assess for signs and symptoms of shock and administer emergency oxygen if available. Ventilations would be used if the patient's respiratory status continues to deteriorate and her respiratory rate drops or she goes into respiratory arrest.

131. **b.** Withdrawal refers to the condition produced when a person stops using or abusing a substance to which he or she is addicted. Dependency refers to the desire to continually use the substance in order to function normally. Tolerance refers to the increase in substance amount and frequency to obtain the desired effect. Overdose refers to the use of an excessive amount of the substance.

132. **b.** Genital injuries, regardless of their location, typically are extremely painful. They can be open or closed wounds, and the severity of bleeding varies. Injuries to the penis usually occur as a result of an accident or assault. Straddle injury, sexual assault and childbirth are the most common situations associated with female genital injuries.

133. **b.** The priority is to get the patient out of the cold. Once the patient is removed from the cold, handle the area gently because rough handling can damage the body part. You should never rub the affected area since this can cause skin damage. The scenario does not suggest any dangers other than the cold environment, so scene safety is not a problem. Reorienting the patient would be appropriate if the patient was confused, and this would be done once you get the patient out of the cold.

134. **d.** In the hot zone, rescue, treatment for any life-threatening conditions and initial decontamination occur. In the warm zone, complete decontamination takes place and life-saving emergency care, such as airway management and immobilization, occurs.

135. **c.** Traumatic asphyxia can result from injuries that often are caused by a strong crushing mechanism or by situations in which patients have been pinned under a heavy object. A patient shot in the chest, one with broken ribs from a fall and one with a sucking chest wound have the least risk for developing traumatic asphyxia.

136. **b.** The first priority with any snake bite is to wash the wound. You would need to keep the injured area still and lower than the heart. Apply an elastic roller bandage. Checking for infection would be done at a later time. Ice is not used with snake bites.

137. **c.** Although identifying the weapon, assessing the patients and following appropriate protocols are important, the top priority is to ensure your own safety. Without this, the other actions would be futile.

138. **d.** Any evidence that you collect while treating the patient for injuries should be isolated, and each piece of evidence needs to be bagged individually in a paper bag to prevent cross-contamination. Plastic bags do not allow air movement and cause the DNA to deteriorate due to moisture build up. You need to follow local protocols and give the evidence to the police as soon as possible.

139. **c.** Excited delirium syndrome is characterized by high body temperatures, increased body strength, insensitivity to pain and agitation.

140. **b.** When performing manual stabilization, call for more advanced medical personnel first and then place your hands on both sides of the patient's head. Next, gently position the patient's head in line with the body and support it in that position. Then maintain an open airway, control any external bleeding and keep the patient from getting chilled or overheated

141. **c.** When establishing rapport, you should speak directly to the patient, maintain eye contact and tell the patient who you are and that you are there to help. Telling the patient to calm down would be inappropriate because the statement can be interpreted as threatening. You should not touch the patient without permission.

142. **a.** A *transient ischemic attack* (TIA), often referred to as a "mini-stroke," is a temporary episode that, like a stroke, is caused by reduced blood flow to a part of the brain. Unlike a stroke, the signs and symptoms of a TIA (which are similar to a stroke) disappear within a few minutes or hours of its onset. If symptoms persist after 24 hours, the event is not considered a TIA but a

stroke. The risk factors for stroke and TIA are similar to those for heart disease.

143. **c.** When a tooth has been knocked out, handle the tooth by the crown, rinse it under running water and place it in a glass of milk or, if milk is not available, place the tooth in clean water or moistened sterile gauze. If the patient is conscious and able to cooperate, rinse out the mouth with cold tap water if available. Control the bleeding by placing a rolled sterile dressing into the space left by the missing tooth. Have the patient gently bite down to maintain pressure. Ice is inappropriate. Do not attempt to reimplant the tooth. Contact a dentist or bring the tooth and the patient to an emergency care center as soon as possible.

144. **a.** Older people are at a higher risk for suicide than the general population because depression is common in the geriatric population and it may be misdiagnosed as dementia or confusion. They do not have an increased tendency for impulsive action, nor do they experience more problems with alcohol abuse. An individual of any age may be reluctant to seek help for mental health problems due to the stigma attached to suicidal thoughts, suicide attempts or general mental health problems.

145. **a.** Someone who is conscious (responsive) and has no spinal injury should be removed from the water. A patient who is unresponsive, lying face-down in the water or has a neck or spinal injury should be cared for in the water.

146. **b.** When controlling bleeding from an open head wound, do not put direct pressure on the wound if you feel a depression, spongy area or bone fragments. Place a sterile dressing or clean cloth over the wound and gently press against the wound and the area around the wound with your hand. Elevate the head and shoulders if spinal injury is not suspected, and use a roller bandage to cover the dressing completely.

147. **d.** When providing care to a patient with an object embedded in the eye, do not attempt to remove the object but rather stabilize it by encircling the eye with gauze or a soft sterile cloth, being sure to avoid applying any pressure on top of the area. Styrofoam® materials are not used to shield the area because small particles can break off and get into the eye.

148. **c.** Crepitus is a grating sound or feeling when an attempt is made to move a fractured bone and is caused by the two pieces of bone rubbing against each other. Angulation refers to an abnormal alignment or angle of an injured limb when it is compared with an uninjured limb. Deformity refers to a change in the shape of a limb when an injured limb is compared with an uninjured limb. Cravat is a folded triangular bandage used to hold other splints in place.

149. **b.** Signs and symptoms of anaphylaxis, a severe allergic reaction, include weakness, nausea, dizziness, swelling of the throat or tongue, constricted airway and difficulty breathing. Itching, hives or a rash suggests a localized allergic reaction.

150. **c.** To apply a binder, wrap the cloth around the patient and the injured part securing it against the body. Place a triangular bandage under the injured part and over the uninjured area to form a sling. Tie the ends of a sling at the side of the neck. A circumferential air splint is positioned around the injured area and then filled with air.

151. **a.** To care for a patient with heat cramps, the most important initial action is to reduce the cramps. First, have the patient rest, then gently massage and lightly stretch the cramped muscles to ease the discomfort. In addition, encourage the patient to drink fluid , such as a commercial sports drink, milk or water, to replace what was lost to perspiration.

152. **c.** For a suspected elbow fracture, do not attempt to straighten or bend the elbow or change its position. Splint it with a sling and binder in the position in which you found it.

153. **b.** Indications of a serious abdominal injury include complaints of severe pain; bruising; nausea and vomiting (possibly with blood); pale or ashen, cool, moist skin; weakness; thirst; and pain, tenderness or a tight swollen feeling in the abdomen.

154. **d.** Evidence of soot or burns around the mouth, nose or the rest of the face may be a sign that air passages or lungs have been burned, possibly leading to airway closure; therefore, your priority would be to maintain an open airway (patency). Emergency oxygen administration may become a priority if the patient develops respiratory distress caused by the burns. The skin is not burned or injured, so protecting the skin is not a priority. Fluid loss typically is associated with deeper or more extensive burns and usually would not be indicated by soot or burns around the mouth or nose.

155. **c.** You should call for more advanced medical personnel if the patient complains of severe pain, the force that caused the injury seems great enough to cause serious damage, the patient

cannot move the body part without pain, if the injured extremity is blue or extremely pale or the patient shows signs and symptoms of shock. Swelling would be expected because blood and other fluids seep into the surrounding tissues.

156. **b.** A blood agent attacks the body's cellular metabolism, disrupting cellular respiration. Blister agents cause the formation of blisters when they come in contact with the skin and mucous membranes. Nerve agents disrupt the chemical recovery phase that follows a neuromuscular signal. An incapacitating agent produces temporary physiological or mental effects or both, rendering individuals incapable of concerted effort in the performance of their duties.

157. **d.** You have already sized-up the scene and performed a primary assessment. The patient is breathing so his airway is open. Your initial action would be to stabilize his head and neck to prevent further injury.

158. **d.** The patient's statement about having no feeling in the hand suggests that circulation to that area is compromised, requiring immediate action. Some pain is expected, but if the patient is complaining of severe pain or pain out of proportion to the visible injury, there is cause for concern. If a bone has fractured, the patient may report hearing or feeling the bone snap or break. A feeling of warmth indicates adequate circulation.

159. **a.** With internal capillary bleeding, bruising around the wound area results, which is not serious. To reduce discomfort, you would apply ice or a cold pack to the areas, ensuring that the cold pack does not come in direct contact with the patient's skin. Elevating the body part, applying direct pressure and maintaining pressure at a pressure point is appropriate for external bleeding.

160. **b.** The patient usually will attempt to ease the pain by leaning toward the side of the fracture, which in this case is the right side and pressing a hand or arm over the injured area, thereby creating an anatomical splint.